The Copy Workshop Workbook

©1993 Bruce Bendinger

The Copy Workshop
2144 N. Hudson • Chicago, IL 60614
(312) 871-1179 FAX: (312) 281-4643

This book is dedicated to Lorelei, Mairee, Claire & "The Bat."
Thanks for making The Copy Workshop work.

A New Edition.

Welcome to the Revolution.

I don't know what geography professors had to say in 1492, but I know how they felt.

Right now, the advertising business is undergoing truly revolutionary changes.

It's growing dramatically – expanding and combining with a wide range of fields– direct marketing, event marketing, public relations and sales promotion – the whole thing people call **"IMC,"** Integrated Marketing Communications.

At the same time, it's contracting dramatically – many large ad agencies, retailers and media companies now offer fewer job opportunities.

Alvin Toffler's "Third Wave," the Post-Industrial Revolution, is crashing around us.

Everywhere you look, things are changing.

Time has compressed.

Now it's fast as a Fax. Or faster.

Options have expanded.

Once upon a time, you dealt with one phone company. At home, your TV tuned in just a few channels. Computers were for big-budget corporations or low-budget science-fiction movies.

Today, the list of possible media channels and marketing tactics is truly mind-boggling.

It's a marketplace that offers far more choices than it did just ten years ago.

Finally…

"The Competition" is smarter.

Nobody's standing still– but if the other guy is pushing harder while you're pushing harder, it can sure feel that way.

These are some of the issues we've wrestled with putting together our New Edition.

THE OLD EDITION.

The Copy Workshop was originally published in 1988.

It was one of the early examples of "desktop publishing."

It went on to become the #1 copywriting book in advertising, as well as the #1 college textbook.

And it turned our little advertising consulting practice into a real publishing company.

Our Mission is to provide "professional-strength" instruction in the fields of advertising and marketing.

OTHER THINGS WORTH MENTIONING:
Alcohol and Tobacco.

Examples of ads for these products appear throughout the book.

Traditionally, these categories demonstrate state-of-the-art advertising techniques.

We've included the examples to demonstrate the techniques – not endorse the products.

Cause-related Advertising.

On the other hand, many examples of good ads for worthy causes are not featured.

We endorse such causes– and public service advertising on their behalf.

But our focus is how to create advertising that helps businesses stay in business and prosper. (Then, of course, you'll earn enough to support worthy causes.)

Ethics.

Sad to say, this ain't no ethics book.

Or a grammar book, as some might note.*

One of the essential forces of advertising and marketing is the search for advantage.

The "break the rules" spirit of the creative mind and the "bend the rules" history of many successful campaigns will continue to produce many examples of questionable ethics.

In our own lives, we've found that ethical questions are seldom those that confront you with bold moral choices– they just sort of sneak up on you. And you do the best you can.

Our best advice is that you be of good heart and good intent in dealings with your clients and your fellow human beings.

In return, we offer our best wishes for your good fortune and great success.

And this book.

An ad from Procter & Gamble dealing with the complex problem of diapers and recycling.

Can we help you?
Call 312-871-1179 and real human beings at The Copy Workshop will do their absolute best to meet your needs.

* One departure from accepted usage is our use of the apostrophe with decades – 60's, etc. Our justification is that it is an implied possessive, i.e. "the decade of the 60's." But frankly, we just think it looks better.

Leonard S. Matthews
President, American Association
of Advertising Agencies (79-88)

SECOND THOUGHTS...
Bruce asked me to add some observations on how things have changed in our industry since The Copy Workshop Workbook was first published.

First, the weather's better.

After retiring from the 4A's in New York, we moved to California and I bought into a small agency in San Diego where my daughter worked.

My son joined us, and it once again proves to me that no matter what size agency you're in, this is a great business when you like the people you work with.

Second, this book is needed more than ever.

Fewer agencies of any size have the time or the resources to train young professionals and this is even more true for a smaller ad agency like ours.

The smaller the agency, the bigger the problem – since you're also missing that group interaction where senior people help the cub copywriter learn on the job.

We have a number of copies of Bruce's book at our agency – and they get well-used by our junior people. It's still the best "How To" book I've ever seen.

I've also found it a real help in getting Account Executives to understand the creative process.

In this New Edition, Bruce has added more emphasis on "Integrated Marketing."

I think that's good.

(continued on next page.)

Introduction.

We've needed a book like this.

It presents the essential creative and business principles needed for one of the toughest jobs in American business – writing effective advertising.

It was written by one of our industry's genuine creative talents – Bruce Bendinger.

I first met Bruce in 1970, when I was President of Leo Burnett. He came to us from one of Chicago's creative boutiques, where he'd won numerous awards. We started him on one of our toughest accounts – P & G's All Temperature Cheer.

Over the next two years, Bruce led a team that built Cheer into the #2 brand in the category with advertising that was engaging, yet effective.

In 1972, we named him a vice-president and Creative Director. He was 27.

Since then, Bruce has established himself as a top creative consultant, doing projects for clients and agencies across the country.

He also spent a few years as Sr. VP, Group Creative Director at FCB/Chicago, where he saved the Pizza Hut account for the agency – with work that helped turn that client's business around.

We worked together again in Washington, DC on Campaign '76 and, over the years, we kept in touch.

When Bruce sent me an early version of the book, I opened it with curiosity... and then delight.

I thoroughly enjoyed it.

It's great reading – Bruce demonstrates contemporary copywriting at the same time he teaches it.

And even though this book was written for advertising copywriters, there's something in it for everyone in our business.

Bruce set out to do a tough job.

I think he's done it wonderfully.

You're going to enjoy this book.

Leonard S. Matthews

Leonard S. Matthews
Former President,
American Association of Advertising Agencies (4A's)

(continued from previous page.)

But I think it's also worth mentioning that this is what the best agencies have done all along.

At Leo Burnett, if it was something that would help a client's business – we did it. And so should you.

I hope this book helps you find new ways to help your clients.

Because media advertising isn't the only way to build our client's brands.

Finally, I'm a genuine fan of Bruce's writing in this book – because it demonstrates the quality and attention that all our work deserves.

Because when we do work we can be proud of; when we do work that builds our clients' businesses; when we work as a team with people we like – there's not a better business in the world.

Len Matthews
Rancho Santa Fe

How to Read This Book.

However you want.

If you think you want to be a copywriter, use it like a good friend. Or a good boss.

If you're already in the advertising business, use it like a set of stretching exercises.

You can do the exercises if you feel like it. Or, better yet, apply some of the principles to your latest assignment– the one that's due tomorrow.

If you're a college student, use it the way your teacher tells you.

And, if you just picked it up because you're curious about advertising… enjoy yourself.

Because having a good time is one of the ways you make great advertising.

Bruce Bendinger

Bruce Bendinger on CBS Morning News.

5

Once upon a time...
copywriting was taught.

It was a skilled craft, acquired through years of apprenticeship and hard work.

But TV, The Baby Boom, and The Creative Revolution changed all that.

The shift from print to television created copywriters with outdated skills.

Then came the 60's.

War Babies, our first TV generation, hit the advertising business about the same time Bill Bernbach's writers and art directors were revolutionizing it.

Creative careers accelerated.

A memorable theme and a decent TV idea turned a writer into a Creative Supervisor.

Escalating salaries and expectations made apprenticeship unaffordable and impractical.

The economy changed.

The easy growth of the 60's slowed in the 70's and staggered into the 80's.

Clients grew nervous.

While slowly, the tempo grew faster.

Now it's the 90's. Faster than ever. Tougher than ever. More choices. More chances.

For small clients, increased media noise made it harder than ever to be heard.

For large clients, growing bureaucracies made it harder than ever to decide.

For agencies, the battle between the rules of research and the rule-breaking spirit of The Creative Revolution just made it harder.

And so it goes.

Haphazardly ever after...

Meanwhile...

You have a job to do.

As a copywriter.

And maybe you're not getting as much help as you'd like. That's what this book is about.

The Objective is to give you some help that will help you do your job better.

The Strategy is to present excellent examples and the principles that make them work.

The Tactic is this book.

The first step of the journey is to become a student of our craft.

Let's Go!

HISTORICAL NOTE #2.

Though a business practice since earliest recorded history, advertising grew and prospered in the USA.

The spirit of advertising seems to be uniquely American – due to a number of unique forces:

The English Language.

An adaptable, democratic and easy-to-use language, English has become the language of business around the world.

Useful concepts and phrases are quickly adapted and adopted.

It's a language made for today's changing marketplace.

Economic Opportunity.

With an abundance of resources and opportunity, America had a population motivated to make the most of it and a government that encouraged and subsidized enterprise.

Democracy

The marketplace is about choice. America was the best place to have a new idea and make it happen.

One of the key players in this process has been the person who shapes the communications of commerce – the copywriter.

An American original.

As we move to a world economy, the need for creative and motivating communication has become a world-wide opportunity.

But it started here.

Index:

THE FIRST SECTION:
We'll start with a look at the early breakthroughs in thinking about advertising problems.

And, we'll take a brief look at some of the forces shaping today's marketplace.

Then, we'll examine the creative or "ideation" process and show you some ways to develop more flexibility in your thinking.

Finally, we'll talk about the way verbal and **visual** communication have to work together.

A MESSAGE FOR READERS WHO AREN'T WRITERS.
Though this book is for copywriters and advertising students, there's something in it for almost everybody.

If you're in business, perhaps it can help you be a more effective marketer.

If you're not, it will probably make you a smarter consumer.

It's an introduction to modern communication techniques.

It can help you learn to solve problems creatively.

It can help you learn to work with others more effectively to solve business problems.

It can make communicating to others easier and more fun.

This is the beginning of one of the most interesting journeys in American business.

Along the way, you may learn a few new concepts and develop a few new skills.

You might even enjoy it.

MORE WORDS.

THE TOUGH SECTION:
It deals with the development of Advertising Strategy and basic Copywriting Techniques.

The Strategy section will help you learn how to write a P&G-style Advertising Strategy statement.

It's a complex topic covered as simply as possible.

Addendums feature a survey of numerous agency strategy formats.

There's a short but important section on what makes for a good Selling Idea and, almost as important, how to sell ideas once you have them.

And an introduction to contemporary Copywriting Style.

ONWARDS...

THE LAST SECTION:
We'll talk about working in the advertising business.

We'll talk about working relationships in the advertising business.

We'll talk about how things can go wrong and how to make things go right. Hopefully.

This section includes discussions of: **Group Creativity, Supervision** and **Team Work.**

We'll talk about copywriting opportunities outside of advertising. (The good news – there are a lot of them!)

We'll talk about building your "Book," and getting a job.

Finally, we'll talk about how it all works together – and what it takes to make a great Campaign!

Assignment #0.

These Assignments are so easy, we won't even give them a number.

Do them anyway.

They're designed to help you start thinking about advertising.

#0/A. MAGAZINE EXERCISE.

- Pick 2 ads you LIKE.
  Tell us why you like them.

- Pick 2 ads you HATE.
  Tell us why you hate them.

#0/B. VCR EXERCISE.

Tonight, when you watch TV, save the commercials and zap the programs.

Now, look at them again.

- Pick the 2 commercials you like best.
  Why did you like them?

- Pick the 2 commercials you like least.
  Why didn't you like them?

#0/C. SCRAP FILE(S).

- Start a file of ads you like.
- Start another file. Start saving ads or articles on subjects or businesses that interest you.

Think of it this way – if you had your own agency, what accounts would you like to have. Or, to think of it another way, what companies would you like to be working for?

Start to save and clip.

#0/D. THE PAPER CLIP ASSIGNMENT.

- Create a print ad for a paper clip.

Make a rough sketch of the ad, write the headline(s) and body copy.

We want you to exercise your imagination.

But, remember, the purpose of the ad is to sell the item. Limit ad size to 8x10.

Since this is a workbook, you might want to clip your ads to this page.
Speaking of Paper Clips…
Here's a classic copywriting assignment from Sears.
Do it now– and then see how you'd do it after reading this book.

Assignment #1.

I CAUGHT MY DAD EATING BARBECUED RICE KRISPIES!

You think I'm joking don't you? I only wish I were. The ghastly truth is that grown ups, not content with eating us children's RICE KRISPIES cereal normally with milk and sugar, are now cooking with them. Look, I came in and there's my dad eating his tea. And he is ~~actually~~ actually eating barbecued RICE KRISPIES! "Your mum cooked it" he says shamelessly. "Barbecued meat loaf in barbecue sauce… it's jolly nice." "Is there any more?" I say cooly, obviously meaning to give what's left to some deserving children. "But you're always complaining about me cooking with RICE KRISPIES.. I didn't think you'd like it." says my mum. "Here's your egg and chips."

We're all ~~domed~~ ~~doomd~~ doomed in lots of trouble.

BARBECUED MEAT LOAVES

BARBECUE SAUCE

Kellogg's RICE KRISPIES. Now everyone's hearing how good they are.

This ad for "Barbecued Rice Krispies" won awards in Great Britain.
It sold a few Rice Krispies, too. Now it's your turn. Create an ad like this one.

ASSIGNMENT #1 (Cont'd)

First, pick your **product.**

Throughout the book, you'll be asked to "pick a product."

Sometimes the categories are very specific and sometimes they aren't.

In this case, your product is either:

A. A product you like –

Cereal, peanut butter , whatever.

B. A service you might offer –

Baby sitting, dog-walking, whatever.

C. An event –

A party, a picnic, lunch, whatever.

D. You –

Think of it as a fun way to do a resumé.

HERE'S HOW TO DO IT:

1. Find an appropriate picture of yourself – snapshot, school picture, etc. That's your **visual**.

2. Decide on your product.

Got it? Good.

If you can find a picture of your product, maybe that should be in the ad, too.

3. Write a **headline**.

It can be a quote, a story title, or a "true confessions" type of headline.

Whatever.

4. Write some **copy**.

Tell us things we should know about your product. Why is it a good product?

What's the **"benefit"** of your product?

Write it like a story or a short theme.

5. You might want to add an extra something at the bottom: a coupon, your recipe for a great peanut butter sandwich, directions to the lunchroom. An offer, a slogan. Whatever.

6. Now put 'em all together in a layout that looks sort of like the Rice Krispies ad.

YOU MAY TRACE THIS FOR YOUR LAYOUT.

As you can see by the Rice Krispies ad, neatness is optional.
It can be typed up nice and neat. Or super sloppy. Whatever.
There's only *one absolute requirement*.
Have fun.

Advertising's Ages.

Claude Hopkins. Copywriter.
In 1908, Lord & Thomas paid him
$185,000 a year! He was worth it.
Hopkins' clients made millions.

* Throughout this book, the words "product" and "brand" are used interchangeably.

In the beginning, advertising agencies were advertising "agents."

They sold advertising "space," primarily in newspapers and magazines, and collected a commission. Today, it's usually 17.65%.

Advertising was "keeping your name before the public." After all, customers who know your name are more likely to buy your product.*

Today, we call that "Awareness" and it's still a priority of almost all advertising.

Then, in the early 1900's, a young man named **Albert Lasker** at the Lord & Thomas agency (now Foote, Cone & Belding) had a revelation.

The advertising business was *not* selling space. Rather, it was selling what was *inside* that space. The advertising itself.

Advertising was *"Salesmanship in print."*

Claude Hopkins, a Lord & Thomas copywriter, was advertising's first great salesman.

In "Scientific Advertising," Hopkins describes the attitude a successful copywriter must develop.

"Don't think of people in the mass.
That gives you a blurred view.
Think of a typical individual, man or woman, who is likely to want what you sell."

Hopkins continues…

"The advertising man studies the consumer.
He tries to place himself in the position of the buyer. His success largely depends on doing that to the exclusion of everything else."

Times have changed.

The truth remains.

Talk *to* people.

One at a time.

PRE-EMPTION.

Hopkins is also credited with inventing a technique known as *"pre-emption."*

You take a product feature or a quality that is generic to the category, and, by pre-empting that feature, you make it yours.

Two early examples were *"It's Toasted"* for Lucky Strike and the claim that Schlitz beer bottles were sterilized with *"Live Steam."*

In fact, all tobacco was "toasted," and all beer bottles were sterilized with steam.

This advertising technique is still used today.

Drink an Orange

Orange juice—a *delicious* beverage—is *healthfulness itself.* California orange juice is rich in flavor and bouquet.

Have you a tendency to overeat?—orange juice provides an aid to digestion that counteracts the ill effects of the heavy meal.

California orange juice is advised by thousands of physicians for the tiniest babies as well as for grown-ups. It provides a needed food

value and aids in the proper assimilation of food.

In short, the fresh, pure, *live juice* of good oranges, which comes to you in Nature's germproof package, is a *natural regulator* that every mother and wife should be careful to serve to the whole family at every meal.

Why forego for even a single day this natural liquid food that makes *all other* foods more healthful?

Sunkist
California Seedless Navel Oranges

Sunkist navel oranges are juicy, sweet, full-flavored and delicious.

They are seedless, firm and *tender.* Because of these facts hundreds of thousands of house-

wives, and famous chefs, prefer them for salads and desserts. Write for free booklet of excellent tested recipes. Try the many dainty dishes you can make with this luscious fruit.

CALIFORNIA FRUIT GROWERS EXCHANGE
Co-operative — Non-profit — Eastern Headquarters
Dept. A99   139 North Clark Street, Chicago

All first-class dealers sell Sunkist Oranges and Lemons. Look for the name "Sunkist" on tissue wrappers, and save wrappers for beautiful silverware.

Use the Sunkist Orange Juice Extractor
10c—from Your Grocer or Fruit Dealer

The Sunkist Juice Extractor is especially designed to extract the juice of the largest as well as the smaller sizes of either Sunkist oranges or lemons. It is a new pattern of unusually large size which is manufactured of heavy tough glass exclusively for us.

We are distributing an enormous number of these at cost simply to facilitate the preparation of orange juice. This gives you, at a minimum price, the best orange juice extractor that fruit experts can devise.

If you cannot secure this from your dealer, send 16c in stamps to cover cost and expense of mailing and we will send it direct to you by parcel post. 24c to points in Canada.

CALIFORNIA FRUIT GROWERS EXCHANGE
Co-operative — Non-profit
Eastern Headquarters
Dept. A99   139 N. Clark Street
Chicago

This Juice Extractor 10c from Your Dealer anywhere in U.S.

This is an exact reproduction of the Extractor, actual size.

COPY BY HOPKINS.

Here's one of Hopkins' most famous ads for Sunkist.

In 1916, this was a new idea for the average American – *Orange Juice!*

The headline was simple and perfect. "Drink an Orange."

Now look at the first copy section.

First, Hopkins focuses on **Consumer Benefits** – good taste and good health.

Next, to support those benefits, he focuses on **Features** or **Attributes** of the product, expressed as **Product Benefits** – such as "Nature's germ-proof package."

Note the use of Informative Captions throughout.

Finally, Hopkins "Asks for the order" and closes with – An Offer.

Claude Hopkins and Albert Lasker actually had a juice extractor designed and manufactured.

They knew it would help increase the use of oranges.

And it worked!

After Hopkins offered good reasons to add orange juice to one's diet, and a "Juice Extractor" for *only 10¢*, America's breakfast habits changed forever.

Palmolive

The successor to ordinary toilet soaps in Particular Homes. Made of Pure Imported Olive and Palm Oils skillfully blended and combined with Cocoa Butter. **Palmolive** is not merely a cleanser, it combines all the virtues of the wonderful ingredients from which it is made. It allays irritation and inflammation and supplies the necessary oils for harsh skins and dry scalps.

Palmolive exercises the skin in that it stimulates the action of the many tiny pores and glands. The removal of all obstacles allows free circulation of the blood, and the delicate nourishment embodied in **Palmolive** supplies just the necessary impetus to restore the skin to its proper condition after cleansing it. Continued use will produce a beautiful, healthy, rosy complexion. There is no complexion that **Palmolive** cannot improve. If your dealer cannot supply you, send us his name and 15 cents and we will forward, prepaid, a full size cake.

Send four cents in stamps, to cover cost of mailing, and the *names of your grocer and druggist*, and we will send one of our beautiful oriental photogravures without advertising upon it, suitable for framing, size 10 x 16 inches. Address,

B. J. JOHNSON SOAP CO., 318 Fowler St., Milwaukee, Wis.-

Image Advertising. *Though Hopkins might deny it, he also did image advertising. Here, he took an unknown soap made of palm and olive oils and created America's leading beauty soap.* **Palmolive!** *Despite the "reason why" copy, the real impact of this ad is visual. Once again, an offer. This time, the art from the ad!*

A $100,000 Dish

New-Type Baked Beans Which College-Trained Scientific Cooks Have Spent Years in Perfecting

It has cost us at least $100,000 to perfect Van Camp's Pork and Beans.

Modern culinary experts—men with college training—have devoted some years to this dish. Able scientists and famous chefs have co-operated with them.

This Was Wrong

Old-style baked beans were very hard to digest. They were always under-baked. Yet the baking crisped them and broke them—made some hard and some mushy.

In the Van Camp kitchens each lot of beans is analyzed before we start to cook. They are boiled in water freed from minerals, because hard water makes them tough.

They are baked in steam ovens by live steam under pressure at 245 degrees. They are thus baked for hours—baked as beans should be—without bursting or crisping a bean.

856 Sauces

The zestful sauce which we bake with Van Camp's would itself give the dish distinction.

But these scientific cooks made 856 sauces before they attained this perfection. This ideal tang and savor came only through months of development.

A far greater accomplishment was to fit baked beans for easy digestion, while leaving them mealy and whole.

This Is Perfect

The result is a new-type dish which will change your whole idea of baked beans. It will multiply their popularity. Above all, it will not tax digestion. And it costs you less—all ready-baked—than do home-baked beans. Please order a trial meal.

VAN CAMP'S

Pork and Beans

Baked With the Van Camp Sauce — Also Baked Without the Sauce

Your first shave

will prove, beyond all doubt, the claims men make for this unique shaving cream

Let us send you a 10-shave tube to try

WE'VE built Palmolive Shaving Cream to a national business success by making few claims for it. We let it prove its case by sending a 10-day test tube free to all who ask. In that way, we've gained leadership in a highly competitive field in only a few years.

130 formulas tried

Before offering Palmolive Shaving Cream, we asked 1000 men their supreme desires in a shaving cream. Then met them exactly.

We tried and discarded 130 formulas before finding the right one. We put our 60 years of soap experience behind this creation. The result is a shaving cream unlike any you have ever tried.

Five advantages

1. Multiplies itself in lather 250 times.
2. Softens the beard in one minute.
3. Maintains its creamy fullness for 10 minutes on the face.
4. Strong bubbles hold the hairs erect for cutting.
5. Fine after-effects due to palm and olive oil content.

Just send coupon

Your present method may suit you well. But still there may be a better one. This test may mean much to you in comfort. Send the coupon before you forget.

THE PALMOLIVE COMPANY (Del. Corp.), CHICAGO, ILL.

- 10 SHAVES FREE -
and a can of Palmolive After Shaving Talc

Simply insert your name and address and mail to Dept. B-1196, The Palmolive Company (Del. Corp.), 3702 Iron St., Chicago, Ill.

Residents of Wisconsin should address The Palmolive Company (Wis. Corp.), Milwaukee, Wis.

The Hopkins Approach.
Note the similarities–
"130 formulas/856 Sauces."
The "Dish" ad positions Van-Camp's against home-cooked beans.
*The "First Shave" ad positions Palmolive against other shaving soaps and offers a **Free Sample**.*
Again, Hopkins changed America's habits.

Famous Copywriters.

Helen Lansdowne Resor.

"She had a dozen ideas to the minute," an associate recalled, *"and kept them coming so fast you couldn't possibly keep up and had to sit down afterwards with a pencil and paper and try to sort them out."*

"She had a brilliant feminine mind," said another, *"that darted and dipped and swooped with terrifying speed and accuracy."*

In many ways, it was a marriage of opposites - but it worked.

Stanley was slow and serious. Helen was quick and smiling.

Stanley was quite conservative. Helen was a leader in supporting women's suffrage and planned parenthood.

Even at a time when women did not yet have the vote, many were prominent in the early days of advertising.

In 1903, the magazine *Profitable Advertising* profiled the careers of 40 women copywriters, advertising artists, agents and advisers.

Other prominent ad women were: copywriter-turned-author **Helen Woodward** (who wrote "Through Many Windows"), **Louise Taylor Davis** (Y&R), **Jean Wade Rindlaub** (BBDO) and the legendary **Bernice Fitz-Gibbon** who wrote copy for Macy's - *"It's smart to be thrifty."* Wanamaker's and Gimbel's - *"Nobody, but nobody, undersells Gimbel's."*

How's this for a story?

Beautiful and talented copywriter meets handsome young account executive.

They work together, fall in love, and marry.

Together, they build the world's largest ad agency. Sound far-fetched? It's true.

In the early 1900's, after graduating from highschool as Valedictorian, **Helen Lansdowne** was writing retail ads in Cincinnati.

First, she wrote for a Cincinnati newspaper and then a local streetcar advertising company.

Meanwhile, a bright young account executive was making a name for himself inventing brand names for clients and developing strategies that appealed to the growing middle class.

His name was **Stanley Resor.**

He hired Helen Lansdowne as a copywriter for his small Cincinnati agency.

When J. Walter Thompson hired Stanley (and his brother) to open a Cincinnati office, Helen went with them.

At the time, many JWT clients had products that were purchased by women. Helen was the right person at the right place at the right time.

"I supplied the feminine point of view.

I watched the advertising to see that the idea, the wording, and the illustrating were effective for women."

Even then, understanding and insight into the consumer made a tremendous difference in the effectiveness of the advertising.

Her ads for Woodbury's Soap increased sales 1000% with – *"A skin you love to touch."*

She was the first woman to appear before the board of Procter & Gamble. But not the last.

She explained the advertising to a room full of men who marketed to women.

In 1911, Stanley and Helen moved to the New York office. In 1916, Stanley was part of the buy-out of the still small JWT. In 1917, they married.

Together, they ran JWT. He ran client service and she supervised creation of the advertising.

She never really had a title.

But then again, she didn't need one.

By 1922, the agency had tripled in size to $10.7 million. They grew to $20.7 million in 1926 and moved into new offices.

Helen supervised the legendary JWT office decor as well as the advertising. She nurtured and supervised a creative staff where women were paid well and treated well.

And they wrote advertising that worked.

SOFT SOAP & HARD SELL.

Here are two famous JWT campaigns.

For Woodbury's, Helen Resor sold softness, romance and sex appeal.

Copy featured a skin-care regimen and an offer of product samples and the art from the advertisement.

For Lux, they sold glamor, luxury, fame... and sex appeal.

Helen Resor upgraded the testimonial format by getting famous people to endorse JWT products.

Stanley Resor called it "the spirit of emulation." Helen called her friends.

The first famous personage was Mrs. O.H.P. Belmont, a leader in New York society at the time – as well as a prominent feminist – she endorsed Pond's in exchange for a donation to one of her favorite charities.

Ads featured Mrs. Reginald Vanderbilt, the Duchess de Richelieu and the Queen of Rumania.

Helen also invited a high-school chum to come work at JWT – James Webb Young. (You'll read a bit about him in Chapter 3.)

Caples, Getchell & More...

The early copywriters invented the craft of copywriting.

Here's some work by a few of the pioneers: John Caples, Bruce Barton, Stirling Getchell, Ned Jordan and others.

John Caples. *BBDO's direct response and copy testing expert.*

To men who want to
Quit Work some day

Here's a famous Caples Headline. (He kept working for 50 years)

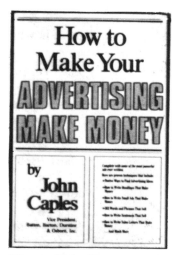

"How to Make Your Advertising Make Money."
© 1983 John Caples

Read all about it.

You can understand Caples' style just by reading the Table of Contents of his well-written and well-organized book – *"How to Make Your Advertising Make Money."*

TABLE OF CONTENTS:

The advertising of the time has an innocent charm. Here is Caples' famous "They Laughed" ad. The style is dated, but the appeals still work.

"Can he really play?" a girl whispered. "Heavens no!" Arthur exclaimed. "He never played a note in his life."

They Laughed When I Sat Down At the Piano But When I Started to Play!~

ARTHUR had just played "The Rosary." The room rang with applause. I decided that this would be a dramatic moment for me to make my debut. To the amazement of all my friends, I strode confidently over to the piano and sat down.

"Jack is up to his old tricks," somebody chuckled. The crowd laughed. They were all certain that I couldn't play a single note.

"Can he really play?" I heard a girl whisper to Arthur.

"Heavens, no!" Arthur exclaimed· "He never played a note in all his life. . . But just you watch him. This is going to be good."

I decided to make the most of the situation. With mock dignity I drew out a silk handkerchief and lightly dusted off the piano keys. Then I rose and gave the revolving piano stool a quarter of a turn, just as I had seen an imitator of Paderewski do in a vaudeville sketch.

"What do you think of his execution?" called a voice from the rear.

"We're in favor of it!" came back the answer, and the crowd rocked with laughter.

Then I Started to Play

Instantly a tense silence fell on the guests. The laughter died on their lips as if by magic. I played through the first few bars of Beethoven's immortal Moonlight Sonata. I heard gasps of amazement. My friends sat breathless — spellbound!

I played on and as I played I forgot the people around me. I forgot the hour, the place, the breathless listeners. The little world I lived in seemed to fade — seemed to grow dim — unreal. Only the music was real. Only the music and visions it brought me. Visions as beautiful and as changing as the wind blown clouds and drifting moonlight that long ago inspired the master composer. It seemed as if the master

musician himself were speaking to me—speaking through the medium of music—not in words but in chords. Not in sentences but in exquisite melodies!

A Complete Triumph!

As the last notes of the Moonlight Sonata died away, the room resounded with a sudden roar of applause. I found myself surrounded by excited faces. How my friends carried on! Men shook my hand — wildly congratulated me— pounded me on the back in their enthusiasm! Everybody was exclaiming with delight—plying me with rapid questions. . . "Jack! Why didn't you tell us you could play like that?". . . "Where *did* you learn?"—"How long have you studied?"— "Who *was* your teacher?"

"I have never even *seen* my teacher," I replied. "And just a short while ago I couldn't play a note.',

"Quit your kidding," laughed Arthur, himself an accomplished pianist. "You've been studying for years. I can tell."

"I have been studying only a short while," I insisted. "I decided to keep it a secret so that I could surprise all you folks."

Then I told them the whole story.

"Have you ever heard of the U. S. School of Music?" I asked.

A few of my friends nodded. "That's a correspondence school, isn't it?" they exclaimed.

"Exactly," I replied. "They have a new simplified method that can teach you to play any instrument by mail in just a few months."

How I Learned to Play Without a Teacher

And then I explained how for years I had longed to play the piano.

"A few months ago," I continued, "I saw an interesting ad for the U. S. School of Music—a new method of learning to play which only cost a few cents a day! The ad told how a woman had mastered the piano in her spare time at home—and *without a teacher!* Best of all, the wonderful new method she used, required no laborious scales — no heartless exercises — no tiresome practising. It sounded so convincing that I filled out the coupon requesting the Free Demonstration Lesson.

"The free book arrived promptly and I started in that very night to study the Demonstration Lesson. I was amazed to see how easy it was to play this new way. Then I sent for the course.

"When the course arrived I found it was just as the ad said — as easy as A.B.C.! And, as

the lessons continued they got easier and easier. Before I knew it I was playing all the pieces I liked best. Nothing stopped me. I could play ballads or classical numbers or jazz, all with equal ease! And I never did have any special talent for music!"

Play Any Instrument

You too, can now *teach yourself* to be an accomplished musician—right at home—in half the usual time. You can't go wrong with this simple new method which has already shown 350,000 people how to play their favorite instruments. Forget that old-fashioned idea that you need special "talent." Just read the list of instruments in the panel, decide which one you want to play and the U. S. School will do the rest. And bear in mind no matter which instrument you choose, the cost in each case will be the same—just a few cents a day. No matter whether you are a mere beginner or already a good performer, you will be interested in learning about this new and wonderful method.

Send for Our Free Booklet and Demonstration Lesson

Thousands of successful students never dreamed they possessed musical ability until it was revealed to them by a remarkable "Musical Ability Test" which we send entirely without cost with our interesting free booklet.

If you are in earnest about wanting to play your favorite instrument—if you really want to gain happiness and increase your popularity—send at once for the free booklet and Demonstration Lesson. No cost — no obligation. Right now we are making a Special offer for a limited number of new students. Sign and send the convenient coupon now — before it's too late to gain the benefits of this offer. Instruments supplied when needed, cash or credit. **U. S. School of Music, 1831 Brunswick Bldg., New York City.**

Pick Your Instrument

Piano	'Cello
Organ	Harmony and
Violin	Composition
Drums and	Sight Singing
Traps	Ukulele
Banjo	Guitar
Tenor	Hawaiian
Banjo	Steel Guitar
Mandolin	Harp
Clarinet	Cornet
Flute	Piccolo
Saxophone	Trombone
Voice and Speech Culture	
Automatic Finger Control	
Piano Accordion	

U. S. School of Music,
1831 Brunswick Bldg., New York City.
Please send me your free book, "Music Lessons in Your Own Home", with introduction by Dr. Frank Crane, Demonstration Lesson and particulars of your Special Offer. I am interested in the following course:

....

Have you above instrument?...............

Name...
(Please write plainly)

Address...

City.............................State.............

THE ADMAN NOBODY KNOWS.

He was a best-selling author, the confidante of Presidents, and a U.S. Congressman.

He was Chairman of the United Negro College Fund and the American Heart Association.

He was a preacher's son named Bruce Barton. He was a copywriter.

His name's still on the door at BBDO – Batten, Barton, Durstine & Osborn.

In addition to his work at BBDO, he wrote continually – articles (he began as a magazine writer) and books.

He combined his religious and advertising backgrounds to write *The Man Nobody Knows*, combining classic parables of Christianity with modern salesmanship.

It was a best-seller.

In a recent book, *The Seven Lost Secrets of Success*, author Joe Vitale lists a number of Barton's classic principles. They include:

• **Discover your real business.** Lipstick or romance? Tires or safety?

• **"Story Selling."** Use the value of parables and stories in delivering your message.

• **The value of sincerity and honesty in effective selling.**

As Barton said...

"The advertisements which persuade people to act are written by men who have an abiding respect for the intelligence of their readers, and a deep sincerity regarding the merits of the goods they have to sell."

In 1937, Barton was appointed to an unexpired term in Congress and elected a year later.

He returned to be President and Chairman of BBDO, but insisted that somebody else run the business.

He just wanted to make ads.

You can't buy a Congressman for $5000. But you can rent him.

By law, an individual PAC (political action committee) can donate only $5000 to a candidate's primary and general election campaign. But that's plenty. Says Rep. Thomas Downey (D., N.Y.), "You can't buy a Congressman for $5000, but you can buy his vote on a particular issue."

An original article in the July Reader's Digest examines how the millions of PAC dollars *have* influenced particular legislation and how "the best Congress money can buy" could *reform* campaign financing.

For 39 million readers, the best reporting their money can buy is in The Digest.®

John Caples of BBDO developed this format for Reader's Digest. Other people write them now, and the account is even with another agency, but these small powerful ads are still winning awards and still pulling in readers for Reader's Digest.

ADVERTISING BUILDS BUSINESSES.

This period demonstrated the power of well-crafted advertising appeals to establish brand name products.

Listerine was a small antiseptic brand 'til JWT Dramatized The Problem of *"Halitosis,"* a semi-scientific advertising word for "bad breath."

Many of the brands we know today were established during this period. With advertising.

Often a bridesmaid but never a bride

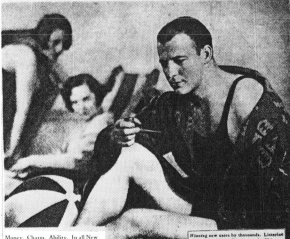

You wouldn't care to meet Marvin

LISTERINE

Listerine gets "Halitosis."

On the left, two hard-working ads that helped build Listerine into a major brand.

As mentioned, they Dramatized the Problem and pre-empted it, with ownership of *"Halitosis,"* a semi-scientific word for "bad breath."

If you can own The Problem, you have a good chance of owning the solution.

J. Stirling Getchell wrote one of the very first POSITIONING ads for Walter Chrysler years before Lee Iaccoca & Avis.

Just one ad, "Look at All Three" helped establish Chrysler as a major auto manufacturer.

Somewhere West of Laramie

SOMEWHERE west of Laramie there's a broncho-busting, steer-roping girl who knows what I'm talking about.

She can tell what a sassy pony, that's a cross between greased lightning and the place where it hits, can do with eleven hundred pounds of steel and action when he's going high, wide and handsome.

The truth is—the Playboy was built for her.

Built for the lass whose face is brown with the sun when the day is done of revel and romp and race.

She loves the cross of the wild and the tame.

There's a savor of links about that car—of laughter and lilt and light—a hint of old loves—and saddle and quirt. It's a brawny thing—yet a graceful thing for the sweep o' the Avenue.

Step into the Playboy when the hour grows dull with things gone dead and stale.

Then start for the land of real living with the spirit of the lass who rides, lean and rangy, into the red horizon of a Wyoming twilight.

JORDAN MOTOR CAR COMPANY, Inc., Cleveland, Ohio

Word Magic...

Is it prose, or is it poetry? The style and vocabulary are dated, but you can feel the appeal of this ad. It tapped into classic imagery – The West– fast horses, fast cars and, perhaps, fast women. What's today's "Word Magic?"

"Look at All Three!

BUT DON'T BUY ANY LOW-PRICED CAR UNTIL YOU'VE DRIVEN THE NEW PLYMOUTH WITH FLOATING POWER"

THOUSANDS of people have been waiting expectantly until today before buying a new car. I hope that you are one of them.

Now that the new low-priced cars are here (including the new Plymouth which will be shown on Saturday) I urge you to carefully *compare* values.

This is the time for you to "shop" and buy wisely. Don't make a deposit on any automobile until you've actually had a demonstration.

It is my opinion that the automobile industry as a whole has never offered such values to the public.

In the new Plymouth we have achieved more than I had ever dared to hope for. If you had told me two years ago that such a big, powerful, beautiful automobile could be sold at the astonishing prices we will announce on Saturday . . . I'd have said it was absolutely impossible.

I have spent my life building fine cars. But no achievement in my career has given me the deep-down satisfaction

A STATEMENT BY WALTER P. CHRYSLER

that I derive from the value you get in this 1932 Plymouth. To me, its outstanding feature is Floating Power. We already know how the public feels about this. Last summer it was news, but today it is an established engineering achievement.

It is my opinion, and I think that of leading engineering authorities, that any new car without Floating Power is obsolete. Drive a Plymouth with Patented Floating Power, and note its utter lack of vibration . . . then drive a car with old-fashioned engine mountings and you will understand what I mean. *There's absolutely no comparison.*

We have made the Plymouth a much larger automobile. It is a BIG car. We have increased its power, lengthened the wheelbase and greatly improved its beauty.

In my opinion you will find the new Plymouth the easiest riding car you have ever driven. Yet with all these improvements we have been able to lower prices.

Again let me urge you, go and see the new Plymouth with Floating Power on Saturday. Be sure to look at all THREE low-priced cars and don't buy any until you do. That is the way to get the most for your money.

FIRST SHOWING NEXT SATURDAY, APRIL 2nd, AT DESOTO, DODGE AND CHRYSLER DEALERS

*Notice how this ad "positions"
Chrysler as one of the three
cars you should consider.*

Y&R

In those days, creating advertising was primarily a copywriter's job.

Then, **Ray Rubicam** broadened the creative process.

First, he involved Research, hiring Northwestern University professor **George Gallup** to study ad readership.

Most important of all, he involved The Art Director in the process.

The result was ads that set new standards for both readership and graphic quality.

His agency, **Young & Rubicam,** set other standards, too.

Rubicam believed, *"Advertising has a responsibility to behave properly."*

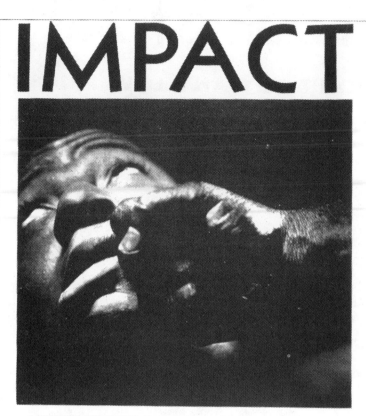

Y&R. An advertising agency advertises itself.
Few "house" ads have been this memorable.
Visual and copy work together, *creating an effect more dynamic than either one by itself.*

28

STEINWAY
The Instrument of the Immortals

There has been but one supreme piano in the history of music. In the days of Liszt and Wagner, of Rubinstein and Berlioz, the pre-eminence of the Steinway was as unquestioned as it is today. It stood then, as it stands now, the chosen instrument of the masters—the inevitable preference wherever great music is understood and esteemed.

STEINWAY & SONS, Steinway Hall, 107-109 E. 14th St., New York
Subway Express Stations at the Door

Steinway. *Classic.*
An early example of IMAGE and POSITIONING.
Note the sense of proportion.
The ad is influenced by design considerations as well as copy.

Rubicam didn't like the Hopkins style of copywriting. He felt,
"You can sell products without bamboozling the public."
Rubicam believed ads should be distinctive.
A good ad was,
"An admirable piece of work."
His philosophy?
"Resist the usual."
Some early Y&R ads are featured here.
They still hold up.

Advertising from back then was a lot different.
The tempo was slower.
But, gradually, the pace quickened.
20th Century technology was creating new consumer miracles: Appliances, convenience foods, automobiles, filter-tip cigarettes, and finally,

TV

Unique Selling Proposition.

Rosser Reeves.
Chairman. Ted Bates & Co.
Author of "Reality in Advertising."
*Inventor. **USP**.*

DEFINITION OF

USP:

1. Each advertisement must make a proposition to the consumer.

Not just words, not just product puffery, not just show-window advertising.

Each advertisement must say to each reader "Buy **this product** and you will get **this specific benefit**."

2. The proposition must be one that the competition either cannot, or does not, offer.

It must be **unique** – either a uniqueness of the brand or a claim not otherwise made in that particular field of advertising.

3. The proposition must be so strong that it can move the mass millions, i.e. pull over new customers to your product.

USP.

This was advertising's child of the 50's.

Rosser Reeves was the father, and his book, "Reality in Advertising," was the New Improved Testament.

The premise was simple.

Find the unique benefit possessed by your product and hammer it home.

Repeatedly.

"M&M's melt in your mouth, not in your hands."

"Colgate cleans your breath, as it cleans your teeth."

In the original Anacin TV commercial, heads full of hammers hammered home the Anacin USP.

Repeatedly.

And Rosser Reeves' agency, Ted Bates & Co., sold carloads of Anacin, Colgate, and M&M's.

The tools of the trade were: slogans, demonstrations, mnemonics, and repetition.

And those tools built businesses.

Repeatedly.

They demonstrated the power of television as an advertising medium.

Repeatedly.

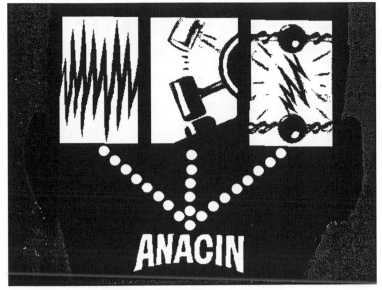

This frame is from the classic Anacin commercial.
It cost $8200 to produce.
It made more money than "Gone with the Wind."

Some commercials were fun to watch.
"Use Ajax (Boom Boom) the Foaming Cleanser."

Today, the discipline of the USP remains, particularly with package goods marketers.

But even Ted Bates & Co. added a new dimension to their USP. It's Unique Selling Proposition plus Unique Selling *Personality.*

Image. The 60's.

Welcome to The Creative Revolution.

REEVES BELIEVES...

"Let's say you have one million dollars tied up in your little company and suddenly your advertising isn't working and sales are going down.

And everything depends on it.

Your future depends on it, your family's future depends on it, other people's families depend on it...

Now, what do you want from me? Fine writing? Or do you want to see the God-damned sales curve stop moving down and start moving up?"

In his spare time, Rosser Reeves wrote short stories and poetry.

But when it came to writing advertising, he was all business. His only gauge for good advertising was "will it work?"

His first lesson –*"You must make* **the product** *interesting, not just make the ad different."*

Copy: "Which hand has the M&M chocolate candy in it?

Not this hand– that's messy, but this hand...

*because **M&M Candies Melt in Your Mouth, not in your hand."***
A Side-by-Side Demo with a ***"Reason Why."*** *It worked.*

The Creative Revolution.

The 60's was the decade of "The Creative Revolution." Three people were instrumental in shaping this dramatic change in advertising.

*All three were copywriters: **David Ogilvy, Leo Burnett** and **Bill Bernbach.***

David Ogilvy.

David Ogilvy hired a model with an eye-patch for Hathaway shirts and wrote a Rolls-Royce headline the world will never forget.

"At 60 miles an hour the loudest noise in this new Rolls-Royce comes from the electric clock."

The title of his book was memorable, too. *"Confessions of an Advertising Man."*

David Ogilvy was a student of the craft of copywriting. His writing combined intelligence, common sense, the lessons of Hopkins, Caples and Reeves, and his own unique wit and style.

Here is Ogilvy's paraphrase of Hopkins.

"I don't write to the crowd.

I try to write from one human being to another human being in the second person singular."

Yet, Ogilvy's contribution moved beyond the rational. It was emotional.

Ogilvy had class. Image.

The style of the man in the Hathaway shirt. The delightfully stuffy Commander Whitehead and *"Schweppervescence,"* a tongue-in-cheek USP.

The dignity of Rolls-Royce with the perfect witty counterpoint.

Ogilvy did advertising that made you like and respect the advertiser. He believed that

"Every advertisement is a long-term investment in the image of a brand."

David Ogilvy. *Copywriter. Though now retired to his French chateau, his agency continues to grow with intelligent ads in the Ogilvy style.*

The Rolls-Royce Silver Cloud—$13,995

"At 60 miles an hour the loudest noise in this new Rolls-Royce comes from the electric clock"

What __makes__ Rolls-Royce the best car in the world? "There is really no magic about it— it is merely patient attention to detail," says an eminent Rolls-Royce engineer.

1. "At 60 miles an hour the loudest noise comes from the electric clock," reports the Technical Editor of THE MOTOR. Three mufflers tune out sound frequencies—acoustically.

2. Every Rolls-Royce engine is run for seven hours at full throttle before installation, and each car is test-driven for hundreds of miles over varying road surfaces.

3. The Rolls-Royce is designed as an *owner-driven* car. It is eighteen inches shorter than the largest domestic cars.

4. The car has power steering, power brakes and automatic gear-shift. It is very easy to drive and to park. No chauffeur required.

5. The finished car spends a week in the final test-shop, being fine-tuned. Here it is subjected to 98 separate ordeals. For example, the engineers use a *stethoscope* to listen for axle-whine.

6. The Rolls-Royce is guaranteed for *three years*. With a new network of dealers and parts-depots from Coast to Coast, service is no problem.

7. The Rolls-Royce radiator has never changed, except that when Sir Henry Royce died in 1933 the monogram RR was changed from red to black.

8. The coachwork is given five coats of primer paint, and hand rubbed between each coat, before *nine* coats of finishing paint go on.

9. By moving a switch on the steering column, you can adjust the shock-absorbers to suit road conditions.

10. A picnic table, veneered in French walnut, slides out from under the dash. Two more swing out behind the front seats.

11. You can get such optional extras as an Espresso coffee-making machine, a dictating machine, a bed, hot and cold water for washing, an electric razor or a telephone.

12. There are three separate systems of power brakes, two hydraulic and one mechanical. Damage to one will not affect the others. The Rolls-Royce is a very *safe* car—and also a very *lively* car. It cruises serenely at eighty-five. Top speed is in excess of 100 m.p.h.

13. The Bentley is made by Rolls-Royce. Except for the radiators, they are identical motor cars, manufactured by the same engineers in the same works. People who feel diffident about driving a Rolls-Royce can buy a Bentley.

PRICE. The Rolls-Royce illustrated in this advertisement—f.o.b. principal ports of entry—costs **$13,995.**

If you would like the rewarding experience of driving a Rolls-Royce or Bentley, write or telephone to one of the dealers listed on opposite page. Rolls-Royce Inc., 10 Rockefeller Plaza, New York 20, N. Y. CIrcle 5-1144.

WOW!! WHAT AN AD!
First, it's smooth as a ride in a Rolls.
Second, it's filled with interesting facts. Ogilvy did his homework.
Third, note the **counterpoint** *– technical facts with a human touch. "The engineers use a stethoscope," "No chauffeur required," "People who feel diffident about driving a Rolls-Royce can buy a Bentley."*
By the way, Ogilvy didn't write the headline – it came from a review in a little known British car magazine. Ogilvy did his homework. Note how the ad ends with an offer. Just like Hopkins.

THE HATHAWAY "STORY."

So what does the eyepatch do?

First, it adds "Story Appeal," increasing interest and readership.

Second, it creates distinctiveness and memorability. (After all, a shirt is a shirt.)

The Eyepatch gives the campaign image continuity.

Third, eye contact. People look back at people. It's natural.

And one is better than none.

The Original Ogilvy

*Ogilvy's first book, **"Confessions of an Advertising Man"** is good. His second, **"Ogilvy on Advertising"** is great! A must read by a master.*

You may not agree with all his "rules," but you have to know them before you can break them.

The Ogilvy Influence.

Here are two first-rate books by two of Ogilvy's business partners:

*"**The New How to Advertise**," by Kenneth Roman (and Jane Maas), is an excellent updated summary of the Ogilvy philosophy.*

*"**Romancing the Brand**," by David Martin of the O&M-affiliated Martin Agency, offers excellent insights into how to put the Ogilvy philosophy to work on a smaller scale.*

The man in the Hathaway shirt

AMERICAN MEN are beginning to realize that it is ridiculous to buy good suits and then spoil the effect by wearing an ordinary, mass-produced shirt. Hence the growing popularity of HATHAWAY shirts, which are in a class by themselves.

HATHAWAY shirts wear infinitely longer—a matter of years. They make you look younger and more distinguished, because of the subtle way HATHAWAY cut collars. The whole shirt is tailored more generously, and is therefore more comfortable. The tails are longer, and stay in your trousers. The buttons are mother-of-pearl. Even the stitching has an ante-bellum elegance about it.

Above all, HATHAWAY make their shirts of remarkable *fabrics*, collected from the four corners of the earth—Viyella and Aertex, from England, woolen taffeta from Scotland, Sea Island cotton from the West Indies, hand-woven madras from India, broadcloth from Manchester, linen batiste from Paris, hand-blocked silks from England, exclusive cottons from the best weavers in America. You will get a great deal of quiet satisfaction out of wearing shirts which are in such impeccable taste.

HATHAWAY shirts are made by a small company of dedicated craftsmen in the little town of Waterville, Maine. They have been at it, man and boy, for one hundred and twenty years.

At better stores everywhere, or write C. F. HATHAWAY, Waterville, Maine, for the name of your nearest store. In New York, telephone OX 7-5566. Prices from $5.95 to $20.00.

Finally, David Ogilvy created an agency. Today, Ogilvy & Mather is one of the world's largest. Much of their success is a result of Ogilvy's philosophy.

Today, his agency abounds with rules and guidelines, which will surprise no one who reads his books.

But Ogilvy himself says, *"I hate rules."*

In the beginning, Ogilvy's image-making was rule-breaking and helped create a whole new style of advertising.

Now Ogilvy & Mather is part of a large agency conglomerate – a result of Ogilvy's one regret – going public.

But his spirit and individuality are still a part of their heritage.

They're still going like sixty.

And the loudest noise is the electronics.

The man from Schweppes is here

MEET Commander Edward Whitehead, Schweppesman Extraordinary from London, England, where the house of Schweppes has been a great institution since 1794.

Commander Whitehead has come to these United States to make sure that every drop of Schweppes Quinine Water bottled here has the original flavor which has long made Schweppes the only mixer for an *authentic* Gin-and-Tonic.

He imports the original Schweppes elixir, and the secret of Schweppes unique carbonation is locked in his brief case. "Schweppervescence," says the Commander, *"lasts the whole drink through."*

It took Schweppes almost a hundred years to bring the flavor of their Quinine Water to its present bittersweet perfection. But it will take you only thirty seconds to mix it with ice and gin in a highball glass. *Then*, gentle reader, you will bless the day you read these words.

P.S. If your favorite store or bar doesn't yet have Schweppes, drop a card to us and we'll make the proper arrangements. Address Schweppes, 30 East 60th Street, New York City.

SCHWEPPES PERSONIFIED.

"Personification" is an interesting technique.

A Person represents The Product.

Here, Ogilvy used Commander Whitehead, who introduced America to Schweppes.

In many ways, he *became* the product. Sophisticated. Attractive. Sociable.

A person who mixes well at parties. Just like Schweppes.

Note the similar layout styles of the Schweppes and Hathaway ads.

Ogilvy studied readership results and determined what he believed were the best layout approaches.

Somewhere West of Ogilvy

Below, an example of modern Ogilvy work – written by Hal Riney, when he ran their San Francisco office.

The San Francisco office became Hal Riney & Partners – just one example of agencies started by Ogilvy people (McCaffrey & McCall is another).

Note the rhythm and rhyme.

Also note the combination of appeals – Visual communication on the left side of the page and a verbal "Reason Why" on the right.

Why the beer from here is better than the beer from there.

If Oregon were like other places you'd expect the beer here to be like other beers.

But in attitude as well as geography, our state is different from places like Wisconsin and Missouri. And that's why Portland brewed Blitz-Weinhard is so different from the beers brewed in Milwaukee or St. Louis.

Natural beer, naturally brewed and naturally aged.

Over the last 30 years or so science has revolutionized the art of brewing.

There are chemicals on the market which can shorten the time it takes to brew beer. And other chemicals which can preserve it once it's bottled. There are machines available to make beer ferment faster, and techniques to make it "age" quicker.

These are cost-saving innovations. But they're not a natural part of the brewing process, so they're not part of making Blitz-Weinhard beer.

At Blitz-Weinhard, we use no additives, no preservatives, no chemicals and no shortcuts. Our product is naturally brewed, naturally fermented and naturally aged.

This means it costs us more to make Blitz-Weinhard. But we believe natural country deserves nothing less than natural beer.

A small brewery.

Once America's demand for beer was supplied by hundreds of small, local breweries. Today, brewing is heavily concentrated in the hands of a few large, national manufacturers with sizable brewing plants located in different parts of the country.

But Blitz-Weinhard is made only at the original brewery in Portland. As a result the total amount of beer we can produce is quite small by industry standards. This means we are able to brew with the extra time, care and attention required to produce the finest product possible.

The hops and barley are better here.

There's a type of barley which grows only in the Northwest, and it is held in high regard by brewers everywhere. It's safe to say that brewers in the East and Midwest would use most of this barley, but for the high cost of shipping it across the country.

Because we're close to the water, we are able to brew Blitz-Weinhard with more of this premium barley than any other brewer is known to.

We also brew our beer with premium cascade hops. This variety was developed by Oregon State University, and has been acclaimed throughout the industry as the equal of Bavaria's famed Hallertau hop. But the Willamette and Yakima valleys are the only areas suited to growing cascade hops, and the relatively small crop assures a premium price - a price we are willing to pay in order to brew Blitz-Weinhard with the finest ingredients available.

Fresher beer is better beer.

Newly brewed beer must spend time in aging vats to bring its flavor to maturity. Aging is necessary to mellow the beer, and to bring out its sparkling clarity.

But once in the bottle, time is the enemy of good beer. In a matter of weeks, it can begin to lose its freshness. Eventually it will become stale and unappetizing.

Because our goal is to supply quality beer only to the people of Oregon, bottles of Blitz-Weinhard don't have to spend weeks or months being shipped long distances, or standing in warehouses. Brewery-fresh Blitz-Weinhard beer can reach the farthest point of our distribution within hours of leaving Portland.

Taste and tradition, guaranteed.

Blitz-Weinhard has been brewing premium beer for Oregonians since Territorial days. We are the oldest continuously operating brewery west of the Mississippi, and throughout our 122 year history, we have tried to follow the basic guiding principle laid down by our founder, pioneer brewer Henry Weinhard.

Spare no time, effort, nor cost to give our customers a perfect glass of beer.

In the spirit of these words, every bottle and can of Blitz-Weinhard beer carries a written guarantee of satisfaction. If you are ever displeased with our product, for any reason, your money will be refunded.

We're aware that other brewers don't offer a guarantee like ours. But when you think about it, there's no reason why they should.

After all, they're not the beer here.

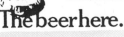

The beer here.

Leo Burnett.

Meanwhile, **Leo Burnett** was building an agency in Chicago, Illinois.

Leo, a loveable man in a freshly rumpled suit, had bowls of apples in the lobby, peas picked in the moonlight, and a slogan that was pure Leo.

"When you reach for the stars, you might not quite get one, but, you won't come up with a handful of mud either."

Everyone loved Leo.

And they loved his advertising.

Leo put red meat on a red background.

He took a little pea company in LeSeur, Minnesota and grew the Jolly Green Giant.

His Chicago agency took a New York cigarette and moved it to Marlboro Country.

Leo's Logo.

Charlie the Tuna, Morris the Cat, the Pillsbury Doughboy, Tony the Tiger and all the other cute cartoon critters of Kellogg's were born at Leo's.

Leo believed in ***"inherent drama."***

He believed it existed in almost every product or service.

Leo believed in Middle America.

His "Chicago-style" advertising showed love and respect for people.

It felt home grown and authentic.

It was. Leo called it,

"The glacier-like power of friendly familiarity."

That friendly strength and the hard-working Middle Americans who thought the way Leo did, grew his agency into one of the largest in the world.

Now there's a big, brawny building in Chicago with his name on it, where thousands of people work every day.

And the apples are still in the lobby.

Leo.

THE BURNETT STYLE.

Strong, simple instinctive imagery.
Each with its own *"inherent drama."*

Marlboro Today.
Burnett rode the brand all the way to #1.

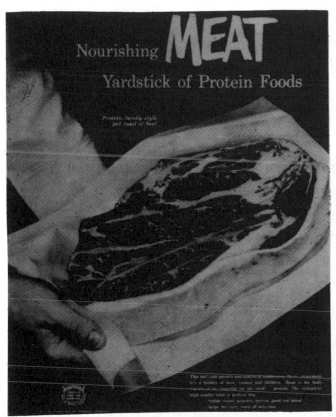

Red Meat on a Red Background. *One of Leo's earliest.*
The power of the ad isn't the words – it's the **Image.**
This black and white rendition doesn't do it justice.
The selling idea, very simply, is **Red!**

Strong brand. Strong Flankers. Strong Heritage.

The Original Marlboro Man.
Projecting the personality of a cigarette.
A cowboy for a cigarette with a British name?
The "glacier-like power" begins to build.
By the way, Leo saw a Life Magazine article
on cowboys – that's where the original idea came from.

The
filter doesn't
get between
you and
the flavor!

Marlboro
THE NEW FILTER CIGARETTE FROM PHILIP MORRIS

Yes, this easy-drawing but hard-working filter sure delivers
the goods on flavor. Popular filter price. This new Marlboro
makes it easy to change to a filter. This one you'll like.

"Blessings on thee, little man, barefoot boy with cheeks full of Kellogg's Corn Flakes."
Classic Work for Kellogg's.

The Burnett Secret.

Here are what I believe to be the four main reasons for Leo Burnett's long-term success:

1. AGENCY TEAMWORK.

The people at Burnett work *together.*

Creative and account people work as equals. They listen to each other, and respect each other.

2. CLIENT PARTNERSHIP.

The Leo Burnett Agency operates as a dedicated business partner.

They have the best interests of their clients at heart. Always.

It is not an act, it is a rock-solid belief.

This builds client respect and trust and unifies the agency around a single-minded goal – *build the client's business.*

3. LONG-TERM CAMPAIGNS

Burnett knows how to stick with an idea. This becomes a tremendous competitive advantage.

The cumulative power of an advertising idea takes time to build.

Of all advertising agencies, Leo Burnett has more long-running campaigns than any other. By far.

They know how to take a simple idea, like *"fly the friendly skies"* for United Airlines, and make it last for 20 years. Make that 30.

Burnett may or may not have better ideas in the first year.

But, over time, they know how to keep a campaign fresh.

They don't change campaigns just because there's a new creative team or a new ad manager.

They know that building the equity and image of a brand is a long-term job.

And they do it.

Year after year after year.

4. HARD WORK.

Nobody outworks Burnett.

It is only possible to work as hard as the people at Burnett.

It is impossible to work harder.

Some successful new agencies, such as Chiat/Day, have this same work ethic.

Once upon a time, when I worked at Leo Burnett, I received a compliment from The Creative Director of the World.

"You know why you're good?" he asked.

"Why, no?" I said, puffing up for some flattery about my unique talent or, perhaps, my keen intelligence.

"You've got stamina." said The Creative Director of the World.

Nobody outworks the Leo Burnett Company.

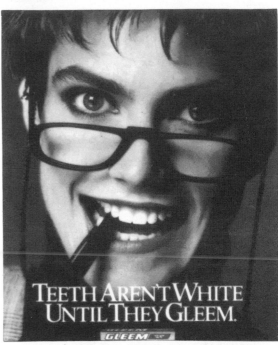

Burnett knows how to keep P&G smiling. A long-term relationship.

Dewar's Profiles.
Another example of
a long-term campaign.
Burnett knows how to
stick with it and
keep it fresh..

I found out about Joan

The way she talks, you'd think she was in Who's Who. Well! I found out what's what with her. Her husband own a bank? Sweetie, not even a bank account. Why that palace of theirs has wall-to-wall mortgages! And that car? Darling, that's horsepower, not earning power. They won it in a fifty-cent raffle! Can you imagine! And those clothes! Of course she does dress divinely. But really...a mink stole, and Paris suits, and all those dresses...on his income? Well darling, I found out about that too. I just happened to be going her way and I saw Joan come out of Ohrbach's!

Ohrbach's

34TH ST. OPP. EMPIRE STATE BLDG. • NEWARK MARKET & HALSEY • "A BUSINESS IN MILLIONS, A PROFIT IN PENNIES"

Ohrbach's. DDB's first client.
Ohrbach's was outspent by ten other retailers, but their advertising gave them greater awareness than the competition.
This ad is a surprise, but you understand it instantly.
DDB won awards for Best Retail fifteen years in a row!

Starting Dec. 23 the Atlantic Ocean will be 20% smaller

EL AL ISRAEL AIRLINES

*EL AL. Here's another DDB Trademark. **Visual Surprise**. DDB's Art Directors gave us a new way of looking at the same old page. Surprise! A new way to say faster.*

Bill Bernbach.

Meanwhile, a copywriter from Grey Advertising opened up a New York agency that set new standards for the entire industry. **Bill Bernbach.***

His agency, Doyle Dane Bernbach, set the tone for advertising in the 60's.

Some people called it "soft sell," but it wasn't. It sold hard. It just wasn't rude.

Bernbach's work was smart. Intelligent.

It didn't talk down to people.

It was honest. Admitting faults and winning sales ("We're Only #2." "Ugly is Beautiful.").

It was funny.

It was classy.

And the graphics knocked you on your ass.

DDB made the writer/art director team the industry standard.

The latest graphics, typography and film techniques were used to create advertising that raised the craft to the level of art.

As Bernbach said,

"I warn you against believing that advertising is a science. It is intuition and artistry, not science, that develops effective advertising."

Yet it was not art for its own sake.

"You must have inventiveness, but it must be disciplined. Everything you write, everything on a page, every word, every graphic symbol, every shadow should further the message you're trying to convey."

Bernbach was not just a leader, he was a teacher. Moreover, he seemed to know how to bring out the best in others.

His people created advertising and agencies in DDB's image: Julian Koenig, George Lois, Mary Wells, Helmut Krone, Ron Rosenfeld, and many others were part of the DDB Creative Revolution.

*Pronounced Bern-<u>back.</u>

40

Today, Bill Bernbach's influence is felt in every advertising award show and almost every agency creative department.

What was it exactly?

He never wrote a book about it, and many of the best DDB ads were written by others.

Bill Bernbach broke the rules but never felt obliged to write new ones.

His philosophy was quite simple, really.

"Find the simple story in the product and present it in an articulate and intelligent persuasive way."

It was all based on an even simpler belief.

"The power of the idea."

You don't have to be Jewish

to love Levy's
real Jewish Rye

Levy's. Surprise! DDB made bread exciting.
Instead of backing off from the ethnic nature of the product, they met it head on.
As a result, they managed to say "The bread for everybody" in a tremendously arresting and distinctive way.
Another facet of DDB style. Taste.
This approach could have been offensive, but it wasn't.

THE DDB PHILOSOPHY.
• Nobody's waiting to hear from us.
• Advertising that nags its way into people's consciousness does only half as much as advertising should.
• Genuinely entertaining, involving or dramatic advertising not only gets people's attention, it gets their affection.
• This kind of advertising multiplies every dollar an advertiser spends.

DDB CREATIVE APPROACH.
• Creativity is as important in developing a strategy as it is in communicating it.
• Creativity that doesn't reinforce the proposition in an ad or commercial isn't creative, it's disruptive.
• Execution isn't a vehicle for delivering a selling message, it *is* a selling message.

SOME DDB QUESTIONS.
• Does it communicate a message that is motivating?
• Is it fresh, appealing, intrusive?
• Is the style and tonality appropriate to the product and the point?
• Do you like the company that manufactures/sells this product?
• Will it help build a long-term personality for the product?

41

VOLKSWAGEN.

Here are some of the most famous ads from DDB's most famous campaign.

Teamwork in action:

Bill Bernbach, Creative Director; Helmut Krone, Art Director; Julian Koenig, Copywriter; & more – courageous clients, and more writers and art directors who kept the campaign burning bright.

IBM's "Think" and "Think Big" were common slogans of the times.

DDB bucked the trend… just like Volkswagen.

Or buy a Volkswagen.

News as Product News.

Bernbach believed in using the timeliness of today's newspaper to make a point for his clients.

When the U.S. had a gas shortage, Volkswagen capitalized on the event with this ad.

They ran the Art Director's rough as the illustration.

It's ugly but it gets you there.

Volkswagen Newspaper Ads kept in touch with the news.

Bernbach believed advertising should be a bit "sociological."

Note the combined use of humor and current events to dramatize the Volkswagen image.

Lemon.

This Volkswagen missed the boat.

The chrome strip on the glove compartment is blemished and must be replaced. Chances are you wouldn't have noticed it; Inspector Kurt Kroner did.

There are 3,389 men at our Wolfsburg factory with only one job: to inspect Volkswagens at each stage of production. (3000 Volkswagens are produced daily; there are more inspectors than cars.)

Every shock absorber is tested (spot checking won't do), every windshield is scanned. VWs have been rejected for surface scratches barely visible to the eye.

Final inspection is really something! VW inspectors run each car off the line onto the Funktionsprüfstand (car test stand), tote up 189 check points, gun ahead to the automatic brake stand, and say "no" to one VW out of fifty.

This preoccupation with detail means the VW lasts longer and requires less maintenance, by and large, than other cars. (It also means a used VW depreciates less than any other car.)

We pluck the lemons; you get the plums.

Lemon. Krone's original headline was "N.G." Then Koenig wrote "This Volkswagen missed the boat"…and then…went to the track (It became the first line of copy). Rita Seldon wrote the classic "Lemon" headline. Krone kept it all on track. Teamwork.

Humorous, but hard-selling. In three words, they sum up one of Volkswagen's major advantages and make you smile.

Relieves gas pains.

Think small.

Our little car isn't so much of a novelty any more.
A couple of dozen college kids don't try to squeeze inside it.
The guy at the gas station doesn't ask where the gas goes.
Nobody even stares at our shape.
In fact, some people who drive our little flivver don't even think 32 miles to the gallon is going any great guns.
Or using five pints of oil instead of five quarts.
Or never needing anti-freeze.
Or racking up 40,000 miles on a set of tires.
some of our economies, you don't even think about them any more.
Except when you squeeze into a small parking spot. Or renew your small insurance. Or pay a small repair bill. Or trade in your old VW for a new one.
That's because once you get used to
Think it over.

This ad was originally a "one-timer" for Fortune.
It was so well received that consumer versions were written.
We'll tell you more about this ad later in the book.

Outdoor *was another important part of the Volkswagen campaign.*
For years. Again and again.

RABBIT TRANSIT.

VOLKSWAGEN DOES IT AGAIN

Avis is only No.2 in rent a cars. So why go with us?

We try harder.
(When you're not the biggest, you have to.)
We just can't afford dirty ashtrays. Or half-empty gas tanks. Or worn wipers. Or unwashed cars. Or low tires. Or anything less than seat-adjusters that adjust. Heaters that heat. Defrosters that defrost.
Obviously, the thing we try hardest for is just to be nice. To start you out right with a new car, like a lively, super-torque Ford, and a pleasant smile. To let you know, say, where you can get a good, hot pastrami sandwich in Duluth.
Why?
Because we can't afford to take you for granted.
Go with us next time.
The line at our counter is shorter.

AVIS.

This was one of the first modern "Positioning" ads.

A marvelous piece of logic.

It made you believe that you got a better deal and better service.

This is an excellent example of 60's style copywriting by Paula Green, with help from Helmut.

Tight and delightful.

Not as fact-filled as Rolls-Royce or VW, but, there was less to say.

A dramatically different layout approach by Helmut Krone (who also wrote the last lines of copy).

It said, "Read Me."

People did.

What a Wonderful Theme.
It communicated the benefit of being better without over-promise.

And, ***it motivated personnel –*** *an important and often overlooked function of advertising.*

We try harder.

YOW! THE NAUGA!!
George Lois created "inherent drama" in Naugahyde™.

"If you have not crystallized it into a single purpose, a single theme that you want to tell the reader, you cannot be creative. For merely to let your imagination run riot, to dream unrelated dreams, to indulge in graphic acrobatics and verbal gymnastics is not being creative."

Bill Bernbach

POW! Campbell's hits the target with a soup aimed at men.

NOW. Make the most of current events to give your ads punch.

Find The W

What makes a great ad?
Ogilvy has guidelines.
Burnett has a feeling.
Bernbach has an idea.

We'll be covering ways to develop ideas and strategies later, but here's a quick review of some of the techniques that the 60's pioneers used.

RE-DEFINE THE PROBLEM.

People at DDB were constantly turning the problems over in their minds.

This was a lot of the "creative" work done. While a lot of headlines were written along the way, the real job was articulating the underlying marketing issue the advertising had to address.

DRAMATIZE VISUALLY.

Even David Ogilvy, the least visual of the three, did this in his best work, *"Dove is 1/4 cleansing cream,"* Commander Whitehead and the Hathaway eye patch all had visual elements.

George Lois, formerly of DDB, looks for *"words that bristle with visual imagery."*

He's an art director who looks for verbal imagery. His goal – *"the blending of verbal and visual imagery – that inexplicable alchemy which causes one plus one to equal three."*

Writers thinking visually and art directors looking for the right words – breaking the boundary between words and pictures.

LOOK INTO TODAY'S WORLD.

Though many 60's ads now seem dated, they were contemporary when they ran.

They featured contemporary language and a contemporary graphic style.

Some of it was cutting-edge and some of it was straight down the middle.

OW!

But one of the reasons these campaigns found a place in popular culture is, that's where they began.

UNDERSTAND THE CUSTOMER

The Creative work of the 60's had a genuine understanding of how people felt. About their lives. About products. About advertising.

Whether it was Ogilvy's intellect generating a tour de force on Rolls-Royce, or Leo Burnett's instinct putting red meat on a red background, *an understanding of the person who would respond to the ads* was a key part of their creation.

Even DDB's Avis campaign had this deep understanding of the customer. Think about it.

The key customer for rent-a-cars is usually a salesman on the road – who probably has a bigger competitor. Just like Avis!

That person knows in his own life exactly what it's like to "Try Harder."

The strength was not just the brains of clever copy or the beauty of brilliant art direction.

It had heart.

It understood the people it was talking to.

So should you.

On December 11th, giant lobsters will invade Downers Grove.

Lock your doors. Bolt your windows. Grab a basket. Live Maine lobsters are heading for the new Eagle Food Center in Downers Grove. Open season begins December 11th.

HOW TO OPEN A SUPERMARKET.
Here's how to add some "Wow" to a supermarket opening.
"Lock your door. Bolt your windows. Grab a basket. Live Maine Lobsters are heading for the new Eagle Food Center in Downers Grove!"

THE POSITIONING ERA COMETH

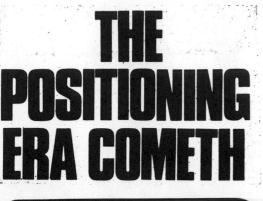

The product era.

In the '50s, hard sell ads predominated.

The image era.

In the '60s, creativity came into vogue.

The positioning era.

Coke | IBM
Hertz | Xerox

In the '70s, strategy will be king.

Positioning.

"The Positioning Era Cometh," headlined the article by Jack Trout and Al Ries.

And it did.

The premise was simple and its promise of profit in the age of product proliferation was irresistable.

The key to success was **positioning** your product properly in the consumer's mind.

"Positioning" was, in itself, a product of product proliferation.

The 70's marketplace was now a teeming pool of products and messages.

The consumer was on overload.

Procter and Gamble was an early practitioner, marketing detergents with distinctly different positions: Tide for clean, Bold for bright, and Cheer, renamed and repositioned as All-Temperature Cheer, for all-temperature washing.

Positioning was tailor-made for the brand management organizations that had become standard in the major advertisers' marketing departments.

In fact, Trout and Ries had started as brand managers at General Electric.

Positioning was a rational explanation for what DDB and Leo Burnett did on instinct.

For example, *"We're only #2"* for Avis was classic "Against" positioning.

It seemed to help people get a grip on what they were doing as they slid through the 70's.

Did it work? Sometimes.

Positioning was a helpful way of thinking for clients and agencies, whether they happened to believe in USP or "image."

Positioning accomodated both views.

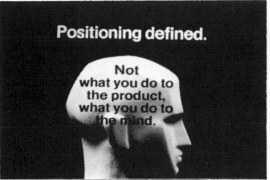

Where is your product "Within the Mind" of the consumer? **That is the first question.**

The Brand Philosophy.
In the battle to increase market share, more and more companies became multi-brand marketers – offering different brands to meet different needs or opportunities in the marketplace.

Successful Positioning.
The distinct positioning for Lite Beer from Miller succeeded in a market where many (including DDB) had failed.

They addressed and solved the marketing problem of trying to market "diet beer."

The use of ex-Jocks combined with the "Less Filling" re-statement of the low-calorie claim, made Lite Beer acceptable in the mind of the heavy beer drinker.

You just focused on where your product stood inside the mind of the consumer.

The search moved from "within the product" (USP) to "within the prospect's mind."

That's the real battleground.

And, perhaps most important, since Positioning was rooted in both marketing and creative thinking, successful implementation demanded cooperation between the "creatives" and the "suits." Marketing and creative people found a common ground.

By the end of the 70's, "Positioning" was part of every major agency's vocabulary and their book was a best-seller.

Today, Trout and Ries continue to maintain their leadership position in marketing thinking with **"Marketing Warfare"** and **"Bottom-Up Marketing."**

Read All **About It.** *"Positioning: The Battle for Your Mind." by Al Ries and Jack Trout.*

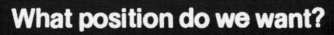

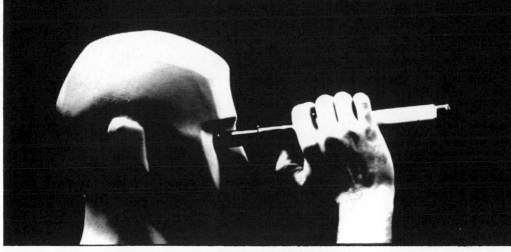

What Position do you want "Within the Mind" of the consumer? **That is the second question.**

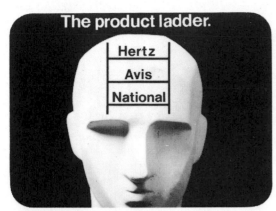

THE BEST POSITION.
Be first in the consumer's mind.
Dominant share of mind results in a dominant share of business.

McDonald's.
Some of the best work of the 70's was Needham's work for McDonald's.

*In many ways, a version of the warm Burnett/ Kellogg's school of advertising, they did a superb job of talking to **you**, with "**You Deserve a Break Today.**" and "**We Do It All for You.**"*

*Great music, warm, human TV production, and, most important, a company totally committed to "**QSC&V**" Quality, Service, Cleanliness, and Value.*

Each ad reinforced those characteristics and supported McDonald's leadership.

Tough to beat.

FOUR BASIC TYPES OF POSITIONING:

1. The **"Best"** or **Leadership** Position.
2. The **"Against"** Position.
3. The **"Niche"** Position.
4. The **New Category.**

Naturally, there are some combinations and variations. First, the basic positions:

The Best Position.

Become first in the mind of the customer.
Once you're there, it's hard to beat.
For example, ask IBM's competitors.
Many beat IBM to the punch with better products. But, in the customer's mind, IBM held onto #1.
Hertz and McDonald's are two other excellent examples of this position.

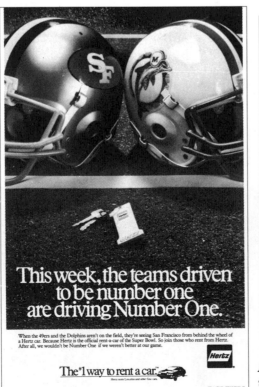

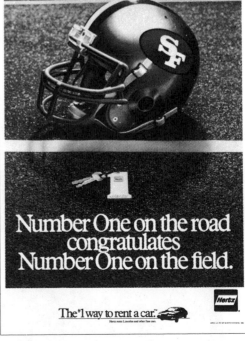

HERTZ. #1 and working to stay that way. Year after year.

The "Against" Position.

It can be a tough road.
But sometimes you don't have a choice.
You suck it up and take 'em on.
Avis had the right idea.
You *do* have to try harder.

*Against the
Against Position.
Hertz works hard
to defend their
#1 position.*

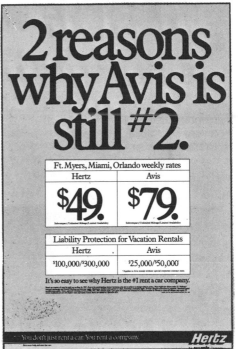

AVIS. The classic "Against" position. Among other things, it can leverage off natural sympathy for the "underdog" and resentment of the "Big Bully." Can be difficult to defend.

The New Category.

By establishing (or inventing) a new category, you have a brand new opportunity to be the #1 brand and take a Leadership Position.

It may be totally new, like **Federal Express**, or, a matter of definition, like **Michelob** (Super Premium Beer).

Sometimes Niches turn into Categories.

**THE MORE POTATO
POTATO CHIP**

NEW PRODUCTS. Are often positioned by comparison to current products.

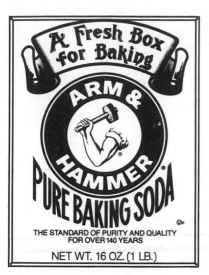

Arm & Hammer Repositioned itself into the refrigerator, turning baking soda into a refrigerator deodorant.

Pontiac. "Wide Track" was more than a claim. GTO and Firebird helped reposition Pontiac from a sedate "Grandmother" image into the "Hot" performance category in the mind of the consumer. Sales accelerated as did the reputation of Pontiac Division Chief John DeLorean.

Re-Positioning.

If you don't like your position, you may want to change your position – from the one you have to the one you want.

That's "Re-Positioning."

During the 70's, a number of marketers, such as Pontiac and 7-Up, revitalized their products by "Re-Positioning."

ALL-TEMPERATURE CHEER.

The All-Temperature Position took Cheer from a weak #5 to a strong #2 in the tough and competitive detergent category.

Cheer moved from a "Whiteness" Position ("New Blue Cheer") to a position associated with a new laundry practice – washing in all-temperatures. They re-positioned the product to match the change in laundry habits caused by new fabrics and brighter colors.

Contemporary "slice of life" commercials not only reflected new habits, they reflected new values, with kids and husbands helping with a traditionally female household chore.

Earlier commercials, with basically the same strategy, featured marginally competent women, slightly confused by their laundry. They were then told to use Cheer by a male authority figure.

The commercials didn't work, even though they did Burke*.

MORAL: The right positioning, or the right *re*-positioning, isn't everything.

You need the right advertising!

* A type of "Day After Recall" research.

Niche Positions.

If you can't have the whole pie, how about a nice slice of it?

That's the "Niche" position.

It establishes leadership in one aspect of a product category.

When it's the right match with a segment of the marketplace, you can be #1 with some of the people all of the time!

Many New Category Products and "Flanker" Brands can also be viewed as "Niche" Positions.

Success depends on identifying a target and doing a better job of matching your product to the needs and preferences of that target.

Market Segmentation is one of the techniques used to help discover a profitable niche in the marketplace.

Virginia Slims. Cigarettes for women!
"You've Come a Long Way, Baby" Executed with a liberated attitude that hit the right note with their target audience.

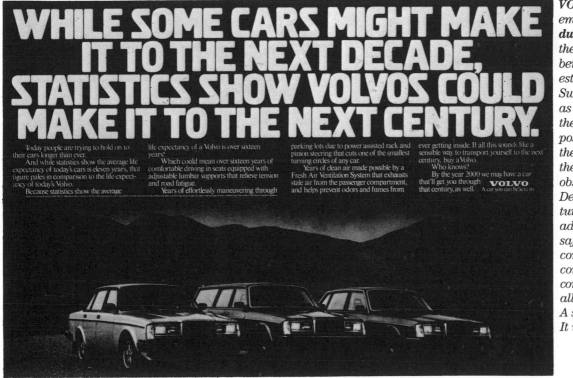

*VOLVO emphasized **durability** and then, the related benefit of **safety** to establish this Swedish import as a major seller in the U.S. First, they positioned themselves **against** the planned obsolescence of Detroit manufacturers. Then, they added emphasis on safety features combined with the company's genuine commitment to overall driver safety. A solid position. It worked.*

The Uncola

7-UP VS. THE COLAS.
In the 60's and into the 70's, 7-Up **Re-Positioned** itself **against** the brown cola drinks.
It worked because they related to something already established within the consumer's mind.

"The essence of positioning is sacrifice – deciding what's unimportant, what can be cut away and left behind; reducing your perspective to a very sharp point of view."

Keith Reinhard

Combinations.

The four basic types of positions can have many combinations and variations.

Some of the ways products are positioned:

1. BY PRODUCT DIFFERENCE.

Generally, all positions work to establish some sort of brand differentiation within the category.

The difference between your product and the competition can be the basis for your position.

2. BY KEY ATTRIBUTE/BENEFIT.

There should be some sort of consumer benefit either stated or implied in your position.

For example, *"The Quicker Picker Upper"* positions Bounty as it communicates a clearly stated attribute/product benefit.

Other more general attributes, such as quality, may have an implied benefit.

Many successful brands have been built by pre-empting the key attribute or benefit generic to the category. Leo Burnett does this often.

3. BY USERS OF YOUR PRODUCT.

Virginia Slims is an excellent example.

Many brands are built by Heavy Users – those who use a great deal of the product.

Another aspect of product usage is known as **"The 80/20 Rule."**

That is, 80% of your business comes from 20% of your customers. For example, 20% of beer drinkers drink 80% of the beer.

Many brands are built with heavy usage and loyalty from a relatively small group of people.

4. BY TYPE OF USAGE.

Michelob was successful with *"Weekends are Made for Michelob."* They weren't as successful with *"The Night belongs to Michelob."* (Some of this was due to the fact the beer market changed.)

Remember, these various types of positionings can be combined.

Years earlier, Shaefer Beer combined Type of Usage with a Heavy-User position.

The result – *"Shaefer is the one beer to have when you're having more than one."*

5. POSITIONING AGAINST A CATEGORY.

Light beer can be positioned against regular beer; discount clothing stores are often positioned against department stores.

6. POSITIONING AGAINST A SPECIFIC COMPETITOR(S).

You can go against the overall leader, as Avis did, or against a specific competitor.

Truck marketers often play this game.

Ford goes against Chevy and vice versa.

Meanwhile, various small Japanese-made pick-up trucks position against each other.

7. POSITIONING BY ASSOCIATION.

This is generally associated with image advertising. It can also be used to reinforce other attributes, such as a firm's heritage in the community being used to reinforce their caring and service – or their old-fashioned recipes.

8. POSITION BY PROBLEM.

Similar to positioning by benefit, only the problem is dramatized more than the solution.

Successful products fulfill needs – that need is often a problem that needs solving.

For example, calcium products that combat the effects of osteoporosis in women.

Federal Express positioned itself against the problem with *"absolutely positively…"*

NOTE: These Combinations were based on work done by Roman Hiebing in "The Successful Marketing Plan," one of the most complete marketing books available. ©1990 NTC.

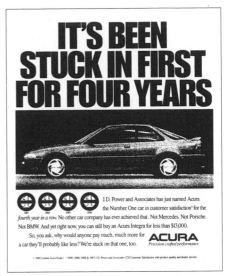

TRYING FOR LEADERSHIP
Acura works to leverage #1 in a survey into building a leadership position.

"Marketing Warfare." This is a marketing book based on military theory.

In today's more crowded marketplace, packed with mature categories – for every winner there's a loser.

It's war! Trout and Ries describe Four Types of Warfare:

Defensive. This is played by #1 in the category and the focus is protecting your position aggressively.

Offensive. This type of marketing is played (or waged) by the #2 and #3 marketers in the category.

Flanking. This is a type of marketing similar to "Niche" positioning and is played by smaller marketers.

Guerilla Warfare, played and waged by the smallest marketers.

Their thinking shows an increasing concern for the use of **Tactics** in the marketplace – actions that result in an improved business position.

This concern is developed further in their excellent book, **"Bottom Up Marketing."**

Assignment #2.

This assignment is designed to help you put some of the historical lessons we've just covered into practice.

Some of the assignments are pretty easy and some are pretty tough.

1. DO A PARODY OF ONE OF THE ADS IN THIS CHAPTER.

Use the product of your choice.
This one's fun!

2. TEAR OUT ADS FROM MAGAZINES.

Pick ads that represent principles or techniques from the different periods. This one's easy.

• Hopkins-style.
  Person to person & pre-emption.
  • 50's-style **USP.**
  • 60's-style **Image.**
  • 70's-style **Positioning.**

3. HISTORY EXERCISE.

Pick a product, any product. (I've done this exercise many times, and I just pick something close at hand.)

Do ads that demonstrate basic techniques from each period. It's tough – but a lot of fun!

A. Do a Hopkins-style ad.
B. Do a 50's-style ad. What is the **USP?**
C. Do a 60's-style ad. What is the **Image?**
D. Do a 70's-style ad. What is the **Position?**

cont'd

They laughed when I sat down to write this assignment.
Some examples people sent in.

This send-up of Ogilvy's Rolls-Royce ad was done by Howard Luck Gossage (Ogilvy was amused).

"At 60 miles an hour the loudest noise in this new Land-Rover comes from the roar of the engine"

AND MORE READING...

From Those Wonderful Folks Who Brought You Pearl Harbor.
Jerry Della Femina
Simon & Schuster

When Advertising Tried Harder. The Sixties: The Golden Age of American Advertising.
Larry Dobrow/Friendly Press

Playing in Traffic on Madison Avenue.
David Herzbrun/Dow-Jones Irwin

Bill Bernbach's Book. A History of the Advertising that Changed the History of Advertising.
Bob Levenson/Villard Books

What's The Big Idea?
George Lois/Doubleday

The Book of Gossage.
Howard Luck Gossage & others
The Copy Workshop

THE 70'S

Positioning: The Battle for Your Mind.
Al Trout/Jack Ries/McGraw Hill

The Image Makers. Power and Persuasion on Madison Avenue.
William Myers/Times Books

And for fun, some paperbacks...
The Space Merchants
Frederik Pohl/CM Kornbluth
St. Martin Press
In this science-fiction farce, ad agencies have taken over the world.
It was written in 1952.
Years later, there was a sequel...
The Merchant's War
Frederik Pohl/St. Martin Press

The 80's.

Trade Ad of the 80's.
Often, the challenge is to get consumers to change their minds. This campaign cleverly challenges the consumer's mindset – by first agreeing with it.

In this case, the target consumers are marketers – potential advertisers in Rolling Stone Magazine.

The Ad of the 80's.
Cointreau on TV in print.

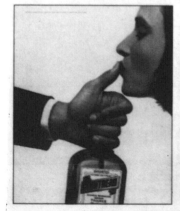

USP. Image. Position.

Every ten years we get a good idea.

What about the 80's? We saw it.

Doug Warren, an agency president who left the business in the 70's, made this observation on his return.

"We now live in a nonverbal society. Impressions are made on a visual basis.

Language mainly serves to reinforce preconceived stereotypes.

Nothing new you say? I disagree.

The change over the past ten years is extreme and will grow stronger...

We respond in an ever-increasing degree on a strictly emotional level triggered by visual stimuli.

Talk all you will about your product's advantages, but the verbiage had better conjure up acceptable visual recall. People no longer have time (and there's growing inability) to isolate or critically examine facts."

He's right.

The successful advertising of the 80's is simpler and more visual.

We are moving from verbal to visual communication...from logical left-brain "perception" to right-brain "reception."

The destination?

Julian Koenig indicated it when he was named to the Copywriter's Hall of Fame many years ago.

"The simpler the better.
'Til form and content
are one and the same."
He's right.

THE PINK BUNNY ANNOUNCES A NEW AGE OF ADVERTISING.

Now advertising makes fun of advertising making fun of advertising.*

With a very competitive point.

The charming "Pink Bunny" ads mask a very tough-minded business decision.

Eveready,™ and their agency, Chiat/Day, discovered that durability was not only the most important claim in the battery category – it was the only meaningful claim.

The leading brand, DuraCell,™ was making exactly that point in their advertising – with a larger budget.

Client and agency made a tough decision– compete with DuraCell, the category leader, on its "home turf." Durability.

When advertising first broke, research demonstrated a high level of confusion.

Eveready's Pink Bunny was being confused with DuraCell's advertising, with it's battery-powered toys.

Chiat/Day knew their challenge wasn't to do it different, but to do it better – to make Eveready more likeable, while establishing the brand's reputation for durability.

Client and agency stuck with it.

Tough marketing. Charming advertising.

That keeps on going. And going…

TWO FOR ONE
Here, The Pink Bunny interrupts a real commercial – for Purina Cat Chow.

Both brands have the same parent company – Ralston-Purina.

TOUGH PROBLEMS.
TOUGH DECISIONS.
The Pink Bunny is a perfect example of the kind of tough-minded decisions you have to make.

Deciding to take on a larger competitor with a smaller budget and "me-too" advertising was a very difficult business decision.

And, after the decision was made, client and agency had to endure about a year of research and trade magazine articles that reported consumers confusing Eveready advertising with the competitor's.

The Pink Bunny had at least two predecessors – a British beer commercial that used the technique of interrupting commercials, and David Herzbrun's campaign for VW of Germany in the 60's.

Major Changes...

You've changed over ten years.

So did advertising.

As we discussed, we must now communicate more quickly and more *visually*.

Advertising also changed because of:

- Changes in the Marketplace.
- Changes in the advertising business itself.
- Changes in our lives. Yours and mine.

As a result, traditional advertising became less effective. Here's what happened:

1. A CHANGED MARKETPLACE.

Fast food hamburgers aren't new anymore.

Neither are small foreign cars or VCR's.

In business after business, we've moved from growing categories, where almost everyone's sales curve went up, to "mature" categories.

There's a big difference.

In mature categories, the growth that comes from people making new purchases and adopting new habits is essentially over.

Sales are "flat"– purchase habits and brand preferences are more established.

In mature categories, it takes more than a clever commercial to get a consumer to change– particularly if that consumer is currently satisfied with their current product.

In mature categories, an established leadership position often makes that leader harder to move.

In mature categories, advertising has a much more difficult task to accomplish.

When Volkswagen established itself in the 60's, with a unique car and unique advertising, it pretty much had the field to itself.

At the time, VW was better built and more reliable than other foreign cars.

Times change.

CAPITALIZING ON BRAND EQUITY.

In today's economy, established brand names have become even more valuable.

Years of advertising and consumer familiarity can make brand names extremely valuable properties.

Many of the mergers and buy-outs involved companies setting very high values on existing brand names.

And they were right.

After all, what would it cost today to establish a brand with the same awareness and familiarity of one that had been around for decades?

One result - Flankers.

Once, common marketing wisdom as practiced by P&G was to establish a new brand with its own unique benefit and position.

Now, it makes more sense for many brands to become families of related products.

The Average American Lives 73.7 Years. (Give Or Take A Few.)

Overweight. Subtract 5 Years.

Stress. Subtract 3 Years.

Excessive Drinking. Subtract 5 Years.

Lack Of Sleep. Subtract 2 Years.

Smoking. Subtract 6 Years.

Poor Diet. Subtract 4 Years.

Lack Of Exercise. Subtract 3 Years.

Your life expectancy isn't determined by statistics alone.

It's determined by the decisions you make every day. Decisions about things like smoking. Drinking. Exercise. Diet. Things that can have a profound impact on the length of your life—and on its quality.

At MedCenters, our goal is to keep you as healthy as we possibly can. So when you're sick, we provide you with doctors and medical facilities that are second to none.

More than 400 doctors, in fact, at 41 Twin Cities locations including the Park Nicollet Medical Center.

But we also have a lot to offer when you're not sick. We can help you make some important decisions about your health. And if you choose, we can help you conquer your bad health habits through information, classes, counseling—whatever it takes.

You see, our commitment to your health is more than a matter of thermometers, pills and stethoscopes. It's a matter of principle.

To find out more, ask your employer. Or write MedCenters Health Plan, 4951 Excelsior Boulevard, Minneapolis, MN 55416.

But don't put it off. Life's too short.

MEDCENTERS HEALTH PLAN

Life-expectancy figures are for illustrative purposes only and can vary widely. Consult your doctor.

Copy in the 80's.
Make the visual work harder.
Keep the words to a minimum.
Also, keep an eye out for new trends in health and diet as well as art and fashion.

The Picture Story.
You read into it your own feelings and experience.

Cutty and denim.

More Copy of the 80's.
Jeff Gorman and Gary Johns for Nike – the brand of the 80's.

IT JUST FEELS RIGHT.

You bet it does.

Mazda saw an open "niche" in the marketplace and went for it – with a well-designed small convertible that was also designed to be profitable with a small production run.

The result – a unique new car that was like nothing else available.

And, guess what, the advertising worked like gangbusters.

In about a year, other car makers responded with their own small convertibles – but by this time, Mazda Miata had established itself as the leader in this New Category.

In "Marketing Warfare," Trout & Ries describe this as **"Flanking."**

Look for undefended ground on the battlefield and take it.

Even a unique automobile, like Mazda Miata, quickly found itself competing with other nifty two-seater convertibles.

A New Category can become mature in a startlingly short period of time.

In a mature category, for each winner, there's usually a loser.

It's "Marketing Warfare."

As a friend at Leo Burnett says, *"Advertising today is selling corn flakes to people who are eating Cheerios."*

This more competitive marketplace is one of the main reasons for the tremendous growth of Sales Promotion – the use of incentives to stimulate consumer purchase behavior and force distribution in a more crowded marketplace.

2. CHANGING MEDIA.

There are not only more media choices – it also costs more.

CPM's (Cost Per Thousand) in mass media have generally risen much faster than the rate of inflation.

As a result, it can cost two to three times more to reach the same number of people as it did ten years ago.

So, unless you can write an ad that's two to three times more effective, your advertising won't have the same impact in the marketplace.

That's why marketers and agencies are always looking for "breakthrough" concepts – ads that are many times more effective.

And that's why many marketers and agencies are looking at alternative media channels, alternative media delivery strategies, and alternative targets.

For example, since it now costs more to reach (and persuade) new customers, why not increase effort against *current customers?*

In many ways, the growth of direct-mail, "frequent-user" programs, "niche" media (like special interest magazines) and various forms of database marketing has been stimulated by the declining cost effectiveness of traditional mass media.

As a writer of messages in the media, you need to know this.

CHANGING CONSUMERS.

We've changed – as "receivers" and customers.

As the number of messages increases, we become less responsive and more selective.

Think about it. It's simply impossible for us to respond to every message.

As a "survival mechanism," we learn to ignore, or, more accurately, we learn to not pay attention. We all do it. We have to.

As Allen Rosenshine, President and CEO of Omnicom said, *"Too much of advertising isn't simply bad, it's simply irrelevant."*

In addition, we're very good at selecting information when we need it.

If the car makes a funny sound on a Winter morning, we'll quickly find and pay attention to car battery ads we usually ignore.

We're all smarter consumers of advertising.

We use it when we need it.

We let it slide by when it's of no interest.

Bottom-line, we pay attention to ads when they're important to us.

Finally, since we're experienced advertising "consumers" – and we're pretty good at it.

Our choice of soft drink, fast food, automobile, laundry detergent and so on, is based on our own real-world experience and our own personal taste.

It's not just ads, that's for sure.

TWO OTHER TRENDS.

Two other things happened to advertising in the 80's: the growth of first-rate advertising in what used to be called "secondary markets" and the effect of the stock market.

1. Smaller Markets.

Minneapolis and Portland are two dramatic examples of the tremendous increase in the quality of advertising in smaller cities.

The technology of advertising production is no longer limited to large markets. Every market has access to good typography, photography and design.

And, while many big marketers have big bureaucracies devoted to "risk management," most small marketers know they need impact.

So… there's often more opportunity for high-impact work with smaller clients, markets and agencies.

2. Stock Markets.

The other major change was due to price differentials between the New York and London Stock Exchanges.

The London Exchange valued agency stocks more highly. The P/E ratio (Price to Earnings) was twice that of the New York Exchange!

This meant Saatchi & Saatchi, based in London, could offer U.S. stockholders almost twice as much.

They bought Ted Bates, Compton, Campbell-Mithun-Esty, Dancer Fitzgerald Sample and others.

Can anyone do this trick? Yes.

Saatchi's accountant, Martin Sorrell, bought a shopping cart company – Wire Plastic Products (WPP).

It was small. It was cheap. It was listed on the London Stock Exchange.

In a startlingly short period, he bought Ogilvy & Mather and JWT, two of the world's largest agencies.

What does this mean to you?

Fewer jobs at these agencies.

And, less money for salaries as the large agencies now have some rather big bank loans.

Advertising that worked.
This was Saatchi & Saatchi's winning campaign for Margaret Thatcher.

These ads typify **the visual attitude** of the 80's.

The Search for Surprise. A sophisticated audience that's seen it all needs new levels of stimulation.

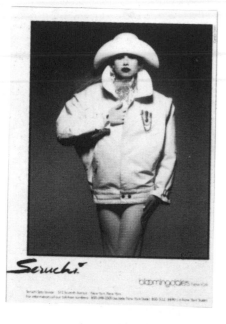

"Graphic Verbalization" says it all.

Some of us have more finely developed nesting instincts than others.

The Passionate Eye of Fashion. *The emotions are communicated without explanation. Visceral Visuals.*

The Surreal Vision. *Schools of art re-emerge as advertising styles. Communication beyond reason.*

An 80's Scrapbook...

The Product As Art. *Chanel.*
What more is there to say?

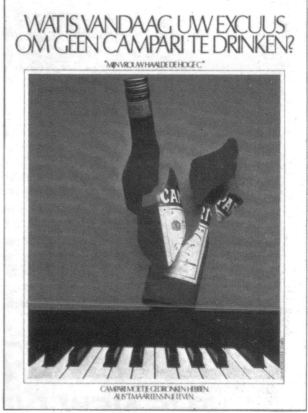

The European Influence.
With many different languages, Europe has a
long history of Visual Communication.
The Poster *is a major advertising art form.*

Product Heritage. *What It Is.*

Another school of Art.
Grade school.

TV in the 80's.

"Today, Sesame Street is brought to you by the letter 'A'." From Sesame Street, to MTV, to high-tech commercials for upscale businessmen, television became a ravenous consumer of the newest video techniques.

And the viewer became more sophisticated.

Today, we've developed a "Channel-Changer Mentality," which zips and zaps through the media environment.

Today's viewer receives and perceives at an ever increasing speed through an ever-wider range of choices in the video environment.

Here are some of the 80's trends:

THE ROCK VIDEO INFLUENCE.

Aggressive and surreal quick-cut imagery driven by a powerful music track.

This is both cause and result of improved ability to receive and interpret visual information.

Marketers now perceive Rock 'n Roll as part of our contemporary cultural heritage and use it as a marketing tool.

Attention Getters. *Party Animals, Joe ("He's lying") Isuzu and the fast-talking Mr. Spleen for Federal Express.*

THE GROWTH OF TECHNOLOGY.

Computers and video technology expanded the techniques available in video production.

What was once "state of the art" is now available at most TV stations and video houses.

Complicated video effects are now easier and more affordable.

CELEBRITY.

Television now adds its own aura to those who stand center stage in our electronic window.

From manufactured celebrities, like The Raisins, Spuds MacKenzie and Bartels & Jaymes, to established celebrities like Michael Jackson, Bill Cosby (and whoever's hot this week).

From nationally recognized "super-models" to the celebrity status generated by local retailers and advertising spokesmen.

It's electronic sizzle.

While the use of celebrities is a common advertising technique, the game of fame in marketing has grown stronger.

The lines of celebrity are blurring, with public figures doing commercials and commercial spokespersons turning into public figures.

DONNA: Looking for a job, Mom?
FERRARO: Very funny.
LAURA: Well, I am.
DONNA: What's it this week Laura, marine biology?
FERRARO: Are we still hoping to be a star of stage and screen?
LAURA: Come on Mom, it's a tough choice.
FERRARO: Sure, it's tough when you can be anything you want to be.
VO: When you make a choice, what's right is what feels right. Diet Pepsi.
FERRARO: You know, there's one choice I'll never regret.
DONNA: Politics?
FERRARO: No, being a mother.
VO: Diet Pepsi. The one calorie choice of a new generation.

WHO IS THAT LADY?
It's a former vice-presidential candidate in a commercial done in the "Hyper-Realism" mode first popularized by Pepsi.

Manufactured Celebrity.
Hal Riney creates "Geezer Chic" for
Ernest and Julio Gallo with Bartles
& Jaymes.

A distinctive home-spun delivery
combined with a sophisticated
sense of humor.

Numerous versions keep the idea
fresh.

Unique. And effective.

"Where's the Beef?" Joe Sedelmeier casts Clara Peller in a
Wendy's commercial and America takes the bait.

MICHAEL J. FOX: Sure.
AVO.: Diet Pepsi, The Choice Of A
New Generation.

The Invasion of the Clutter Busters. Novelty and celebrity combine with special effects to get America's attention.
During the 80's, production budgets exploded and large sophisticated marketers like Pepsi set the standard.
Meanwhile, network TV audiences shrunk as America discovered cable TV and the remote control channel changer.

66

"Here's the Chief!" Wendy's agency casts Founder Dave Thomas in a Wendy's commercial and he becomes their latest celebrity.

Parody Products.

Advertising became its own context during the 80's.

Once rare, commercials now regularly use other well-known commercials as a reference.

Above, a Chicago radio team does a hip spoof of the Bartles & Jaymes advertising.

Below, local car dealers ("Where you always save more money.") push pepperoni for local Pizza Huts.

And a national campaign for Coca-Cola is created and produced by a group of Hollywood directors, challenging the agency's traditional role as the source of creativity in advertising.

The Invasion of the Butter Busters. *Consumer concerns with health and food content, like cholesterol, combined to good effect to get American marketer's attention. It's "The Right Thing To Do." and the light thing to do. During the 80's, the marketplace exploded with a thousand points of "light", and "lite" and kept going into the 90's. Meanwhile, promotions grew bigger than ever and some commercials look like they're edited by a channel changer.*

HARDERFASTERBETTERMORE!

Just in case you didn't think there was enough to worry about – it's all happening faster than ever, too.

Computer-based information and production technology have accelerated the pace of business.

In the 80's, business moved from Fed-Ex to FAX machines.

That's just one example.

There's not time for all of them.

"INTEGRATED MARKETING COMMUNICATIONS."

by Don Schultz, Robert Lauterburn and Stanley Tannenbaum. NTC.

The first book written for "IMC" – the new phrase for the new age of advertising.

It provides an excellent summary of the reasons for IMC growth and a first look at IMC planning.

Now it's the 90's.

A maturing marketplace, more expensive media, and more experienced consumers have all made a big change in advertising.

It all happened in the 80's.

Well, now it's the 90's, and the world is changing faster than ever.

Today, the challenge for advertising to be fresh and relevant is even greater.

And so is the pressure to "play it safe."

The challenge to reduce risks and conserve resources in a less effective environment competes with the challenge to break through the clutter and make an impact.

Often, that means risk – it's riskier than ever to change. It's riskier than ever *not* to change.

And that's why advertising has become a much tougher business.

The good news? Well, as Toffler said –

"The transition to a knowledge-based economy sharply increases the demand for communication and swamps the old image-delivery systems."

We need people who can think.

We need people who can communicate.

And we *really* need people who can do both.

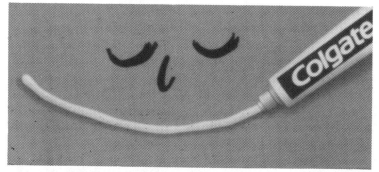

Fast Communication. See how quickly Colgate communicates the Benefit. This is communication that works in any language – since it's all Visual.

68

Assignment #3

1. NAME A PRODUCT.

_____

2. WRITE A GOOD REASON TO BUY IT.

_____

3. VISUALIZE IT!

No words. Just a picture.

You can tear one out of a magazine or just write a description of your visual – but it must be *visually driven!*

4. START A FILE OF SOME OF YOUR FAVORITE VISUAL COMMUNICATIONS.

AN 80'S READING LIST:

Here are some books worth looking at. Each deals in its own way with the major changes in our economy and our society during this period:

Future Shock
Alvin Toffler

The Third Wave
Alvin Toffler

Powershift
Alvin Toffler

The Medium is the Message
(or Massage)
Marshall McLuhan

The Responsive Chord
Tony Schwartz
Anchor Press/Doubleday

Media. The Second God
Tony Schwartz/Random House

Toffler deals with the Post-Industrial Revolution, one of the three great revolutions in human history – which happens to be going on right now.

McLuhan is difficult (even he wasn't always sure what he meant), but thought-provoking. (He was introduced to the world by the legendary San Francisco copywriter, Howard Gossage.)

Tony Schwartz is a copywriter turned Media Consultant who puts McLuhan into a practical context.

(His **"Resonance"** Theory appears at the end of Chapter 2.)

In business, the **"Excellence"** books by **Tom Peters** are worth your attention. **"Passion for Excellence"** is the most enjoyable. **"Liberation Management"** is the latest.

These books had a great impact on the way people think.

For a less optimistic view of the 80's, there are a number of business books – **"Barbarians at The Gate"** is one of the better ones.

You can also impress your friends by reading a Harvard Business Review Article, **"Managing our way to economic decline"** by **Robert H. Hayes and William J. Abernathy**. (It's reprint # 80405).

Finally, you might enjoy **"Emperors of Adland"** by **Nancy Millman**, and **"Whatever Happened to Advertising?"** by **Martin J. Mayer**.

SLAM-DUNK MARKETING!

A page on the back of Rolling Stone announces the premiere of **Charles Barkley vs. Godzilla** on the MTV Music Awards.

Is it an ad promoting another ad?

Is it a promotion?

Is it event marketing?

Is it the shoes?

It's an excellent example of the thinking which turns Barkley vs. Godzilla into more than a TV spot.

Stations get PR footage on the shooting of the commercial – sports shows feature it along with the latest scores.

Charles Barkely is interviewed and asked what Godzilla is really like. It's all in fun, but there's some serious marketing going on.

Meanwhile, posters and other promotional materials head toward the retail outlets (along with the shoes), to make it an event in the stores as well as in the media.

That's how NIKE and their agency, Wieden & Kennedy, turn a single commercial into a multi-dimensional media event – including a monstrous amount of free media coverage.

That's Integrated Marketing Communications in action.

The 90's. Now.

In *"PowerShift,"* Alvin Toffler makes an important point as he chronicles our progress through the Post-Industrial Revolution.

He notes that the value of information is approaching the value of things.

Mazda Miatas and Macintosh Computers contain a lot of information and smart thinking as well as metal, plastic, rubber and silicone.

Think about it.

It's not just metal, it's *mental.*

It means the information content we add to manufactured goods is more important than ever.

It means that the people who produce useful information in this Information Age will be more important than ever.

Whether you produce ads, marketing plans, computer programs or some new form of information, there's a need for you somewhere in this complex, fast-changing marketplace.

Communications will be more important in this Information Age. And our communication options are increasing rapidly.

How do we think about these incredible new opportunities? In a word, *"integrated."*

THINKING INTEGRATED

Marketers in the 90's have to develop a whole new way of thinking. So do copywriters.

Today, your message can go through a wider range of channels. You have more options.

Today, you can tailor your message to a wider range of groups – from consumers and the trade to your fellow employees. Still more options.

And you have to make them work together.

An excellent example of integration in action was Apple's introduction of the Macintosh.

A LOT MORE THAN "1984."

There was a lot more to Apple's 1984 intro than the spectacular "1984" commercial.

Though everyone seems to remember the commercial, it only ran *once* – in the Super Bowl.

Look at what else was going on.

For months, PR people had been briefing the technical and business press – stories were timed to break in newspapers and magazines.

They prepared informative print advertising, multi-page "FSI's" (Free Standing Inserts) and even sponsored entire magazines.

Other hard-working TV commercials featured specific Product Features and Benefits.

Apple was even into publishing. Three whole magazines came into existence with the active cooperation of Apple executives.

Two monthlies, *MacWorld* and *MacUser* and *MacWeek* – a specialized weekly.

Other important target groups, from retailers to software developers, were involved in special Apple programs.

They were reached through a combination of direct communications, events (such as demos and Sales Meetings), advertising in specialized media and an outreach program Apple called "Evangelism."

Posters for the store, brochures, banners and T-shirts helped with the introduction.

So did special interactive software programs that allowed customers to walk into a store and immediately interact with a Mac.

Apple's agency, Chiat/Day, prepared much of the advertising materials.

Other materials were prepared by a variety of groups, including Apple's own in-house creative department.

On January 24th, Apple Computer will introduce Macintosh. And you'll see why 1984 won't be like "1984."

If you go to the bathroom during the fourth quarter, you'll be sorry.

This print ad helped to make "1984" an even more important event.

71

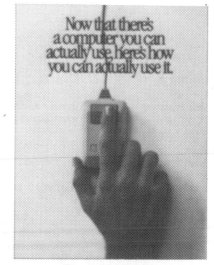

The Apple Look.
Clean graphics. Bright copy.
Right to the point. And click.

We can tell you
all the terrific ways
Apple Desktop Media℠ can
help you express your ideas.

But
we'd rather
show you.

The
World of
Apple
Desktop
Media

Apple Sales Tools.
When it takes more than
an ad to tell the story.

These groups worked together – consulting with each other and developing a common look for all the materials.

They even developed a common type face, "Apple Garamond" (Garamond condensed, 80%).

MANY TARGETS, MANY CHANNELS.

Since the beginning of advertising, talking to your target as a single individual has been critical to developing effective communication.

But you may have multiple targets.

For example, dealers and software developers were critical for Macintosh's success – even though they're not exactly customers.

Meanwhile, you have to reach large important groups of consumers who may not have much in common with each other – including the way they'll use your product.

Grade School Teachers, Art Directors and Accountants are good examples.

Each group has specialized needs.

Apple even went so far as to develop an Electronic mail system – "AppleLink" to help keep in contact with these diverse groups.

Integrated thinking helps you deal with the wide range of communication needs of a product like Macintosh – from high-impact TV to small newspaper ads for local dealers.

Now, let's look at another example.

The Apple Catalog

Apple Catalog.
The Direct Approach.

72

Smart Choices.

In today's marketing environment, there are more options than ever – including more media *channels.*

Today, copywriting is more than crafting the right message – it's crafting the right way to *deliver* that message.

SMART MARKETING BY SMARTFOOD.

When Frito-Lay purchased SmartFood, they bought more than a brand.

They bought a marketing plan.

To establish SmartFood as a unique, non-traditional snack food brand, SmartFood, and their smart agency, Mullen, decided to do it with non-traditional media forms.

Instead of a 30" TV commercial, which would have appeared on TV with lots of other 30" TV commercials for snack foods, they consciously chose alternative media channels.

Outdoor. Radio. Unusual direct mail.

And sampling.

People dressed as six foot bags of SmartFood distributed the product in high-traffic areas across the country – from malls to ski slopes.

The result, a highly distinctive introduction that created a highly distinctive brand personality.

In truth, SmartFood was flavored popcorn – tasty, but not tremendously new and different.

The choice of media channels differentiated this product as much as the advertising itself.

Smart.

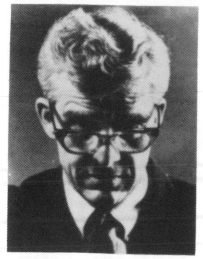

His agency was in an old San Francisco firehouse – no one knew how to start a bigger fire in the media with fewer ad dollars.

Gossage was also committed to larger causes – one concern was how media was being taken over by advertisers – he thought of it as hot dog vendors taking over a football game.

Howard Gossage – The First "IMC" Copywriter?

Howard Gossage wrote ads – but his ads were more than advertising.

His advertising launched fads, contests, social movements, books, the Beethoven sweatshirt and mountains of free publicity.

On a lark, he introduced the world to Marshall McLuhan. (You can read about it in Tom Wolfe's *"The Pump House Gang."*)

His agency's ads for the Sierra Club helped launch the modern environmental movement.

Another Gossage ad for a small Caribbean country was debated in the House of Commons.

Gossage understood how advertising could play a part on a larger stage – acting as a catalyst for a larger media presence.

When he conceived an ad, he also thought about how it could grow into something larger.

Today, that's part of what we call "Integrated Marketing Communications," or "IMC."

Gossage simply thought it was a smart way to make the most of his clients' small ad budgets.

IS THIS YOUR SHIRT?

If so, Miss Afflerbach will send you

your [EAGLE] label

THIS is a two-color striped button-down shirt designed and tailored by Eagle Shirtmakers and sold everywhere by fine men's stores. Many of them admire our shirts so much they sell them under their own names. High praise indeed, and we should like to reciprocate by advertising their (our) shirts. But it's hard to know just where to start. Obviously we can't say things like "None Genuine Without This Label" when they are all quite genuine, you know. And it would be silly to say "Try An Eagle Shirt Today!" when it is likely you already have a drawerful; even though you didn't know it until just this minute. So all we can suggest is that you send in for your Eagle label. Write Eagle Shirtmakers, Quakertown, Pennsylvania; Attention Miss Afflerbach.

Eagle Shirts *hired Gossage to establish them as a maker of quality shirts – they were a "private label" manufacturer with no consumer reputation. Unique ads in* **The New Yorker** *did the job – generating record levels of consumer response. The response to this campaign was topped off with a unique form of integrated marketing – they were published as a book, "Dear Miss Afflerbach." By this time, everyone knew Eagle Shirts.*

BE THE FIRST ONE ON YOUR BLOCK TO WIN A KANGAROO!

That's how Howard Gossage got you to think about Australia's airline – Qantas.

Gossage believed contests, offers, coupons and surveys were a great way to involve readers and dramatize some important aspect of the product.

Most of his ads included a **Response Device.**

Gossage Today. This ad for The Nature Company by the San Francisco agency Goodby Berlin Silverstein owes a debt to the work of copywriter Howard Gossage and art director Marget Larsen.

It's a disarmingly unique and persuasive piece of communication, beginning literally with a "bird's eye view" of the product.

GOOD GOSSAGE!

Here are three other examples:

1ST INTERNATIONAL PAPER AIRPLANE COMPETITION

Gossage saw unique creative opportunity in the most common advertising tasks.

This began simply as a project to sell Scientific American to advertisers – it was noted Scientific American readers flew a lot.

By the time the dust settled, the contest had generated tons of press coverage. Advertisers and magazine readers alike became more aware of Scientific American.

Contest entries were actually made into a book!

BEETHOVEN SWEATSHIRTS

A small classical FM station asked Gossage to help them stay in business.

The result – a Beethoven sweatshirt!

He also used it as a tie-in with another client, Ranier Ale.

It was a classic Gossage event. "Coach Stahl wants you to walk to Seattle."

After it began, newspapers treated it like a news story. Free PR!

PINK AIR.

Pink Air spoofed advertising years before The Pink Bunny - it was a campaign for Fina Gas.

It had contests, (Your Chance To Win 15 Yards Of Pink Asphalt), premiums (Pink balloons and valve caps), and the world's longest slogan.

[Our Motto] "If you're driving down the road and you see a Fina station, and it's on your side so you don't have to make a U-Turn through traffic and there aren't six cars waiting and you need gas or something, please stop in." Plus coupons for pink valve caps and credit cards.

☞ **RESPONSE/INVOLVEMENT** ✍

Gossage's agency ran as many as seven coupons in one ad (for The Sierra Club).

He believed it was an important way to involve readers. It did!

In Gossage's ads, you could:
- ❏ Sign up to walk to Seattle.
- ❏ Get recipes for Irish Coffee.
- ❏ Vote for Pride or Profit.
- ❏ Vote for or against billboards.
- ❏ Fill out a survey on your stereo listening habits.
- ❏ Write your Congressman, The President or the IRS.
- ❏ Get a free Eagle Shirt Label.
- ❏ Order a Beethoven Sweatshirt.

Formats, Forces &

Three things seem to be true about the most effective 90's advertising.

1. It uses the familiarity of formats.

2. It leverages forces in the marketplace.

3. It breaks through "The Fourth Wall" and shares the consciousness of its audience.

The Live-Action Cartoon.

Nike and Wieden & Kennedy take a familiar format and two familiar characters and combine them a whole new way.

Forces at work – SuperStar meets SuperStar. Michael Jordan soars beyond reality into fantasy.

The Fourth Wall breaks with broad takes to the camera punctuated with sight gags start to finish.

FORMATS VS. FORMULA.

Formulas may not work, but formats do.

A "Formula" is a prescribed way of communicating things. Sometimes they work, and sometimes they're just phony and unpersuasive.

Formats, however, supply *context* – a reference frame for the viewer to get to your message.

While still allowing any style, any attitude, any content, they provide important clues and cues.

Newscasters, music videos, documentaries and sit-coms are all examples of familiar formats.

FORCES VS. FADS.

Fads are short-term trends that come and go.

If it's style rather than substance, hopping onto a trend is usually unpersuasive.

Forces are underlying values in the culture and the marketplace. They can be very dynamic, even if they've been around for centuries.

Saturn's positioning is a superb example of tapping into contemporary cultural forces in a way that connects with the way people feel.

When your advertising can tap into these forces, the result can be powerful.

"Integration," is one of those forces – using other media forms to reinforce a message.

Think Global. Act Local. Here, Edy's Ice Cream identifies with the Chicago market as well-known local aldermen debate their favorite flavors. A relatively new brand taps into local tradition and becomes a "hometown" brand overnight. It even makes the national news. This commercial breaks another wall – the one between politics and business.

"The Fourth Wall."

Good advertising often breaks barriers.

Years ago, advertising that made fun of advertising was generally frowned upon.

Today, it's a way of identifying with the viewer – another way of getting on the consumer's side of the communication.

Sometimes it's obvious. Sometimes it's merely a shared awareness – an attitude.

One way or another, good advertising usually breaks some sort of barrier.

As you look at advertising you like, see how each uses Formats and Forces to build clear and persuasive communication – and how each breaks a barrier between advertiser and consumer.

Breaking "The Fourth Wall."

When an actor plays to the audience, or looks into the camera, "The Fourth Wall" is broken.

Playwrights and screenwriters are generally advised to avoid this.

Advertising shatters this wall with regularity, making the audience a more active participant.

Boys on the Block

The Social Documentary.
McDonald's reinforces its relationship with the American family and the American Work Force.

Maximum value from a spot about minimum wage jobs.

Current social concerns are forces that give this ad extra impact.

The Fourth Wall is broken with shared understanding.

Saturn. Positioning for the 90's – a Mission for the 21st Century.
Saturn has a Mission – "to be the friendliest, best-liked car company in America." To fulfill their Mission and achieve that position, they had to break a wall – that wall was an attitude – the attitude of many American car buyers toward American cars.

They break the wall emotionally and make you feel good about the car (and the company) without making a single product claim or mentioning that the company is General Motors.

A simple documentary format shows people and their values.

The human forces of caring about your job and America's unique love for the automobile are virtually pre-empted by Saturn.

CHERYL SILAS had a highway collision, was hit twice from behind, and then sold three cars for us.

Saturn breaks other barriers as well – like their dealer advertising.

All dealers are called "Saturn of (City Name)," positioning them differently from other dealers.

And advertising them differently.

Has the wall been broken?

Initial surveys indicated that the second-choice of Saturn buyers was <u>not</u> an American car.

The Smiths sent the Bartons, who sent the McGees, who sent the Thompsons, who sent the Riveras, who sent the Jacksons...

The fact that so many new Saturn owners are dishing out high praise for their car-buying experience isn't anything you'd call "dumbfounding." To the contrary. Unless we're missing something, we happen to think that's how most people respond to being treated fairly.

M.S.R.P. of the 1991 SL2 is $12,195 including retailer preparation and freight production. See license and options additional. ©1991 Saturn Corporation.

THE 90's. NOT NEW.

As Don Schultz of Northwestern University points out – one group of marketers has practiced "Integrated Marketing Communications" for years. Small companies.

Smaller "business-to-business" marketers have been *thinking integrated* since marketing began.

The small business-to-business marketer knows how to integrate his communications all by himself:

- **Advertising in trade journals**
- **Direct mail to customers**
- **Conventions and Trade Shows**
- **Press releases to trade press**
- **Incentives for the sales force**

Whether or not all the right decisions are made, the small marketer is fairly familiar with the marketing and selling options available.

The small marketer's small agency is often a partner. Smaller agencies supply a range of "IMC" services:

- **Advertising • PR**
- **Brochures & Catalogs**
- **Sales Meetings • Trade Shows**
- **Newsletters • Corporate ID**
- **Package Design**

Other smaller businesses, such as single-store retailers, practice their own brand of IMC:

- **A sale (promotion)**
- **A newspaper ad**
- **A mailing to customers**
- **"Co-op" advertising**
- **Incentives to sales people**
- **Telemarketing**
- **Bus bench backs**
- **Flyers handed out in the mall**

All are IMC tactics appropriate for a small retailer.

Without even knowing it, many of them "think integrated."

For larger marketers, it's a lot more complicated. Budgets are bigger, and so are the organizational problems.

Different departments have different budgets – one person runs Sales Promotion, another runs PR and someone else handles the agency.

Simple things become complicated as larger marketing organizations try to "think integrated."

The 90's. Now What?

Today, copywriting isn't just about how you write – it's about how you think.

Today's copywriting opportunities cover everything from national ads to personalized letters in your mailbox – from catalogs to interactive computer discs.

TV opportunities range from 30 seconds to 30 minutes.

Today, there are more opportunities than ever for creative communication.

Create a promotion. Stage an event.

Publish a book.

Send in the coupon. Call the 800#.

Watch the enclosed video.

Never before have there been more choices and more opportunities.

And never before has it been more difficult.

COMPLICATED. BUT SIMPLE.

To do the job in the 90's marketplace, you'll need three things:

Integrated Thinking. Even if you're just working on a segment, your thinking should cover the full range of the marketing task.

Smart Choices. At the planning stage, you'll have to choose from a wide range of options - a range that keeps growing every day.

Persuasive Communication. That's still the copywriter's job – persuasive writing that knows how to talk to your target(s).

And that's what the rest of this book is about.

DENNIS HOPPER with son
HENRY LEE HOPPER in babyGap
pocket-t and overalls.
Photographed by Herb Ritts.

baby GAP

The Basics Still Work.

National and global advertisers still realize the importance of a strong Product Story.

So do consumers.

Even while new values and new presentations generate new excitement in the marketplace, a strong simple demo can still do the job.

Easy Spirit demonstrates comfort and fashion with a spirited basketball game played in high-heeled shoes.

Product and personality. The Gap blends the two, featuring portraits of "cutting edge" individuals looking comfortable in The Gap's simple fashions combined with other clothes - just like in the real world.

The "Individuals of Style" campaign was developed by The Gap's own in-house Advertising Department.

Smart merchandising and smart advertising helped The Gap grow from a jeans store into America's second largest clothing brand.

They also developed "Flankers" – GapKids and Baby Gap.

Smoking Out New Opportunities.

Wrigley Spearmint Gum, saw a Problem as an Opportunity, taking advantage of increased smoking restrictions by positioning their product as an alternative with smokers. With a strong simple visual device (substituting the No Smoking symbol for the "O"), they quickly communicate the thought "When You'd Like to Smoke But Can't." The brand had been on an eight year sales decline – until these ads. The first year, sales increased 5%.

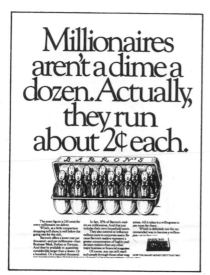
"THE PERSONAL MEDIA NETWORK"

Keith Reinhard, head of DDB/Needham, wants you to think about *"The Personal Media Network."*

What is the media experience from the point of view of the individual Target Customer?

And what is the best time to reach him or her for your product?

It includes places and habit patterns – when and why they read, watch TV, or listen to radio. For example, is the media for information, entertainment of background?

It also includes things you might not think of as media, like the package itself.

Thinking like this can help pizza companies decide to advertise just before halftime on a football game.

Thinking like this can help you add in-store advertising to complement your TV schedule.

Join the family. 3

Assignment #4A.

Here's an initial "stretching" exercise to help you think about the range of "IMC" opportunities.

Discover your own "Personal Media Network."

1. Track yourself through a typical day – what "media" are part of your network?

Me
Wake Up

Go to Sleep

2. When and where were the best opportunities to reach you?

3. How does your "Personal Media Network" differ on the weekend?

Millionaires or Minimum-Wage?
As these ads indicate, you reach them in dramatically different places - in an upscale business magazine or at the counter of a fast food restaurant.

#4B. You Do It.

One of the ways we can develop insight into others is to develop insights into ourselves.

The excellent work for NIKE is an example of advertising most people enjoy.

They work very hard to "Just do it."

How do they persuade us?

Let's compare things we like and ads we like and see if we can't find the "truths" about both.

- Make a list titled "Things I Like."
- Make a list titled "Ads I Like."
- Now, think a bit. What "truths" are there about advertising that persuade you?

Not just things you want to own, but attitudes and images that touch you. Write down a few "truths" that are true for you.

Learning what it takes to persuade ourselves is the first step in learning to persuade others.

"THE PERSONAL TRUTH"

Dan Wieden, head of Wieden & Kennedy, wants his agency to discover *"The Personal Truth"* in the products they advertise.

How do they relate to the individual customer's feelings and experience?

Their NIKE advertising includes products for a wide range of activities – each has a different reason for being in people's lives.

The NIKE advertising tries to match up against the personal values attached to those activities.

Their advertising to women is dramatically different from that aimed at competitive tennis players or older runners.

Thinking like this helps NIKE advertising "ring true."

Even their celebrity advertising is crafted to allow you to empathize with the individual.

So the advertising's not just about NIKE – it's about *you*.

"Just do it" is a theme that gathers strength as each commercial adds its own "truth" to the NIKE image.

Different Groups. Different Approaches. *This "Design Your Own Shoe Laces" Promotion takes a "Foot Loose" approach for casual footwear.*

Two Brains Are Better Than One.*

YOUR "LEFT BRAIN"
Logical
Verbal
Math
Words
Facts
Memory
Conservative
YOUR "RIGHT BRAIN"
Associative
Visual
Geometry
Music
Playful
Asks "What If?"
Imaginative

*

The two major modes of human brain hemisphere function were first described by psychobiologist Roger W. Sperry. His research was honored with a Nobel Prize.

**

The connection between the two sides of the human brain is called the **Corpus Callosum.**

It literally lets the right hand know what the left hand is doing.

And… women have a larger Corpus Callosum than men.

That's right, on average, women have many more connections between the left and right hemispheres of the brain!

First, your brain has two sides.
Left and right.
The left side of your brain is connected to the right side of your body.
And vice versa.**
The left side is logical and verbal, rational and conservative.
It does not take risks.
The right side is different.
It is intuitive, visual, liberal and imaginative.
The left side reads.
The right side feels.
A well-organized Ogilvy-style "reason why" communicates to the left side of the brain.
Bill Bernbach's ads surprise the right side.
The right side of your brain listens to music. (But not always.)
The left side does math. (But not geometry.)
And, while both sides work together, it's important to consider how you will be communicating.
Emotionally or rationally.
"Image" or "reason-why."
Visually or verbally.
Or both.

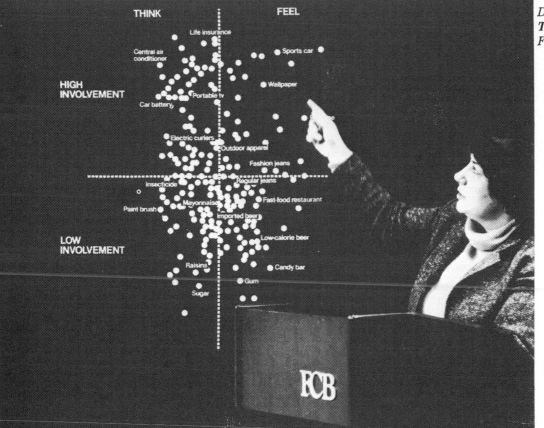

Dona Vitale explains **The Grid.** *From the FCB Annual Report.*

The FCB Planning Grid.

The folks in the Research Department at Foote Cone and Belding developed something called **The Vaughn Grid** (Richard Vaughn was Research Director of FCB's L.A. office – his original article can be found in the ADDENDUM at the back of this chapter).

It's now known as **The FCB Grid for Advertising Planning.** Or, "The Grid."

It's a pretty useful tool.

"The Grid" takes this emotional vs. rational difference, plus a number of other advertising theories, (Economic, Social, Psychological and Responsive) and organizes the whole thing into a "playing field."

THE FCB PLANNING GRID.

The Horizontal dimension goes from the Rational to the Emotional. **THINKING** to **FEELING**.

The Vertical dimension is **INTEREST** level – it goes from **LOW INTEREST** to **HIGH INTEREST**.

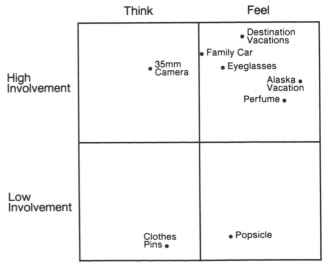

INTO THE GRID.

Here's a 3- Step Process for using The Grid:

1. WHERE THE PRODUCT FITS.

First, place the product category in what you believe is the proper place on The Grid.

2. WHERE THE BRAND FITS.

Next, decide where your brand fits

within the product category.

3. WHERE THE BRAND ATTRIBUTE FITS.

Finally, decide where the distinguishing product attribute of your brand fits.

So, for example, you could have a relatively emotional brand in a rational category. And vice versa.

EXAMPLE: ARCHWAY "THE GOOD FOOD COOKIE."

While the cookie category tends to be "lower right," Archway, a leading baker of oatmeal cookies, developed a "Good Food" position in the early 80's - a relatively "high think" position.

This matched up with other marketplace phenomena, such as increased concern about ingredients and good news about oat bran.

Now, how do you use the Grid?

You use **The FCB Planning Grid** as a helpful technique and mental exercise for determining your advertising approach.

It helps you relate the type of product you're selling to the mind of the target consumer. (Remember Positioning?) Because each of us is a different type of consumer, depending on what we're buying. Consider...

WHERE IS YOUR PRODUCT ON THE GRID?

Thinking/High Involvement: like a 35mm camera, or a costly office machine advertised to an office purchasing agent?

Thinking/Low Involvement: like clothes pins or a floor cleaner or motor oil?

Feeling/High Involvement: like perfume, fashion, motorcycles, or cosmetics?

Feeling/Low Involvement: like a Popsicle, candy bar, soft drink, or cigarette?

Get the idea?

IT CAN BE BOTH.

As the SAAB ad at the end of this chapter demonstrates, selling messages can contain elements of *both* thinking and feeling.

You may decide to sell your product in a rational way when others are selling theirs emotionally.

The key is to make a rational strategic or tactical decision – even if the logical conclusion is to be emotional.

There may be alternative hypotheses as to the proper placement of your product on **The Grid.**

This, in itself, can lead to interesting discussion and, hopefully, a better decision.

Thinking or Feeling.

High Involvement or Low.

All have their place.

In the heart.

And mind.

"Exploding the Dot."

Many of the techniques of advertising involve developing mental flexibility.

Learning one way of thinking about things. Then another.

Here's one that's *almost* the exact reverse of the Planning Grid.

After you determine where you want to place your dot on the Grid, "Explode" it!

Turn your focus inside out and look at the types of forces pushing the dot in different directions, related to: the consumer, the product experience and the purchase decision.

READING LIST: TWO BOOKS ARE BETTER THAN ONE.

Every day, there are more and more books examining aspects of left and right brain thinking.

There is a fascinating technique for teaching you to draw **upside down!** It generates right brain/visual connections in left brain/verbal people.

"Writing the Natural Way" by Gabrielle Lusser Rico helps you hook into associative areas of the right brain and unlock your writing creativity.

"A Whack on the Side of the Head" by Roger Von Oech, a Silicon Valley Creativity Consultant, is a lot of fun.

"Whole Brain Thinking. Working from Both Sides of the Brain to Achieve Peak Job Performance," a business book based on Roger Sperry's Nobel Prize winning research on split brain theory, by Jacquelyn Wonder and Priscilla Donovan.

Read a few of them.

You'll be a more effective and creative thinker.

And, you'll have more fun.

Maybe twice as much.

HIGH INVOLVEMENT "THINKING"   HIGH INVOLVEMENT "FEELING"

LOW INVOLVEMENT RATIONAL   LOW INVOLVEMENT EMOTIONAL

Often, these forces can be expressed as little "quotes" about the feeling or thinking involved.

Here's an example for Old El Paso, a leading brand of Mexican food.

There's more than one way to think about advertising.

But this is one of the best.

"EXPLODING THE DOT." OLD EL PASO MEXICAN FOOD.

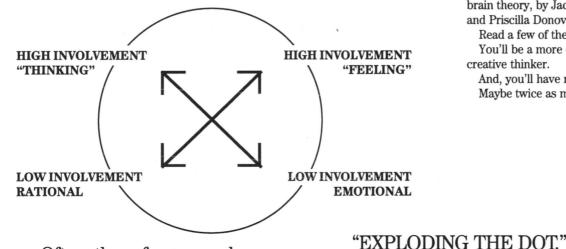

HIGH INVOLVEMENT "THINKING"
Initial decision – High Risk-
"What do I do?" Challenge
Meal Planning – New Recipes,
Procedures.
A good way to serve good nutrition.

LOW INVOLVEMENT RATIONAL
Success – Low Risk/No Risk
Good, Easy, Economical.
America's Favorite Brand of
Mexican Food.
An economical way to serve good food.

HIGH INVOLVEMENT/"FEELING"
Initial decision – High Risk -
Fear of embarassment
Success – Creative Satisfaction
A creative way to enjoy a meal.

LOW INVOLVEMENT EMOTIONAL
– Fun & Flavor.
A fun, exciting meal.
"¡Ole!"

Assignment #5.

1. RIGHT TO LEFT.

Take a right brain (Emotional) ad.
Make it a left brain (Rational) ad.

2. LEFT TO RIGHT.

Pick a left brain (Rational) ad.
Do the opposite.
Make it a right brain (Emotional) ad.

3. GRID EXERCISE.

Draw The Grid.
Make a list of 10 different products.
Place them on **The FCB Planning Grid.**

4. BOTH SIDES.

The SAAB ad on the right appeals to both.
Pick another product with *both* rational and
emotional appeals.
Write an ad that appeals to both.
(It can be a spread.)

5. "EXPLODE THE DOT."

Take the product from #4 and show the various
forces at work in all four sections of The Grid.
Repeat the process with a second product.

FOR THE RIGHT SIDE OF YOUR BRAIN.

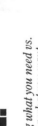

SAAB

The most intelligent car ever built.

A CAR FOR THE LEFT SIDE OF YOUR BRAIN.

The left side of your brain, recent investigations tell us, is the logical side.

It figures out that $1 + 1 = 2$. And, in a few cases, that $E = mc^2$.

On a more mundane level, it chooses the socks you wear, the cereal you eat, and the car you drive. All by means of rigorous Aristotelian logic.

However, and a big however it is, for real satisfaction, you must achieve harmony with the other side of your brain.

The right side, the poetic side, that says, "Yeah, Car X has a reputation for lasting a long time but it's so dull, who'd want to drive it that long anyway?"

The Saab Turbo looked at from all sides.

To the left side of your brain, Saab turbocharging is a technological feat that retains good gas mileage while also increasing performance.

To the right side of your brain, Saab turbocharging is what makes a Saab go like a bat out of hell.

The left side sees the safety in high performance. (Passing on a two-lane highway. Entering a freeway in the midst of high-speed traffic.)

The right side lives only for the thrills.

The left side considers that *Road & Track* magazine just named Saab "The Sports Sedan for the Eighties." By unanimous choice of its editors.

The right side eschews informed endorsements by editors who have spent a lifetime comparing cars. The right side doesn't know much about cars, but knows what it likes.

The left side scans this chart.

Wheelbase	99.1 inches
Length	187.6 inches
Width	66.5 inches
Height	55.9 inches
Fuel-tank capacity	16.6 gallons
EPA City	19 mpg*
EPA Highway	31 mpg*

The right side looks at the picture on the opposite page.

The left side compares a Saab's comfort with that of a Mercedes. Its performance with that of a BMW. Its braking with that of an Audi.

The right side looks at the picture.

The left side looks ahead to the winter when a Saab's front-wheel drive will keep a Saab in front of traffic.

The right side looks at the picture.

The left side also considers the other seasons of the year when a Saab's front-wheel drive gives it the cornering ability of a sports car.

The right side looks again at the picture.

Getting what you need vs. getting what you want.

Needs are boring; desires are what make life worth living.

The left side of your brain is your mother telling you that a Saab is good for you. "Eat your vegetables." (In today's world, you need a car engineered like a Saab.) "Put on your raincoat." (The Saab is economical. Look at the price-value relationship.) "Do your homework." (The passive safety of the construction. The active safety of the handling.)

1982 SAAB PRICE** LIST		
900 3-Door	5-Speed	$10,400
	Automatic	10,750
900 4-Door	5-Speed	$10,700
	Automatic	11,050
900S 3-Door	5-Speed	$12,100
	Automatic	12,450
900S 4-Door	5-Speed	$12,700
	Automatic	13,050
900 Turbo 3-Door	5-Speed	$15,600
	Automatic	15,950
900 Turbo 4-Door	5-Speed	$16,260
	Automatic	16,610

All turbo models include a Sony XR70, 4-Speaker Stereo Sound System as standard equipment. The stereo can be, of course, perfectly balanced: left and right.

The right side of your brain guides your foot to the clutch, your hand to the gears, and listens for the "zzzooommm."

Together, they see the 1982 Saab Turbo as the responsible car the times demand you get. And the performance car you've always, deep down, wanted with half your mind.

*Saab 900 Turbo. Remember, use estimated mpg for comparison only. Mileage varies with speed, trip length, and weather. Actual highway mileage will probably be less. **Manufacturer's suggested retail price. Not including taxes, license, freight, dealer charges or options desired by either side of your brain.*

This is the original article by Richard Vaughn which formed the basis of The FCB Planning Grid. It also covers the "Learn/Feel/Do Circle," which we'll cover in the following Addendum.

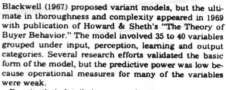

Advertising Age

Magazine

The Consumer Mind: How To Tailor Ad Strategies

Planning models are not all-purpose cures, but guides to organizing advertising goals.

BY RICHARD VAUGHN

Advertising is unlike the direct communications between two people which involves a give-and-take experience. It is a one-way exchange that is impersonal in format. To compensate, advertising must often make greater use of both rational and emotional devices to have an effect. People can selectively notice or avoid, accept or reject, remember or forget the experience, and thereby confound the best of advertising plans.

To understand how advertising works, it's necessary to explore the possibilities people have for thinking, feeling and behaving toward the various products and services in their lives. This isn't easy because we are all capable of being logical and illogical, objective and subjective, obvious and subtle simultaneously. Everything considered, it's not surprising that a unified theory of advertising effectiveness has eluded us for so long.

Four traditional theories of advertising effectiveness have long been prominent in marketing:

Economic: A rational consumer who consciously considers functional cost-utility information in a purchase decision. Economic theory says consumers act in their own financial self-interest. They look for maximum utility at the lowest cost. Rational, methodical calculation is presupposed, so price-demand equations are used to calculate aggregate consumer behavior. Consumers must have functional information to make a decision. This old, much-revered theory most often applies to commodity items. It is highly respected by economic forecasters and is the only theory widely publicized by U.S. government regulatory agencies.

Responsive: A habitual consumer conditioned to buy thoughtlessly through rote, stimulus-response learning. Responsive theory tells us consumers are lazy and want to buy with minimum effort. They develop habits through stimulus-response learning. The process is nonrational and automatic, as repetition builds and then reinforces buying activity for routine products. Information serves a reminder/exposure, rather than thoughtful purpose.

Psychological: An unpredictable consumer who buys compulsively under the influence of unconscious thoughts and indirect emotions. Psychological theory explains consumer behavior as ego involvement: The personality must be defended or promoted. This is essentially unpredictable, undeliberate and latent as psychic energy flows between the id, ego and super-ego. Implicit product attitudes are more important than functional benefits for products that touch people deeply.

Social: A compliant consumer who continually adjusts purchases to satisfy cultural and group needs for conformity. Social theory describes consumers as basically imitative. People watch what others buy and comply/adjust to get along or to be inconspicuous. It's an emotional, insecure behavior. Group role, prestige, status and vanity concerns are involved. Opinion leaders and word-of-mouth communication are important for the visi-

Richard Vaughn is research director, Foote, Cone & Belding/Honig, Los Angeles.

ble products affected.

While these theories have had proponents who defended them as sole explanations of consumer behavior, most marketers now consider them at best only partial explanations. These theories were most topical in the 1950s.

Which theory is right? They all have some truth. *Economic* motives dominate much consumer behavior, especially on expensive products and those with highly functional benefits. But *responsive* buying also prevails; many routine items require little or no thought, and purchase habits, once established, can serve indefinitely. *Psychological* issues complicate our understanding because many items can have "symbolic" overtones. The same is true of *social* motives since numerous products have public meaning. Thus, at various times and for different products, each theory might play a part in consideration, purchase and consumption behavior.

While these theories have enough face validity to make them interesting, they lack the specificity to make them practical. Also, which theory to use in a situation and how to blend it with other theories are constant and frustrating problems.

Time and the efforts of consumer theorists have moved beyond these simpler explanations to more dynamic notions of how consumers respond to advertising.

Many consumer behavior models were developed in the early 1960s. They took a variety of forms, but most were patterned after Lavidge and Steiner's "Hierarchy of Effects" model in 1961.

This model proposed that consumer purchase of a product occurred via a sequential hierarchy of events from awareness through knowledge, liking, preference and conviction. It was a major step toward integrating the implications of the economic, responsive, psychological and social theories. In principle at least, rational concerns could coexist with habituation, ego involvement and conformity motives. Although research has been unable to verify the model, it has been conceptually useful and, because of its common sense qualities, remains today the intuitive, implicit model accepted by most marketing managers.

Andreason (1963), Nicosia (1966) and Engel-Kollat-

Blackwell (1967) proposed variant models, but the ultimate in thoroughness and complexity appeared in 1969 with publication of Howard & Sheth's "The Theory of Buyer Behavior." The model involved 35 to 40 variables grouped under input, perception, learning and output categories. Several research efforts validated the basic form of the model, but the predictive power was low because operational measures for many of the variables were weak.

Despite their detail, these second generation models remedied defects in the basic hierarchy model:

• Consumers might proceed through the sequence imperfectly (stop/start, make mistakes).
• Feedback would allow later events to influence earlier activities.
• Consumers could skip the process entirely and behave "illogically."

In a return to simplification, the following summary adoption process model appeared in 1971 (Robertson). It included the main features of earlier models.

This modified hierarchy model proposed that some consumers, under some conditions, for some products, might follow a sequential path. The dotted lines are feedbacks that can alter outcomes. Other decision patterns (on the right) track consumers as they violate the formal sequence of the hierarchy. Thus, consumers can learn from previous experience and swerve from the awareness-to-purchase pattern.

This scheme preserved the LEARN-FEEL-DO sequence of most hierarchy models but made it more flexible. It also helped explain purchase behavior without the presence of measurable product knowledge or attitude formation. Shortly after the arrival of this model, however, other hypotheses appeared.

The new theories are not models as much as explanations for conflicting results from consumer research. They are, respectively, "Consumer Involvement" and "Brain Specialization." They have been introduced to explain why consumers are interested in some purchase activities more than others and how consumers perceive different messages during purchase consideration.

Briefly, "Consumer Involvement" suggests a continuum of consumer interest in products and services. On the high side are those that are important in money cost, ego support, social value or newness; they involve more risk, require paying more attention to the decision and demand greater use of information. Low involvement decisions are at the other extreme; they arouse little consumer interest or information handling because the risk is small and effort can be reduced accordingly.

It's hard to define this concept because involvement can include consumption as well as purchase situations. Basically, the money, time, complexity and effort involved in buying and using products demand that the consumer make value judgments. Some decisions are important enough to get a lot of effort, others are not.

As the stakes rise, more attention must be given to the decision to avoid making a bad buy. The lower risk product has a lighter penalty for a mistake, and less anxiety about the outcome. The implication: Involvement level

(Continued on Page 46)

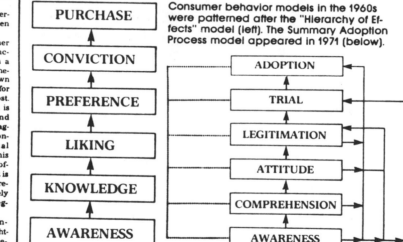

Consumer behavior models in the 1960s were patterned after the "Hierarchy of Effects" model (left). The Summary Adoption Process model appeared in 1971 (below).

| PURCHASE |
| CONVICTION |
| PREFERENCE |
| LIKING |
| KNOWLEDGE |
| AWARENESS |

| ADOPTION |
| TRIAL |
| LEGITIMATION |
| ATTITUDE |
| COMPREHENSION |
| AWARENESS |

Advertising Age, June 9, 198

The Consumer Mind

(Continued from Page 45)

affects receptivity to advertising.

"Brain Specializat on" proposes that anatomical separation of the cerebral hemispheres of the brain leads to specialized perception of messages. The left side is relatively more capable of handling linear logic, language and analysis—in short, the cognitive (thinking) function. The right side is more intuitive, visual and engages in synthesis—the affective (feeling) function. The implication: Advertising response will vary depending upon the thinking or feeling communication task involved.

This subject is quite topical, and enthusiasm for it is producing considerable marketing speculation. The physiological evidence is limited and there is no empirical support for it in a marketing context. However, it's not necessary to endorse right/left brain theory to use the principle that people are capable of both thinking and feeling reactions to stimuli.

Both of these theories have compounded the discussion about how advertising works. The balance of this article is an attempt to regain perspective.

In order to provide a structure that will integrate the traditional theories and LEARN-FEEL-DO hierarchy models with consumer involvement and brain specialization theories, a new approach to advertising strategy is called for. This requires building a matrix to classify products and services.

Here are the pieces for this new model:

- "Thinking" and "Feeling"
- "High" and "Low" involvement

This outline suggests that there are purchase decisions where thinking is most involved and others where feeling dominates; there are situations that are more important and those that are less so. The combination of these reference points produces a strategy matrix that encompasses most of the traditional theories as well as the various LEARN-FEEL-DO hierachy models just discussed.

Thinking and feeling are a continuum in the sense that some decisions involve one or the other, and many involve elements of both. The horizontal side of the matrix conveys this hypothesis and further proposes that over time, there is movement from thinking toward feeling. High and low importance is also a continuum, and the vertical side of the matrix displays this. It is suggested that over time, high importance can decay to relatively low-importance.

Four quadrants are developed in the matrix, with the dotted line in the following diagram indicating a soft partition between them. The solid line arrows visually depict the evolution of consumer tendencies as importance wanes and thinking diminishes with respect to particular products and services. The quadrants outline four potentially major goals for advertising strategy: To be informative, affective, habit forming or to promote self-satisfaction.

What does this matrix reveal? Each quadrant:

- Helps isolate specific categories for strategy planning;
- Approximates one of the traditional consumer theories (economic, psychological, responsive, social);
- Suggests a variant hierarchy model as a strategy guide;
- Implies considerations for creative, media and research.

The following detailed chart expands upon these points. Taking the quadrants separately, a number of strategy possibilities are suggested:

Quadrant 1: High involvement/thinking (informative). This implies a large need for information because of the importance of the product and thinking issues related to it. Major purchases (car, house, furnishings) probably qualify and, initially almost any new product which needs to convey what it is, its function, price and availability. The basic strategy model is the typical LEARN-FEEL-DO sequence where functional and salient information is designed to build consumer attitudinal acceptance and subsequent purchase.

The economic model may be appropriate here as well. A consumer here might be pictured as a "THINKER." Creatively, specific information and demonstration are possibilities. Long copy format and reflective, involving media may be necessary to literally "get through" with key points of consumer interest. If strategy research has defined the significant message to be communicated, recall testing and diagnostic measures will help evaluate the effectiveness of a proposed ad.

Quadrant 2: High involvement/feeling (affective). This product decision is involving, but specific information is less important than an attitude or holistic feeling. This is so because the involvement is related to the person's self-esteem (psychological model). Jewelry, cosmetics and fashion apparel might fall here. A functional example: Motorcyles. The strategy requires emotional involvement on the part of consumers; basically, that they become a "FEELER" about the product.

The model proposed is: FEEL-LEARN-DO. Creatively, executional impact is a possible goal, while media considerations suggest dramatic print exposure or "image" broadcast specials. Copy testing won't get much help from message recall since the effect is likely to be nonliteral; attitude shift testing or emotion arousal (autonomic, psychogalvanometer) tests may be more helpful in determining advertising effect.

Quadrant 3: Low involvement/thinking (habit formation). Product decisions in this area involve minimal thought and a tendency to form buying habits for convenience. Information, to the extent that it plays a role, will be any point of difference that can be meaningfully exploited. Most food and staple package goods items likely belong here. Brand loyalty will be a function of habit, but it's quite likely most consumers have several "acceptable" brands. Over time, many ordinary products will mature and descend into this commodity limbo.

The hierarchy model is a DO-LEARN-FEEL pattern which is compatible with the traditional responsive theory. It suggests that simply inducing trial (coupons, free samples) can often generate subsequent purchase more readily than pounding home undifferentiating copy points. This consumer can be viewed as a "DOER." Creatively what is required is to stimulate a reminder for the product. Media implications might include small-space ads, 10-second IDs, point of sale pieces and radio.

The ideal advertising test would be a sales measure or lab substitute; recall and/or attitude change tests may not correlate with sales and therefore be misleading. This is a troublesome quadrant because so many commonly used products and services are here and require very detailed and careful planning effort.

Quadrant 4: Low involvement/feeling (self-satisfaction). This low involvement area seems to be reserved for those products that satisfy personal tastes—cigarets, liquor, candy, movies. Imagery and quick satisfaction are involved. This is a DO-FEEL-LEARN model with some application of the social theory because so many products here fit into group situations (beer, soft drinks).

This consumer is a "REACTOR" whose logical interest will be hard to hold and short-lived. Creatively, it's basic to get attention with some consistency. Billboards, point of sale and newspapers might apply here. Copy testing will need to be sales oriented because recall and attitude change may not be relevant.

These comments are meant to be thought-starters rather than a formula for planning. The options clearly depend upon the category, brand, sales trends and marketing objectives. Also, it's not necessary to be restricted to just these four possibilities in using this matrix. For example, two other hierarchy models are available:

- Between quadrants one and three, a LEARN-DO-FEEL sequence might apply as consumers go directly from information to trial.
- Between quadrants two and four, a FEEL-DO-LEARN model suggests acting upon an initial feeling and purchasing.

Also, some products conceivably belong between quadrants 1 and 2 or 3 and 4, requiring elements of both learn and feel simultaneously. The options for placing products in the proper area are challenging indeed. But by thinking a product through the system, using available research and management judgment, the advertising strategy implications can become clearer and more manageable.

What this model says is that consumer entry into a product should be determined for information (learn), attitude (feel) and behavior (do) issues to develop advertising. We help do this using basic consumer research. The priority of learn over feel, feel over learn, or do over either learn-feel, has implications for advertising strategy, creative execution, media planning and copy testing.

To appreciate fully what this change means, recall that the LEARN-FEEL-DO sequence has been endorsed for years as the only "legitimate" model of advertising effectiveness. Its linearity has been forced into situations where it simply didn't apply. But it is only one of several models. Furthermore, it's no longer a straight line concept, but rather, circular.

Unfortunately, few advertising strategies are simple. Many products have learn, feel and do in varying degrees, best represented perhaps by overlap.

The fundamental hypothesis of this model can now be stated: An advertising strategy is determined by specifying (1) the consumer's point of entry on the LEARN-FEEL-DO continuum and (2) the priority of learn *vs.* feel *vs.* do for making a sale. Specifically, the strategy issue is whether to develop product features, brand image or some combination of both.

- To the extent a brand has hard news, with distinct features, and can link its name to them, the sale centers on "learning," with "feeling" and "doing" coming after.
- Lacking such information, where a product gives its users an identity via intangible/emotional features leading to an image, the sale centers on "feelings" and proceeds to "learning" and "doing."
- As brands endure and achieve fixed places in the consumer's mind, buying may become routine and consist primarily of "doing" with very little conscious "learning" or "feeling."

The more the strategy matches consumer purchase experience, the better the advertising will be "internalized" or "accepted." Advertising may now have to be the right communication "experience" for the consumer as well as th[illegible]e same way. Sometimes communication of key information and salient emotion will be needed to get a sale; at other times consumers will need one, but not both; and often buying may occur with little or no information and emotion. The purpose of strategy planning is to identify the information, emotion or action leverage for a particular product, build the appropriate advertising model and then execute it.

This planning model is not an all-purpose cure. It's a guide to help organize the advertising objectives for a product. The account team has to use product research to determine the brand's leverage and then build a strategy that incorporates creative, media and copy testing projects. If done properly, the parts should fit together. #

How Advertising Works: An FCB Planning Model

THINKING → FEELING (HIGH INVOLVEMENT ↓ LOW INVOLVEMENT)

	THINKING	FEELING
HIGH INVOLVEMENT	**1. INFORMATIVE (THINKER)** CAR-HOUSE-FURNISHINGS-NEW PRODUCTS **MODEL:** LEARN-FEEL-DO (Economic?) **Possible Implications** **TEST:** Recall, Diagnostics **MEDIA:** Long Copy Format, Reflective Vehicles **CREATIVE:** Specific Information, Demonstration	**2. AFFECTIVE (FEELER)** JEWELRY-COSMETICS-FASHION APPAREL-MOTORCYCLES **MODEL:** FEEL-LEARN-DO (Psychological?) **Possible Implications** **TEST:** Attitude Change, Emotion Arousal **MEDIA:** Large Space, Image Specials **CREATIVE:** Executional Impact
LOW INVOLVEMENT	**3. HABIT FORMATION (DOER)** FOOD-HOUSEHOLD ITEMS **MODEL:** DO-LEARN-FEEL (Responsive?) **Possible Implications** **TEST:** Sales **MEDIA:** Small Space Ads, 10 Second I.D.'s, Radio; POS **CREATIVE:** Reminder	**4. SELF-SATISFACTION (REACTOR)** CIGARETTES-LIQUOR-CANDY **MODEL:** DO-FEEL-LEARN (Social?) **Possible Implications** **TEST:** Sales **MEDIA:** Billboards, Newspapers, POS **CREATIVE:** Attention

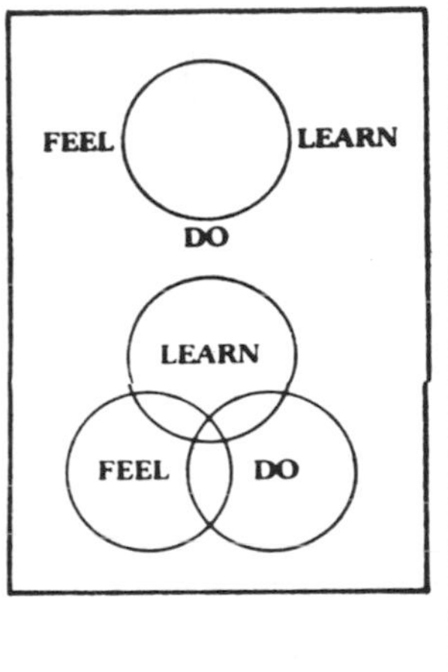

*

We're not sure whether this is an understatement or an overstatement – but it makes you think.

So do these "Going Out of Business" advertisements...

**

Ditto.

***

"AIDA"

This is the more common acronym for the process:

Attention
Interest
Desire
Action

However, "interest" and "desire" overstate the case for many product categories.

"Awareness" and "Attitude" seem more accurate.

And easier to remember.

Think Better Three Ways.

This Addendum will cover three additional ways to think about advertising!

One is a hierarchy –
The Four A's of Advertising.***

One is circular –
The Learn/Feel/Do Circle.

One is subjective –
Resonance.

Let's begin with the beginning.

A IS FOR ADVERTISING.

Advertising isn't a thing.

It's an active relationship.

It's something that happens *to* a person, whether reader, viewer, listener or someone not paying much attention.

It's not just the ad, it's *the response* to the ad.

It's not what happens in the ad, it's what happens *inside the person.*

That's how advertising works. Advertising that does not do that merely "talks to itself."

It may be handsome. The client may love it.

Hey, you might even win an award.

But it probably won't work very well.

How *does* advertising work?

Advertising works on four levels, which we'll call **The Four A's of Advertising.**

ATTENTION
AWARENESS
ATTITUDE
ACTION

Let's take them one by one…

First, advertising has to get **ATTENTION.**

Breaking through to get attention is also one of the toughest jobs.

You're not only competing with a lot of other messages done by other skilled ad people, but people are very good at tuning out what doesn't interest them.

The thing to remember is that the ad doesn't have to jump out at you. It's even better when people jump into the ad.

When people notice your ad, to some extent, they remember it.

And, a certain percentage of these people will buy your product. Generally, this will be a greater percentage than those who don't know your name or notice your ad.

Overcoming all the barriers to communication and getting ATTENTION is advertising's first job.

Second, advertising must build **AWARENESS.**

You want your advertising to move from merely being noticed to being *remembered.*

It occupies a space in the conscious or subconscious mind or memory.

This is usually a cumulative process and building awareness is a constant goal of virtually all advertising. It takes time, and that often means sticking with it – but it's worth it!

At this second level, advertising has an ongoing existence *inside* people.

If they remember the right thing about you, a greater percentage of these people will be disposed to buy your product.

Third, advertising works to reinforce or change **ATTITUDE.**

ATTITUDE is the feeling people have toward your product.

Attitude is more active than Awareness.

"Nobody's waiting to hear from us."
Bill Bernbach

"Nobody reads advertising. People read what interests them; and sometimes it's an ad."
Howard Gossage

"It's important to be visually brave; to do something that goes beyond the ordinary and captures attention. That, as we know, is 50% of the battle; to turn the prospect's head, to pay attention to what's being said."
Susan Gillette, DDB Needham

"AIDED" AND "UN-AIDED" AWARENESS.

One of the basic research techniques used to measure advertising's effectiveness is to measure "Awareness."

In its simplest form, you ask people what ads or products they remember.

As in, "Do you remember any beer commercials?" or "What brands of beer do you remember?"

The percentage of people who remember your brand or advertising is called Awareness or **"Un-Aided Awareness."**

If your brand or commercial is not mentioned, the person is then asked, "Do you remember such and such a beer commercial, or such and such brand of beer?"

If the answer is "Oh, yeah," or something to that effect, this percentage is **"Aided Awareness."**

First, your ad must be noticed.
Second, it must be remembered.
Third, it must become important.
Fourth, it must work.

ASK FOR THE ORDER:
Look for ways to *activate* the consumer in your ads.
Invite them into your store.
Ask them to try your product.
Make them an offer.

When there is an Attitude toward a product, people can usually tell you how they feel.

Attitude can be positive, negative or neutral.

To state the obvious, you want to build a positive attitude toward your product. However, some advertising works to build negative attitudes toward the competition. Political advertising is a good example.

An attitude is usually the result of some type of experience:
- an ad,
- a product experience,
- imagery of the product name or package,
- "Word of Mouth" (a powerful force),
- All of the above (Integrated Marketing Communications).

A major long-term job of advertising is to build or shift Attitudes toward the product, and about the product.

Often this shift has specific strategic focus, i.e. improve reputation for quality.

The better the Attitude, the better the sales.

Finally, there is **ACTION**.

The relationship is externalized and the person actually acts!

He buys the product, sends for a brochure or writes his Congressman.

Sometimes you can move someone all the way to ACTION in only one ad.

Direct Mail, for instance, does this all the time. People send for a product or more information on the basis of one ad or mailing.

Retail advertising is also Action-oriented.

Retailers measure advertising effectiveness by store traffic and sales.

But with all advertisers, even those concerned with short term sales, or even survival, the action of advertising is also a long-term cumulative process that builds with each ad.

For every advertiser, advertising is part of a long-term process…even when it's designed for short-term results.

Once more, that process is…
gain **ATTENTION**,
build **AWARENESS**,
shift **ATTITUDE**…and
motivate **ACTION**.

THE 4 A's OF ADVERTISING.

2. The "Learn/Feel/Do" Circle.

It's called the Learn/Feel/Do Circle.

It describes the ways people involve themselves with products.

You may have noticed it in Richard Vaughn's article explaining **"The Grid."** They showed three overlapping circles labeled **"Learn," "Feel,"** and **"Do."** (Fig. 1)

Learn. We read about a product in an ad, or look at the label.

Feel. We may have feelings about the product or product category.

Do. We buy a product, use it, and experience it.

Generally, these three circles are shown as one circle, which we call the **Learn/Feel/Do Circle** *(Fig. 2)*.

This simple little figure describes a sequence that can be very helpful in how we think about advertising.

TWO SIMPLE RULES.

1. You may enter at any point on the circle.

Your initial experience with a product may be "Learning," "Feeling," or "Doing."

2. You may go in either direction .

The sequence of experience can go in either direction.

 Think about it…

> "*Every advertisement is a long-term investment in the image of the brand.*"
> **David Ogilvy**

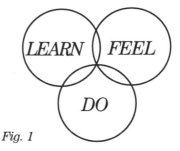

Fig. 1

Fig. 2

THE LEARN/FEEL/DO CIRCLE

93

Do/Learn/Feel

For example, what is the process by which your customer gets involved with your product?

For a new snack food, he may try it first (DO), find out how it tastes (LEARN), and then FEEL.

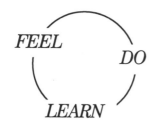

Feel/Do/Learn

For a new perfume the advertising might create feeling first. She thinks it might be her perfume (FEEL), tries it at the store (DO), and finds out (LEARN).

Get the idea?

Resonance.
Is not just the message or the consumer. It's the way the two interact...

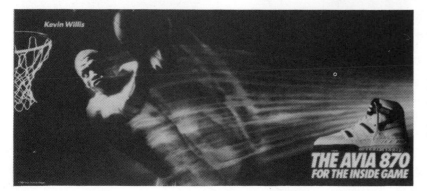

Think about the *process* by which people can involve themselves with your product and with your advertising.

For example, a High Involvement/Thinking type of product may encourage you to try to "teach" people about your product with a long copy ad – **Learn/Feel/Do.**

For an inexpensive snack like SmartFood, perhaps you should encourage sampling – **Do/Learn /Feel.**

Different approaches may find you entering at different parts of the circle.

Think about how your target customer will relate to the product and the advertising.

Think of the point of entry.

Then think of the sequence.

The Learn/Feel/Do Circle is an excellent conceptual tool for thinking about the dynamic you wish to create with your advertising:

What do you want them to **learn**?

What do you want them to **feel**?

What do you want them to **do**?

Hierarchies, Grids and Circles…

Now, how do they all work *together* inside of the consumer? That's **RESONANCE.**

3. Resonance.

Advertising happens *inside* people.

As a writer and producer, Tony Schwartz has been responsible for some of the most powerful and effective ads ever run - the "Daisy" commercial helped create a landslide victory for Lyndon Johnson.

He's also made some very important contributions to the way we think about communications.

Let's take a look at his "Resonance" Theory.

THE "RESONANCE" THEORY.

When you achieve "Resonance," your external message relates to the internal values and feelings of the person you're talking to. Here's how Mr. Schwartz describes it.

"Resonance takes place when the stimuli put into our communication evoke <u>meaning</u> in a listener or viewer...

The meaning of our communication is what a listener or viewer gets <u>out</u> of his experience with the communicator's stimuli."

The two ads on this page resonated to me.

They may or may not speak to you.

Resonance demands an understanding of what is already inside the consumer's mind.

"It concentrates on evoking responses from people by attuning the message to their prior experience."

Hopkins would say,

"The advertising man studies the consumer. He tries to place himself in the position of the buyer."

Tony Schwartz says,

"The skillful electronic communicator should be aware of what is inside the minds of the people he wants to reach so that he can find a link between his material and those who receive it."

End of Addendum.

Ads to Remember.
The quick little emotional vibration off the double meaning in the St. Pauli Girl ad creates Resonance.
 At least, it did for me.
 Pick out some ads that resonate with you - study how they work on you and how you respond.

Resonance in Action.
A little girl with a daisy... a countdown... a nuclear explosion... and a message to vote for Lyndon Johnson.

How to Have an Idea.

Creativity.

Every year, in speeches, seminars, meeting rooms, classrooms and Creative Directors' offices, someone asks,

"What is Creativity?"

Answering this question has become a minor industry in itself.

Since a completely satisfactory answer will never be given, this situation will continue to provide steady employment to the chronically over-qualified.

However, what we're really interested in is how the mind associates and combines learned information in fresh new ways.

This is called "Having an Idea," or "ideation," and a key part of your job is to work with and develop ideas that help your client's business.

The business of advertising is about having ideas. So let's talk about it.

Here's what Arthur Koestler said in his book, "The Act of Creation."

"All great innovations consist of sudden shifts of attention and emphasis onto some previously neglected aspect of experience...They uncover what has always been there (yet) they are revolutionary."

Here's what Leo Burnett said,

"Creativity is the art of establishing new and meaningful relationships between previously unrelated things...which somehow present the product in a fresh, new light."

And here's what James Webb Young, a well-known copywriter of his time, said in 1944.

"An idea is nothing more or less than a new combination of old elements."

It's Not Creative Unless It Sells.

Not True.

This is a popular advertising slogan. Catchy, but incorrect.

An ad may be quite creative but not sell, and, it may or may not be the ad's fault.

The product, or some other aspect of marketing, such as distribution or pricing may be at fault.

Could you sell an Edsel?

An ad may delight both agency and client for its creativity, but miss the mark with the customer.

Creative, but not effective.

On the other hand, a very ordinary and unimaginative ad may be quite effective in the marketplace if the message is strong and the product and value are above average.

Even if the ad itself is not very "creative," it may sell very well.

96

The Creative or "Ideation" process appears to have certain stages:

1. PREPARATION.

Collecting input. "Doing your homework."

During the preparation stage, information goes into the Left Side (Verbal/Storage/Memory) of the brain.

2. FRUSTRATION.

Unless the answer is obvious, the result is often frustration.

The answer is not achieved through simple logic – so the Left Side doesn't quite know what to do with all this information. You're frustrated.

Emphasis shifts to the other side of the brain.

3. INCUBATION.

Now the Right Side of your brain goes to work, shuffling through the information – consciously or subconsciously, associating new and old information in new combinations.

You may actually want to "sleep on it."
Mull it over. It's a natural process.

4. ILLUMINATION

AHA! The light bulb goes on!

Two previously unrelated elements connect.
Congratulations, you've just had an idea.
Don't always expect a blinding flash of light.

As Leo said, "The secret of all effective originality in advertising is not the creation of new and tricky words and pictures, but putting familiar words and pictures into new relationships."

5. EVALUATION.

Now, you have to decide whether or not your idea is a *good* idea.

This is a major problem for many talented creative people – they have lots of ideas, but can't tell their good ones from their bad ones.

Here we bring back the Critical/Analytical Left Side for an opinion.

James Webb Young.
JWT Copywriter & Educator.
Developed successful direct-mail business in spare time.
Wrote "A Technique for Producing Ideas."
It's only 61 pages long and a classic. Read it if you can find it.

LEARN TO BE #2 ON A GOOD IDEA.

True story.

The client and agency were in an idea session for a new TV spot.

Nike had just signed Bo Jackson.

At one end of the table, they were having fun naming famous "Bo's."

Bo Derek, Beau Brummel, Little Bo Peep, etc.

Someone said, "Bo Diddley."

The CD's ears perked up – Jim Riswold recognized an idea that could work.

By next morning, it was written.
Which is how it often works.
It wasn't the CD's idea.
But he knew what to do with it!

THE
COPYWRITER
- - - - - - - -

by John E. Matthews

**WHAT TO DO UNTIL
THE IDEA COMES.**
From "The Copywriter"
by John Matthews.
Here are some little mechanical tricks
I've found helpful, and that you can add
to your own collection of "what to do
until the idea comes."

The first trick is simply the mechanical process by which you write. Do you
use a typewriter, a ball-point, a stubby
black pencil, a tape recorder?
[Note: This piece was written "BC,"
before computer–Ed.]

Whichever you use, try switching to
something else whenever the blank
moment comes up. Perhaps you'll
discover that there's a strange and
wonderful two-way communication
between your brain and the writing
mechanics.

Sometimes if you start talking instead
of typing, the brain will get back in
working order. (It's kind of like kicking
a flat tire. It may not inflate the stupid
thing, but it makes you feel you're
"taking action.")

Another category that works is called
"brain jiggling." This covers anything
that goes bumpety-bump-bump – from
driving your car down a country road to
taking a train ride.

All kinds of locomotion belong to this
group – even jogging around the block.
I admit that many pedestrians on
Michigan Avenue (or Madison Avenue,
for that matter) may think it odd to see
an apparently civilized person jogging
up the street.

But we are not out to impress such
pedestrian observers; the main thing is
to get your brain working again.
[Note: Written Before Jogging– Ed.]

cont'd on following page

Evaluating ideas is also one of the critical roles of The Creative Director.

The difference between having ideas and knowing which are the *good ideas* is mainly one of Evaluation, learning to be critical of your own work in a positive way.

Evaluation might also involve additional "ideation" to shore up the weak spots of the initial idea or to take your idea "one more step," by using it as part of a new combination.

6. ELABORATION.

Working it out.

Copy and layout.

This is the other hard part.

Having ideas, even good ones, is really pretty easy. Making them work is work.

And *that's* how to have an idea.

FOUR ADDITIONAL POINTS ABOUT THE IDEATION PROCESS:

1. If Illumination doesn't come right away, you might not have done enough Preparation.

If your preparation is not complete, you may be missing that critical element of insight.

Every successful copywriter talks a lot about becoming immersed in the product and in the prospect. This is *key* to Preparation.

Prepare thoroughly and then allow your intuitive process to sort it out. (Remember, Incubation may take some time as well.)

A few thoughts while you tough it out.

Einstein said, *"The supreme task of the physicist is to arrive at those universal elementary laws from which the cosmos can be built by pure deduction. There is no logical path to these laws; only intuition resting on experience can reach them."*

And jazz pianist Thelonius Monk said, *"Sometimes I play things I never heard myself."*

You can do it. Be Prepared.

2. Selling an idea can be even harder than having one.

A new idea can be threatening.

Koestler says this about the shock of new ideas, *"They compel us to re-value our values."*

After all, others have *not* gone through your ideation process.

Sometimes the best approach is to walk your audience through the process you went through.

Step-by-step–from Preparation to Frustration to Illumination.

And then Evaluation and Elaboration.

Give them time to get comfortable with a new thought. (Like cheap underwear, the mind, once stretched, never reverts to its original shape.)

On the other hand, your idea might not be accepted because it's *too obvious!*

Just as a maze can be solved by going backward, the creative act is sometimes diminished in retrospect. The path that was once unclear is now there for all to see.

"Aha," becomes, "of course."

Leo Burnett had this to say about new ideas…

"Great copy and great ideas are deceptively simple."

Trout and Ries agree.

"The best positioning ideas are so simple that most people overlook them."

If this is the case, dramatize your concept's *simplicity.* (People don't always have to know how clever you are.)

In every case, emphasize to the client or the people you work with, how this idea relates to *their* needs and solves *their* problems.

Help *your* idea become *their* idea.

Another brain-jolter calls for walking down the street and entering the first shop you spot that you have no business in. Or have never been in for any reason whatever.

Now there's one school which contends that a couple of afternoon hours in a good movie will work wonders in regenerating creative cells.

I've always considered this "cinema-system" most unimaginative; something which could be construed by laymen as merely the lazy Copywriter's excuse to goof-off an afternoon.

Much more ingenious and inspiring (and filling) is the system I have discovered of reactivating the brain via the stomach.

This system is extemely practical; it can be applied during your lunch hour.

It merely involves changing your luncheon habits drastically.

You frequent the Imperial House? Try Woolworth's lunch counter, a veritable creative wonderland!

Usually have a social lunch?

Make one anti-social.

I don't claim to know what makes this system work so well. But work it does. And it can save hours of waiting for a cold typewriter to thaw.

Ordering Information:

When we called John Matthews to ask for permission to use this piece, we asked him if he had any remaining copies of this old favorite of ours.

John called back a few weeks later to say he'd found the last few copies and he was sending them to us.

So… if you want to add this classic to your collection, you can now order **"The Copywriter"** *from The Copy Workshop. While Supplies Last.*

3. Your idea isn't always the right idea.

Try to be objective about your ideas. Many bright creative people are victimized by their inability to know their good ideas from their bad ones and to confuse *their* idea with the *right* idea. This is compounded by a competitive reluctance to like other people's ideas.

Learning to tell good ideas from bad ideas is a tough skill to develop.

Since it's a bit like predicting the future, you'll never be perfect at it.

As a start, try to learn to like the best idea…no matter whose it is.

Evaluation is another important part of this process. Get other opinions.

Try to become objective about your ideas. (It ain't easy.)

And learn to keep going.

Remain open to new insights and new ideas. What seemed like the destination may be only a stop along the way – a piece of a larger puzzle.

4. It's hard work. You may need help.

Once you get an idea, even a great one, you have to work to make it work.

And you probably need help.

Elaborate.

Learn to get others to help you make your idea work better and work harder.

Working together on ideas is one of the joys of this business. As Norm Brown of FCB said, *"Work is fun."*

Bill Backer, of Backer Spielvogel Bates wrote a wonderful book on the topic, *"The Care and Feeding of Ideas."* Read it.

There are many ways to Elaborate.

The root word is "labor."

Once you get an idea, your job hasn't ended. It's just begun.

Idea Exercises:

1. PREPARATION.
List the types of source material you can assemble for Preparation on a product assignment.

2. MORE PREPARATION.
List other types of product-related experiences you can generate at the Preparation stage.

3. ILLUMINATION.
Describe two times you have experienced Illumination. Short paragraphs.

4. FRUSTRATION.
Describe two times you have experienced Frustration.

How was this resolved?

The Idea Box.

James Webb Young recommends that you write each fact on an index card.

One fact (or idea), one card.

Keep adding cards and place them all in a box – or wrap them with a rubber band.

After you've put them all down, put them aside for as long as you can.

Then go back to the pile and, as you review the cards, write down new ideas as they emerge.

EXAMPLE:
A new combination
of old Elements.
Garbage bag + Jack-o-Lantern.
Turning lawn & leaf bags into
pumpkins pumps up sales in the
fall for plastic bag companies.
A simple idea.
Don't you wish you'd
thought of it!

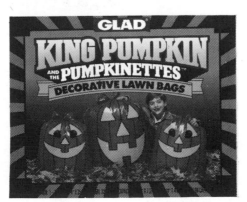

12 TIPS TO GET STARTED.

Here's some practical advice from John Caples. (There's a lot more in his wonderful book, "How to Make Your Advertising Make Money.")

1. Don't wait for inspiration.
2. Start with something easy.
3. Write as if talking to a companion.
4. Write a letter to a friend.
5. Forget the "Do's" and "Don'ts."
6. Describe the product.
7. Make a list of benefits.
8. Write what interests you most.
9. Get inspiration from others.
10. Copy successful copy.
11. Start by writing headlines.
12. Write fast and edit later.

READING LIST:
Here are some books on "How to Have an Idea."

The Act of Creation
Arthur Koestler/Pan Picador (1975)

**A Technique for
Producing Ideas.**
James Webb Young/Crain Books

DeBono's Thinking Course
Edward de Bono/Facts on File.

**The Office.
A Facility Based On Change.**
(Available through
Herman Miller Furniture)

Some of the books listed in the previous chapter also deal with the subject of "Ideation."

Zen Copywriting.

In Zen archery,
the archer and the act become one.

The copywriter's job
is much the same.

Imagine
the destination
before you begin
the journey.

Your job is to take
information
and images
and ideas
and make them
what they were
meant to be.

You must
organize them,
imagine them,
write them,
and
sell them.

As your journey progresses,
your destination will be seen more clearly.
As your skills develop, your arrows
will fly closer to the invisible
target's center.

That's your job.

Imagine
the future.
Make it
come
true

.

Q: *How many Zen Masters does it*
   take to change a light bulb?
A: *Two. One to change the light bulb.*
   One to not change the light bulb.

Two aspects of Zen are accomodating
contradictory thoughts and being in
touch with the moment.

Both are important in advertising.

For example, we take small products
that play a minor role in people's lives
and make them seem important.

It's a business you must really take
seriously to be successful. Yet, take it
too seriously, and it makes you crazy.

Good advertising has an intuitive sense
of the moment – a knowing without
knowing.

It is often hard to explain.

The Way of Zen.
Alan Watts/Vintage Books N.Y.

Zen in the Art of Archery.
E. Herrigel/Pantheon, N.Y.

Zen and The Art of
Motorcycle Maintenance.
An Inquiry into Values.
Robert M. Pirsig

Shogun. James Clavell
   (The book is better than the movie.)

Ad Haiku.

Let's do some **Haiku.**
a Japanese poem form
of only three lines.

First five syllables
then in the middle seven
followed by five more.

It's five seven five
a rhythm made from phrasing
that doesn't need rhyme.

How to do Haiku?
Feel the thought within the thing.
Put it on paper.

You can Haiku, too
Just start at the beginning
let the writing flow.

Haiku Exercises:

1. TRADITIONAL HAIKU.
   Based on an object or scene in nature.

2. DO A HAIKU.
   about a tool or kitchen appliance.

3. HOW TO HAIKU.
   Do a Haiku about how to do something.

4. MOVIE REVIEW HAIKU.
   Do a Haiku about a movie or TV show.

5. ADVERTISING HAIKU.
   Do a Haiku about a brand name product.

"A space traveler in an Einsteinian Universe moving in what he believes to be a straight line will eventually end up where he started.
This is also true in some parts of New Jersey."
Psychology Today, 4/83

ZEN ADDENDUM:
INSIDE & OUTSIDE.

When working on a problem, I try to go *inside* the problem.

Into the product.

Into the Target Consumer.

Into the relationship between people and product.

Yet, it's also true that the answer, or part of it, may be *outside* – at the cutting edge of art, fashion, or music.

Or a unique combination of concept and circumstance.

But, to get outside, I believe that sometimes you must go so far in that you come out the other side.

Just like in some parts of New Jersey.

Once you go inside a problem deeply enough, you can almost feel yourself standing outside.

A good copywriter can go both ways...all at once.

That's why, as a copywriter, you must continually broaden your outside perspective at the same time you journey inside the products you advertise and try to get *inside* the minds of the people you talk to.

ZEN READING LIST:

Want to know more about Zen? Don't get carried away, but I believe that a general understanding of Zen can help in doing your job.

PAPER NAPKIN HAIKU.
This can be a lot of fun with the right group of people – at a restaurant, or wherever.

One person starts a Haiku – five syllables.

The next person writes the next line – seven syllables.

A third person does the third line – five syllables.

Try it.

Art Director Appreciation.

Advertising is a team sport.

Copywriters and Art Directors depend on each other. No business relationship is closer.

Except perhaps in a trapeze act.

A major factor in how well you succeed in this business will be based on how well you work with an Art Director.

Earlier, we discussed the left and right sides of the brain.

There is a parallel here in your contributions to the creation of an ad.

THE ART DIRECTOR IS VISUAL
— Right Side.

THE COPYWRITER IS VERBAL
— Left Side.

Your contributions reinforce each other.

This was part of Rubicam's revolution and the genius of the DDB approach.

The amount of time the two of you spend developing an ad can be different, too.

After you write something brilliant, like "New and Improved," the Art Director may have to spend hours making it look right.

A storyboard can take a day or two, particularly if the visuals have to be thought out and the rendering has to be of good quality.

After you sell the ad, the disparity continues.

For print ads, shooting, re-touching, typesetting, and key-lining are the Art Director's responsibility.

On the other hand, you have to spend more time with Clients and Account Executives (you're the verbal one, remember?).

The point is, while the two of you are partners, even parents, your jobs are very different.

And the better you team up, despite these very real differences, the better the two of you will do. Together.

Here are a few hints for successful teamwork:

1. DON'T FINISH TOO FAST

Put thumbnails, roughs, and headline ideas up on the wall. Let it incubate.

2. TALK ABOUT TYPE.

Type is one important way to establish tone of voice. What sort of attitude do you want your words to project?

The typeface can even influence the headline itself. (And vice versa.)

Certain words look better in certain type faces. Talk about it. Try your hand at press type.

Learn a layout program on the computer.

This is a key decision. You're entitled to a vote!

3. STORYBOARD OR KEY FRAME?

Chances are, you don't need to do a storyboard right away.

Learn to present with *key frames.*

An office filled with un-sold storyboards is a monument to wasted time.

4. BE A FRIEND.

There may be much in your backgrounds that is different. Still, there is much that you share.

And that will grow with time.

The two of you are literally the parents of your creations. You have responsibilities and obligations to each other and the product of your combined talents.

Invest time and energy in that relationship and it will pay off in the work you do.

Together.

GRAPHIC DESIGNERS VS. ART DIRECTORS

Fine artists and great graphic designers aren't necessarily good advertising art directors.

Fine design may arrange the page with pleasing proportion.

Fine art may express the artist's feelings and touch the heart (and the wallet) of the gallery-goer.

Good advertising art direction motivates action in ordinary people!

It grabs the casual reader and moves him in a desired direction.

It may invite him in, or pop off the page and poke him in the eye.

Whatever the effect, it can't just sit there looking nice.

It must be noticed.

The advertising art director uses art and design to accomplish objectives.

They are means to an end.

For the same reason, excellent essayists, journalists, novelists, poets and playwrights are not necessarily good copywriters.

And vice versa.

MAKE THE LAYOUTS ROUGH AND THE IDEAS FANCY.

STAVROS COSMOPULOS

COSMOPULOS, CROWLEY & DALY, INC.
ADVERTISING/MARKETING
250 BOYLSTON ST., BOSTON, MASS. 02116
266-8800

Q : How many art directors does it take to change a light bulb?

A : Does it have to be a light bulb?

One of the finest practitioners of the Art Director's art is **Helmut Krone.**

Mr. Krone was one of the influential AD's at DDB.

Here is one interview with Mr. Krone done for The Wall Street Journal.

On the following pages is another – a classic view of the Art Director's role.

Hear what Helmut has to say.

5. THE MEETING IS THE MEDIA.

You probably think you do ads for print and television. Wrong.

You do meetings!

Your medium is not the magazine page or TV screen. It's the meeting room wall and the walnut conference table.

Visualize The Meeting:

How big is the room? Where is the wall?

Where are the people you'll be presenting your ads to? Who are they?

You'll have to make an impact in that space.

Own the room with the power of your work.

Attack the Wall!

Get the theme up nice and big. Give the meeting a headline.

Have a simple right brain visual to go with all that left brain verbiage.

Remember, if you don't do the meeting right, the ads don't run.

Or worse.

Another team wins.

KRONE ALONE

In 1950, a 25-year-old designer saw The Art Directors Club annual exhibition dominated by a very new and very small advertising agency. The designer's name: Helmut Krone. The agency: Doyle Dane Bernbach. The rest is history. Here, from a recent conversation, are the singular views of DDB's executive vice president, a creative director, and a member of the Art Directors Hall of Fame, with creative talent so extraordinary the late Bill Bernbach suggested he should be included in this series.

On early ambitions:
I was interested in industrial design and architecture. At 21, I had two interviews scheduled. First, with a designer named Robert Greenwell who was doing freelance ads for a magazine. The second with Raymond Loewy. Greenwell offered me $40 per week. I said, "Gee, that's great." I never interviewed with Loewy. And never looked back. I tell my children, it's not so much what you do but how you do it. Kids today spend half their lives agonizing over their first move, first job. It doesn't matter, it's how you tackle your work. Stop worrying so much and just do *something*.

On advertising:
I was Bauhaus-based. My idol was Paul Rand. Advertising? If you had any respect for design—any self-respect—and you wanted to tell your mother what you were doing, you worked *around* advertising, but *not in it*. So I worked for Greenwell, in pharmaceuticals, in fashion, for publishers—but not for the hard-core advertising agencies. I had to wait for Bernbach to start his agency. I came here in 1954. I was 29, and one of four art directors.

On alternatives:
I have always said there were only two people for whom I could work: Bill Bernbach and myself. Bill did more than start an agency. He made advertising *respectable*, a profession, a high art. We argued a lot. With genuine disagreement but real affection. We could fight like cats and dogs because we *knew we were both after the same thing*.

On television and print:
I'm not crazy about *things that move*. I like things that stand still; that you can study, hold in your hand, look at, contemplate. That's what I hate about television commercials. They're happenings. They go by and you don't even remember the details. In a print ad, you can study them. There's a point to caring about details in print. If you can give a photo just an extra ounce of *caring*, just a touch of inspiration, it shows. While I do my share of TV, I'm known as the print maven around here. I really do like it. After all these years, the idea of the *page* continues to fascinate me.

On work:
Beauty and style are qualities I count as secondary. If they are in the work, they come along for the ride. The only quality I really appreciate is *newness*, to see something no one has ever seen before. New comes at 11 o'clock at night, after you've spent all day hunched over the board. I have worked with a couple of geniuses. I spend long hours making up for not being a genius.

On confidence and clients:
I am very insecure. Nothing I do ever turns out exactly right. It's never what I expected. I like to work with clients. I need their judgment. All I know is that what I'm doing is new. The client can tell me if it's right. I hate presentations: agency

people filing in with a big portfolio, taking out their acetate-wrapped comprehensives and saying, "Here. Make a decision." I like to have clients work with me. I show them scraps of paper. I pull things out of the wastebasket, tissues off the wall. I say "What do *you* think? Should I keep going?" It's not a matter of giving clients what they want. It's a matter of making sure you're on the same wave length.

On working with writers:
I talk with the writer. We come up with a concept. The writer leaves. But I stay. I want to *top* the concept. I want to lay something on top of the concept that's totally unexpected. Most people go home. I don't. For my work begins *after* we've settled on a headline and picture. The next day, the writer will see the ad. It'll have the headline and the picture we discussed. But it won't look or feel the way they thought it would. And that's unnerving to some writers.

On staying ahead:
I try to have some idea of what I want to do even before I know what has to be done. So before I get an assignment, I know what my attack will be, even before I know the product. You can't explain this to a client. They don't understand the process. But I believe you can bend and twist the idea to fit the problem, and come up with something totally new. Does it sound crazy? Bernbach used to say, "First, you make the revolution. Then you figure out why." Thinking ahead isn't unfair to the client. It gives him a head start.

On ads as information:
I think people want *information*. They don't get it from advertising. Say you're buying a tape deck. Well, you're up against it—especially if you read the ads. You know the formula. A double-entendre headline. Nice photo. But *no real meat* in the ad. Because the people who did the ad don't think you *really* want to know. Advertising people argue that it's good to make it simple. But that's not the point. People want to know. Advertising ought to give them the information they need.

On the page as a package:
The page ought to be a *package* for the product. It should look like the product, smell like the product and the company. If it's a highly technical product—like the Porsche—that's how the page ought to look and feel. I tried to make the Porsche ads look a little like what you see when you raise the hood of the car. It's a *package* for Porsche. Every company, every product needs its own package.

On ideas and making them work:
Good ideas announce themselves. A bell rings. But that's just the start. To stage an idea at the level where I want to work, to do work that's *out at the edge*, you need to know about the tools. Type, photography, illustration, are tools. You need to know how they work, to know nearly as much about them as the people who specialize. For if you can't use the tools, you can't really make a good idea work.

On drawing pads:
Some people begin by drawing layouts. I can't work that way. I begin by *thinking*. I don't want to be influenced by that first scribble. Scribbles can box you in. Think first. I don't want to design *ads*. That's why I've spent my life fighting logos. Logos say "I'm an ad, so turn the page." I don't just leave out the logo. I give the client something better. And it doesn't look like an ad.

On The Wall Street Journal:
Form follows function. That was the Bauhaus revolution. The Journal is Bauhaus. Its form follows its function: information, organized for the reader, gathered for business reasons. I've said you ought to be able to identify your ads if you hang them upside down, forty feet away. The Journal *is* The Journal; there's no mistaking it. I've also said the graphic image ought to reflect reality. The Journal *looks* like business, and it *is* business. Of course, I read The Journal. Of course, I like to see my ads in The Journal. I have had a lifelong fascination with *the page*, and no publication gives me a bigger page than The Journal. As an art director, I am in the business of *staging* ideas for our clients. The Journal does a magnificent job of *staging* advertising.

The Wall Street Journal.
It works.

Advertising Age
Features

CREATIVE MAN HELMUT KRONE TALKS ABOUT THE MAKING OF AN AD

By Sandra Karl
Doyle Dane Bernbach, New York

Q. Is it true that you are a perfectionist?

A. I resent the charge. A perfectionist is someone who finishes the backside of a drawer, which I consider completely unnecessary. I spend a lot of time on the front, but I am definitely not interested in the backside of the drawer.

I feel that there's this imaginary line, and you have to get over that line. As soon as I feel I'm over that line, I quit. I don't go any further. I'll leave a thing without all the ends pulled in as soon as it's over that line.

Q. You mean you have a certain standard, and when you reach it, you stop?

A. Yes, just like everybody else. Now, maybe that line is in a different place for me. It all depends on where you place that line. For example, in engravings or television production, I feel that I'm not a stickler no matter what anyone says. If the page has the effect I was after, I'm not interested in petty little corrections.

Q. How did you come to work on Volkswagen when DDB first got the account?

A. I got on Volkswagen because I was the only one who'd ever heard of the car. I had one of the first Volkswagens in the U. S., probably one of the first 100, long before I ever worked here.

And just to show you how wrong a person can be—and how fallible I am—I was dead set against the Volkswagen campaign as we did it. I felt that the thing to do with this ugly little car was to make it as American as possible, as fast as possible. Like, let's get Dinah Shore also. What's that thing she used to sing? "See the U.S.A. in your Chevrolet." I wanted "See the U.S.A. in your Volkswagen." With models around the car and tv extravaganzas.

Q. But it was on Volkswagen that you changed the look of ads. You changed the way the copy looked.

A. Well, first let me say that on Volkswagen I felt so strongly that we were doing the wrong thing—even though I contributed my third to it, certainly—that I finished up three ads, went on vacation to St. Thomas, depressed, came back two weeks later and I was a star.

Q. You say you contributed your third. Not your half?

A. My third, Bill Bernbach's third and Julian Koenig's third.

Q. What was Bill Bernbach's third?

A. Mostly in keeping me from doing the other. Also, the whole concept of speaking simply, clearly and with charm belongs to him. There was nothing new about the Volkswagen idea, the only thing was that we applied it to a car.

Probably eight years before that, Bernbach did an ad for Fairmont strawberries, where he showed a whole strawberry in the middle of a big page—just one life-size strawberry. And the headline was: "It seemed a pity to cut it up." What they were selling were the only whole frozen strawberries on the market, the point being that a strawberry has to be perfect in order to keep it whole.

Volkswagen is not any different from that ad that he did a long time before. The only thing different about it was its application to cars—and that's different enough. I took traditional layout A, which had always existed—two-thirds picture, one-third copy, three blocks with a headline in between. But I changed the picture. The picture was naked looking, not full and lush. The other small change was the copy, which was sans serif rather than serif.

Q. And nobody had ever done that before?

A. Not with that layout, no. It was an editorial look, but with sans serif type.

Q. The look of the copy was very different. The use of "widows" which we spoke of once before.

A. I actually cut those "widows" into the first Volkswagen comps with a razor blade and asked Julian Koenig to write that way. I deliberately kept the blocks from being solid, and when I felt that a sentence could be cut in half, I suggested it just to make another paragraph.

I wanted the copy to look Gertrude Steiny. The layout in that case actually influenced a new copy style, which Bernbach later referred to as "subject, verb, object."

Q. You mean the layout came before the copy style? The copy style came about because of the way it would look on a page?

A. Definitely.

Before then, it was usually the art

In his 14 years at Doyle Dane Bernbach, Helmut Krone has, until now, refused interview requests. That hasn't kept him from winning nine New York Art Directors Club medals, dozens of other awards and the title of vp-director of special projects at the agency. After numerous tries by Sandra Karl of the DDB pr office, he agreed to an interview for the agency's house publication. Attired in his newest outfit—cowboy pants, suede shirt and neckerchief—he sat back and talked to Miss Karl about his work, how and why he does it. Here is the interview taken from the October "DDB News."

director's job to get writers to fill out "widows," so that they could have a neat, No. 2-looking gray wash on the page.

As far as layout is concerned—which I consider a lost art—I feel that almost no one is looking around for a brand new page, a new way of putting down the same old elements, a new way of breaking up that 7x10" area.

Q. You're saying that they should be?

A. Yes, but everybody wants to belong to the current club. There's safety in that, I suppose. And they want to show they're smart enough to recognize what's good, what's "in." They think being current, being fashionable is being new. And it's really the opposite of new.

If you get a medal in the Art Directors Club, the chances are that what you did was not an innovation. I'd say that about almost every medal that I've gotten. They were for innovations that were already a year or two old, and, therefore, easy to digest.

If people say to you, "That's up to your usual great standard," then you know you haven't done it.

■ "New" is when you've never seen before what you've just put on a piece of paper. You haven't seen it before and nobody else in the world has ever seen that thing that you've just put down on a piece of paper. And when a thing is new, all you know about it is that it is brand new. It's not related to anything that you've seen before in your life. And it's very hard to judge the value of it. You distrust it, and everybody distrusts it. And very often, it's somebody else who has to tell you that that thing has merit, because you have no frame of reference, and you can't relate it to anything that you or anybody else has ever done before.

Alexey Brodovitch at the New School was the one who put me on to "new." Students would bring in something to class that they thought was spectacular, but he'd toss it aside and say: "I've seen this once before somewhere." And he wouldn't even discuss it.

Q. What was his reaction when you did something he'd never seen before?

A. I never did anything he'd never seen before while I was in his class. I wasn't ready.

And now that I've done all that talking about "new," let me contradict myself and take a swing at the current trend toward "doing your own thing."

I asked one of our writers recently what was more important: Doing your own thing or making the ad as good as it can be. The answer was: "Doing my own

CREATIVE MAN HELMUT KRONE TALKS

Advertising Age, October 14, 1968

thing." I disagree violently with that. I'd like to propose a new idea for our age: Until you've got a better answer, you copy. I copied Bob Gage for five years. I even copied the leading between his lines of type. And Bob originally copied Paul Rand, and Rand first copied a German typographer named Tschichold. The thing to do when you get a requisition is to find an honest answer. Solve the problem. Then, if through the years a personal style begins to emerge, you must be the last to know. You have to be innocent of it.

Q. I'd wanted to ask you about the Avis layout. That was new too, wasn't it?

A. Yes. I remember going home on the train one night with Bob (Gage). Everybody at that time was doing Volkswagen layouts. In fact, the headlines were getting smaller and smaller, and the fashion at the time was to write three meaningful words, so strong in themselves that you could set them in very small type.

We had a discussion about this on the train, and he said: "How much smaller can headlines get before they become invisible?" And I thought about it. I was working on Avis currently and looking for a page style. Now that's very important to me, a page style. I feel that you should be able to tell who's running that ad at a distance of 20 feet.

Q. Just by the page style?

A. Just by the page style. You can tell a Volkswagen ad from a distance of 30 feet,

Think small.

Big illustration area, small type in Volkswagen ad was reversed for Avis.

Avis is only No.2 in rent a cars. So why go with us?

We try harder.
(When you're not the biggest, you have to.)
We just can't afford dirty ash-trays. Or half-empty gas tanks. Or worn wipers. Or unwashed cars. Or low tires. Or anything less than seat-adjusters that adjust. Heaters that heat. Defrosters that defrost.
Obviously, the thing we try hardest for is just to be nice. To start you out right with a new car, like a lively, super-torque Ford, and a pleasant smile. To know, say, where you get a good pastrami sandwich in Duluth. Why?
Because we can't afford to take you for granted. Go with us next time.
The line at our counter is shorter.

and an Avis ad from a distance of 40 feet.

Anyway, to get back to this headline thing. I started thinking about what he'd said, how absurd it was getting with these headlines getting smaller and smaller. So what I did was I took the Volkswagen style and turned it inside out: The headline became big, and not in the middle, I put it on top. The picture became small, and the copy became large. It was very carefully, methodically done, very coolly arrived at. It was *not* inspired. It was a mathematical solution. I made everything that was big, small, and everything that was small, big.

Q. Anything else?

A. Why don't you come clean and ask me why I'm so slow.

Q. Okay. Why are you so slow?

A. I have no defense, only a reason. Though a New Yorker, I had a German upbringing. And I'm the recipient of the best of such an upbringing as well as the

victim of the worst part of it.

A German son is always wrong until he's proved himself to be right. He is a know-nothing and has everything to prove. It gives you a certain insecurity which is the opposite of "chutzpah." You tend to rework things and believe they're never good enough, because, after all, you're a "know-nothing."

David Ogilvy once said: "An agency ought to be on time, just like a good tailor." But in defense, I'd like to say that I've got the best tailor outside of Rome—and he's always late!

Q. Do you enjoy it, the work?

A. I don't know. I go back and forth. Advertising is stupid. Advertising is great. Advertising is totally unnecessary. Advertising is the most vital art form of our day. It depends on what week it is, I think they're both true.

I didn't plan out my existence. "I'm going to do this for two years, this for three years, and then I'll be a vice-president, and so on." I never heard of stock options.

All I did was keep my nose on the board. I worked my ass off. I worked just like my father and mother worked. My father was an orthopedic shoemaker and my mother was a seamstress, and I believe that they were probably the best shoemaker and seamstress in America. I believe that with all my might. And I guess that's how it all happened. They used to work their heads off. And people said they were the best. #

These exercises are designed to help you learn to think more visually.

WORK BACKWARDS!

Learn to become more of a visually-driven writer.

Rough out visuals first.

Write words to pictures.

Try to think about products in a totally non-verbal way and see what essential communication imagery you discover. Then, write the words.

Visual Exercises:

1. THE ART CENTER EXERCISE.

Do an ad for **LAVA**™ Soap that communicates with *only a visual!*

No headline. No copy.

2. THE PRESS-TYPE EXERCISE.

Get a sheet of Press-Type™ or Letraset™ or one of the other commercial press-on types.

They're available at most art supply stores.

Pick a type face that appeals to you and press out a few words that feel appropriate in that face.

3. VERBALIZING VISUALS.

Pick three ads you like.

Verbalize why you like them *Visually.*

4. PLAN A MEETING.

Do a rough chart of the meeting room and the wall space. Outline materials needed.

More Words.

This section of the book will deal with:
1. Basics of Strategic Thinking and Salesmanship.
2. Principles of effective copywriting style.
3. Copywriting for different media.

How to Copywrite.

Copywriting is a job.
A skilled craft.
Verbal carpentry.
Words on paper.
Scripts to time.
And one more thing.
Salesmanship. Our first lesson is:

SALESMANSHIP = STRATEGY + STRUCTURE + STYLE.

While we'll cover a wide range of topics, it's really all about persuasion and salesmanship.

There are things that may change with time and circumstance.

And some things will stay the same.

It will always be a combination of artistry and common sense, hard work and easy answers, smart thinking and dumb luck.

Things may get complicated, but there are still simple fundamentals everyone can learn.

And while there will be many exceptions to general rules, you have to know them before you can break them.

This is the general process –
You'll develop a STRATEGY.

From that Strategy, you'll generate a SELLING IDEA – an idea that helps sell.

Then, you'll give it STRUCTURE – to make your Selling Idea easy to understand.

And, you'll do it with STYLE.

STRATEGY + STRUCTURE + STYLE.
That's SALESMANSHIP.
And that's your job.

"Advertising is salesmanship in print."

John Kennedy
Copywriter, Lord & Thomas

The quote is dated.
The reality remains.
Salesmanship.
The ad you write has to *sell*.
It must persuade.
Persuasion is more than
Communication.
It is active.
It does not merely inform.
It influences.
It motivates.
It *moves*.

"They don't call it work for nothin'."

Jerry Bieberle, Old Friend

110

Well, how do you sell?

Developing a Strategy begins with clearly defining your Objective – a statement of what you want to accomplish. Before you can have a Strategy, you must have an Objective.

Discovering the Objective is your first step.

The Objective is a statement of the mission to be accomplished and, sometimes, the Problem to be solved (i.e. *"The Problem the Advertising Must Solve"*).

Oh, and by the way...

There are many types of strategies.

MARKETING STRATEGIES.

Many companies have a large, complex document called a **Marketing Strategy.**

This covers a wide range of things related to selling products, such as pricing, distribution and other factors of the marketplace.

There are also **Promotional Strategies,** which focus on promotional tasks, and **Public Relations Strategies** which focus on communications goals for publicity and unpaid media. There are even **Packaging Strategies.**

In this book, we will focus on developing and executing an *Advertising* Strategy.

ADVERTISING STRATEGIES.

Advertising works with a shorter document. It may be called an **Advertising Strategy,** a **Communication Strategy** or **Creative Platform** – or something else.

It is part of the larger Marketing Strategy.

An Advertising Strategy generally indicates what the advertising should communicate and to whom it will be addressed.

From now on, when we say "strategy," that's what we mean.

The ad you write is an execution of your Strategy – it is a **Tactic.**

M.O.S.T. = MISSION, OBJECTIVE, STRATEGY, TACTICS
Some definitions and examples:
Mission – Principles by which a company is run.

An example, Apple Computer's stated mission: *"Our goal is to put Macintosh computers in the hands of as many people as possible."*

A Mission helps a company maintain focus in a complicated business environment.
Objective – A specific task to be accomplished.

An Objective Statement for a Marketing Strategy might be: *To double unit sales of low-end computers next quarter.*

An Objective Statement for an Advertising Strategy might be: *To convince decision-makers (parents and small business owners) that our entry-level computers offer the added-value of the Macintosh operating system.*

Defining Objectives is key to developing good Strategies.
Strategy – How you will meet an Objective. There are often alternate strategies to choose from – even when objectives are clear.
Example: *Our strategy will be to:*
　　a.) *increase advertising,*
　　b.) *offer price-off incentives,*
　　c.) *provide easier financing,*
　　d.) *lower the retail price,*
　　e.) *some or all of the above.*
The chosen (or "recommended") strategy is the best hypothesis as to how to meet the objective.
"On-Strategy." When something is "on-strategy" it conforms to the strategy (hypothesis).
"Off-Strategy." When it is "off-strategy" it fails to conform to the recommended strategy. It may or may not meet the objective and may represent an alternate hypothesis.
Tactics – Specific planned actions that execute the Strategy.

Ads, sales materials – the whole range of marketing communications tools are tactics. So is a sales call.
Example: *Advertising featuring Mac Classics starting at $999.*

While the final result is a straightforward sequence, the path to achieving it can be more like putting together a puzzle – or solving a mystery.

Clues – bits of information – help you along the way. Perhaps an insight into your Consumer, an interesting Product fact, or even something you pick up from the competition's advertising.

You often find yourself testing hypotheses – like a scientist (or a detective).

Even when you miss, you learn.
So you aim better next time.

Determining an Objective, developing a Strategy, executing a Tactic.

This is the path you will travel.

From that Strategy, and all the thinking that went into it, you will develop a **Selling Idea**.

The step after that is Structuring the Sale - structuring the framework that presents your Selling Idea. Or, in simpler terms, making it easy to understand.

Remember, advertising is communication written with a consciousness of the *receiver*.

Writers may write for themselves.

Copywriters write with others in mind.

It's *receiver-driven* communication.

The presentation of your idea must have a Structure that is easy for the person receiving the message to follow and understand:

A BEGINNING.

Getting Attention.
Inviting involvement.
Establishing context.

A MIDDLE.

Developing your Sale.
Adding Support or Credibility.
Reinforcing Memorability.

AN END.

Building Awareness.
Shifting Attitudes.
Motivating Action.
Achieving the Objective.

Your last step isn't a step at all.
It may be a hop, a karate kick or a pirouette.
It's Style.
And, once more, this is our message.

> Discover The Objective.
> Develop a Strategy.
> Generate a Selling Idea.
> Structure the Sale.
> With Style.

SALESMANSHIP = STRATEGY + STRUCTURE + STYLE

Discovering The Objective.

Where *are* you going?

This question must be answered first.

This is **The Objective** – the mission to be accomplished.

Often, your first mission is to find it.

Here are some ways to help you get started.

1. THINK ABOUT THE CUSTOMER.

Remember, the fact you wish to sell a person something is both assumed and irrelevant.

What is that person's current state of mind?

Perhaps it is total ignorance.

If that's the case, building *Awareness* may be your Objective.

In some cases, it may be the only Objective you need.

Building Awareness is an implicit and important part of almost every Ad Objective.

The better you know the person you're talking to, the better you'll understand what you must accomplish. Remember Hopkins,

"The advertising man studies the consumer. He tries to place himself in the position of the buyer."

To envision the target, you must envision the Target Consumer.

Think about a *person*.

Not a number!

Demographic information can help, but you must use it as a tool to imagine *the real live person*.

This copywriter **understood the consumer.** *A very thoughtful ad, with empathy and insight into the difficulty of maintaining and losing weight.* *A* **Product Benefit** *that leads to a* **Consumer Benefit.**

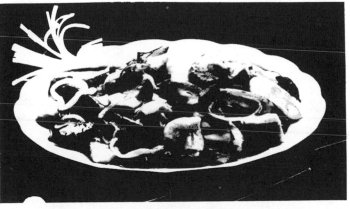

ANNOUNCING THE TASTE YOU USED TO CHEAT FOR.

Bald, rubbery, hard-boiled eggs. Endless vistas of cottage cheese. The relentless boredom of carrots and celery.

Conventional diet food is enough to drive you *off* a diet.

Happily, Weight Watchers 19 *New* Frozen Meals are good enough to drive

you on.

Like this Chicken Oriental in a snappy soy-spiked ginger sauce with crunchy Chinese vegetables.

Lean, juicy beefsteak smothered in a thick, brown gravy.

Lasagna dripping with spicy tomato sauce.

Yes, even *Sausage Pizza.* Now you can have them. Even if you're on a diet.

So if you're really serious about dropping those extra pounds, our exciting new taste can help.

After all, how can you go off your diet, if the taste you want is on it?

WEIGHT WATCHERS 19 NEW FROZEN MEALS. TRY IT. YOU'LL DIET.

113

An Ancient Prejudice Has Been Removed

"TOASTING DID IT"—
Gone is that ancient prejudice against cigarettes—Progress has been made. We removed the prejudice against cigarettes when we removed harmful corrosive ACRIDS (pungent irritants) from the tobaccos. Thus "TOASTING" has destroyed that ancient prejudice against cigarette smoking by men and by women.

"It's toasted"
No Throat Irritation-No Cough.

CIGARETTES

Understanding the Consumer
helped Claude Hopkins and others build a new market for cigarettes.

 Note the use of the pre-emptive "It's Toasted" theme line.

Think about that person in real life…and how your product fits into their life.

 Psychographic information can help. Much of the "Lifestyle" work, such as **VALS (Values and Life Styles)**, can provide you with valuable insights and help you get to know your customers.

 VALS offers a way of looking at people and getting to know them.

 Focus Groups can help, too.

 Listen to real people talk about their real lives and how the products you want to sell them fit into their lives.

 Much of this is **Usage** information– information that helps you understand how the product fits into people's lives.

 Sometimes it can be as simple as talking to people who've purchased the product.

 In general, customers can be a valuable source of good ideas.

2. THINK ABOUT THE PRODUCT.

Describe the product and what it does.
For example, let's say you're working on…

 • Toothpaste plus mouthwash.

 • A convenient diet product.

 • Spicy fried chicken.

We've just listed **Product Features** (sometimes called **Attributes**).

 They're, quite simply, features of the product.

 Now, how do these features become benefits for the person you'll be talking to?

 • A cleaner breath?

 • An easy way to lose weight?

 • A unique exciting flavor?

 These are **Product Benefits** – benefits *of* the product to the consumer.

 If the Product Benefit is meaningful, you'll probably want to communicate that Product Benefit to your Target.

114

It's dry!
But so shiny it looks wet.

Mr. Clean's lemon fresh formula never leaves dull streaks when it dries, even when you don't rinse. Mr. Clean cleans your whole house right down to the shine.

Mr. Clean. The man behind the shine.

Advertise Your Advantage.

Historically, products that advertise their advantages have done well…when the advantage was worth advertising.

Communicating the Product Benefit may be your Objective.

Or, perhaps, the Product Benefits is only a step on the ladder leading to a higher benefit…a benefit *within* the consumer –

• A fresher breath (and greater personal attractiveness),

• A smaller dress size (and greater personal attractiveness),

• A more enjoyable meal.

This is a **Consumer Benefit**.

This is the benefit that the consumer receives. Communicating the Consumer Benefit may be your Objective. It often is.

Though, as you may notice, a number of different products can deliver fairly similar Consumer Benefits – some of those benefits we call **Values**.

GIVE A TOY
A CHILD
FOR
CHRISTMAS.

KAY BEE
STOREWIDE CHRISTMAS SALE

LADDERING.

ATTRIBUTES, FEATURES, BENEFITS & VALUES.

Much strategic discussion focuses on what factor to emphasize. Sequencing these factors is called "Laddering."

Here are generally agreed upon definitions listed "bottom to top:"

Attribute (Product Attribute) Characteristic of Product, usually inherent or natural – *Applesauce comes in wide-mouth glass jars.*

Product Feature Aspect of Product, usually based on some manufactured or designed aspect –*Applesauce spoons smoothly out of the jar.*

Product Benefit. A benefit to the consumer, usually based on a Product Feature or Attribute – *Applesauce is easy to serve.*

Consumer Benefit. (or Customer Benefit) A benefit usually based on how the Product Benefit delivers a positive result to the consumer – *I save time and my children get extra nutrition (which tastes good – so they'll eat it).*

Values. The human dimension reinforced by the Benefit – *I'm a good mother because I serve Applesauce.*

Laddering is the process of moving through this sequence.

The general method is to ask people *why* is that Feature (or Benefit) important. The answer generally moves you up the "ladder."

A continuing issue is where to focus.

Generally, the farther down the ladder you are, the more product- specific your message and the more you are differentiating your product.

The higher up you are the more you are dealing with what's important in the consumer's life – and the more generic your benefit. (All nutritious foods reinforce nurturing values!)

This is a major area of strategic choice. We offer only definitions.

Not answers.

Values are about internal needs and self-image.

Every product we use relates in some way to values that are important to us.

The part of us that nurtures.

The part of us that wants to succeed.

The part of us that wants to have a good time.

Determine the aspect of the consumer – the Value – that's most important for your product.

For our products, the Values might be:

• A better self-image/greater personal attractiveness (for the mouthwash/toothpaste).

• A better self-image/greater personal attractiveness (for the diet product – if it works).

• Reinforcing self-image as a "taste leader" (for the spicy fried chicken). Pleasure-seeking.

Values are important – but remember, they're not exclusively about your product. For example, most nutritious food products can reinforce a woman's nurturing maternal values.

Consider…

How does the benefit *within* the product manifest itself *within* the consumer? And what aspect of the sequence is "ownable?"

Leo Burnett's **"inherent drama"** lives here.

Place yourself *between* product and people.

See how they interact. There is *movement* there and there is depth – active, dynamic and a lot deeper than it might look at first.

For example, as I learned long ago, the practice of washing clothes in all temperatures is also about the families that live in those clothes.

From Product Features to Product Benefits to Consumer Benefits to Values. Find out what is most meaningful.

You may discover your Objective is communicating that unique dimension.

Or… you keep looking.

MILK.
IT DOES A STUDENT BODY GOOD.

3. THINK ABOUT THE COMPETITION.

The competition is important, too.

Most Marketing Plans and Strategies consider "Source of Business." If you win, who loses?

(Sometimes new usage will be the source of overall business. For example, soft drink consumption has grown – people drink less water.)

Even if you don't compete directly in your advertising, you should consider what other similar products are already *inside* the consumer's mind.

Think of what associated benefits, images and habit patterns are already out there.

Think about what's going on in the marketplace. Most of all, think about what goes on *inside* the consumer's mind when he or she thinks about the product category.

Where do you want your product to be?

Answering that question and then achieving it is **Positioning.**

Establishing a distinct position for your brand versus the competition may be The Objective.

If it is…

1.) Don't underestimate the expense and effort it might take to achieve that position.

2.) Realize establishing that position may not generate increased sales. (i.e. "diet beer.")

HAVEN'T YOU WAITED LONG ENOUGH FOR A NEW IDEA IN BIRTH CONTROL?

Today.
The Sponge vs. "The Pill."
Here's some hard-hitting, provocative positioning in an area that used to be Taboo for advertisers – Birth control. Whatever your views, these ads will get your attention.

"Hitting The Sweet Spot,"
by Lisa Fortini-Campbell –
the first U.S. book on Account Planning.
[Available from The Copy Workshop.]

To be successful, Trout and Ries maintain
"Your position must be:
 1. A unique position.
 2. With broad appeal."
And Rosser Reeves in his **USP**…
"The proposition must be one that the competition either cannot or does not offer.
It must be unique – either a uniqueness of the brand or a claim not otherwise made in that particular field of advertising."
Person… Product… and Competition.

"THE SWEET SPOT" & "THE STRATEGIC TRIAD"

Consumer Insight is one factor that can help you unify these elements.

One Consumer Insight concept is called *"The Sweet Spot."* You want to hit it.

But first you have to find it.

Finding it is the result of insights into the consumer, the consumer's feelings and attitudes about the product category and feelings and attitudes toward your specific brand.

Consumer Insight + Brand Insight = Sweet Spot

These same three factors – customer, product and competition – are the general basis of many types of business strategy development.

Together, they are often referred to as "The Strategic Triangle" or **"The Strategic Triad."**

Your Objective is most likely involved with some combination of these same three factors: customer, product and competition.

But, in advertising strategy, there is a fourth dimension which you must consider.

Now you must think about…

THE PROBLEM!

4. THINK ABOUT THE PROBLEM.

Ask yourself a very simple question…

"What's The Problem?"

The *real* problem.

Is it the product (Heaven forbid!), the image, lack of awareness, the sales force, the sales volume, the ad budget, or unrealistic expectations?

Sometimes it's the ads and, almost always, the ads are the easiest thing to change.

But there are often a few other factors squirming around in the stew.

Peel the onion.

Put yourself in your client's shoes, your customer's mind, and the account exec's briefcase.

Turn the situation upside down and inside out. And vice versa.

Let it incubate.

You might even ask a few more questions.

Why? Because there is *danger* here!

Don't Solve The Wrong Problem!

It's not uncommon to have large numbers of bright, well-informed people focused on the wrong problem.

It's not uncommon to enter situations where people passed the real problem and its solution a long time ago.

Trout & Ries again,

"The best positioning ideas are so simple that most people overlook them."

And Leo Burnett said,

"Great copy and great ideas are deceptively simple."

Simple, but not easy.

In their Creative Work Plan, Y&R focuses on "The Problem the Advertising Must Solve."

In virtually every agency planning system, some part of the document addresses this issue in one way or another.

What's the Problem?

Tough Problems/Tough Ads.
Here, the message is dramatized through contrast.
Each ad qualifies its target charmingly and disarmingly.
Each appeals to the instincts of a certain type of person.

119

Problem/Usage/Consumer Benefit
"Morning Breath" was an engaging way for SCOPE to tell a simple story that contained a combination of strategic elements.

Some SCOPE commercials also position the brand against the competition (Listerine) by mentioning "Medicine Breath."

Visualize The Problem.

What Problem can the *advertising* solve?

Think about it. Even though there are a lot of problems out there, what is the problem that advertising should address?

The right answer to this question can give your whole advertising program a clear focus.

While The Problem may indeed be contained within The Strategic Triad, it often seems to have a life of its own.

And getting a handle on that slippery little devil is often key to determining your Objective.

Sometimes, you'll find the problem has already been identified. Only people don't realize it.

Do a little historical research: old memos, old ads, people who used to work on the business.

There are discarded ideas and valuable insights scattered about just about everywhere.

Some of them are good ideas orphaned by pure circumstance.

And some are *terrific!*

If you can make one of them get up and walk, your reputation may be enhanced by the miraculous nature of your deed and the gratitude of those whose ideas you have saved.

But… *be sure to acknowledge the original authors of the idea!*

This can be a tricky area.

Some will be generous and appreciative. Others will not.

By making a point of giving credit where credit is due, you will at least protect yourself from being branded as a thief.

Meanwhile, remember that your obligation is to see to it that the product gets *the best ideas available.*

No matter whose.

Wherever you find it, whoever thought of it, whatever it is, you must know the answer to The Question – **"What's The Problem?"**

Jay Chiat notes,

"The creative process is really a very structured thing that has to do with problem-solving.

George Lois says,

"You should be able to distill a marketing problem – which precedes the advertising solution – into one simple sentence."

Once you have an answer, you may proceed.

You now understand The Problem.

Solving The Problem is often The Objective of your advertising.

It usually combines key aspects of the Product, the Customer and Competition.

A cautionary note – your conclusions may not lend themselves to widespread publicity.

For this reason, it is not uncommon to have both stated and unstated Objectives.

For example, the *stated* Objective might be,

"To give the sales force a rallying cry."

The *unstated* Objective might be,

"Now that we've got the product fixed, let's get the sales force to try and get it back into the stores again."

Or, worse yet, you may have to re-convince turned-off customers who have already been burned once, while dealing with a client who refuses to acknowledge the problem.

Now *that's* a Problem.

If you're still not sure of your Objective... go back to where you started...

THINK ABOUT THE CUSTOMER.
THINK ABOUT THE PRODUCT.
THINK ABOUT THE COMPETITION.
THINK ABOUT THE PROBLEM.
and... COMBINE THEM!

THE BUD LIGHT PROBLEM.

Their problem was at the bar, when the customer said, "Gimme a light," which could mean Miller "Lite," the leading light beer, or any light beer.

How could they communicate in a fresh, memorable and persuasive way that people should order a Bud Light?

That was the problem.

The answer was the "Bar Call" campaign, originally planned as a few ten second commercials.

This simple solution to the problem has become a successful campaign.

Advertising that effectively solved The Problem.

Q. WHAT'S BAND-AIDS' STICKY PROBLEM?

Let's say you're at Y&R, working on Band-Aid™ brand bandages.

What's the problem your advertising should solve?

You already have dominant share and have product in the medicine cabinets of most of America.

Your major usage is by mothers of active young children (2-10, the "Owie Age."), who use them to deal with the common cuts and scrapes of childhood.

Awareness is high.

Image is positive.

People, for the most part, already have the product in the house.

What, then, is "The Problem the Advertising Must Solve?"

Look for the answer at the end of this chapter...

5. COMBINE THEM.

That's right, think of everything.

All at once.

Sometimes the answer is simple and obvious, and sometimes it's subtle.

Look for patterns of reinforcement.

"Pattern recognition."

Basically, it's the ability to see a pattern based on incomplete information.

It's the way some people recognize new and emerging trends *before* the hard data is in.

Sometimes it's called "intuition," knowing something based on a few clues.

Advertising thinking is often like that.

Pattern recognition can be key to identifying new marketing and advertising opportunities.

It may be a trend in art or fashion, or a changing lifestyle.

It may be rooted in old-fashioned values or it may be a new-fashioned product.

It may be one person in a Focus Group, one customer, or a salesperson out in the field.

The challenge is to recognize it.

Feel the forces at work.

Think of it as a playing field…

Positioning opportunities that have been left open by the competition.

Problems unsolved.

Benefits undramatized.

Needs unmet.

Targets to be hit.

You will find your Objective at a conjunction of these forces.

As Lite discovered, not so long ago.

The Objective

when discovered, will be *synergistic*.

The Objective is not a static statement describing a distant future, it's a *dynamic system* that describes an achievable goal.

Meeting The Objective will create or reinforce forces that will move your business forward.

Because once you know where you're going, you can start to figure out how to get there.

For example:

• Solving The "Diet Beer" Problem.

• Solving the "Gimme a light" Problem.

• A memorable way to get people to use SCOPE in the morning.

• Getting women to use more Band-Aids.

• And more…

When you discover the Objective, you not only describe target, you unleash a force that helps aim the arrow and powers it to your goal.

It's all synergistic – it all works together.

Whatever your Objective, you must have one before you can take the next step.

STRATEGY.

How you get there.

The path you must travel…

A. HOW TO GET MOTHERS TO USE MORE BAND-AIDS.

Y&R discovered an important opportunity – after the Band-Aid was initially applied, a scab formed and the old Band-Aid (which was now a bit dirty) was taken off and the scab protected the cut.

However, *re-applying a Band-Aid to protect the scab* promoted better healing. The cut was not re-opened and the scab was not knocked off (or picked off by the child). On average, cuts healed faster when a Band-Aid was used for this purpose.

The Problem became – Mothers do not realize that they can promote better healing by re-applying a Band-Aid to protect the scab.

Advertising which focused on this point promoted increased usage which resulted in increased sales.

DISCOVERING OBJECTIVES.
Let's review some of the things you can do to Discover your Objective:

1. Think about the Customer.
   A. Consumer Information. Customer Profiles, Demographics, Usage Studies, Sales Data.
   B. VALS. Studies of consumer Values and LifeStyle.
   C. Focus Groups.
   D. Talk to consumers. You'll learn a lot from one-on-one interviews.

2. Think about the Product.
   A. Use the product.
   B. List Product Features and Product Benefits.
   C. List Consumer Benefits and Values.
   D. Do some "Laddering."

3. Think about the Competition.
   A. Do a "Store Check." Look at the competition in the marketplace. Compare package, price, in-store promotions and performance.
   B. Clip competitive print ads. Make a clip file. If possible, tape a few competitive TV commercials.
   C. Look for articles on the product category. Read trade magazines. Try the library or clipping services.
   D. Talk to customers. Find out why they like your competition. Find out the competition's weaknesses.

4. Think about The Problem.
   Some common advertising and marketing problems –
   A. Low Awareness. Consumers unaware of product.
   B. Old product didn't perform. (If current product doesn't perform, try removing yourself from Problem.)
   C. Pricing Problem. (Hard to solve with advertising alone.)
   D. Distribution Problem. Consider trade as Target.
   E. "Political" Problem. Obvious answer not recognized, irrational bias, office politics, etc.
   F. Budget Problem. Not enough money to do job, unrealistic expectations, too many things to do, etc.
   G. Advertising Problem. Previous advertising did not "work." (Find out why before you write new ads.)

Strategy.

How *do* you get there?

That's strategy.

Strategy is a subject taught at great length and expense in business schools across the nation.

Seminars abound. Sober businessmen endorse its healthful benefits.

But sometimes, strategy is like the weather – where everyone talks about it, but less is done than most will admit.

And sometimes it's not like the weather at all – because wherever you go, it seems to be pretty much the same.

Brand names for less.

Better than the rest.

Best value. Quality and service.

Today, many businesses seem to have pretty much the same strategy.

Once upon a time, some companies had MBA's and Marketing Departments and some companies didn't.

Strategies offered important differentiation.

Today, all companies have MBA's and Marketing Departments – in many cases, strategy is becoming a commodity.

But, to be a successful copywriter, you have to learn about strategies.

What makes them different?

What makes them the same?

And, most of all, what makes them work?

Moreover, you have to know strategies because every new idea, particularly the brightest and most startling, is in immediate danger of being cursed with that most loathsome of criticisms..."*It's off-strategy!*"

Maybe it is, and maybe it isn't.

But the minute your work is criticized with this comment, your credibility sinks to that of a new puppy…charming, perhaps, but not quite house-broken.

That's why you have to learn strategy.

In strategic development, market facts of varying accuracy and relevance are linked with hypotheses of varying validity in a long complex sequence.

And in the process, many businessmen forget that a strategy is an hypothesis.

It's a theory, a blue print, a road map.

It's a "best guess."

It's an art, not a science.

Here's how Kenichi Ohmae, author of "The Mind of the Strategist," described the process.

"In business as on the battlefield,
the object of strategy is to bring about the
conditions most favorable to one's own side.
In strategic thinking, one first seeks a clear
understanding of the particular character
of each element of a situation, and then makes the
fullest possible use of human brainpower
to restructure the elements
in the most advantageous way.
Phenomena and events in the real world
do not always fit a linear model.
Hence, the most reliable means of dissecting a
situation into its constituent parts and then reas-
sembling them in the desired pattern
is not a step-by-step methodology
such as systems analysis.
Rather, it is that <u>ultimate nonlinear</u>
<u>thinking tool,</u> the human brain.
No matter how difficult or unprecedented
the problem, a breakthrough to
the best possible solution
can come only from a combination of rational
analysis based on the real nature of things,
and imaginative reintegration
of all the different items into a new pattern,
using <u>non-linear brain power.</u>"

TACTICS, STRATEGIES & OBJECTIVES:

Strategists ask,"What *should* I do?"
Tacticians ask,"What *can* I do?"

The strategist is concerned with consistency and pay out over the long haul.

The tactician is concerned with effectiveness and short-term results.

Sometimes the tactics available to you can determine what strategies and objectives are possible.

And, sometimes, tactics can help you discover the best strategy. Hal Riney says, *"I don't know what the Strategy should be 'til I do the creative."*

"Marketing Warfare" and **"Bottom-Up Marketing"** by Trout and Reis are good sources for examining this "bottom-up" way of thinking.

Below is a graphic description of the strategic thinking process.

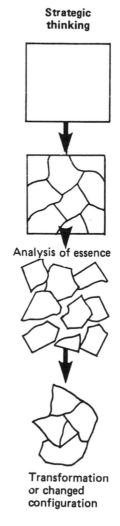

Strategic thinking

Analysis of essence

Transformation or changed configuration

From "The Mind of The Strategist" by Kenichi Ohmae. (A great book!)

The process of strategic development can be complex. Yet, its essence is simple.

Simply put, an Advertising Strategy answers the question,

"How do you sell the thing?"

To be a successful copywriter, you must be a successful salesperson.

And, to survive in the complex world of an advertising agency, you *must* become involved in developing and understanding strategy.

Strategies are instinctive to good salesmen.

"That suit looks good on you."

"You're going to love this restaurant..."

"An offer you can't refuse."

P&G defines it this way...

"Advertising Strategy is that portion of a brand's marketing strategy which deals with advertising copy.

It is a statement which identifies the basis upon which we expect consumers to purchase our product in preference to competition."

A successful strategy must have the potential to persuade. Remember Bernbach.

"Advertising is fundamentally persuasion."

Your strategy must be able to generate movement in the marketplace.

It must *sell.*

On the following page is the basic thinking on Copy Strategy taught to trainees at P&G and to people who work for their many ad agencies.

Those who leave P&G for other jobs take these lessons with them, as do agency people who work on their business.

It has become a standard industry view on the subject of Copy Strategy.

Copy Strategy.

A copy strategy is a document which identifies the basis upon which we expect consumers to purchase our brand in preference to competition. It is the part of the marketing strategy which deals with advertising copy.

The fundamental content of a copy strategy emerges directly from the product, and the basic consumer need which the product was designed to fulfill.

A copy strategy should state clearly the basic benefit which the brand promises and which constitutes the principal basis for purchase.

While not mandatory, the strategy may also include:

- A statement of the product characteristic which makes this basic benefit possible.

- A statement of the character we want to build for the brand over time.

PURPOSE OF A COPY STRATEGY.

Copy strategy provides guidance and direction for a brand's advertising.

It should be a long-term document, not subject to judgment changes.

The copy strategy provides guidance and direction for the agency's creative people. It prescribes the limits within which an agency is to exercise its creative imagination, while being flexible enough to allow latitude for fresh and varied executions.

The copy strategy provides a common basis upon which to evaluate and discuss merits of an advertising submission in terms of intent and idea content.

A clear copy strategy can save a great deal of creative time and energy, because it identifies those basic decisions which we do not intend to review and rethink each time we look at a new piece of advertising.

CHARACTERISTICS OF A GOOD COPY STRATEGY.

Here are some things which characterize a good strategy statement:

- It's clear.

The basis upon which the consumer is being asked to buy our brand in preference to others should be quite clear to everyone involved.

- It's simple.

Key here is that the number of ideas in the strategy be kept to a minimum.

- It's devoid of executional considerations.

The copy strategy identifies *what* benefits we are to present to consumers, avoiding executional issues which deal with *how* these benefits are to be presented.

-It's inherently competitive.

The copy strategy should provide the answer to the question "Why should I buy this product rather than some other?"

SOME COMMENTS ON CONVENTIONAL WISDOM ABOUT STRATEGIES.
It is generally believed that…

1. Strong strategies beget strong tactics.

This is probably true.

But what if your strategy is *not* resulting in strong, motivating communication that is meaningful to the consumer?

• Perhaps the people creating the tactics aren't good enough.

• Or, perhaps, the strategy itself is not inherently persuasive.

If a strategy is strong, you *should* be looking at a wide variety of persuasive communications based on that strategy.

If you're not, it's not unreasonable to conclude that you should be taking another look at the Strategy as well as the people who are executing it.

2. A mediocre execution of a correct strategy is better than an excellent execution of an incorrect strategy.

Yes, but there are limits to what is generally accepted to be true.

For example, a commercial that makes fun of your target consumer probably won't work very well – no matter how on-strategy it might be.

Concurrently, some alternate strategies may be as persuasive (i.e., "as correct") as the recommended strategy.

In this case, all bets are off.

How to Write a Strategy.

The purpose of this section is to show you the basic format for writing an Advertising Strategy.

We can't tell you how to write the *right* strategy, but we can tell you how to write one that:

1.) makes sense

2.) is written in a format that will be clear to everyone who reads it.

Writing Strategies takes practice.

The more you do it, the better you'll get.

Just being aware of strategies that have worked (and failed) in the past can be a big help.

It also helps to work with good people – for developing a Strategy is usually *a team effort:* Research, Account Management, Clients, Creatives, even Consumers (in the form of Focus Groups or Account Planners) can be a part of that team.

As a mental process, it involves logical analysis, intuitive thinking, high-minded hypothesizing and tough-minded negotiation.

And even though it's often complicated and frustrating, strategic development can be tremendously exciting and satisfying – as you work with others to shape the future of a business.

Let's get started.

On-Srategy or Off-Target?
This clever visual tells its Target (people who eat Kentucky Fried Chicken) that they're "Bucketheads." How persuasive do you think it is?

There are numerous formats for writing an Advertising Strategy.

The one we'll start with is a simple format that has been used by many clients and agencies, including Procter & Gamble and Leo Burnett.

It has three parts:

1. AN OBJECTIVE STATEMENT.

The Objective is stated *within* this first section of the Strategy.

It combines the advertising's Objective Statement with a description of the Target Consumer and the name of the Brand.

2. A SUPPORT STATEMENT.

This indicates the Support you will use to help you attain the Objective.

It may be a "Reason Why" for the Benefit, or it may be something else. It is sometimes called the "Reason Why'" Section.

3. A STATEMENT OF TONE OR "BRAND CHARACTER."

This describes either the "Selling Attitude" or the long-term values of the brand.

This is how it looks.

Advertising Strategy is that portion of a brand's marketing strategy which deals with advertising copy. It is a statement which identifies the basis upon which we expect consumers to purchase our product in preference to competition.

P&G would say that a strategy "customarily contains the following information."

1. A Statement of the basic benefit which the product promises and which constitutes the principal basis for purchase of the brand.
2. A Statement of the product characteristic which makes it possible for the product to deliver this basic benefit.
3. A Statement of the character we strive to build for the product.

**Advertising will (Verb)
(Target Consumer) that (Product/Brand)
is/will/provides
(Statement of Objective/Benefit).**

Support will be (Support/Reason Why).

**Tone will be
("Selling Attitude" Adjectives).**
– or –
**Character of the (Brand)
will be seen to be
(Description of "Brand Character.")**

A Strategy is
• Simple
• Clear in Intent
• Contains no executional elements.

That's it. Simple. But not easy.

1. The Objective Statement.

Our Advertising Objective Statement starts simply…"**Advertising will…**"

Obviously, it will *do* something.

We need a verb.

"Convince," "persuade," and "communicate" are the verbs most commonly used.

"Remind" has also been used; *"Put a JELL-O out tonight"* was a Reminder Strategy.

We prefer "convince." It demonstrates confidence and reminds us that we are talking about *persuasion*, something that will occur inside the consumer's mind.

Next, the Strategy defines who we're talking to…**The Target Consumer.**

Hopefully, this will be more than a simple statement of demographics.

"Women 18 to 45" may be correct, but "mothers" or "traditional homemakers" may be closer to a real description of your target.

"Usage" is another good way to describe your Target Consumer.

It's often helpful to include some phrase describing the type of person you're targeting.

Remember, you're talking to a **person.**

A real person. Describe that person.

Your description may be qualitative (taste-oriented, price-conscious, etc.) or quantitative (18-45, A&B Counties, etc.). Or both.

It may be broad, it may be narrow, but try to give your target *dimension*.

Look for the important characteristics that your target consumers have in common.

STEP-BY-STEP: ARCHWAY "GOOD FOOD COOKIE" ADVERTISING STRATEGY:

Background: In the early 80's, Archway Cookies, a small national brand, was caught up in "The Cookie Wars."

Large marketers, such as Frito-Lay and P&G, entered the cookie category while Nabisco and Keebler defended their positions aggressively.

Archway moved to a strategy based on a "Niche" position.

While other cookie companies competed with chocolate chip and other chocolate varieties, Archway developed a strategy based on its strength in *oatmeal* cookies.

Even broadly based products have Target Consumers that can be described with insight.

Y&R places great emphasis on this – they call it **"Prospect Definition."**

Y&R believes it's critical to understand what's important to consumers.

They believe prospects should be defined in terms of: product usage, demographics and psychographics (life styles, attitudes, etc.)

This is rooted in the origins of copywriting.

"The advertising man studies the consumer. He tries to place himself in the position of the buyer."

Often, simple descriptions of the target are backed with additional in-depth information.

For example, your strategy may refer simply to *"men who drink premium beer."* This will be backed with additional information – such as attitudes toward sports, women and their job.

Broadly defined targets may have important subgroups described in support material.

Here are some typical examples:

> *Women who wash confidently in
>   all temperatures.*
> *Working mothers.*
> *Fashion-conscious women, 18-35.*
> *Young adults concerned about nutrition.*
> *Adults who wear eyeglasses.*

Now, add the name of your Product.

That should be easy.

So far, your strategy reads

**"Advertising will (convince)
(Target Consumer) that (Product)
is/will/provides…**

Now it gets tough.

**ARCHWAY COOKIES
OBJECTIVE STATEMENT.
Part One. Target Consumer**
*Advertising will convince
adults who eat cookies*

Though much cookie consumption is by children, Archway is basically an adult product.

This was supported by a wide range of market research as well as focus groups that addressed this specific issue.

A key question – were adults naturally "migrating" to the brand, or was Archway an "old" brand with an eroding customer base.

Research focused on this key issue.

The answer – adults naturally "discovered" Archway Cookies as they looked for something "more home-made" and less sweet.

Additional barriers were discovered to increased consumption by children.

Information about Archway purchasing habits, which skewed older and female, was used to assist in media selection.

A decision was made to advertise both to older consumers, who were the most loyal Archway customers, and to younger adults who were "migrating" into Archway's market.

**ARCHWAY COOKIES
OBJECTIVE STATEMENT
Part Two. Advertising Objective
*...that Archway Oatmeal Cookies
are uniquely nutritious
and delicious.***

Strategy is about choice.

Archway's major strategic decision was to focus mainly on their popular Oatmeal Cookies.

Rather than advertise the whole line, the decision was made to focus on Oatmeal-based varieties (over 30% of sales).

The Benefit was actually based on an Attribute – oatmeal.

Oatmeal naturally has good nutritional characteristics and, even more important, a wholesome, positive image with consumers.

The decision was made not to overstate "healthy" aspects, but rather to depend on the inherent "good nutrition" of oatmeal – this was a unique claim in the category.

Taste was added to the benefit claim to remind everyone that we were talking about cookies, but was a secondary part of the benefit statement since it was generic – cookies taste good.

What's the Objective?

What is the movement in the consumer's attitude which, if accomplished, will result in selling the product?

Sometimes, in the case of products with a clear dimension of difference, it's communicating product *superiority* in a persuasive fashion:

It might be a general superiority such as "It's the best" (often hard to prove) or "It's better" (easier to prove).

It may be superiority in a specific dimension of product performance.

It's usually some form of superiority, uniqueness or differentiation.

The movement may be psychological – such as "confidence" or "satisfaction."

Or it might be tangible – "feels soft" or "tastes terrific!"

Your product might be:

Easier – Convenience Strategy

Cheaper – Economy Strategy

Better quality for the price – Value Strategy.

Your product might be a Service, or a combination of Product and Service, which adds other dimensions.

Sometimes this movement is rational, sometimes it's emotional – every time it's important.

A key consideration is that it be *meaningful.*

Many well-supported strategies have failed because, when you got right down to it, the difference was not meaningful to the consumer.

Either it wasn't important enough, or it wasn't worth the extra price (products that do more often cost more).

Ask this question – What is it we want the person to believe or feel about our product or service?

And will that cause the person to purchase?

Here's an example for Cascade Dishwashing Detergent.

"Advertising will convince automatic dishwasher owners that Cascade provides virtually spotless end results.

This is a clear statement of what they want their advertising to communicate.

In this case, their Objective is communicating the Benefit of "virtually spotless end results." The movement in the consumer's mind is increasing conviction that Cascade delivers in this dimension of product performance.

The word "virtually" clearly communicates that neither the advertising nor Cascade can promise or deliver *completely* spotless results.

If you have a clear idea of the movement in the consumer's mind you wish to achieve, you understand The Objective.

In the case of products without dramatic differences or with multiple benefits, this may not be clear. (A common strategic problem.)

Once you've developed your Objective or Benefit Statement, your strategy reads

"Advertising will (convince)
(Target Consumer) that (Product)
is/will /provides
(Objective/Benefit).

You've just finished the first section of the Strategy.

A simple statement that sets out the mission to be accomplished by your advertising.

However, saying it isn't enough.
You need help.
"Support will be..."

DISCOVER THE BENEFIT.

In general, you will want to discover the Benefit a consumer derives from the product.

You may wish to ask yourself these questions.

Is it a **Product Benefit**?
i.e. "spotless end results."

Or is it a **Consumer Benefit**?
i.e. "I'm a good homemaker."

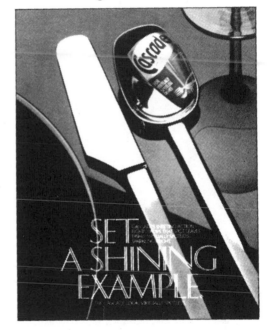

A statement of the basic benefit which the product promises consumers and which constitutes the principal basis for purchase of that brand.

2. The Support Statement.

The second section of the Strategy begins **"Support will be..."**

Generally, Support is the reason you can provide the benefit mentioned in the Objective Statement. For example...

> **"Virtually spotless end results will be attributed to the sheeting action produced by the Cascade formula."**

The Objective is communicating the Benefit which is the reason for buying Cascade.

Support is the *reason* you provide the benefit.

Sometimes this is clear and simple – Cascade's "sheeting action" is a *"reason why."*

And sometimes it isn't simple at all.

Many ambitious strategies have failed because of an unrealistic attitude toward this critical issue, promising more than they can deliver or pricing themselves higher than people are willing to pay.

Others failed because the Strategy sounded great in the meeting but could not be developed into distinctive and motivating advertising.

Again, **"What's for sale?"** **"Why buy?"**

You should be able to provide a simple answer.

Finally, Support and Objective are *linked.*

What can you deliver as Support to meet your Objective?

Here are some of the more common issues related to developing your Support.

The first relates to "Laddering."

ARCHWAY COOKIES SUPPORT STATEMENT

Support was based on the inherent nutritional characteristics of oatmeal cookies with additional emphasis on other emerging health concerns – such as palm oil.

A low-calorie claim was added later ("ounce-for-ounce lower in calories than most other cookies in your store.")

Archway's other varieties were used as further support for Archway uniqueness.

Support will be:
Archway Cookies are made with nutritious oatmeal,
Archway Oatmeal Cookies are naturally low in sodium and fat – they contain No Palm Oil.
Archway has many unique varieties.

Longer ads, like 60" radio spots, went deeper into the Support Section. Shorter ads, like in-store posters, concentrated on the first points.

It's wrought from pure silver and writes like pure silk.

You will find writing with the Parker sterling silver Premier fountain pen anything but drudgery.

In fact, it's entirely possible you will find it something of an inspiration.

We can't promise it will give you the wisdom of an Oscar Wilde, although holding the solid silver body does lend itself to contemplation. (It's 92.5% pure, as pure as sterling silver comes.)

When you do finally write, the words will flow with such uninhibited smoothness there will be nothing to block the way should a profound thought happen to wander along.

Thank the nib for that. And the extremes we go to

making it. The nib takes three weeks to manufacture, because we do it almost entirely by hand.

We fashion it from 18K gold to make it flexible to the touch. Then at the tip we mount a tiny pellet of ruthenium, a metal four times harder than steel and ten times smoother.

The ruthenium tip is sculptured under a microscope—a deft operation any surgeon could envy. But an even more delicate task follows.

The nib must be split with a cutting disc only .004" wide. Literally fine enough to split hairs.

Finally, the nib is tumbled in walnut shells for eighteen hours to leave the gold incomparably smooth.

Only after all this, not to mention 131 inspections along the way, will the craftsman who made the nib sign the certificate allowing us to sell you this pen.

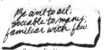

Buy the Parker Premier and even if you never write anything magnificent, at least you will never write anything but magnificently.

◆ PARKER

PRODUCT BENEFIT VS. CONSUMER BENEFIT.

It's common for enthusiastic debate to focus on these relationships. In fact, it never stops.

Here's an example…

Is the Objective communicating a Consumer Benefit (or Value) with the Product Benefit as Support ("You're a Good Mother because you serve Yum Nut Peanut Butter to your kids.")?

Or, is the Objective communicating the Product Benefit with a "Reason Why" as Support ("Yum Nut Peanut Butter tastes better because it's made with more nuts.")?

Strategically, this is a good question.

And a good case can often be made for both sides of the argument.

Consumer Benefits are generally regarded as strategically superior – yet, in one survey, TV commercials that focused on Product Attributes or Benefits were judged more effective and distinctive.

Product Benefit as Support for Consumer Benefit. Great manufacturing is the Reason Why. Great writing is the Benefit.

LOOKING FOR SUPPORT?

Often, while discovering the Objective, material for Support has been generated in the process:
Product facts.
- Product Benefits.
- Consumer Needs.
- Consumer Benefits.
- Competitive Advantages.
- Positioning Opportunities.
- Whatever It Takes to Solve The Problem.

It's Better. See!

The P&G Philosophy.
Better Products. Strong Strategies. And, if possible, **Visual Demonstration** of Benefit or Superiority.

"The key to successful marketing is superior product performance.

If the consumer does not perceive any real benefits in the brand, then no amount of ingenious advertising and selling can save the brand."

Ed Harness
Former P & G Chairman

Product Benefits also are termed Features. This terminology is usually used by those who do not believe in Product Benefits.

The only thing certain is that this will continue to be the subject of strategic discussion.

TYPES OF SUPPORT.

"Reason-Why."

This type of support is often a product fact, such as Cascade's sheeting action. This is particularly true with package goods.

Combinations.

Sometimes it's a *combination* of facts that allows you to provide a specific benefit.

"Support is that Special K is low in calories and sugar, high in protein."

It's common to link two Product Benefits to create a Consumer Benefit or a larger Product Benefit. Here are three examples:

A. The classic Value equation links Quality and Price. **Price/Quality = Value**

B. Liquid laundry detergents combine *special* cleaning properties (removal of stains or collar soil) with *general* cleaning effectiveness to build their position.

C. Convenience and Good Taste is a common combination for many prepared foods.

Yet, the Benefit is relatively single-minded (i.e. "Easy to serve a great tasting meal.")

"Permission to Believe."

This is a subtler type of support. Generic claims such as product performance or good taste can be shaped to become a "permission to believe" that your product delivers that benefit in a unique way.

Joy cleaning "down to the shine" or 9-Lives tasting good enough for finicky Morris lets you believe the products perform as advertised.

Sometimes color is added to products to visualize a colorless technical improvement. (This is "Nine Wheel Logic.")

Support is almost ephemeral.

We find **"image"** here.

Objective and Support are often linked by imagination, artistry, and ad budgets.

The linkage between Marlboro and the imagery of Marlboro Country is an act of will supported by heavy media expenditures. The heritage of the name is of English nobility – it's not Western at all.

The "Life Style" imagery of many campaigns, particularly those for beer and soft drinks, seeks to place the product in a certain type of environment with certain types of people.

Usually, fashion advertising does not persuade you by talking about their unique stitching process, but by projecting a look (visual support) and an attitude.

Some aspects of image are based on a brand's long-term heritage.

But the result of those feelings and attitudes on the part of consumers can be very substantial. It can be as strong and powerful as any logical "reason why."

GENERIC BENEFIT. UNIQUE SUPPORT.

In theory, the more unique and distinctive your Support, the more it will be Support for your Product's Benefit. The Benefit may be generic, but the Benefit plus the Support (the proposition) should be a unique construct.

As Rosser Reeves' USP states, your Support should be **"unique."**

"The proposition must be one that the competition either cannot or does not offer.

It must be <u>unique</u> – either a uniqueness of the brand or a claim not otherwise made in that particular field of advertising."

Come to where the imagery is.

That's the theory.

In reality, many successful brands manage to reinforce their leadership and dominate by staking claim to a generic attribute common to the category.

Many dominant brands have established positions with benefits generic to the category.

It's the modern version of Claude Hopkins' **"pre-emption,"** Rosser Reeves' **USP** and Leo Burnett's **"inherent drama."**

One of the key issues in developing a winning strategy is determining what benefit position you can establish and how you can support it.

LINKAGE.

One important concern is establishing *linkage* throughout the strategy.

This means you must *link* an Objective that can be accomplished with Support that can be delivered.

Whether your Support is a product-based fact or pure imagination and attitude, these two parts of your Strategy must be well-connected.

It's common for Objective and Support to be linked – it's inherent in the relationship.

"Reason Why" Linkage.

As discussed, classic package goods strategies try to provide a logical "reason why."

As P&G would say, *"A statement of the product characteristic which makes it possible for the product to deliver this basic benefit."*

P&G brands are based on superior product performance supported by an extraordinary commitment to marketing superior products.

This is not always possible.

Many products compete in areas where there is no specific "reason why." Or, where the "reason why" is either not motivating or "ownable."

A statement of the product characteristic which makes it possible for the product to deliver this basic benefit.

A "Reason Why." Support Statement.

For example, shiny floors in the floor wax and floor cleaner category.

If this is the case, you have to look for another type of linkage.

Associative Linkage.

Naturally, emotional/associative linkage is not as strong as rational/logical linkage.

For this reason, Image Strategies can seem a bit flimsy when you look at them on paper.

They are much more dependent upon provocative copy, exceptional production values, hefty media budgets, and patience.

In Image advertising, the Support is often *visual.* For example, Marlboro cowboys and the scenery of Marlboro Country.

If Support can be distinctively visualized, so much the better – "Seen/Associated" is a measure of advertising effectiveness.

You should also remember that "image" is more difficult to measure in research and takes a longer time to build.

When working with an Image Strategy, you must be *extremely* tough-minded about what it will take to make it work in the marketplace.

While there is certainly some linkage in image campaigns… men drink beer and teenagers enjoy soft drinks… much of the communication happens on an emotional level.

Imagery.

Music.

Style.

The communication is this product is *associated* with this sort of:

A) People, B) Activity,

C) LifeStyle, D) Imagery,

E) All/Some of Above.

Target Consumer as Support.
Common "Positioning" Strategy.

SUPPORT STATEMENTS CAN BE
SPECIFIC:

*"Special K helps control weight.
Support will be that Special K
is low in calories and sugar,
high in protein."*

SUPPORT STATEMENTS CAN BE
GENERAL...

*"Support will be visual
representation
of the spirit and flavor of
Marlboro."*

(With 20/20 hindsight, that's how I'd
write a Marlboro Support statement.)

For example,

"The night belongs to Michelob."

This is an excellent example of associative linkage and the result is entertaining advertising utilizing the imagery of the evening.

And More Linkage.

To strengthen your Strategy further, it is often helpful to establish *additional linkage* between the Benefit and the Target Consumer.

For example, "Less Filling" was a benefit that appealed to Lite Beer's Target – the heavy beer drinker. So did the visual support – ex-jocks who enjoyed it.

Like a good ad, a solid Strategy **resonates.**

All of the elements work together to build the sale. As the saying goes,

*"A good Strategy hangs together
or the people who wrote it hang separately."*

SOME FURTHER CONSIDERATIONS.

Is Support Single-Minded?

A laundry list of attributes is not Support. Support in a Strategy should reinforce a single-minded path to the Objective.

Multiple Benefit Strategies (i.e. "Tastes better/Costs less") must be clearly superior to those that focus on a single benefit.

However, by *linking* two pieces of Support, it is sometimes possible to achieve a single-minded benefit.

Is Your Support Clear?

When you read the Strategy, do you understand *why* a person should buy this product?

Does it make sense?

Does it seem important?

And, finally…

Does It Feel Like You Can Sell the Product with It?

Sooner or later, you've got to write an ad.

Will your Support support you?

This may seem like an obvious question, but the "pre-sold" nature of the people writing strategies often makes them more eager to be persuaded than the consumers to whom they'll be advertising.

If your Support is supportable, write it down. (If it isn't, keep writing.)

Now your strategy will read:

"Advertising will (*convince*) (*Target Consumer*) that (*Product*) is/will/provides (*Objective/Benefit*).

'Support will be (*Support*)."

That's what you say.

Tone is how you say it.

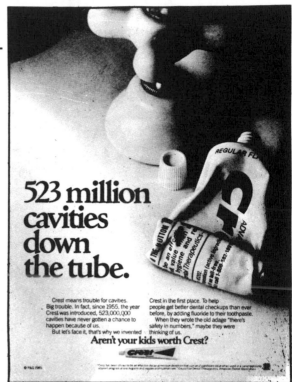

523 million cavities down the tube.

Crest means trouble for cavities. Big trouble. In fact, since 1955, the year Crest was introduced, 523,000,000 cavities have never gotten a chance to happen because of us. But let's face it, that's why we invented Crest in the first place. To help people get better dental checkups than ever before, by adding fluoride to their toothpaste. When they wrote the old adage "there's safety in numbers," maybe they were thinking of us.

Aren't your kids worth Crest?

"Reason Why" Support.
Product performance as Support for
a Consumer Benefit.
"No Cavities!"

ARCHWAY COOKIES
OBJECTIVE & SUPPORT.
Most of the time, communicating a benefit will be your Objective.

In the Archway strategy, Oatmeal implied a nutrition benefit unique to the cookie category.

Note the ways in which the first two statements are <u>linked.</u>

Advertising will convince
adults who eat cookies that
Archway Oatmeal Cookies
are uniquely delicious
and nutritious.
Support will be:
Archway Cookies are made with
nutritious oatmeal.
Archway Cookies are naturally
low in sodium and fat – they
contain no Palm Oil.
Archway has many unique
varieties.

Even *unique* is used as linkage.
Unique varieties can be Support for unique taste (uniquely delicious).
This is not an accident.

3. The Tone or Brand Character Statement.

Your Strategy may also have a third part – a Tone or Brand Character Statement.

Over the years, there has been a movement away from "Tone" or "Tone and Manner" statements, which describe the character of the advertising, toward statements which describe the character of the brand – *"long-term brand values."*

This is particularly true with clients such as P&G, who view Advertising Strategies as long-term documents which, ideally, should be in place over a number of years.

Over that period of time, P&G believes that while the *tone* of the advertising may vary, the *values* represented by the brand should remain constant.

WHEN TO USE A TONE STATEMENT.

There are many cases where a Tone Statement can be a very helpful addition to the Strategy.

Many clients are not P&G and your Advertising Strategy may be in a more or less constant state of revision. If the advertising isn't "working," the Strategy is one of the things you have to look at.

In these cases, Tone Statements can be very helpful as you firm up your strategic direction.

They can be a place for additional insights into the Target or the best advertising style for the product category.

As a practical matter, there are only Tone Statements for new brands with no heritage.

The Right Tone.
The Right Brand Character.
This award-winning advertising has the right tone for its target – men who fish.

It also strengthens the character of the brand.

Whether you use a Tone or Brand Character Statement, your ads should do both jobs well.

142

In situations where you are trying to **re-position** a brand, reach consumers in a new way, go after a new target, or deal with a **"rejector base"** (former customers who no longer purchase your brand), "long-term brand values" may actually be a hindrance and a Tone Statement more helpful.

WHEN TO USE A BRAND CHARACTER STATEMENT.

Currently, Brand Character Statements are preferred by major marketers and agencies.

For Flanker Brands, there will usually be a Brand Character Statement based on some variation of values of the "Mother" brand.

When your brand advertises to diverse groups, a Brand Character Statement can help focus on values that endure across groups.

By the way, when writing a Brand Character Statement, be patient – developing a Brand Character Statement everyone can agree on may take a little time.

Brand Character Statements can be tough to write and Tone Statements are relatively easy.

For example, is the brand "warm," "feminine," "womanly," "female" or "motherly?"

Even though a number of people may *feel* the same way about a brand, they may express it differently.

In summary…

Tone Statements are short-term and about the Advertising.

Brand Character Statements are long-term and about the Brand.

You should learn to write both.
We'll start with the Tone Statement.

MORE ON TONE VS. BRAND CHARACTER…

I like Tone Statements for the same reason P&G *does not* like them – they are "about the advertising."

After all, this is an Advertising Strategy we're writing.

I've found that Tone Statements can offer an important opportunity for people to talk about how they think the advertising should "feel" just as you're getting ready to create it.

This can be important input during creative development and a helpful reference frame when the advertising is presented.

That's why, as a practical matter, I find Tone Statements very helpful.

The Tone Statement.

The Tone statement begins

"Tone will be…"

Tone is the *how* of the Strategy. It's key to the type of advertising you will create.

A key Strategic question in developing the Tone Statement…

"How will you relate to the Target Consumer?"

The **Tone** of your Strategy is the first step in determining the style of your advertising.

More from Bernbach:

"Great execution becomes content.

It brings what you have to say to the eyes and ears of your audience believably and persuasively."

DDB Strategies contained what they termed a **"Tone and Manner"** Statement.

The right Tone will help put you on the right track to great execution.

Essentially, determining the desired Tone will be based on your knowledge of your product, how to talk to your target consumer, and the competitive environment.

Sound familiar?

It's The Strategic Triad – only this time it's about feeling and attitude.

The Tone Statement functions as a right-brain/ emotional description of your Strategy.

Here are two examples:

Tone will convey the spicy fun of Popeyes' New Orleans heritage.

(Popeyes Famous Fried Chicken '81-83)

Tone will be compatible with today's competitive fast-food environment.

(Popeyes Famous Fried Chicken '85-'87)

As you might imagine, Popeyes' Tone State-

ARCHWAY COOKIES TONE STATEMENT.

Tone will combine the importance of good nutrition with the fun of cookies.

A major concern was that we didn't forget that cookies taste good and are fun – that's why people buy them.

In this regard, the Tone Statement related to the Objective Statement.

It also clearly signalled that commercials should have entertainment value – not just nutritional value.

ment changed because their advertising environment (the competition) changed.

A good Tone Statement can help you focus your Strategy and your Tactics (the ads) on your Target Consumer.

Tone is a guide for how to talk to your target.

The descriptions in your Tone section should be *meaningful* to your target and helpful to the people creating and judging the advertising.

Will it be intrusive and newsy?

Or honest and empathetic?

Rational or Emotional?

Or both?

In addition, it's not uncommon to revise your Tone section as you find out more about how to talk to your target. Often, the facts of an Advertising Strategy are right before the feelings are.

While not executional, the Tone Statement helps guide the execution in the proper direction and it indicates the type of communication which the target will respond to.

Proper Tone, executed with Style, helps create a "Selling Attitude."

Once you've completed your Tone Statement, your Strategy is written.

It reads…

**"Advertising will (*convince*)
(*Target Consumer*) that (*Product*)
is/will (*Objective*).**

Support will be (*Support*).

**Tone will be
(*"Selling Attitude" Adjectives*)."**

And that's how a complete Advertising Strategy looks when you use a Tone Statement.

Now let's talk about the alternative…

**SOME EXAMPLES
OF TONE STATEMENTS:**

*Tone will reflect the fun
of the pizza eating experience.*

*Tone will be fashion-conscious
and "state of the art."*

*Tone will be intrusive
and bring excitement
to a major improvement
in a low-interest category.*

A statement of the character we strive to build for the product.

The Brand Character Statement.

Clients like P&G and agencies like Y&R do *not* believe in Tone Statements.

Y&R says,

"As usually written they are meaningless. If the rest of the Strategy is clear, they are unnecessary."

At Y&R, they address this issue with something they call the "Prospect Definition," which treats the target in depth. (We'll cover the Y&R Creative Work Plan in an Addendum which follows.)

At P&G, they've evolved to what they call **Brand Character Statements** which describe the enduring values of their brands – these values are viewed as an important part of a brand's equity in the marketplace.

Here are some Brand Character Statements for a few familiar brands:

Crest is the dedicated leader in improving dental health for the family.

Coast is a product that is exhilarating to use.

Pampers – pre-eminent reputation as the leader in baby care... a warm and affectionate attitude toward babies.

Camay – the soap of beautiful women.

These statements describe the "enduring values," "long-term values" or "core values" of the brands.

In developing a Brand Character Statement,

ARCHWAY COOKIES BRAND CHARACTER.

"The Good Food Cookie."
This positioning line was also their Brand Character Statement.

ARCHWAY COOKIES PROMOTIONAL STRATEGY

Remember, Strategy isn't just Advertising Strategy.

When Archway shifted to their "Good Food Cookie" position, they made another important strategic shift with their Advertising program – they integrated it with their Promotional program – *they focused on promoting their promotions.*

In the cookie category, about 90% of purchase decisions are made in the store.

So, let's be real, if you're displayed at the end of an aisle with a good cookie at a good price, you're going to sell some – *whether people saw your advertising or not.*

The new promotions supported the Advertising Strategy and the new "Good Food" position with themes like "Did You Have Your Oatmeal Today?"

But remember, the advertising program also supported the promotions, and this fact was communicated to the grocery trade – which helped get displays into stores.

So, in many cases...
the advertising worked
before **it ran!**

In developing a Brand Character Statement, review all the relevant aspects of the brand history: packaging, graphics, target customer values – everything you can think of.

Then distill it to its essence.

Try to describe the brand as you would a person – look for the adjectives and phrases that best personify the brand.

What does your brand stand for?

Within all this information you should find the essential elements you need for building a Brand Character Statement.

Brand Character Statements can begin, *"The Character of the Brand will be seen to be"* or in whatever way seems appropriate.

Remember, this is a long-term document.

Don't worry if it takes a while. And don't worry if you have to revise it a few times 'til you finally get it right.

And (instead of a Tone Statement), this is the third element of your Advertising Strategy.

Now your strategy reads...

"Advertising will (*convince*) (*Target Consumer*) that (*Product*) is/will (*Objective*).

Support will be (*Support*).

Character of (*Product*) is (*"Brand Character" Statement*)."

And that's an Advertising Strategy with a Brand Character Statement.

Now let's try writing a few.

STRATEGY READING LIST:
Here are some of the better books in this field.

The Marketing Imagination
Theodore Levitt/MacMillan N.Y.

Positioning & Marketing Warfare
Trout & Reis/McGraw Hill

The Mind of The Strategist. Business Planning for Competitive Advantage
Kenichi Ohmae
Penguin Business Library
ISBN 0-1400-91289
(My personal favorite)

The Y&R Traveling Creative Workshop
Hanley Norins/Prentice-Hall
ISBN 0-13-973116-4

The Making of Effective Advertising
Patti & Moriarty
Prentice Hall/ISBN 0-13-547290-3

Planning for R.O.I. Effective Advertising Strategy
Wells, William D/DDB Needham
Prentice-Hall/ISBN 0-13-679466-1

Planning for R.O.I. Workbook
Prentice-Hall/ISBN 0-13-679473-4

Also recommended:

Passion for Excellence
Peters & Austin/Harper & Row

Small is Beautiful
E.F. Schumacher/Harper & Row

Further Up The Organization
Robert Townsend/Alfred A. Knopf

NEW PRODUCTS.

A new product is a strategy brought to life. Thinking up new products is good exercise for thinking up new strategies.

It's usually developed with a Target Consumer in mind, and offers a unique benefit with a product-based "reason why."

Its reason for being is usually a need in the marketplace.

So, let's try a few.

Here are some helpful hints:

• Focus on a problem that needs solving.

• Think of current trends and growing needs.

• Your best ideas may come from a familiar area.

• Your new "product" could also be a new service. Or a combination of product and service – like lawn care.

• A **good name,** often one that communicates the benefit, can also help make a new product successful.

For the moment, you can ignore
• **Technology limitations**
• **Price considerations**
• **Size of the market**

(Many new product ideas are developed for small and/or emerging markets.)

By the way, in the real world, **80% of new products fail!**

Good luck.

Assignment #6.

1. INVENT A NEW PRODUCT.
  • What is it?
  • Who is Your Target Consumer?
  • What is The Benefit?
  • What is Support for your Benefit?
  • What should the Tone be?
  • What about Brand Character?
  • What is the *Name?* (It should describe your product in an appealing way.
  • Does this suggest any Advertising themes?

2. WRITE YOUR STRATEGY.
  Product Description:

  _____

  _____

  Brand Name: _____.

  "Advertising will _____

  _____ **that**

  _____ **is/will/provides**

  _____.

  Support will be _____

  _____.

  Tone will be _____

  _____.

  Brand Character is _____

  _____.

  Advertising Theme:

  _____

  _____.

Here's a New Product based on an Old Product!
Tom Brancky at Starkist realized that Tuna could be convenience food.
  The result – a Tuna Salad Lunch Kit.
  Instant understanding by consumers and instant sales accelerated by engaging coupon ads like this – combining established brand heritage with a brand new idea.

Strategy Worksheet:

PRODUCT: _____

PRODUCT DESCRIPTION: _____

_____

_____

TARGET CONSUMER: _____

_____

_____

PRODUCT BENEFIT(S): _____

_____

_____

CONSUMER BENEFIT(S): _____

_____

_____

SUPPORT: _____

_____

_____

TONE OF ADVERTISING: _____

_____

BRAND CHARACTER: _____

_____

ADVERTISING THEME IDEAS:

_____

_____

_____

MISC: _____

_____

NOTE: You may want to make copies of this.

Having trouble picking a product?
Grab something close at hand.
Or have someone pick it for you.
Remember, in the real world, you
have little control over assignments.

Products with the strongest benefit and greatest competitive advantage usually generate the strongest strategies.

ALTERNATE STRATEGIES.

The three major determinants for alternate Strategies are:

• **Competition**
   (Source of Business)
• **Target Consumer**
• **Message Selection (Benefit)**

Here are some examples:

Competition.

Stove Top Stuffing could have been a side-dish, but Stove Top decided to focus on the most popular side-dish, which was the major "source of business," potatoes.

"Stove Top Stuffing, instead of potatoes" clearly defined the competition as it communicated the Benefit – a nice change of pace.

Target Consumer.

Many years ago, P&G advertised JIF peanut butter exclusively to kids.

After all, most peanut butter was consumed by kids, and they influenced similar purchases – like cereal.

However, P&G found this was a purchase decision made by *mothers*.

"Choosy Moms Choose Jif" was the result of this change in focus.

Message Selection.

Attributes, Features, Product Benefits, Consumer Benefits, Values – a single product offers many choices.

Apple began advertising Macintosh as *"The Computer for the rest of us."*

While this appealed to many early Mac adopters, this "Against" positioning alienated many business people – a key market for Apple's Objectives.

BBDO's new line, *"The power to be your best"* successfully communicated to both Target Groups.

Instead of Potatoes

Assignment #7.

PICK AN EXISTING PRODUCT.

1. MAKE A LIST.
   • Target Consumer options.
   • Benefit options.
   • Support options.
   • Tone options.
   • Brand Character options.

2. WRITE YOUR "BEST BET" ADVERTISING STRATEGY.

"Advertising will _____
_____ **that**
_____ **is/will/provides**
_____.

Support will be _____
_____.

Tone will be _____

Brand Character is _____

Advertising Theme:

_____

_____

3. WRITE A "NEXT BEST BET" ADVERTISING STRATEGY.

"Advertising will _____
_____ **that**
_____ **is/will**
_____.

Support will be _____
_____.

Tone will be _____

Brand Character is _____

Advertising Theme:

_____

Assignment #8.
Business Building Ideas:

Good ideas build business.

Whether it's putting a box of Arm & Hammer Baking Soda in your refrigerator, or making some Rice Krispies Treats, ideas like these can lead to powerful advertising.

Your Assignment:

Have an idea that will build a company's business. Then, write an ad about it.

It might be:

- A new use for the product
- A new target for the product
- Something else.

Your idea should be for an existing product or service.

Your idea should be one that generates "plus" business.

It's a simple assignment, but it'll help teach you to think about advertising problems in an important way – because everyone's looking for ideas that build business.

DUAL TARGETS AND SECONDARY BENEFITS.

Programs can often have more than one target. For example, many products have to communicate to the trade as well as the consumer.

After all, if it's not in the store, it doesn't matter how good the ad is.

To sell more jeans this year, push the right buttons.

And, a single product may have different customers who buy it for dramatically different reasons – an example, Apple Computers.

If you have dramatically different Target Groups, you may have to integrate more than one Strategy into the advertising process.

Remember, Secondary Targets can be of Primary Importance.

Here, Lee Jeans talks to the trade. And it's a good fit.

124 salesmen in one room and not a single ounce of polyester.

NEW...THE TASTE OF RICE KRISPIES TREATS IN A CEREAL.

From Secondary Usage to New Product.
Kellogg's discovered consumer familiarity with their Rice Krispies Treats recipe created a ready market for a ready-to-eat cereal based on that recipe.

Notice how the ad also addresses a potential problem – people might think of it as dessert not breakfast.

That's why secondary copy works to reassure mothers with a chart indicating "Less sugar than most kids' cereals."

CONVENIENCE STRATEGIES.

Convenience is becoming ever more important for "time-poor" Consumers.

Convenience strategies generally focus on some factor of product usage and performance and related benefit.

Faster, easier, less mess, etc.

Support may be simple and single-minded (New Formula), or more complex (New Formula, new package with competitive performance results).

You may also need a bit of "quality re-assurance." But the communication should be simple.

SUPERIORITY STRATEGIES.

These focus on a dimension in which your product is better than something else.

It may be a competitor, your own previous product, or no product at all!

Support is often a Reason Why.

IMAGE STRATEGIES.

They're tough to write because the focus and benefit are less tangible.

Sometimes the focus is *Attributes* (The independent magazine for independent women).

Sometimes it's *Associative* (Sunkist Orange Soda and Beach Boys).

Sometimes it's *Assumptive*, or *Pre-emptive* ("This Bud's for you" – Reward for a job well done.)

Sometimes, as in the case of much fashion advertising, it's pure *Attitude*.

Assignment #9.

1. CONVENIENCE STRATEGY.

Product: _____

"Advertising will _____
_____ that
_____ is/will/provides
_____.

Support will be _____
_____.

Tone will be _____.

2. SUPERIORITY STRATEGY.

Product: _____

"Advertising will _____
_____ that
_____ is/will/provides
_____.

Support will be _____
_____.

Tone will be _____.

3. IMAGE STRATEGY.

Product: _____

"Advertising will _____
_____ that
_____ is/will/provides
_____.

Support will be _____
_____.

Tone will be _____.

152

4. SERVICE STRATEGY.

(Bank, law firm, baby sitter, shop by phone, etc.)

Service: _____

"Advertising will _____
_____ **that**
_____ **is/will/provides**
_____.

Support will be _____
_____.

Tone will be _____.

5. WRITE 3 THEME LINES FOR EACH OF YOUR PRODUCTS AND STRATEGIES.

Convenience Product: _____
_____
_____
_____

Superiority Product: _____
_____
_____
_____

Image Product: _____
_____
_____
_____

Service/Name: _____
_____
_____
_____

Making Services Tangible.
Here, a bank offers a specific
product with a specific benefit.

SERVICE STRATEGIES.
These are a combination of Tangibles & Intangibles.

For example, a restaurant has both the Tangibles of food and price and the Intangibles of service and overall experience.

An airline sells you a seat and a dinner on a plastic tray.

But the intangibles of efficiency and comfort are more important.

Financial services offer a difficult combination – most benefits, like "make you rich," cannot be claimed with certainty.

Financial services are both high-interest (it's your money, so you're interested) and dull (a lot of talk and numbers that are hard to understand complicated by legal restrictions).

This can make simple communication difficult.

Things like "friendly service" are hard to guarantee, and service, as Mr. Levitt points out in "The Marketing Imagination," is *"generally only recognized in its absence."*

People notice bad service, but take good service for granted.

Your service may emphasize Tangibles or Intangibles.

Or both.

Briefs, Blueprints & Work Plans.

There's no single "right" way to write an Advertising Strategy – though you will find most Strategy systems have a lot in common.

Let's look at a number of popular formats:

Y&R Creative Work Plan.

This classic system begins with four elements:

1. A STATEMENT OF THE KEY FACT
based on an analysis of all pertinent facts.

2. A DEFINITION OF THE PROBLEM
which the advertising must solve in light of this Key Fact. This is *"The Problem the Advertising Must Solve."*

This should be a *consumer* problem and stated from the consumer point of view.

3. THE ADVERTISING OBJECTIVE
This stems from the Problem.

All of this information helps you develop...

4. THE CREATIVE STRATEGY
In the Y&R system, the Strategy is

"designed to achieve the objective, which will solve the problem that the key fact has defined."

The Key Fact and the **Problem** are related.

For example, research might show that people think your product has an inferior taste, even if they haven't tried it.

The Problem the Advertising Must Solve: *"Our brand has a poor taste reputation."*

This would then relate to the **Objective** – *"To overcome our poor taste reputation with consumers."*

WRITING THE WORK PLAN.

At Y&R, writing the Work Plan is the job of the Copy or Creative Supervisor.

This may be one of the reasons for their exceptional record of unique, on-target work.

The Work Plan must be written before creative work begins.

Its prime purpose is

"to set creative people free... in the right direction."

Y&R Creative Strategy.

The Strategy must include:

A. PROSPECT DEFINITION.

The Prospect Definition defines prospects in terms of:

- Product usage
- Demographics
- Psychographics

Sometimes, facts are not available. If this is the case, use an "educated guess."

B. PRINCIPAL COMPETITION.

The Principal Competition statement gives *"a clear idea of the arena in which your product will do battle."*

In the case of a new or unique product, use a "Reason for Being."

C. PROMISE/CONSUMER BENEFIT.*

The best argument your brand can offer.

The **Promise** Statement has four guidelines:

1. The Promise should be phrased in terms of *"what the product will do for the consumer."*

2. The Promise should be as *competitive* as possible.

3. The Promise should *motivate* prospects in the direction that will accomplish your Objective.

4. The Promise should *not* be written in actual advertising terms.

D. REASON WHY.

A statement that *supports* the Promise. Each statement must be "sharp, clear and specific."

*

In some versions of the Work Plan, this is known as the "Promise," in others, it is termed the "Consumer Benefit."

WORK PLAN AT WORK

Here's an example - a Creative Work Plan for SANKA®.

1. KEY FACT

29% of coffee-drinking households say they are concerned about caffeine, but resist trying SANKA® Brand.

2. CONSUMER PROBLEM THE ADVERTISING MUST SOLVE.

Prospects don't think SANKA® Brand would taste as good as caffeinated coffee, and they also resist its somewhat medicinal image.

3. ADVERTISING OBJECTIVE

Convince prospects that *SANKA® does indeed taste as good as caffeinated coffee* and has the added benefit of being caffeine free.

4. CREATIVE STRATEGY

A. Prospect Definition:
Our prime prospects are mildly concerned about caffeine but haven't switched to decaffeinated coffee. They are probably somewhat more hyper than the average coffee drinker, more health aware, and perhaps even self-conscious about giving in to a decaffeinated coffee.

B. Principal Competition:
The regular coffee prospects are currently drinking. Secondarily, any other decaffeinated coffee they may consider switching to.

C. Promise/Consumer Benefit:
You will be surprised how good SANKA® tastes, and it has the advantage of being caffeine free.

D. Reason Why:
1. In blind taste tests, SANKA® brand decaffeinated coffee is at parity and sometimes superior to competitive caffeinated coffees.
2. Good taste has helped it become the third largest coffee brand in America.

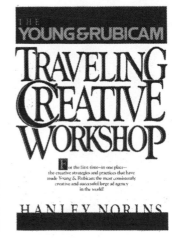

**The Young & Rubicam
Traveling Creative Workshop**
by Hanley Norins
Prentice Hall

GE Focus System.

General Electric is a client that produces numerous communications In-House.

Their Advertising and Sales Promotion Operations division developed a simple three-step process that helps them do effective work.

It has an advantage in that it can be implemented quickly. At GE, you could be writing consumer information on light bulbs one day, and technical ads for atomic power plants the next.

Here's how it works.

1. Focus on the receiver.

First, you must know the Receiver.

Singular, not plural.

You must know this audience as a person, with needs and wants beyond your product.

2. Focus on the proposition.

"The Proposition relates what we know about the product to what we've learned about the Receiver."

The Proposition is a strategic statement, not a headline. But, if you just set the proposition in type and ran it with a picture of the product, "you'd have something useful."

GE believes it relates to a "Key Fact" (Y&R) and a "position," (Trout & Ries) the way they are perceived by the Receiver.

3. Dramatize the Proposition.

With the proposition as the basis, the challenge becomes "break the boredom barrier."

Find a way to communicate the Proposition in a dramatic way.

THREE KINDS OF THINKING.

This classic system calls for three different kinds of thinking:

Thinking about the Receiver involves *Analytic* thinking (and empathy).

Thinking about the Proposition requires *Strategic* thinking.

Dramatization demands *Creative* thinking.

Leo Burnett Strategy Worksheet.

THIS FORMAT BREAKS THE MOLD.

Many successful Burnett campaigns worked, but did not fit traditional Strategy formats.

The key was Leo's "Inherent Drama," stated here as "Key Drama."

Often this allowed Burnett to capture generic benefits with unique executions.

This Worksheet allows you to include these unique properties as well as more traditional approaches.

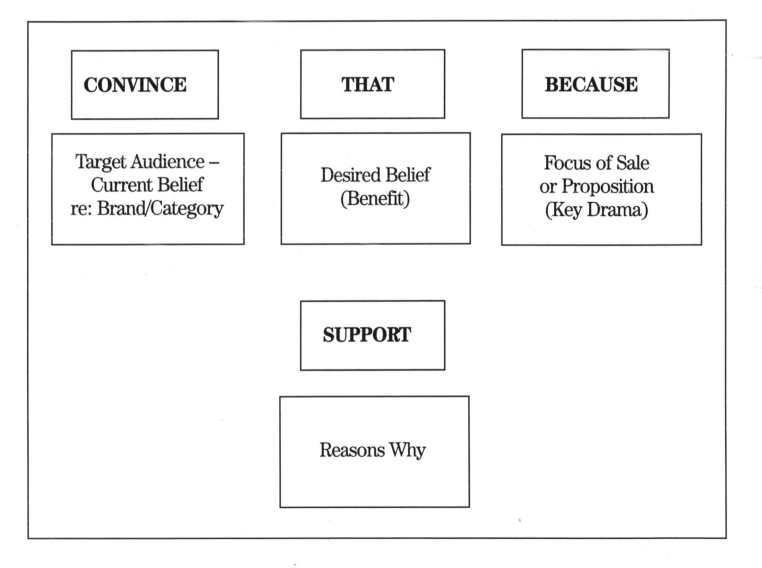

CONVINCE

Target Audience –
Current Belief
re: Brand/Category

THAT

Desired Belief
(Benefit)

BECAUSE

Focus of Sale
or Proposition
(Key Drama)

SUPPORT

Reasons Why

The "R.O.I." System.

ROI stands for "Return on Investment."

At DDB/Needham, it also means that "Great advertising is distinguished by three fundamental qualities: Relevance, Originality and Impact."

Their ROI Strategy System is like the Y&R Work Plan, but there are important exceptions – particularly in the inclusion of certain tactical elements (demonstrations) and a Media section.

The System is built on five questions:

1. What is the purpose of the advertising?

The ROI process focuses on the specific desired behavior and source of business.

2. To whom will the advertising be addressed?

The target section should have both demographic and psychographic information.

DDB/Needham looks for "Aiming Points" which allow you to think specifically and personally about your target. An example would be "Cereal eaters who are interested in sports" for Wheaties.

3. What competitive benefit will be promised and how will that promise be supported?

(See Sidebar.)

4. What personality will distinguish the brand?

This may be treated simply or in great detail.

5. When, where, and under what circumstances will the target be most receptive to the message? What media will deliver that message to the target at the lowest possible cost?

ROI integrates media planning into the strategic process. A key part of this is the concept of *"aperture,"* the time that *"a customer is most likely to notice, be receptive to, and react favorably to, an advertising message..."*

Account Planning & The Creative Brief.

Agencies such as Chiat/Day have added a *third force* to the development process.

In addition to Account Executives and Creatives, they now have **Account Planners.**

The Planner is responsible for the advertising's *target audience relevance.* A key part of the process is developing **The Creative Brief.**

Here is a sample outline:

1. What is the Opportunity and/or Problem the advertising must address?

A brief summary of why you are advertising. Take the consumer's point of view, not "sales are down," but, rather, "consumers are choosing cheaper alternatives."

2. What do we want people to do as a result of the advertising?

3. Who are we talking to?

Try to develop a rich description of the Target Group. Indicate their beliefs and feelings about the category. Avoid demographic information only. Add personality and lifestyle dimensions.

4. What's the Key Response we want?

What *single* thing do we want people to *feel* or *notice* or *believe* as a result of the advertising?

5. What information/attributes might help produce this response?

It could be a key product attribute, or user need the brand fulfills, etc. Avoid a laundry list.

6. What aspect of Brand Personality should the advertising express?

7. Are there media or budget considerations?

8. This could be helpful...

Any additional information that might affect the creative direction.

WHAT'S A BRIEF?

It's originally a British term for a document that "briefs."

One of the places Account Planning began was the Marketing Department of JWT, London where they evolved a two-step system.

First, they positioned the Brand with a **Brand Strategy Summary.**

Then, they prepared a "Brief" for the Creative Department to clarify the issues that were key to developing effective advertising.

This is known as **"The Creative Brief."**

WHAT'S AN ACCOUNT PLANNER?

"The Planner's ongoing function is to accumulate, originate and synthesize data pertinent to the advertising's target audience; to independently pre-test, post-test and monitor – as an ongoing account assignment – both the advertising itself and the dynamics at work in its marketplace."

WHAT'S A BACKGROUNDER?

Before you can write a Strategy, you often need a lot of background – information about the brand.

A "Backgrounder" is usually some form of questionnaire designed to collect and organize that information so the Strategy can be developed.

IF YOU'D LIKE TO KNOW MORE ABOUT YOUR CUSTOMERS...

Just ask.

Here's a handy start at a good questionnaire.

Don't be reluctant to do a few "one-on-one" interviews.

A lot of people think they're better than Focus Groups. Not to mention quicker and cheaper.

So, get out your clipboard and go talk to a few customers.

CUSTOMER QUESTIONNAIRE

How long have you shopped at
_____?

When did you first discover
_____?

What was your first impression?

Why do you keep coming back?

What would you say to a friend who had never tried_____?

What similar places do you shop, and why do you like these places?

"Backgrounders."

Before you write a Strategy, a "Backgrounder" can help organize information in one place.

Here's an example of a "Backgrounder" for a local or regional business.

This one's for a local TV station or cable company. You can write one to suit your needs.

---

1. Name and Location.

For a local advertiser, one of the most important communication tasks is your Name and Address (maybe your phone number, too).

Name:

Location(s):

Addresses and/or Location Identifiers (Intersections, etc.):

Phone Number:

Do you have any unique graphics, such as logo or signage?
(Attach copies. Indicate source of "master" graphics.

Do you have any existing slogans or advertising themes?
(Attach examples of print ads, flyers, brochures and/or radio scripts.)

2. Products and Services.

Tell us about what you make and sell and/or what services you provide. Don't just make a list – let us know some of the things that make your company special – because those are some of the things you'll want to tell potential customers or clients.

Do you have any existing materials that describe your products or services? (Attach brochures, menus, catalogs, etc.)

3. Your Customers.

Tell us about your customers.

Chances are your new customers will be a lot like the customers you have now. They'll live in the same area and have many of the same characteristics.

Let us know what you think is special about you and your company.

Do you have any letters or customers' comments?
(Attach examples – not originals!)

By the way, don't forget that good advertising can also reinforce your current customers' attitudes as well as bring in new customers.

That means, with a good commercial, you should see your current customers more often, as well as new customers.

If you'd like to know more about your customers, just ask them.

"Blueprints."

This is a document of a type used by many agencies to organize an advertising assignment.

It can be used as a worksheet or a job order.

You can use it to build a Strategy Statement.

A TYPICAL CREATIVE BLUEPRINT.

It usually includes:

• **Product Description**

• **Target Audience(s):**

Demographic, Psychographic or Usage.

You may indicate both primary and secondary audiences.

• **Competition:**

Products or services that might be selected instead of yours. Source of business.

• **Problem Advertising is to Solve**

Sometimes this is listed as Purpose.

• **Advertising Objective**

• **Features and Benefits:**

Rank in order of importance.

• **Positioning:**

Your positioning statement.

• **Tone/Manner**

• **Premise/Proposition:**

A sentence that clearly communicates what should be said in the advertising - focus of Sale. It should be clear, but not executional in nature.

WHAT'S A BLUEPRINT?

It's a common term for a format that combines background and Strategy – often referred to as a "Creative Blueprint."

And, just as often, it may be called something else.

As you can see, it combines elements from things like the Y&R Creative Work Plan and Trout & Ries' "Positioning."

WHAT'S THE DIFFERENCE BETWEEN A BRIEF AND A BLUEPRINT?

Attitude and intent.

A Blueprint tends to lay out the dimensions of a project as objectively as possible.

A Brief tends to be more subjective.

At it's best, a Brief tries to inspire as it generates enthusiasm and insight.

At it's worst, a Brief presents a biased view and may force a solution not supported by the facts of the situation.

WHAT WORKS FOR YOU?
Just as an ad reflects the personality of the advertiser, your Strategy, or Brief, or Blueprint can say something about you and your company.

Your approach to Strategy is a big part of how you do your job.

You'll "own" your Strategy even more with a Strategy format to call your own.

Larry's Brief.

This particular format is used by Larry Asher of Seattle, WA. It reflects places he's been and his own approach to solving problems.

It's based on a format developed by Borders, Perrin & Norrander, which was produced after an extensive survey of agency strategy systems.

Larry added a space for "Strategy," so that there was a place for the basic selling proposition.

Creative Brief.

WHO are we trying to reach?
Describe the target audience.

WHY do these people buy or use this product / service? Explain the consumer benefits.

WHAT is the objective of this project?
Briefly, but concisely, define the results we're after.

HOW does the client's product / service compare to the competition's?
Don't sell, just tell pros and cons.

WHERE is the communication running?
Discuss media alternatives that seem appropriate.

WHEN is a realistic deadline for solutions?

HOW MUCH is allocated to accomplish the task?
Please give approximate dollar range.

STRATEGY What is the best possible selling strategy for this assignment?

WHATEVER else is pertinent information.
Mandatories, cautions, etc.

Assignment #10. Build Your Own Brief.

1. WRITE A STRATEGY FORMAT THAT WORKS FOR YOU.

You may feel free to borrow from any part of this section and use any combination of elements.

Your format may be a single form or a two-part process (i.e. Backgrounder & Brief).

2. GIVE YOUR FORMAT A NAME.

Have that name reflect the "Brand Personality" you wish to project.

Again, you may borrow from elements already presented in this section.

3. FILL OUT YOUR BRIEF.

Take a product you know something about and see if your format works.

4. DO A LITTLE "HYPOTHESIS TESTING."

Now, see how your format works for a few other products you're familiar with.

If you're really feeling ambitious, write some ads based on your Strategy Format.

SECOND THOUGHTS.

Don't forget secondary audiences and secondary benefits.

In many businesses there is a second audience that's very important.

For the food marketers, it's the grocery trade.

For computers, it's dealers and "opinion leaders."

For office equipment, it's secretaries and "decision-makers."

Many complex products, like computers and office equipment, may have additional benefits or features that appeal to those making the final purchase decision.

For example, if both copiers are reliable, which has the best service?

Or the best price?

Or the best lease?

Or…?

IS A TIGER A "BIG IDEA?"
It was for a cereal and a gasoline. How about a lion or a panther? Who knows? Nobody.
Hey, "Nobody" may be a Big Idea, too.

FROM "GRRRR!" TO "R-R-R-R!"
"R-R-R-Ruffles have R-R-R-Ridges" is still a memorable Selling Idea.

Sprint. *dramatizes their Benefit of quality sound by hearing a pin drop over the phone.*

Selling Ideas.

Now that you have a Strategy, your next step is generating a Selling Idea.

We've discussed "How to Have an Idea." Now let's look for an idea for our advertising.

First, your idea should be a *Selling* Idea.

Some say it should be a "Big Idea," but I believe this tends to confuse the issue.

Ideas become Big Ideas only in retrospect — *after* they've performed in the marketplace.

In the beginning, it's all conjecture.

But, to some degree, we're all competent to judge a Selling Idea. It's an idea that sells.

Tony the Tiger sells Sugar Frosted Flakes by saying *"They're Grrrrreat!"*

"Put a Tiger in Your Tank" sold the power of Exxon around the world with universal imagery.

Some of it depends on the strength of the idea itself — and some on how well you execute.

So, how *do* ideas sell?

Let's list a few ways and see if we can understand Selling Ideas better:

1. DRAMATIZE THE BENEFIT.

If you have no other type of idea than this one, you can do very well in the business: Slogans… Dramatic Demos… Mnemonics… Tony the Tiger saying, *"They're Grrrreat!"* and Mr. Whipple squeezing the Charmin *dramatize* the Benefit.

George Lois looks for words that *"bristle with visual possibilities."*

They dramatize all or part of your Strategy in a memorable way.

2. A DISTINCTIVE SELLING PERSONALITY.

The Volkswagen campaign did this marvelously well. Each ad projected a personality consumers could identify with.

Positioning campaigns often do this.

Avis and Dr. Pepper (I'm a Pepper) used a Selling Attitude to reinforce their position.

The position itself can be a personality.

Much fashion advertising does this.

From good old Levis to the latest designer jean. They sell style… with style.

Beers also seek to achieve a personality… only in the case of beer, many of them are fighting to have the *same* personality.

There's a good reason for this. Many of them have the exact same Target Consumer.

3. A UNIQUE SELLING ENVIRONMENT.

A Selling Environment relates to the Selling Personality, but it's subtler.

Marlboro moved from "The Marlboro Man" to "Marlboro Country" – An Environment.

Sunkist Orange Soda became a major soft drink by utilizing imagery and an environment with almost universal appeal for its audience: California, the beach, The Beach Boys, girls in bikinis, surfing, and the Sunkist name.

Graphics can create a Selling Environment.

Your typeface, the overall sense of design, even a photographic attitude (like Nike) can create this Selling Environment.

Sometimes it's the Idea itself and sometimes it's complementary to the main Selling Idea.

For example, McDonald's Selling Environment – the best-run, friendliest, cleanest food chain in the industry (QSC&V – Quality, Service, Cleanliness and Value) – has played a consistent role in all of their advertising over the years.

Our image.

A MUSICAL PERSONALITY & SELLING ENVIRONMENT.
United Airlines unifies their Selling Environment with music.

In the latest version of their long-running campaign, Leo Burnett unifies United's advertising with a powerful musical theme, **"Rhapsody in Blue."**

The audio environment also adds a Selling Personality to every ad – around the world or close to home.

Sunkist Orange Soda's Selling Environment. The Beach.

What color is your brand?
With Levis, it's easy to know.
Dockers makes it easy, too.
Think. What color are you?

With increased visual emphasis, your graphic environment becomes more important.

Color Values can reinforce your Selling Idea. Like Levis and The Blues. Or Dockers' "Colors."

Is color a Selling Idea? Yes it is.

Leo Burnett knew it instinctively.

Red meat on a red background.

4. SOMETHING ELSE.

Sure, why not?

For example, *Dramatize the Problem*.

"Halitosis," a dramatic way of saying "Bad Breath" back in the 30's – built the Listerine business. Today it's "Morning Breath."

Federal Express dramatized their benefit, delivering a package on time, by giving the Problem unique dimension.

Name Awareness Mnemonics may also be Selling Ideas. Like Ken-L-Ration Kibbles and Bits.

Or Rolaids. Or local retailers who sing their phone number over and over and over again. We're taking time to make a simple point.

A Selling Idea Is an Idea that Sells.

Yet, in the complex advertising process, an abundance of opinion can cloud this simple issue.

Your advertising should have a Selling Idea.

This idea, which will emerge from the Strategy, may be quite simple, even though the path you traveled may have been long and hard.

166

Many advertising people labor long and hard searching for the "Breakthrough" so advanced no one can understand it or describe it.

Work hard, but do not be confused.

Selling Ideas should be strong and simple.

"Great copy and great ideas are deceptively simple," said Leo Burnett.

Build your Selling Ideas strong and simple and they may grow up to be Big Ideas.

But in the beginning, your Problems will be:

First, having an idea that sells.

Second, *selling* your Selling Idea.

From having the Selling Idea, we'll move to selling the Selling Idea...

The next part of your journey...

But first, let's think about Selling Ideas.

Selling Idea Exercises:

1. List the most memorable ad campaigns you can remember.

How many were you able to list?

In your own words, write down what you think the Selling Idea is.

2. Name two Selling Ideas that dramatize the Product Benefit.

Other products probably offer the same benefit. How did they make it unique?

3. Name two Selling Ideas that project a Selling Personality or a Selling Attitude.

How are they different from others in the category?

4. Name two Selling Ideas used by a Service.

Is there a symbol involved?

5. Name two Selling Ideas that dramatize a Problem.

Other products may solve the same problem.
How did these products build distinctiveness?

THE PURPOSE OF A SELLING IDEA.

To register the Brand's strategic objective – memorably – over the Competition.

It's the primary executional ingredient and the main thread of executional continuity.

THREE PRINCIPLE VARIABLES:
1. Substance – Meaningfulness or desirability to the consumer.
2. Credibility – Capable of being believed. However, it's OK if it's a bit of a challenge.
3. Provocativeness – Thought-provoking method of expression.

JUDGING SELLING IDEAS.
Is it faithful to Strategy?
Does it have genuine substance?
Is it credible yet challenging?
Is it provocative?

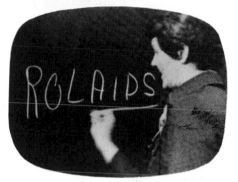

How do you spell "sell?"

167

Assignment #10.

Take the Strategies and Theme Lines you wrote in Assignments #6, #7, and #8.

Pick your three favorites. If you have no favorites, write some new ones.

1. DEVELOP ONE SELLING IDEA FOR EACH PRODUCT AND STRATEGY.
   How do they develop Visual Drama?
   How do they reinforce Name Awareness?
   How do they communicate The Benefit?

2. PRESENT YOUR SELLING IDEAS AS PRINT CONCEPTS, TV KEY FRAMES OR BOTH.

New Product.

NAME: _____

SELLING IDEA: _____

_____

Product #1.

NAME: _____

SELLING IDEA: _____

_____

Product #2.

NAME: _____

SELLING IDEA: _____

_____

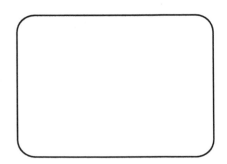

"Where is that big black bag going with that little man?"
It's Leo Burnett, off to make a sale.

Sales Power!
How to Sell Your Ideas.*

How well you sell ideas is as important as how good those ideas are.

So, how *do* you sell ideas?

First, it's pretty complicated.

Second, it's based on understanding *the other person's point of view.*

To help make it all a little simpler, here are a few helpful hints on selling ideas we call, **"Sales Power."** (Note the little list with S.P. initials.)

- STRATEGIC PRECISION
- SAVVY PSYCHOLOGY
- SLICK PRESENTATION
- STRUCTURAL PERSUASION
- SOLVING THE PROBLEM

Let's go step by step.

1. STRATEGIC PRECISION.

First, your Selling Idea must be "on Strategy."

Whether the Strategy is developed instinctively by an individual, or at great length by a committee, your idea should be perceived as an expression of that Strategy. So...

Before You Talk about the Idea, You Have to Talk about the Strategy.

It could be as simple as this...

"Basically our Strategy was to build awareness among teen-agers for your new clothing store."

Or it could be a full-blown presentation – a "Dog & Pony Show."

Strong Strategies Make for Strong Selling Ideas.

An idea that relates strongly to your strategy has the potential to be a strong Selling Idea.

Emphasize that strength.

And once you get the idea, and believe in it, that's the first thing you say to sell the idea.

It's a good idea because it's "on Strategy."

Of course, you'd better be prepared to tell people *why.*

Best of all, you'll be communicating that you understand the Strategy and believe it.

2. SAVVY PSYCHOLOGY.

As you talk to people, think about how *they* feel. Not how you feel. The principle of writing good advertising is the same as presenting good ideas – it's "receiver-driven."

Learn to involve others in your Selling Idea.

That's the next step to selling ideas.

Everyone wants to get with a winner – including your boss and your client.

It might be as simple as communicating that you have a winning idea. And, the earlier you start, the better.

Get others involved.

Invite early input from the AE and the Research Department. (Use it at your discretion.)

Look for information that bolsters your case.

As Leo says, *"Plan the sale as you write the ad."*

Look for ways to make your idea better.

Someone else may have a valuable addition to your idea – and may also become a valuable ally.

Pay particular attention to the psychology of the Target Consumer. The Target Consumer's question is "What's in it for me?"

In fact, that's *everybody's* question.

Understanding that question is solid psychology – show how your Selling Idea answers it.

WHAT IF YOUR IDEA ISN'T "ON STRATEGY?"

If your idea is *not* "on Strategy," you must either have a different idea, or... a different Strategy!

Do not ignore this risky second option. Here's why:

Some strategies look nice on paper, and sound nice in the meeting room, but when it comes time to execute them, they don't lead to strong executions.

For example, Federal Express could have had a strategy that emphasized the benefit of on-time delivery.

Yet, happy normal people receiving their packages on time may not be powerful persuasion (Emery tried this, with no great success).

So Federal Express *dramatized the problem!*

Suddenly, the executional stage opens up – memorable comedic dramas and characters develop into a powerful **resonant** campaign that every businessman can relate to.

Because every businessman has experienced the pressure of the deadline, when it *"absolutely positively has to be there overnight."*

STRONG STRATEGIES MAKE STRONG SELLING IDEAS.

If they're not coming, it may be you, or... it may be the Strategy.

If that's the case, look at the Strategy, look at the work, and try to figure out what's wrong.

Good luck.

ACCOUNT PLANNERS = CONSUMER PSYCHOLOGISTS.

Here's where Account Planning can really help.

A good Account Planner brings consumer insight into the equation when you need it most.

You can gain early insight into how the consumer feels about the category and how they'll react to the advertising.

Savvy Psychology in action!

"Selling is an art of passion. When you're passionate about an idea, it shows."
Tom McElligott

HELPFUL HINTS FOR BETTER PRESENTATIONS:
• **Psychological and Physical:**
  You should be confident, likable… and persuasive.
  Learn to tell a joke or a story. Have a few you know.
  Learn about "body language" and get comfortable.

• **Scripts, Outlines and Talking Points:**
  Outline your opening remarks.
  Write down your closing arguments.
  Rehearse answers to the toughest possible questions.
  Learn to work from notes. (I use a clipboard.)
  Talk about:
    Consumer Needs.
    Consumer Benefits.
    Product Benefits.
    The Strategy's Strength.

• **Overall:**
  Show that you know your stuff.
  Show that you care about the client's business.
  Show that you're the one who can solve tomorrow's problem.
  And finally…

• **Practice:**
  Practice reading copy aloud.
  Practice presenting the storyboard and the script.
  Practice might not make you perfect, but it will make you a better presenter.

Try to look at your Selling Idea from another person's point of view.

Remember, your idea has to meet *their* needs. Not yours. That's why you must learn to relate your idea to the needs of your audience.

Next, you must become accomplished at presenting your Selling Idea to others.

3. SLICK PRESENTATION.

A good presentation makes people *want* to do the ads. If you sell well, people see themselves.

Two team members are vital partners for success at this stage of the game – the Account Executive and the Art Director.

First, the Account Executive.

Remember, he or she wants to win, too.

Get together to rehearse or discuss your presentation, even on an informal basis.

It'll help you *both* get ready for the meeting.

Even if it's on a cocktail napkin on the flight to the client meeting, rehearse the meeting with the AE. Often, you can get the AE to make some of the key arguments on behalf of the Selling Idea.

But, these days, talk is not enough to carry the day. It's only one step – the rational / verbal.

You must address the emotional / visual part of your presentation. *Show Time!*

A Presentation Needs Great Art Direction.

That's why your other important partner is the Art Director. He'd better like the idea – and it should show – with great graphics, loving layouts, juicy comps, terrific key frames or storyboards, and maybe a few extras.

How about a big title card with the campaign Theme? Maybe a button for the sales force?

Your work should sell itself – **visually.**

How tight should layouts be?

Look at it this way. A good layout or storyboard, just like a good presentation, should make you *want* to do the ad.

172

It doesn't have to be tight –
but it must be enticing.

The Meeting is The Media –

That means you've got to get good at presenting your own work.

Like copywriting, it's a skilled craft.

4. STRUCTURAL PERSUASION.

You persuade by meeting other people's needs.

They won't do it for you, but they'll do it for themselves.

So let's talk about what you're going to talk about. Remember Bernbach...

"Persuasion is not a science, but an art."

Art has form. So does persuasion.

Your point of entry is critical.

This is the Beginning. This is Context.

It's *"tell 'em what you're going to tell 'em."*

In everything you communicate, whether it's the first sentence in your ad, or the opening thought in your presentation, you must be concerned with that vital first step.

Remember, in today's cluttered communications environment, you're competing for people's attention – even in a meeting.

The first impression is critical.

So, what *do* you say first?

Do you say, "Here's my great idea." Wrong!

Think about it…

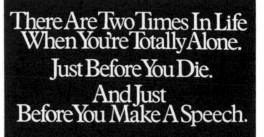

IT'S TRUE!

One of the main reasons most people don't present well is that most people are afraid to present.

It's natural.

Avoidance is natural, too.

You have to work on presenting even though you probably don't want to.

It's natural.

To cheer us up before a meeting, an Account Executive friend would pat someone on the shoulder, smile warmly, and say, "Remember… we're all in this alone."

At least he was honest.

Good Luck.

HERE ARE SOME OF THE THINGS I GO THROUGH.

I take notes – lots of 'em.

When other people talk, I make notes. It's helpful, and it's clear to everyone that I'm listening.

Just like Leo, I'm planning the meeting as well as the ad.

I usually start with a rough outline of the presentation with Titles and Subheads for each part of the Presentation sequence.

As it's coming together, I try to think about the toughest questions that will be asked and try to have answers ready.

I'm always looking for ways to strengthen the Selling Idea and the presentation using other's suggestions.

It makes the Selling Idea stronger and the Selling Team larger.

The more people who believe in the Selling Idea, the better the chance it will sell.

173

*W*hat *do* you say first?
  The first step is a lulu!
  The first step you take affects
every move you make.
  Attention and involvement.
  Resonance. Impact.
  Whatever it takes.
  Be careful.

Remember...
Even Clients have Clients.
Every client has a problem.
Your job is to help solve it.

**PRACTICE
THIS SEQUENCE:**

Start where people *are*.
Problems and Opportunities.
Objectives and Strategies.
Then... the Selling Idea.
Conclude with how it
Solves The Problem.

For example, when dealing with an opposing point of view, the first thing you might want to do is agree with that opposing point of view.

It can encourage those who might not agree with you to hear the other side of the story.

You might start with "Here's the problem."

Or, you might acknowledge other points of view before your own... whatever.

But whatever you do, have an idea of what you're doing and where you're going.

Help them move from where they are to where you want them to be. To do this, organization and sequence are essential.

That's why it's *vital* that you develop the habit of structured, organized thinking.

Don't forget the importance of the emotional/visual part of your presentation.

And remember, you only have one first chance.

5. SOLVE THE PROBLEM.

Clients have needs. And Clients have Clients.

Chances are, the Big-Shot you're presenting to works for an Even-Bigger-Shot who likes to ask tough questions about the advertising.

Make it easy for your Client to answer those tough questions.

You must give him answers as to how this Selling Idea and these ads *Solve The Problem.*

Every Client has a problem.

Hey, if he didn't, he wouldn't need you.

And that's the last helpful hint...

Solve the Client's Problem and You'll Sell the Selling Idea.

The more your Selling Idea can be seen to solve *their* Problem, the better the chance *your* Selling Idea will become *their* Selling Idea.

And that's how to sell ideas.

Now, we'll talk about doing it with STYLE.

174

Salesmanship = Strategy + Structure + *Style!*

Style is the final part of our Salesmanship formula. Some would say it's the most important.

How well you sell often depends on creating the right Selling Attitude.

It isn't just *what* you say, it's *how* you say it.

Successful salesmanship is more than well-structured facts and benefits.

It's Hopkins, *person-to-person.*

It's Bernbach and *the art of persuasion.*

It's Burnett and *inherent drama.*

Style is the personal dimension of the creative process.

Your charm, your wit, your warmth, your skill, your strength, your intelligence, and, most of all, your understanding, all play a part.

Salesmanship is also Showmanship.

Style.

```
┌────────────────────────────┐
│   OUR FAMOUS FORMULA       │
│   Discover the Objective   │
│   Develop the Strategy     │
│   Create a Selling Idea    │
│   Structure the Sale       │
│   And... finally           │
│   Do it with Style!        │
└────────────────────────────┘
```

Early McElligott.
One trait of Tom McElligott's early print is the use of old pictures with contemporary copy .

How to Write with Style.

You must talk person to person.

You must develop a short straightforward writing style.

You must talk *to* people, not at them.

These are the characteristics of good copywriting style.

How are they achieved?

Today's lesson is:

Readin'
Writin'
Rhythm 'n
Re-Writin'

Here's what we'll do:
First, **The 4 R's of Copywriting.**

Then, basic principles of modern copywriting style.

Then, we'll have some fun as we put those principles to work in print, radio, and TV.

WHAT IS STYLE?

It's whatever it takes to earn extra attention and deliver that extra dimension of persuasion.

Impact, Image, Involvement, Awareness, and all those other words we like to use in meetings depend on advertising that's special.

Because advertising must be more than well-structured information.

It must have enthusiasm, conviction, and artistry.

Here's a thought from Bill Bernbach:

"There are a lot of great technicians in advertising. And, unfortunately, they talk the best game.

They know all the rules.

They are the scientists of advertising. But there's one little rub.

Advertising is fundamentally **persuasion...** *and persuasion happens to be not a science, but an art."*

It's difficult to think things through to the point where Objective and Strategy are understood and the Structure of the Sale is clear.

Yet, you must do more.

Bill Bernbach had more to say:

"We're all concerned about the facts we get and not enough concerned about how **provocative** *we have made these facts to the consumer."*

Even Hopkins agrees: *"Try to give each advertiser a becoming style. To create the right individuality is a supreme accomplishment."*

Objective and Strategy.

Structure and Style.

Put them all together – that's Salesmanship.

And that's your job.

"Most great advertising is direct. That's how people talk. That's the style they read."

Jerry Della Femina

The Science of Hopkins. Take this easy test. Compare modern copywriting style to that of Claude Hopkins. Then, send for a **Free Offer!**

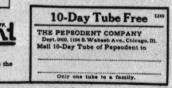

The New Writing.

As the world tuned into the tube, a new writing style emerged.

Post-television copywriting.

It's a style that evolved with the new world of information.

Today, we read, hear, and feel our way through a flow of information.

We inhale, skim, and absorb.

We take bites, bits, and chunks and then change the channel, turn the page, or just tune out 'til we see or hear something of interest.

We have evolved from readers to "viewers" even when we read.

We graze as we gaze.

Today, we're all more selective and demanding consumers of information.

It's casual and natural.

Channel changer in hand, we zip and zap as we interact with our information.

Contemporary copywriting must meet these new realities.

Literary traditions based on novels, short stories, essays, and other pre-electronic forms are being replaced by those based on news, song and the cadence of conversation.

Yet, most writing is still taught as a logical, literary, left-brained skill focused on the writer with an interested reader.

Copywriting is different.

In copywriting, the most important person is not the writer, but *the receiver.*

Are you with me? Good.

AN EDITORIAL.

In school, most writing assignments are exercises in grammar, vocabulary, and reading comprehension – done for the approval of a teacher.

In most cases, you're required to fill a certain number of pages – so brevity is penalized.

As a result, you've been taught to over-write!

Furthermore, you're probably carrying the writing baggage of years of overexposure to overwritten material.

In school, long words are preferred to short ones. Complex concepts win out over simple statements.

The lecturing language of education is preferred to the rhythm of conversation.

This verbal inflation has been encouraged by bureaucrats, lawyers, politicians, and the academic community.

Advertising communication must work in the real world.

Instead of marginally interested teachers, you must talk to totally uninterested consumers.

You don't have to demonstrate your broad vocabulary, flaunt your superior intellect, or get a good grade.

As Julian Koenig said, *"Your job is to reveal how good your product is, not how good you are."*

End of editorial.

The Art of Bernbach.
Visuals and words combine to create surprising impact.

Readin'.

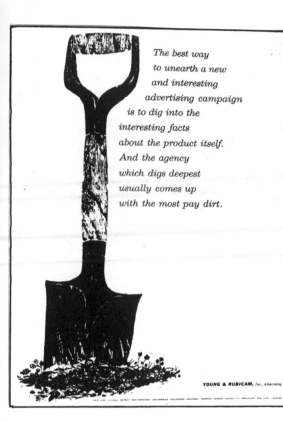

The best way to unearth a new and interesting advertising campaign is to dig into the interesting facts about the product itself. And the agency which digs deepest usually comes up with the most pay dirt.

YOUNG & RUBICAM, Inc., Advertising

Before you can write clearly about a subject, you must understand it.

It means assembling information.

Digging for facts – the Preparation stage of the creative process.

Much of the difficulty of not knowing what to say is rooted in not having anything to say.

This can be a difficult problem for a copywriter, particularly with so-called *parity* products, older products and other advertisers without much news.

It seems like it's all been said before.

Nonetheless, your copywriting must contain *substance.* Interest is maintained with content as well as style.

Credibility must be earned.

And that takes work.

Read all about it.

Take notes. Make lists.

Read memos, fact sheets, magazine articles, and anything else you can lay your hands on.

Involve yourself with the product.

Dig.

A TRUE STORY.

While still a copywriter, Dan Nichols, who became a top commercial director, sat down, dumped a box of cereal in the middle of his kitchen table, and counted the raisins!

That's how *"Two Scoops of Raisins in a box of Kellogg's Raisin Bran"* was born.

You won't find the answer staring into space, getting stoned, feeling alienated, insecure, or above it all.

You must get *into* the product and the people who use it. Dig.

ORGANIZATION, MAN.

Since the creation of ideas is based on new combinations of previously expressed ideas, the greater your resources, the greater your chances of achieving the best combination.

My own technique is to accumulate piles of notes, random scribblings, memos, magazine articles, competitve ads, and product literature.

I let my subconscious Incubate and Organize during this period. And I start as soon as possible. Because even though the due date may seem far off, these things can sort of sneak up on you.

When the pile is a certain size, or the deadline is approaching rapidly, I'm ready to write.

First, I try to organize the material in an orderly, rational way. This gives me a chance to review it again and see if some initial ideas still hold up.

Then, having dealt with the material to some degree in a right *and* left-brained way, I see where it takes me.

Over time, you'll find yourself working with an ever-growing data base, and you'll also find that experience will help you arrive at your destination faster with fewer clues.

FOR MORE INFORMATION.

For complex projects, some people recommend the use of note cards.

I generally use an outline, which I continually revise and update. A word-processing computer makes this relatively easy.

If there are still gaps, I try to fill them in.

Do not neglect the accumulation of *visual* information, either.

Art shows, galleries, a wide range of magazines, movies, and television should also be on your "reading list."

Finally, learn to read people.

It's life on The Learning Curve.

"*Good* writers come in all sizes, shapes, and ages.

What they all seem to have in common is the ability to hear, to listen, to understand – and to distill what they hear and learn into something that's human and persuasive."

Jay Chiat

"*In* art, the only thing you can teach is the mechanics.

When it comes to creativity, that you do by trial and error, by exposing yourself to different things.

I think also you must have the kind of sponge that absorbs."

Paul Rand

GOOD ADVICE.

In "A Technique for Producing Ideas," James Webb Young recommends two types of reading:

1. General Reading.

To expand the range of experience critical in idea producing.

2. Specific Reading.

Related to the products, people and problems at hand.

**HOW TO BUILD
A VOCABULARY
FOR YOUR PRODUCT:**
1. Find Your Verb.
2. Add Adjectives.
3. Pick Up the Pieces.
4. Organize Your Thinking.

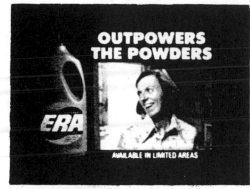

Find Your Verb!
*This verb helped us position a
new liquid detergent against
powdered detergents.*

A Fresh New Verb *brings new
energy to a familiar product.*

Activate the Benefit.
*"Turn up the Volume" adds
energy to Agree's Conditioning
Benefit.*

Writin'.

The next step to quality copywriting is to build
a working vocabulary for your product:
- Nouns, verbs and adjectives
- Slang and jargon
- Interesting ideas
- Facts and figures
- And figures of speech

These are the building blocks for your copy
blocks.

Much of this material will originate in your
notes and the process of reading about your product and working on your Strategy.

Use a Thesaurus if necessary, but you should
try to avoid obscure words.

Your language should be easy to understand.
Here's what you should look for:

1. FIND YOUR VERB!

Your job is to *move* people.

The first things you should look for are **verbs**
associated with your subject.

Verbs *activate* your writing – they are key to
successful persuasion.

Many successful campaigns are based on active
verbal constructions:

"We Try Harder"
"Fly the Friendly Skies"
"Play it Kool"
"Give a Damn"

Can you think of a few?

VERBS *ACTIVATE* YOUR ADS!

Write in the *active* voice. Jump. Fly. Do whatever you want. Don't just sit there. Act now!

Off-the-road

The proliferation of flying cars in *Newsweek* concerns me. Air traffic controllers don't deserve the added stress.

First the April 1 issue, with ads from Mitsubishi, Hertz and Volkswagen.

Then the VW ad runs again in the April 8 issue, along with one from Volvo.

Dr. Jung may have been right about a collective unconscious.

Jay W. Hillis
President, Uplifting Ideas
Seattle

Reprinted from <u>Advertising Age.</u>

2. ADD ADJECTIVES.

Be selective.

Advertising adjectives should be like Baby Bear's porridge. . . "Just right."

They should clarify, inform, and intensify.

They should resonate with the Target.

They should relate to the Strategy.

After adding up all the adjectives that meet your objectives, ask one question.

Is there one adjective strong enough to build a campaign on?

It may be the only one you need.

An Absolutely True Story.

*The original line for Federal Express was **"When it has to be there overnight."***

As Director Joe Sedelmeier was casting the commercial, one actor did a marvelous job with

"Absolutely. Positively."

The agency realized this added extra drama and intensity to the need for Federal Express, and extra memorabilty to their theme.

*This adjective adds **attitude**.*

This adjective intensifies.

Adjective as Headline.

These handsome ads for Centurion bikes communicate their three lines of bikes quickly and charmingly.

This tactic is affordable in Biking specialty magazines for a powerful cumulative effect.

The Product As Adjective.

Many product names are based on adjectives – it's a good Name Awareness device.

This series from Absolut Vodka is an award-winning example.

But be sure that you don't jeopardize your brand name. It makes lawyers absolutely crazy.

ABSOLUT HARING.

ABSOLUT PERFECTION.

ABSOLUT GENEROSITY.

ABSOLUT WARHOL.

Are you using the right car for your gasoline?

The Civic CRX HF — Honda

Folds flat for easy storage.

The Civic Wagon — Honda

3. PICK UP THE PIECES!

Find unique combinations of words and ideas that relate to your product, your product category, and the Strategy.

Pick 'em up and jot 'em down.

Assemble things like:

- **familiar phrases**
- **cliches and puns**
- **endorsements**
- **and "reasons why."**

Build your arsenal.

It's a jungle out there.

Double Feature.
From Honda.
"Are you using the right car for your gasoline?" *features a* **Verbal Double** *which takes a familiar phrase and turns it around to add double-meaning.*
The ***"Folds flat for easy storage"*** *ad features a* **Visual Double** *where the double-meaning works off the visual.*

Storehouse Small Space.
The writer of these storehouse™ ads uses familiar phrases and easy puns to add extra style. Each phrase ties into a Selling Feature of the featured product.

HOT OFF THE PRESS

Here's the latest in high-pressure laminate designs. Our collection includes lots more than you see here. All our laminated furniture is custom-made. And you can choose among 30 distinctive finishes and colors. So come in and let's laminate!

storehouse

SOCIAL BUTTERFLIES

Relax and enjoy a classic butterfly chair. It's comfortable indoors or out, and comes in a dozen happy colors. Canvas covers and wrought iron frames also available separately. Come in and start your collection.

storehouse

LIGHT SWITCH

Now it's as easy to change the color of your shade as it is to change a light bulb. Baked enamel shade comes in 5 colors and 3 sizes to use as a swag lamp or with our sleek floor and table lamp bases. Possibilities are endless! Come see the lights.

storehouse

PEPPERMINT PATIO

Fresh from Denmark. Broad stripes on bright chairs. A brilliant umbrella for table or beach. Club chairs fold for portable comfort. Red-and-white or blue-and-white on white lacquer. It's lots of color. Not lots of cash.

storehouse

184

4. ORGANIZE YOUR THINKING.

Now you're ready to write. Finally.

You have many of the pieces of the puzzle.

Now you have to put them together. Take a short break. Think.

Utilize the Incubation stage of the creative process.

Think about the path you must travel...

Take your time.

Focus past initial concerns... like what headline to write... or when your assignment is due.

Think of the target with your arrow in the center. Now, describe your destination.

Think of Themes.

And Variations.

Start writing.

TENDER LOVING FARE

Whoever said, "...'tis love that makes the world go round," was probably eating chicken soup at the time.

In particular, Campbell's® Chicken Noodle Soup.

We've got history on our side. It's what mothers traditionally served when someone needed good old-fashioned comforting.

And mother really did know best.

That's because it's just about impossible to find a more soothing food than Campbell's Chicken Noodle Soup. Or a more satisfying food. Or a food that simply makes you feel better.

So when you need some tender loving fare, and sometimes we all do, treat yourself to a hot, delicious bowl of Campbell's Chicken Noodle Soup.

Chicken Noodle Soup. Three little words that say something about love.

Campbell's has a full line of low sodium soups for those people who are on a salt-restricted diet or have a concern about sodium.

A Familiar Phrase.
You don't associate this phrase with a bowl of Tomato Soup. The surprising combination creates an interesting ad.

Re-Phrase Familiar Phrases.
The gentle pun, replacing "Fare" with "Care," is a natural extension of Campbell's "Soup is Good Food" Campaign.

In the lower ad, the inversion created by adding "Not" to a variation of this familiar phrase adds new interest and Attention.

HEALTH INSURANCE

One of the best ways to insure good health, is to eat a well-balanced diet that includes nutritious foods like Campbell's Soup.

That's not just our opinion. The fact is university researchers found that soup plays a significant part in a nutritionally healthy diet.

That Campbell's Tomato Soup up there, for instance, is an important source of vitamin C. While Campbell's Vegetable Beef contains more than 1/3 of the day's allowance of vitamin A in just a single serving.

And not only are most Campbell's Soups a rich source of nutrition, they're also light on your stomach, and easy to digest.

So when you're picking out a good health insurance policy, remember to pick up a few cans of your favorite Campbell's Soups.

If you have any questions, talk to one of the best insurance agents around. Mom.

CAMPBELL'S SOUP IS GOOD FOOD

ALL CALORIES ARE NOT CREATED EQUAL

Most of us think of calories as being all bad. They're not. You need the energy they provide.

However, some foods provide more nutrients with their calories, than others and work harder for you nutritionally.

In other words, some foods have more nutrients per calorie than others.

And soup is one of those foods.

SOUPED-UP CALORIES

Most Campbell's Soups are dense in nutrients, so you get a higher level of nutrition with fewer calories than you get from many other foods.

MORE NUTRIENTS IN SOUP CALORIES

Because of their nutritionally hard-working calories, many Campbell's Soups are more nutritious than other good foods. Calorie for calorie, Campbell's Tomato Soup has more Vitamin C than carrots or apricots.

And soup is one of these foods.

Campbell's Vegetable Soups are excellent sources of Vitamin A. Campbell's Minestrone, for instance, has more Vitamin A per calorie than eggs.

And some Campbell's Soups supply other recognized, but less well-known nutrients called "trace elements" which the body needs in small but essential amounts to function properly.

So get the benefit of the hard-working calories in Campbell's Soups, with an added dividend. The calories in Campbell's Soups taste great!

SOUP IS GOOD FOOD

Theme &

A good Theme will usually make a good outdooor board.

A good Theme will usually work with a variety of visuals.

Most great advertising campaigns have a great theme – a strong set of words that give your campaign a "War Cry."

An advertising theme, whether it's a campaign line or a headline, will focus on the one thought you want your Target to remember.

And, for that reason, it should be *memorable*. It should have that certain something which makes it stick in the mind.

By this time, you will have given the subject considerable thought.

You've probably written a few early theme lines and headlines and copy lines.

Sometimes it's hard to know which is which. Write it all down. . . everything.

Because the more you write, the better the chance you'll be right.

Imagine the destination.

Let the Strategy give your thoughts direction and the Objective give you focus.

Send your thoughts to the words that describe the Benefit. Or the Problem.

Again, how do you get their Attention and what do you want them to remember?

And, of all the things you've written, which of them is the right thing?

You may write two dozen theme or headline ideas (or more), yet you must end up with one.

How do you reach that goal?

How will you know you're right?

First, **it'll make sense.**

Second, **it'll feel right.**

Third, **someone else will like it.**

Fourth, **it will inspire more great ads.**

Let's try some Variations on your Theme.

Variations.

Take your Theme, your destination, as your new starting point.

If you've prepared, there should be a natural flow of **Variations**.

Look for **Structural Relationships** that make for strong communication.

Write 'em down, you may need 'em later when you present your idea.

Let your thinking flow. Go with it.

Write various variations on your ideas.

Try different possibilities.

See where they lead.

Turn them inside out and upside down.

Play with the ideas. Have fun. Be prolific.

Get it all on paper.

It won't be all good, but at this stage, it's more important to just write it all down.

This is one of the most enjoyable parts of our business. . . enjoy it.

Respect your first idea, but don't fall in love with it right away.

Write Down Everything You Can Think Of!

See what generates additional thoughts.

Write 'em down.

If you have time, sleep on it.

Utilize the right-brain Incubation process.

When you're done, sort it out and take a look at what you've written.

When you're through, certain phrases and constructions will emerge.

Some things will work better than others.

And, without seeing a single sentence, I'll tell you the one single trait that will distinguish your best writing… Rhythm.

THE NATURAL WAY TO WRITE.

One of the most interesting approaches to writing is explored in **"Writing the Natural Way"** by Gabriele Lusser Rico (©1983 Houghton Mifflin).

In her book, she shows you how to tap into the associative connections you have in both sides of your brain.

She discusses a technique called **"Clustering,"** a non-linear brain-storming process that you can do on a sheet of paper. It looks like this...

Instead of an outline, you start with "Clusters" of words and concepts that form chains and patterns of meaning.

She also helps you focus on **"cadence,"** the natural rhythm of words to **"attune the inner ear of your design mind."**

A fascinating book.

Highly recommended.

HOW DO YOU KNOW YOU'RE RIGHT?

First, it'll make sense.

Second, it'll feel right.

Third, someone else will like it.

Fourth, it will inspire more great ad ideas.

Rhythm.

GOOD COPY'S GOT RHYTHM.
1. Short, Simple Sentences.
2. Active Verbs and a Positive Attitude.
3. Parallel Construction.
4. Alliteration, Assonance, and Rhyme.
5. Puns, Double-Meanings and Word Play.

All good copy's got rhythm.

As a copywriter, your writing must *move* people – and much of it depends on the rhythm of your writing.

You should look for:

1. SHORT, SIMPLE SENTENCES.

Good copy gets to the point.

One idea follows another, maintaining the reader's interest.

Not only does this force your copy to be easy to understand, it creates a tempo.

Movement. Cadence.

As Leo said,

"Great advertising writing, either in print or TV, is always deceptively and disarmingly simple. It has the common touch without being or sounding patronizing."

As Winston Churchill said,

"Little words move men."

Or, as Ed McCabe said,

"Show me something great and I'll show you a bunch of monosyllables."

One. Two. Three.
Punch. Punch. Punch.
Easy to read and easy to understand.

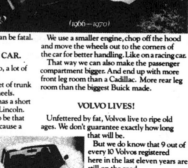

Ed McCabe's Macho Style.
  Tough as a Volvo.
  Hard-hitting and to the point.
    "You can't eat atmosphere."
    "It takes a tough man to make a tender chicken."

2. ACTIVE VERBS AND A POSITIVE ATTITUDE.

Good copy should be written in the active voice. It should *move*.

In most cases, you should write in a positive, assertive manner.

You should present a *positive* attitude about your product.

Every sentence with a passive verb should be examined critically.

So should every sentence that contains a negative.

In "comparison advertising" and certain types of positioning, it's occasionally necessary to be negative.

But be careful.

Remember, Avis said,
"We Try Harder."
It wasn't, "We're not #1."

Even negatives can be positive.
The upbeat rhythm of the copy generates a positive feeling – even with the negative words.

In Fredericksburg you can sleep in a bed that's right out of the 18th or 19th century. You'll awaken to a delicious breakfast (go ahead and cheat on your diet—we won't tell). And you can spend the day looking for bargains in the more than 70 antique shops in our renowned historic district. Now wouldn't it be a crime to miss out on all of that?

For more information about our bed & breakfast selections or other get-away packages, call or write the Fredericksburg Visitor Center.

Fredericksburg, Virginia
706 Caroline Street, Box SP3, Fredericksburg, VA 22401. Phone 1-800-67VISIT.

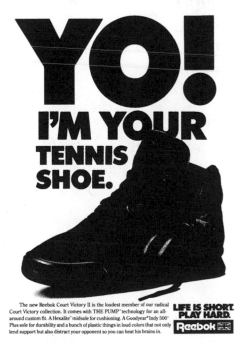

The new Reebok Court Victory II is the loudest member of our radical Court Victory collection. It comes with THE PUMP™ technology for an all-around custom fit. A Hexalite™ midsole for cushioning. A Goodyear® Indy 500® Plus sole for durability and a bunch of plastic things in loud colors that not only lend support but also distract your opponent so you can beat his brains in.

LIFE IS SHORT. PLAY HARD. Reebok

An upbeat attitude can help make products more desireable.
You just know you're going to have fun in these nifty new shoes from Reebok.

A Good Slogan Should Make a Good Button.

189

*"Make it simple
Make it memorable.
Make it inviting to look at.
Make it fun to read."*

Leo Burnett

3. PARALLEL CONSTRUCTION.

Good copy is well built.

Your sentence structure should be consistent.

Your phrasing should be consistent.

Verbs should generally be in the same tense.

Pronouns should be kept under control.

Is it first person plural (we), second person (you), or third (he, she, they)?

Be consistent.

Consistency creates clarity.

The structure of your thinking will be reinforced by the strength of structured writing. And the memorability of your phrases will increase.

Here are some examples:

*"Better Things
for Better Living."*

*"The Quality Goes in
Before the Name Goes On."*

*"It's a Good Time
for the Great Taste."*

*"What You Want
is What You Get."*

Many memorable sentences and many memorable ads make use of parallel construction.

So should you.

"I don't know who you are.

I don't know your company.

I don't know your company's product.

I don't know what your company stands for.

I don't know your company's customers.

I don't know your company's record.

I don't know your company's reputation.

Now—what was it you wanted to sell me?"

MORAL: Sales start **before** your salesman calls—with business publication advertising.

McGRAW-HILL MAGAZINES
BUSINESS • PROFESSIONAL • TECHNICAL

*Note how
parallel construction
makes this ad
work harder.*

190

191

Alliteration makes the words "march."

4. ALLITERATION, ASSONANCE AND RHYME.

Good copy sounds good.

You should make use of the phonic characteristics of the words you use.

Alliteration – is the similarity of the first letter or sound of words, usually consonants.

For example, *"Let it be Lowenbrau"* used a rhythmic double alliteration of the "L" and the "b" in "Lowenbrau."

This creates a distinctive theme which could be used by no other beer.

Assonance – is subtler. It relates to the internal similarity of words, usually vowels. *"Invest in Karastan,"* has both assonance *and* alliteration.

Do you see which is which?

Rhyme.

Finally, rhyme has its reason.

A rhyme is memorable.

The early epics of civilization were poems for a very simple reason – they were easier to remember.

Back then, it was an oral tradition – poems could be passed along and re-membered in a way prose could not.

For this same reason, a well-turned rhyme can nail your message in people's memories.

From *"Winston tastes good like a cigarette should."*

To *"Plop Plop Fizz Fizz Oh What a Relief It Is!"*

The power of the poem is proven. And it keeps your copy movin'.

*This looks like a **Rhyme**, though the sounds are different. Emphasis on the "ier" focuses on Napier's superiority.*

Sail By Mail.

In our new brochure, you can sample nine different cruises without leaving home.

Bermuda. Nassau. Mexico. South America. And, of course, the whole wide Caribbean.

For seven days, or eight, or ten, or even fourteen.

Just send us the coupon. Or see your travel agent. And plan a vacation that can give you something to write home about.

Royal Caribbean
Ships of Norwegian Registry.

Song of America · Sun Viking
Song of Norway · Nordic Prince

Name

Address

City   State   Zip

For your free copy of Royal Caribbean's new cruise vacation brochure, see your travel agent.
Or send this coupon to Royal Caribbean Cruise Line, P.O. Box 012864, Miami, FL 33101.

RHYME TIME

"*Rhyming forces recognition of words. You also establish a rhythm and that tends to make kids want to go on. If you break the rhythm a child feels unfulfilled.*"

Dr. Seuss

Tide with Bleach

Knocks your socks off.

Skinless. Boneless. Quarter Less.

Save a quarter on Hormel Chunk Pink Salmon.
Big chunks of skinless and boneless salmon packed fresh in Alaska.
Ready to use in your favorite recipes.

MANUFACTURER'S COUPON | NO EXPIRATION DATE

25¢ Off Hormel Chunk Pink Salmon
The Casual Cuisine.

203832

© 1987 Geo. A. Hormel and Co.

JEEPERS CREEPERS, WHERE'D YOU GET YOUR BEEPERS?

Flopcorn vs. Popcorn

Drippy is dippy.

SEN-SEN CONFECTION

5¢

BREATH TAKING REFRESHMENT

Dandy Candy Keep It Handy

Reg. Trade Marks

5. PUNS, DOUBLE-MEANINGS AND WORD PLAY.

Good copy is clever. Sometimes.

When these devices work, they can make your copy richer and more interesting.

And they're fun to write.

But, BEWARE!

When they don't work, they're confusing.

Worse yet, they provide the reader with an excuse to not take you seriously.

This danger is increased by the fact that while puns are fun, and double-meanings twice as interesting as regular writing, every one we write will not be worth keeping.

Don't be clever at the expense of clarity.

The pun is *not* the lowest form of humor.

The lowest form of humor is a smart-ass ad that wastes the client's money.

Write as much clever copy as you can. (You will anyway.)

Just don't use all of it.

Double and Triple Meanings add extra power to this 60's ad for an "Anti-Machine" candidate.

Outdoor is a great place

for a play on words.

Most people see it more than once.

New Deal on Canadian Club.
Today only. Limit one per customer.
East Hennepin at University Avenue.

With today's old price on Blatz, we expect to be mobbed.
Today only. Limit one per customer.
East Hennepin at University Avenue.

Good Price For A Change.

Getting your oil changed doesn't have to drain your pocket. Just $9.95 will get you fresh oil and a new filter at Hall's new service department, now until November 30th.
So if you're ready for a change, come to Hall. We're spilling over with new service specials.

Oil & Filter Change Special $9.95.

Includes 5 quarts of oil and a filter change
Offer good with this coupon until November 30th, 1983

Hall Service/Parts
Pontiac/GMC • Honda • AMC • Jeep • Renault

We're Big On Service.
Virginia Beach Blvd., west of the Lynnhaven exit 486-3000

The copywriter and Art Director took the same old story-PRICE-and made it nice.

There's nothing sadder than a washed-up jock.

That's why the guys who wear jocks and the guys who buy them prefer Bike jocks. Because Bike makes deluxe jocks for serious athletes. The best combination of comfort, support and durability.
We've spent years researching the materials that go into Bike jocks to find the best feel in the material that will hold up under the toughest conditions. Like the highest quality heat-resistant rubber to hold its

shape time after time in the roughest washing machines and dryers. And special combinations of double-weave rayon and cotton and nylon-reinforced porous knit, so they dry quicker, keep their support longer, and keep that great feel from the minute you take them out of the box.
The Bike 10 and Pro 10. They outperform other jocks. That's what makes them superjocks; that's what makes them Bike jocks.

BIKE

Solid Strategy with Supporter.

Visual puns, using old art give this retailer a distinct and inviting personality.

195

Puns, Double-Meanings, and Word Play.
When they work, they speak for themselves.

The Double. Double Meaning is achieved
by reversing one aspect of a common cliché...
A negative becomes a positive in an intense and startling way.

Ugly is only skin-deep.

It may not be much to look at. But beneath that humble exterior beats an air-cooled engine. It won't boil over and ruin your piston rings. It won't freeze over and ruin your life. It's in the back of the car for better traction in snow and sand. And it will give you about 29 miles to a gallon of gas.

After a while you get to like so much about the VW, you even get to like what it looks like.

You find that there's enough legroom for almost anybody's legs. Enough headroom for almost anybody's head. With a hat on it. Snug-fitting bucket seats. Doors that close so well you can hardly close them. (They're so airtight, it's better to open the window a crack first.)

Those plain, unglamorous wheels are each suspended independently. So when a bump makes one wheel bounce, the bounce doesn't make the other wheel bump. It's things like that you pay the $1585* for, when you buy a VW. The ugliness doesn't add a thing to the cost of the car. That's the beauty of it.

©Volkswagen of America, Inc. *Suggested Retail Price, East Coast P.O.E., Local Taxes and Other Dealer Delivery Charges, if Any, Additional.

197

TWO OUT OF THREE AIN'T BAD.

SAM SCALI
Inducted into the Art Director's
Hall of Fame, 1984

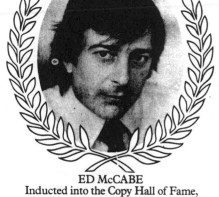

ED McCABE
Inducted into the Copy Hall of Fame,
1974

MARVIN SLOVES

All of us at Scali, McCabe, Sloves would like to congratulate Sam Scali on his induction into the Art Director's Hall of Fame.

We're very proud.

We're also proud of the fact that Sam is not alone. He joins his partner, Ed McCabe, who entered the Copy Hall of Fame in 1974.

And that makes Scali, McCabe, Sloves something very rare indeed: an advertising agency with two founding partners in the Hall of Fame.

Both of these men are advertising legends for good reason. Together, they have created some of the most renowned advertising of all time.

If you're interested in talking to a great art director or a great copywriter about your advertising, Sam and Ed aren't hard to find. They still come to work every day.

Or, if you'd like to talk to the person who does most of the talking for Sam and Ed, call Marvin.

There is, unfortunately, no such thing as a Management Hall of Fame.

But Marvin Sloves is a great reason for creating one.

SCALI, McCABE, SLOVES, INC.

800 Third Avenue, New York, N.Y. 10022 (212) 421-2050 Offices in: Houston, Melbourne, Montreal, Toronto, London, Düsseldorf, Mexico City

© 1984, Scali, McCabe, Sloves, Inc.

6. GOOD COPY VS. GOOD GRAMMAR.

In general, good copy is good English.

Copywriters are allowed **three exceptions** to the general rules of good grammar:

1. Sentence Fragments.

For effect and brevity, sentence fragments can often make copy better.

And clearer.

Overuse will create a choppy effect.

Like this.

But judicious use of the sentence fragment can strengthen and shorten your copy with no loss of communication.

2. Beginning a Sentence with a Conjunction.

Because we often write one-sentence paragraphs.

And because we often have more than one thing to say.

Or for some other reason. . .

The use of conjunctions or connectors at the beginning of sentences is acceptable.

But don't overdo it.

3. Ungrammatical Usage.

As Will Rogers said. . .

"A lot of people who don't say ain't ain't eatin."

When used for effect, slang or bad grammar is permissible.

English is a wonderfully flexible language.

New words and usages emerge constantly.

Contemporary advertising copy should reflect contemporary usage, realizing that copy targeted at teen-agers might not please high-school English teachers.

But this should be done with care.

As writers, we have a responsibility to treat our language with respect.

After all, we make our living with it.

NOW WHAT?
After you've done all that, what do you do?
You do it again. . .
That's **Re-Writin'**.

& Re-Writin'.

How do you re-write right?

Chances are, you have little experience with the degree of disciplined editing and re-writing commonly practiced by good copywriters.

But a few new habits can help get you started becoming a tighter re-writer.

THE MORE THE BETTER.

Tom McElligott's been known to write 200 headlines before getting the one he likes.

How many did you write?

Have you looked at them with a critical eye?

And, then, did you write a few more?

Now, look at the **Structure** of your writing.

Look at your opening section. **The Beginning**.

Most openings are overwritten. (After all, you were just getting warmed up when you wrote it.)

You must condense and distill.

You must be immediately interesting, involving, and informative. *Immediately!* Not eventually.

Get the most meaning into the fewest words.

Create a rhythm and try to hold to it.

As you move toward **The Middle**, think about your Strategy.

Which sentences and phrases deliver the Support most clearly and persuasively?

Build on these thoughts.

The End of your ad should wrap the package beautifully. With a ribbon.

It should meet your Objective strongly, memorably, dramatically, and… with Style.
Reward the Reader.

Put the cherry on the sundae.

Ask for the Order.

Tell 'em what you told 'em.

A skillful wrap up will reinforce the rightness of your writing. And your re-writing.

Q. How many copywriters does it take to change a lightbulb?

A. I'm not changing it!

200

REQUIRED READING:
The Elements of Style.
Strunk & White.

So far, so good. You've been tough, but fair.

And you've cut your copy.

Congratulations.

Well, it's not enough to be tough.

You gotta be brutal.

Next, you might wish to review the rules represented in ***The Elements of Style.***

The Table of Contents provides a handy check list and guide.

Pay particular attention to the sections on Style and Composition.

These rules should become either memorized or instinctive. (Why not take a look at them right now… we'll wait.)

VISUALIZE YOUR COPY.

Another new habit you need to develop is **visualizing** your printed copy.

Not typing on a page, but type in an ad.

As you write body copy, you should begin to have an idea of how your finished copy should look.

CHARACTER COUNT.

As you develop the layout, work with the Art Director to generate a rough **character count.** Here's how:

First, select the desired *type size.*

Type size is measured in "points."

This book is in 16.5 point type.

This is 14 point. This is 12 point. This is 9 point.

Next, look at the layout.

Count the average number of letters on an average line and the number of lines.

A little bit of mathematics and you've got your character count.

Set your typewriter or word-processing program to the number of characters in each line and you'll start to see how your copy will fit.

If your computer will let you put the actual point-size on your screen… better yet.

& Re-Writin'…

It's possible to write excellent advertising copy to almost any length. Long or short.

Most beginning writers over-write.

That's why this next habit is so important.

FORGET WHO WROTE IT.

If you're going to become a good re-writer… **forget who wrote it!!!**

You must become as objective as possible about your own work.

Failure to do this is the downfall of many talented copywriters.

Even though you wrote every one of those wonderful words, that doesn't mean someone else wants to read them all.

Even though it was tough to write it the first time, that doesn't mean you can't make it better the second time. Or the third.

And even though you love to write, that doesn't mean you are obliged to fall in love with every word. Cut 'em.

Someone has to cut the copy. Let it be you.

COPYWRITERS WHO MAKE THE CUT KNOW HOW TO CUT COPY.

Here's a thought from Bill Bernbach:

"*You must have inventiveness, but it must be **disciplined**. Everything you write, everything on a page, every word, every graphic symbol, every shadow, should further the message you're trying to convey.*"

He's right. Re-write.

As a final bit of cruelty, take a look at the part of your copy you like best, the part you really didn't want to cut.

It's probably a piece of "business" or **"schtick*"** used for extra entertainment, extra interest or extra attention.

---

*

In the 60's, the Yiddish vaudeville term **"schtick"** was commonly used by copywriters. (Groucho Marx's cigar and eyebrow wiggle were his own "schtick.")

In advertising, "schtick" refers to a wide range of devices, both good and bad.

202

Your piece of "business" may be:

- A joke in the headline that's woven in and out of the body copy of a print ad.
- A joke in a TV commercial that is set up at the front and paid off at the back.**
- A running gag in a vignette sequence.
- Humorous background action in a TV commercial.
- A clever turn of phrase.
- Etcetera.

Remember, the objective of your ad's "business" is to help your client's business.

Do not lose sight of this fact.

The talented people at DDB agree:

*"Creativity that doesn't reinforce the proposition in an ad or commercial isn't creative, it's **disruptive.**"*

Take a look at your ad one more time.

Is it as strong and persuasive as you can make it?

How will it help your client's business?

You must ask yourself these questions now, for someone else will surely ask them later.

If you can answer these questions satisfactorily, you're in business.

Though taste and writing habits may vary, these are the underlying principles of good copywriting style: *Readin', Writin', Rhythm, 'n **Re-Writin'**.*

Review your work and your work habits.

Keep doing it until the process is a natural part of your approach.

Learn to cut your copy!

Be your own toughest critic.

Shorter *is* better.

Less verbal and more *visual.*

And, in conclusion…

write tight.

RE-WRITIN' EXERCISES:

Practice makes perfect.

And writing is work.

It's good work, but it's work nonetheless.

If you plan on writing for a living, that simply means you must work on your writing… for as long as you write.

That also means you should learn to treat it as an enjoyable task.

So… have fun.

Here are some things you can do to help improve your skills (in addition to re-writing everything you write one more time).

1. Read *Writing the Natural Way.*

It's a fresh new way to develop a fresh approach to writing.

2. Read *The Elements of Style.*

This is still the definitive book on writing style.

If you've read it, read it again.

3. Re-Read this Section.

It's a short section, but don't confuse lack of length with lack of content.

There are a number of principles here that should become your own.

Start by reading this section again, and memorizing the catch phrases.

You might even want to take a red pencil and see if you can tighten it further.

** The final clever line at the end was also sometimes known as the **"clitchik."**

14. Typing & Typography.

To improve your print writing, widen the margins and narrow the measure on your typewriter.

Or the margins on your computer's word-processing program.

Too many copywriters type with narrow margins and wide lines.

This is fine for letters, novels and term papers.

But it's a _terrible_ way to write advertising copy.

A column of advertising copy is usually 30 to 50 characters wide.

(40 is a good place to start.)

You will also notice that many of your sentences are broken up in the middle of important phrases.

As you rewrite your copy, _adjust_ the words and phrases so that copy "breaks" naturally.

If possible, "lines should be broken the way they are spoken."

If the layout is in process, your art director can give you an estimated character count.

To create readable copy, you must understand how your copy relates to the page.

And you must work to help your art director achieve his objectives as well as your own.

Typography is the joint responsibility of the writer and the art director.

It's a team sport, remember?

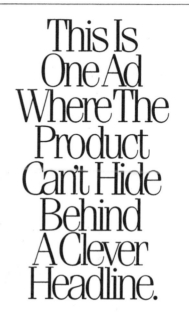
Exercises:

1. RESET THE MEASURE ON YOUR TYPEWRITER (OR COMPUTER) TO BETWEEN 30 AND 50 CHARACTERS.

2. READ A TYPE BOOK.

3. PICK UP A MAGAZINE YOU CAN SPARE.
TEAR IT APART.
PICK THE TYPOGRAPHY YOU LIKE BEST.
PICK THE ADS THAT ARE EASIEST TO READ.
PICK THE MOST INTERESTING.
PICK THE THREE WORST, TYPOGRAPHICALLY.

4. PREPARE A BRIEF PRESENTATION ON THE TYPOGRAPHY YOU LIKE BEST.

                    Sample Print Format.
Job Description Here: (Sometimes,
Client Name   the info goes
"Title Optional"   on this side.)

VISUAL: (Visual Idea Indicated Briefly)

HEAD: Headline Goes Here.

SUBHEAD: Subhead, if any, is indicated.
(or, SUB)   A subhead before the headline may
             be called a PRE-HEAD (or "EyeBrow").

COPY: Write your copy with a rough
             approximation of the column width.
                Use a second TAB to indent your
             paragraphs.
                I usually set the first TAB after the
             longest indicator on the left.
                Some people use Margin Release to
             set the left hand headings, and then
             use the first TAB for indentations.
                Get it?

SUB: If You Have Additional Subheads,
             Add Spacing Between Sections.

COPY: Then, add another line of space
             when you go back to the copy.
             Most typewriters don't have *italic*
             or **boldface.** <u>Underline.</u>
                Then, be sure to indicate the proper
             type "color" on the copy before it goes
             to the type house.
                Write tight.
                Because…

THEME: Good Copy Looks Good.

206

Sample Radio Format.

Client Name
"Commercial Title"
Commercial Length: 60"
Version/Date (optional)

ANNCR: Writing radio's quite simple really.
            Just remember to indicate who's talking on the left.
            I'm the Announcer, but you can call me "ANNCR."

SFX: DOOR OPENS/FOOT STEPS

MAN I: Hey, just dropped in to remind you...

ANNCR: Of what?

MAN I: ... that in radio, people interrupt each other a lot.

ANNCR: Really? Hadn't noticed.

MAN I: Maybe if you wore your headphones once in a while...
            (MISC. NOISE IN BACKGROUND) okay, cue the jingle.

MUSIC: MUSIC UP

VOCAL: Radio! Radio!
            Listen to the Radio!
            (MUSIC UNDER)

ANNCR: That's right, listen to the radio...

MAN I: And be sure to read your script at a nice pace.

ANNCR: Naturally.

MAN I: (TALKS FAST) Not so fast that you have to
            rush and sound like you're late for something...

ANNCR: Naturally.

MAN I: (SLOWLY) And not so slow that... hey, could we have
            some more music?

ANNCR: Certainly.

VOCAL: Your words are going to glisten
            Every time you listen
            to the R-A-D-I-O!

SFX: APPLAUSE/WHISTLES

LOCAL   (5")

ANNCR: Write it right and the next radio commercial you
            hear may be yours. Void where prohibited.

MUSIC BUTTON

We hope you're ready to write.

There are a lot of opportunities coming up in this section – to put our principles to work – in print.

Print Principles.

Many complain about the lack of skilled print copywriters in our electronic media age.

Yet, print is the easiest medium to master.

It's relatively simple to produce.

There's a lot of it that needs doing.

And, it holds still.

Many books focus on various types of print *headlines*, such as types of appeals.

This book focuses on types of print *ads*.

Headlines can vary, but the underlying structure of print ads has remained fairly constant.

As far as this book is concerned, there are *six basic types* of print ads:

1. THE ONE LINER.
2. NEWS (INCLUDING "DEMOS").
3. THE SPIRAL.
4. THE STORY.
5. THE SERMON.
6. THE OUTLINE.

And, of course, COMBINATIONS of these.

Some may think there are more than six types and some may think there are fewer. (For example, ads that work and ads that don't.)

But you'll find that it's quite comprehensive.

Try to become familiar with these different ad types, and be able to write them as needed.

Remember, every good ad has an *underlying structure*.

And there's more than one way to write one.

Let's look at a few.

A QUICK CHECKLIST.
Here are some of the things we just talked about…

Build Your Vocabulary:
1. Find Your Verb.
2. Add Adjectives.
3. Pick Up the Pieces.
4. Organize Your Thinking.

Good Copy's Got Rhythm!
1. Short Simple Sentences.
2. Active Verbs and a Positive Attitude.
3. Parallel Construction.
4. Alliteration, Assonance, and Rhyme.
5. Puns, Double-Meanings, and Word Play.

1. The One Liner.

The essence of the message.

One simple statement that says it all.

This is generally the best way to start writing on a project. And the most challenging.

Whether it's a theme line, headline, poster, outdoor board, or caption this is the test of great copywriting.

Remember, the visual can perform much of the communication.

The Two Liner.
Sometimes your One Liner needs an answer.

Let's Pitch In To Build A New Ballpark.

Classic. *This One Liner by Ed McCabe positioned Horn & Hardart restaurants.*

You can't cover up a bad haircut.

7 South 8th for Hair

Horn & Har   But it's good.

Face Value. *Use it.*
Faces can speak volumes.

Two of the most famous names in America sleep together.

CANNON MILLS

Chivas Regal
*King of the
One Liners.*

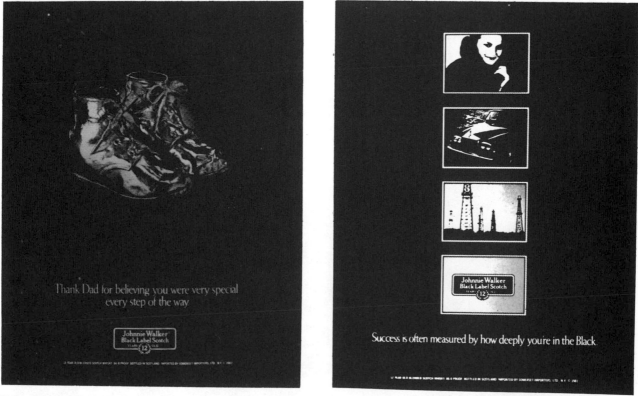

Following in Chivas's footsteps…

*here's some **"Black"** humor.*

Get 'em Quick!
With writing and visuals
that communicate instantly.

Great One-Liners wind up making great outdoor.

Strong visuals ...

make copy stronger.

211

Assignment #11: Starting Your Agency.

Congratulations! You just started an agency. Here are your four clients:

1. DENTAL FLOSS.

(It may be Johnson & Johnson or a brand name you invent.)

The Benefit. Flossing removes plaque from teeth and prevents gum disease.

The Problem. Unpleasant and inconvenient.

The Target. People with teeth (30+).

2. A VEGETABLE.

Pick your own. You may advertise the vegetable generically, (i.e. "Carrots") or, you may give them a brand name, i.e. "UpDoc Carrots."

You should probably do a little background research on your chosen vegetable.

The Objective. Increase consumption.

3. A SERVICE.

You may choose either:

Individual professionals – accountants, doctors, lawyers.

Service organizations – health or financial services (banks, brokers, etc.).

Other service jobs – babysitters, barbers, bartenders – maybe a service company (lawn care).

4. COPYWRITER'S CHOICE.

Pick a product that you can buy in a store.

List: Objective, Benefit, Target, and Problem.

5. WRITE A STRATEGY FOR EACH.

Use a consistent Strategy format.

NOTE: For the following print exercises, you may change any part of your Strategy at *any* time for *any* of your products for *any* reason you wish. (For example, different Benefits or Targets.)

Assignment #11 (cont.): Themes & One Liners.

Now, let's do some writing…

6. WRITE A THEME AND A ONE LINER FOR EACH OF YOUR CLIENTS.

Stick to the Strategy.

7. WRITE A FEW MORE.

Remember, the more you have to choose from, the better your final selection will be.

Famous Faces. Make you look good.

Famous smiles depend on the Water Pik Appliance.

TELEDYNE WATER PIK
You'll feel good about it.

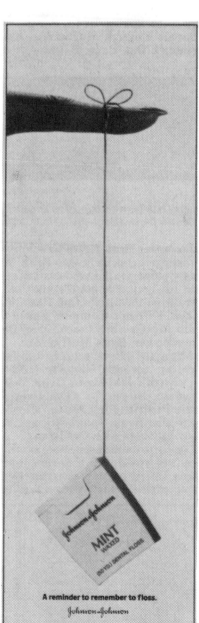

A reminder to remember to floss.

Johnson & Johnson

To find out more about flossing and dental floss, ask your dentist, or write:
American Dental Association
Bureau of Health Eductation
211 East Chicago Avenue
Chicago, IL 60611.

BACKGROUND: Dental Floss.

Flossing removes plaque (a thin, sticky, colorless film containing harmful bacteria that constantly forms on the teeth) and food particles from between the teeth and under the gumline – areas where your toothbrush can't reach.

Tooth decay and periodontal disease often start in these areas.

How to Floss.

1. Break off about 18 inches of floss and wind most of it around one of your middle fingers.

2. Wind the remaining floss around the same finger of the opposite hand. This finger will "take up" the floss as it becomes soiled.

3. Hold the floss tightly between your thumbs and forefingers, about an inch of floss between them. There should be no slack. Using a gentle sawing motion, guide the floss between your teeth. Never "snap" floss into gums.

4. When the floss reaches the gumline, curve it into a C-shape against one tooth. Gently slide it into the space between the gum and the tooth.

5. Hold floss tightly against the tooth. Gently scrape the side of the tooth, moving the floss away from the gum.

6. Repeat this method on the rest of your teeth. Don't forget the back side of your last tooth.

Flossing Hints.

• Establish a regular pattern and time for flossing.

• Think of your mouth as having four sections. Floss half of the upper teeth, then the other half. Do the same for your lower teeth.

• If you do not have good finger dexterity, you may find it helpful to use a commercial floss holder.

• Ask your dentist or dental hygienist for advice.

• Most children cannot floss their own teeth until about age 10. Even then flossing should be supervised.

• Improper flossing may injure your gums. Remember to be gentle when inserting floss between your teeth and under the gumline.

• Your gums may bleed and be sore for the first five or six days you floss. As the plaque is broken up and the bacteria are removed, your gums will heal and the bleeding will stop.

• Flossing can improve your breath – as it removes the bacteria in plaque.

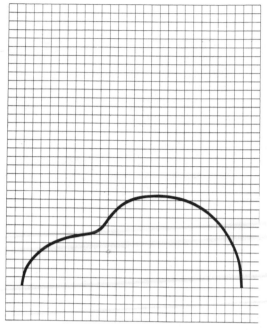

Is the economy trying to tell you something?

ⓦ

Volkswagen used the news.
Bernbach believed advertising should be "sociological," in tune with current events, reinforcing the feeling that the product was also in touch with the times.

Or buy a Volkswagen.

News Item. *Gas shortage.*

2. News.

People read print for new information.

When an ad seems to contain worthwhile information, it's more likely to be read.

New information is usually a good reason to run an ad, whether it's a new product or new price.

Yet, most retailers have sales, and new products (or product improvements) are not exactly front page material.

So, the copywriter's challenge is to make product news seem like more than the same old story.

The day after man landed on the moon, an ad appeared in newspapers across the country.

The ad was from good old Volkswagen.

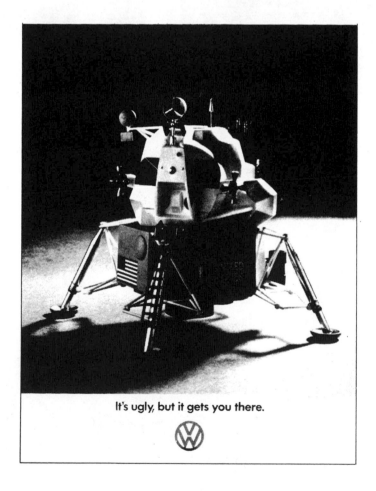

It's ugly, but it gets you there.

ⓦ

IS IT NEWS?

Many products compete for attention.

And it's easy to get lost in the blur.

The two videotape ads shown below are quite well done.

Yet, it's hard to figure out which is which.

You must *differentiate*.

Or your good news will be no news.

*VW made news by taking **a single product feature** (air-cooled engines) and dramatizing it during a New York water shortage. They took news and made it **theirs**.*

Two nice ads. But which is which and who is who? *It's crowded out there – lots of similar products, often in the same size packages wth similar benefits. Advertising is one of the major ways you can **differentiate** your product from the competition.*

Sometimes no news is good news. Here, Heinz reinforces its leadership position.

REVOLUTIONARY NEW KIND OF DRAIN OPENER INVENTED; UNCLOGS DRAINS IN 1 SECOND

NO LYE OR ACID

Worry of Handling Chemicals Over

Up to now, virtually all liquid and crystal drain openers have contained either lye or acid. Lye and acid can, if misused, burn the skin.

Drain Power Ends Worries

Drain Power contains neither lye nor acid. Instead it uses the pressure principle to do the job. (See caption under main illustration.) So a double worry has been removed from everyone who has ever had a clogged drain

to contend with. No acid or lye to worry about handling. No acid or lye to store around the house.

As with many pressurized products like hair sprays, window cleaners, etc., the Drain Power can carries U.s standard warning: Caution: Use only as directed; intentional misuse by deliberately concentrating and inhaling the contents can be harmful or fatal. Use with adequate ventilation to avoid vapor buildup. Keep out of reach of children.

Drain Power Now Available Wherever Drain Openers Are Sold

Look for our bright red package at: Supermarkets; Hardware Stores; Discount Houses; and Do-It-Yourself Centers.

COSTS NO MORE TO USE THAN LEADING LIQUID LYE

Drain Power is not only far faster than the leading liquid drain opener, it actually costs no more to use.

When used according to directions, you can get only two uncloggings from a bottle of the liquid drain opener. Average cost per can for unclogging is 40-45 cents.

But you can get at least five uncloggings from a can of new Drain Power

Average cost per use? 40-45 cents!

Safe to Pipes

What effect does Drain Power have on the average plumbing system?

Tests across the country show Drain Power will not harm structurally sound plumbing systems or septic tanks in any way.

Non-Polluting —Boon To Homes With Septic Tanks

One out of four houses in the U.S. relies on septic tanks or cesspools instead of sewers to carry off wastes.

There is a delicate balance to the bacterial processes which make these systems work.

Drain Power, which contains no lye or acid, will not interfere with septic tank and cesspool systems.

Things To Remember Before Using Drain Power

Almost all sinks, basins and tubs have an overflow vent. When using Drain Power, the overflow vent must be covered. Otherwise, Drain Power's clog-releasing power can cause splashing.

Many homes have back-to-back basins in adjacent rooms.

That brings up the same type of problem as the overflow vent. In this case, cover the second drain opening and vent if applicable.

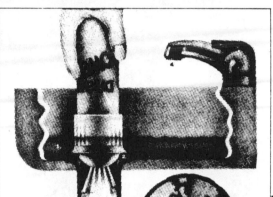

New Product Opens Clogged Drains In One Second Without Harmful Caustics. Drain Power is extremely easy to use as this illustration of a kitchen sink shows. **1.** Fill sink with 1-2 inches of cold standing water. **2.** Remove strainer or stopper from drain and quickly insert nose of Drain Power can into drain opening. **3.** Push bottom of can firmly downward for one second. Miraculously, the drain is opened. **4.** Run hot water for one minute to flush loosened particles down drain.

METHOD CALLED MIRACULOUS

Unclogs With Pressure Instead of Lye or Acid

New Product Is Aptly Called Drain Power®

CLIFTON, N.J.—The Glamorene Products Corporation has announced the invention of an entirely new kind of drain opener which seems destined to make conventional liquid and crystal drain openers all but obsolete.

The new product, called Drain Power, works in a totally different way. Unlike old-style liquids and crystals, Drain Power contains no lye or acid. Instead, it works by pressure

Women With Problem Drains Rejoice

Beats the Plumber

Glamorene officials, normally cautious about praising new products, are ecstatic about Drain Power.

Edward H. Page, Director of Marketing, said, "In less time than it would take a woman to dial her plumber's telephone number, Drain Power can have her sink or tub running freely again. And she won't have to worry about handling lye or acid to do the job"

One Shot Does Job

Drain Power works by releasing a shot of propellant into the drain. This sends pressure waves through the drain water which push the clog through the pipe and into the sewer instantly. With no laborious emptying of the sink, no annoying measuring of chemicals, no frustrating waiting time

In recent tests one shot of Drain Power was more than ample to clear out completely clogged or sluggish drains and make them fast running in 86 percent of the cases. Note: f an extraordinary object should fall into your drain a fork, for example Drain Power will probably not be able to dislodge it. No drain opener can That's a job for a plumber

---

INVENTION WORKS AT SPEED OF SOUND; MAY MAKE OTHER DRAIN OPENERS OBSOLETE

Drain Power may be the world's fastest drain opener you can buy in stores.

Performance figures recently released by the Glamorene Products Corporation of Clifton, New Jersey, manufacturers of the new drain-opening product are, in a word, mind boggling.

Gilbert Pittet, Research Product Manager at Glamorene, and one of the inventors of Drain Power, explained that Drain Power works by releasing a propellant in the drain water. This sets up a shock wave which travels in a straight line through the drain water at the almost unbelievable rate of 4,700 feet per second—the speed of sound

ing at high speed loosen the clog in the pipe on impact and push it through the pipe and into the sewer or septic tank.

It takes one second or less for this to happen, according to Edwin Kolodny Director of Research and Development. The sink or tub can then be used immediately. A comparison of the waiting time before a drain can be used between Drain Power and conventional drain openers is impressive to say the least.

(See chart at left.)

Clogged and/or Sluggish Drains: Minimum Wait After Use*	
Drain Power	1 second
Leading Crystal	15 minutes
Leading Liquid	30 minutes

*As per package directions

Half-Billion Drains in U.S.

It is estimated that there are over 400 million drains in year-around houses in the U.S.—all with the potential of clogging up.

Massive Clog Of Human Hair, Grease, Soap And Coffee Grounds Dislodged In One Second As Drain Power Beats Liquid And Crystal Drain Cleaners In TV "Race"

NEW YORK —Cameramen and stagehands watched in amazement as Drain Power's incredible speed was demonstrated during the video taping of a television commercial in a New York studio.

The "plot" of the commercial was extremely simple. First, three glass drains

were deliberately clogged with human hair, congealed grease, soap curd and coffee grounds. Then, an actual TV "race" took place.

At the words "Ready, Set, Go!", two women hurriedly poured and spooned liquid and crystal drain openers into their respective drains.

Giving the competition a clear head start, the third woman walked up to her drain, inverted her can of Drain Power, gave the can a firm downward push and—whoosh- her drain was open and free-running again.

The competition? Still clogged long after Drain Power had cleared the drain.

How much news is there in a drain opener?
This copywriter did his homework and made a dull product interesting.

DEMONSTRATE YOUR ADVANTAGE.

If you've got something to say, *show it!*

Anything that demonstrates something is called a **"Demo."**

There are different kinds of demos.

There are **Side by Side** demos.

There are **Product Usage** demos.

And a lot more kinds of demos.

As we will demonstrate.

Product Usage Demonstration.

Visualize Your Benefit. *Visual adds value to the low price.*

Advertise Your Advantage. *Here's a "Side by Side" Demo for Sandtex™ House Paint. Again, **visual reinforcement** of the message. Saying it is fine. Showing it is better.*

THE "GOOD DEED" DEMO.

When you're demonstrating for someone else's good, you generally generate a Positive Attitude.

Also, you usually have a good opportunity for Visual Drama.

Even though the subject may be *negative*, you demonstrate that you're "The Good Guy."

Here are some examples.

When you get a chance to demonstrate for a worthy cause, the result can be some extremely powerful advertising.

Nice Products.
Doing nice things
for nice people.

A charming demonstration of a problem.
The actual product – children's clothes–
is not that unique. Neither is the benefit
dramatic – clothes that children can get on
and off more easily.

Yet, the copywriter and art director
combine charming visual demonstration
with writing that adds additional drama
in a warm and humorous way.

*When you give people a hand, or show that you care about them, it can give your message **Added Value**.*

218

The Moral High Ground. *Gives you extra leverage. Right makes might.*

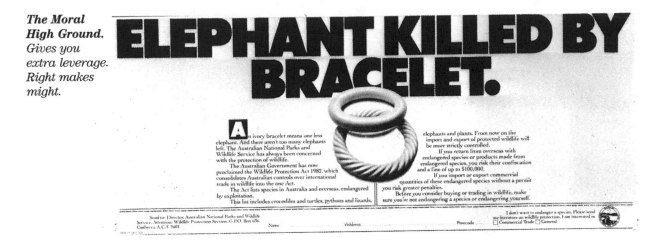

ELEPHANT KILLED BY BRACELET.

An ivory bracelet means one less elephant. And there aren't too many elephants left. The Australian National Parks and Wildlife Service has always been concerned with the protection of wildlife.

The Australian Government has now proclaimed the Wildlife Protection Act 1982, which consolidates Australian controls over international trade in wildlife into the one Act.

The Act lists species in Australia and overseas, endangered by exploitation.

This list includes crocodiles and turtles, pythons and lizards, elephants and plants. From now on the import and export of protected wildlife will be more strictly controlled.

If you return from overseas with endangered species or products made from endangered species, you risk their confiscation and a fine of up to $100,000.

If you import or export commercial quantities of these endangered species without a permit you risk greater penalties.

Before you consider buying or trading in wildlife, make sure you're not endangering a species or endangering yourself.

Send to: Director, Australian National Parks and Wildlife Service. Attention: Wildlife Protection Section. G.P.O. Box 636. Canberra. A.C.T 2601.

I don't want to endanger a species. Please send me literature on wildlife protection. I am interested in ☐ Commercial Trade ☐ General

Name _____ Address _____ Postcode _____

IF YOU WERE TWO YEARS OLD, COULD YOU TELL THE DIFFERENCE?

MINNESOTA POISON CONTROL SYSTEM

Here, a local car dealer stands out from the crowd with a strong message — one that clearly identifies him as a "Good Guy" in the community.

DRINK AND DR~~IVE~~.

Ⓖ Gus Paulos Chevrolet

Danger brings Drama. *With the right words, even a quiet photograph can be dramatic and dangerous.*

How do you do a good Demo? It's all in knowing how to handle it.

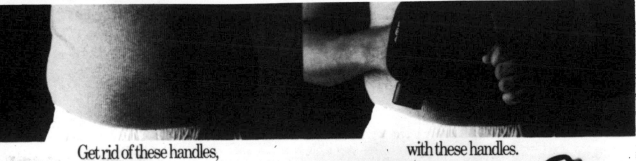

Get rid of these handles, with these handles.

By adding Heavyhands to your walking, running or dancing, you can lose from 30% to 300% more calories while you tone and strengthen major muscle groups *throughout* your body. Find out more at your sporting goods store. **Heavyhands** from AMF.

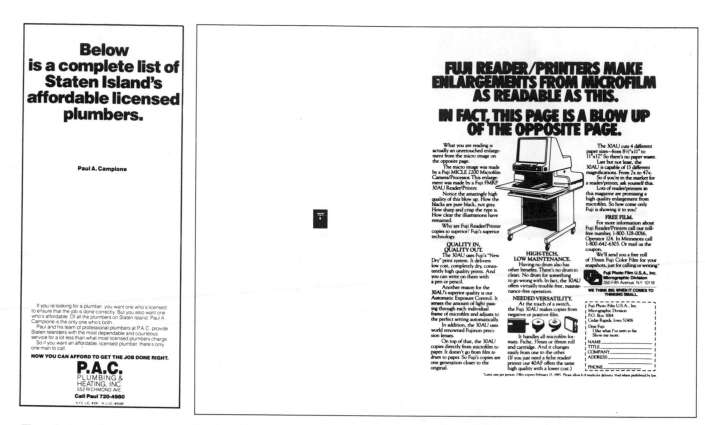
The ad above demonstrates the unique qualifications of this advertiser – a local plumber!

Product Features and Product Performance.
You will often be called on to demonstrate product features that may not be easily demonstrated. Often, a combination of features creates performance.

The ad above demonstrates the end result as a single Benefit. Features are the "Reason Why." A good approach for an expensive machine sold to rational businessmen.

The ad below appears to demonstrate the difference. The real difference between the Toshiba TV and others would be hard to see in a magazine.

THE EXPLANATION.

This ad demonstrates and explains a complex product both visually and verbally.

To bring a bright idea into full bloom, you have to see it clearly from all angles—the forest *and* the trees.

Now you can with ThinkTank,™ the first software designed to process ideas.

ThinkTank helps you sharpen an inspired thought, weed out a weak one, set priorities, weigh alternatives.

Just put your thoughts into the flexible outline format, to organize and expand, edit and evaluate. It's like a spreadsheet for ideas.

While all this structuring helps your brainchild take shape, it won't inhibit the natural flow of creative juices. Because entering an idea onto ThinkTank is as easy as scribbling it on a cocktail napkin. All you need is simple English.

Just let your thoughts flow — from "pie in the sky" concepts to the "nuts and bolts" details. And build more professional proposals, marketing plans, legal briefs, case reports, engineering specifications, research notes, action items, hot lists and to-do lists.

ThinkTank is already a bestseller for the IBM PC, XT, and compatibles and the Apple II family. And now it's ready for the Macintosh.

Call 1-800-556-1234, Ext. 213 (in Calif., 1-800-441-2345, Ext. 213) for the store nearest you. And see what's really on your mind.

The First Idea Processor.

THE CLAIM.

This ad seems to demonstrate by making a claim in a dramatic fashion.

The media itself serves as the demonstration.

AMAZING COFFEE DISCOVERY!

Not a powder! Not a grind! But millions of tiny "FLAVOR BUDS" of <u>real</u> coffee . . . ready to burst instantly into that famous MAXWELL HOUSE FLAVOR!

Utterly unlike old-style "instants" . . . just as quick but tastes so different!

In the famous Maxwell House kitchens this superb, roaster-fresh coffee is actually brewed for you. At the exact moment of perfection the water is removed by a special Maxwell House process—leaving the millions of miracle "Flavor Buds"!

100% Pure Coffee—No Fillers Added!

Just add hot water . . . and the bursting "Flavor Buds" flood your cup with coffee as delicious as the best you've ever brewed. One sip and you'll never go back to old ways!

Saves you money, too! The large economy-size jar saves up to 75¢ compared to three pounds of ground coffee!

See how the Flavor Buds "come to life" in your cup!

MAGNIFIED VIEW of new miracle "Flavor Buds" shows how utterly different they are from old-style powders and grinds.

THE INSTANT you add hot water, the "Flavor Buds" burst—releasing flood of rich, delicious Maxwell House flavor!

Reach for the jar with the stars on top!

A Product of General Foods

The only instant coffee with that GOOD-TO-THE-LAST-DROP flavor!

Assignment #12.

1. MAKE "NEWS" FOR EACH OF YOUR FOUR PRODUCTS (FROM ASSIGNMENT 11).

Write at least one ad for each product:

A. At least one should feature **Product News.**

B. At least one should use a **Demo.**
What kind of Demo is it?

C. One should relate to a **Current Event.**

2. FOR ONE OF YOUR PRODUCTS, CREATE THREE DIFFERENT DEMOS.

Describe them in a short paragraph or try to **visualize** them with a sketch and a caption.

EXTRA! EXTRA!
READ ALL ABOUT IT!

---

3. NEWS STORY.

Grab a news story from this week's news. Then, figure out a way to turn it into an ad for some product involved in or related to the news story.

4. TESTIMONIAL.

Create a unique **Testimonial** using a famous personality of your choice.

5. PRICE NEWS.

Write a **Sale** or **Coupon** ad for one of your products. Make it feel exciting.

6. GOOD DEED DEMO.

Do a **"Good Deed" Demo.**

Use one of your current clients or select another product, service, or worthy cause.

Maxwell House Coffee.
Legally, you can only say "new" for 6 months.
This ad ran for over 2 years.
Note how the writer generates a feeling of excitement with a rational copy story.
This is very much a Hopkins-style ad.
By the way, do you know who first used the phrase, "Good to the Last Drop"? **Teddy Roosevelt!**

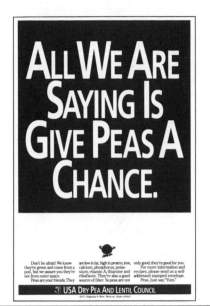

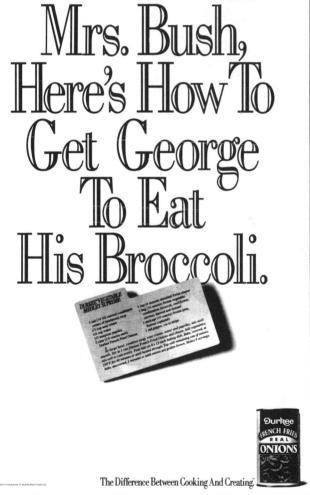

Fresh Vegetable Advertising.
Look what happens when you add a little news value.

THE HEADLINE SAYS IT ALL.

And, at the same time, it makes you want to know more.

The copy keeps building through the Middle, with good writing and strong Support keeping your interest.

Each time around, you add a little more – to reward the reader for his or her continued involvement.

All leading you to The Conclusion.

That's it – The End.

3. The Spiral.

This copy format expands the information as it goes along.

The Spiral is very flexible – from headline to end-line, the story is stated and re-stated.

This approach is based on traditional news-writing principles.

Reporters never knew where the editor would cut the story.

Copywriters never know when the reader will stop reading.

The key is to repeat yourself without seeming to repeat yourself.

This section was a Spiral.

A Spiral often starts with a Visual.

Here, similar visuals dramatize the subject matter – the copy gets quickly to the point.

In one case, a health care provider wants to help you "stand up to osteoporosis."

In the other, a furniture retailer – featuring prices on orthopedic furniture "that won't break your back."

Bright writing. Front to back.

Even the media buy – a long skinny ad – helps reinforce the subject matter.

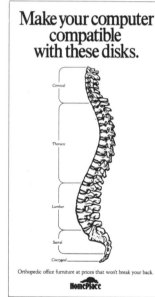

Similar visuals
work well for different products.
Each arrow spirals in its own direction
and each ad makes a different point.

224

It'll feel better in a Rabbit.

Nothing else is a Volkswagen.

You know where you're headed.

Sure you've got confidence. Ambition. A good income. But do you have the American Express Card? If not, you should. Because the Card's a must for any forward-thinking individual.

With it, you're welcomed at major airlines, car rental counters, fine restaurants, hotels and more than 100,000 shops. Worldwide.

And there are other rewards like $75,000 automatic travel insurance and emergency Card replacement. So if you know where you're headed, get the Card. And you might get there a little faster. © American Express Company 1982

THINGS ARE TOUGH ALL OVER.

Fortunately so are Volvos.

Volvos are so tough, in fact, that 9 out of every 10 registered here in the last eleven years are still on the road.

Things being what they are, we can't guarantee the Volvo you buy will survive for eleven years.

But in this cruel world, your best defense is a strong offense.

Road, Tulare County, Indiana

Hole, New York City

Curve, Butte, Montana

225

Reverse Spiral.
Humor is added by stating the reverse of what the audience expects. But the Structure is still the same.

Assignment #13.

Start somewhere interesting and go where you should go. That's really all there is to it.

First, figure out where to start.

1. START SOMEPLACE INTERESTING.

Pick one of your products and start with something the reader might find interesting – the Benefit, the Product, the Problem. Whatever.

Now, write a Headline.

2. WRITE SOME COPY.

Next, write some body copy Spirals.

It's easy.

Your Headline will focus on one part of the Strategy, (perhaps stopping along the way for a SubHead) and your Copy Flow will spiral through the important parts of your message.

Just write something that feels like an ad.

3. MAKE A CHECKLIST.

Next, take a look at the way you spiraled through the Strategy and indicate how you did it.

Here's an example:

Part of Ad	Part of Strategy
Visual	√ Target Consumer
Headline	√ Consumer Benefit
SubHead	√ Product Benefit
Copy Flow	√ Target Consumer
	√ Product Experience
	√ Product Benefit
	√ Consumer Benefit
	√ Product Name
Theme	√ Consumer Benefit.

Do it once, just for fun.

Spiraling through your Strategy will become instinct. Common sense will guide your Structure.

In a very natural way, you'll develop an underlying sense of sequence and Structure.

The key – just do it.

Try to become aware of what you're doing – but don't become too self-conscious about it – and it should start to come naturally.

4. The Story.

Once upon a time, this was a common format.

Many early print ads were stories, such as Caples' famous "They All Laughed."

Today, this format tends to be under-utilized in print, though still widely used in TV.

Testimonials and **Case Histories** are types of ads that may take a Story approach.

It's an entertaining way of talking about your product. Try it.

Set the scene and establish characters.

Establish dramatic conflict, bring in your hero (usually the Product), and pay it off.

Make your story come alive, and make your ad an enjoyable journey.

VW Case History.

"It was the only thing to do after the mule died."

The Baker Street Solution

"Holmes, I'm at a loss," said the Baron. "This is expensive scotch, but the taste is sadly lacking. A family curse, I fear."

The Baron's dog growled menacingly.

"Let me see the glass, Baron," said Holmes.

We watched silently as he held the glass up to the light, swirled the liquid gently, and then thoughtfully dumped the ashes of his pipe into the Baron's scotch.

The dog whined.

"Now let me see the bottle," said Holmes.

"This bottle has passed through many hands," observed Holmes. "Baron, you've been supporting a sinister network of middlemen, and your scotch has nothing to show for it but the price tag." He turned to me.

"Watson, that case we started last night."

"The Baker Street Scotch?" I replied.

"Precisely," said Holmes. "Bring in a bottle." He turned to the Baron. "If you can find us three six ounce tumblers, each with no less than three small cubes of ice, I think we can have this solved before dinner."

The Baron and I were back in a moment. Holmes carefully poured the Baker Street Scotch over the small cubes of ice.

"Observe," he said. "This scotch was imported and bottled by a small, little known group of frugal businessmen. Their prices would satisfy even a Scot. As for the quality…"

Holmes paused and lifted his glass.

"Gentlemen, to the Baker Street Solution."

We sipped.

"Holmes, this is incredible," said the Baron. "My family and friends will be forever in your debt. I don't know how you do it."

"On the rocks with a twist," Holmes replied.

$4.95 FIFTH Code 407

Product Heritage.
Some product stories are fiction.
But entertaining nonetheless.

FACT OR FICTION.

Whatever story you decide to tell, remember to search for the *"inherent drama"* in the product and the people who use it.

If you do, you'll probably find a story worth telling.

And live happily ever after.

Product Story.
Here's everything you wanted to know about how they make Timberland Shoes. The copywriter's craft reflects well on the craft of the manufacturer.

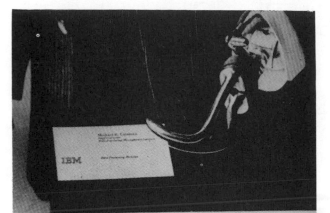

The man behind this hand is Michael Coleman.

The company behind this man is IBM.

There's a story behind both of them.

After the Marines and Vietnam, Coleman earned his MBA and began selling computers for IBM. Promotion followed promotion, and he now teaches our customers how to get the most out of their computers.

His success doesn't surprise us. People with disabilities keep proving that they are as capable as other workers.

As reliable.

As ambitious.

And just as likely to succeed.

At IBM the proof is everywhere, in every part of our business.

The same is true at other companies.

Yet, some people just won't believe that the disabled can do the job.

It has to make you wonder who's handicapped…

And who isn't. IBM

IBM Testimonial.
The visual is so strong, no headline is necessary.

WHY TIMBERLAND HAS TAKEN AN APPROACH TO MAKING SHOES THAT'S YEARS BEHIND OTHER COMPANIES.

Over the years, the shoe industry has seen many changes. Materials that cost less, machines that turn out more shoes—changes that have enabled manufacturers to make shoes faster and more economically.

But not necessarily better.

At Timberland, we've always believed the only way to make shoes is the way shoes were made years ago.

TIMBERLAND'S HANDSEWN MOCCASIN CONSTRUCTION.
THE ART OF HANDSEWING TAKEN TO ITS ULTIMATE.

Consider just the materials.

Where other companies may be satisfied using less expensive leathers, Timberland uses only premium full-grain leathers. In fact, on the average, we believe we invest more money in leathers and soles than any of our competitors.

They cost more in the short run but, because they hold up better, they're worth more in the long run.

We use only solid brass eyelets, so they won't rust. Nylon thread and chrome-tanned rawhide laces because they last longer. And long-wearing rugged Vibram soles that are unbeatable for resistance to abrasion.

But what we do with these materials is even more impressive.

We all know how comfortable slippers are. Well, before the outer soles are attached, our handsewns are actually leather slippers to which we add full mid-soles. Ours provide excellent support on the bottoms of the shoes, while the tops form molds around the feet. (In other words, our shoes conform to the feet instead of vice versa.)

Here, Timberland handsewers take over.

Where others are often satisfied machine-sewing the vamp and kickee, our handsewers sew every stitch by hand. One at a time.

In addition, unlike machine-sewn shoes, Timberland handsewns are dampened and made on the last. Then, they're allowed to dry on the last, ensuring no wrinkles on the uppers.

But, more important, this total control by man instead of machine results in handsewns that, unequivocally, are the finest, most comfortable shoes in the world.

WE'RE COMBINING OLD WORLD CRAFTSMANSHIP WITH NEW WORLD SELLING.

A lot of companies would be satisfied merely making a product as good as our handsewns.

But Timberland isn't a lot of companies.

Soon, we'll be launching a major advertising campaign for our handsewns.

We'll also supply you with a complete package of p.o.p. material.

The reason for all this? Very simple.

Surely, we take great pride in how well Timberland handsewns are made.

But we take even greater pride in how well they sell.

Timberland

228

SUCCESS STORY.

Today, stories like this would never get through the Legal Department.

They were done before TV, but they still feel like TV commercials.

A comic book approach, like the Fleischmann's Yeast ad, and the Charles Atlas ad on the previous page, can be an effective way to tell your story.

Credibility might suffer, but you'll probably get great readership.

By the way, when George Gallup first surveyed newspaper readership, guess what part of the paper he found was read the most?

The comics!

One other thing. *"Eat 3 cakes of yeast a day?"*

YUCHH!

Product Stories.
Something old. Something new.

Pier Pressure.
Keep 'em coming back for more.

Assignment #14.

This Assignment can be a lot of fun.

The "Store Story" Exercise helps you go from just writing ads to thinking about all the things it takes to make a business work.

1. WRITE A STORY FOR EACH OF YOUR FOUR PRODUCTS.

Try for a range of Story-types: Product Stories, Testimonials, Case Histories, Fact and Fiction. Even a comic book.

Generally, you'll want it to be a story about how your product solved a problem – but try to look for fresh ways to tell your Story.

2. THE STORE STORY.

This engaging ad for Banana Republic is an excellent example of what we're talking about.

A. Create Your Store. You can create one from your imagination or pick your favorite shop (and maybe present the assignment to pitch some freelance). Here's a handy check list:

Store Name.

What Need does it fill in the Market?

What Products will you sell?

What Services will you offer?

Who is your Target Customer?

(Don't forget the Location.)

B. Write an **Introductory Ad.**
Tell the story of why you started your store.

C. Write a **Product Story Ad.**
It should be a good ad for your store as well as a good ad about the product.

D. Write a **Customer Story Ad.**
(Probably a Case History or Testimonial.)

E. Write a **"Why We're Having a Sale" Ad.**
Name the Sale.
Any other Promotional Ideas?

Banana Republic: A Short History
   Chapter 1

Never buy clothing by the pound from someone you don't know...

It was the Summer of '77 when we
came upon the Spanish Paratrooper
shirts--shirts made to go through
wars. Our kind of shirts. We were
not retailers, but an artist and a
writer who enjoyed dressing in our
own way--in functional,well-made,
natural-fabric safari-style clothing.
We spotted those shirts in a damp
warehouse in a dark Madrid alley and
had them shipped home to
the U.S. That's when
we learned...never to
buy clothing by the
pound. When we
unpacked the
shirts,
we also
found a
lot of old
airplane
parts...

Mel & Patricia Ziegler

THE PREMIER PURVEYOR
NOW AT NORTHBROOK COURT
OF TRAVEL & SAFARI CLOTHING

BANANA ✶ REPUBLIC
TRAVEL & SAFARI CLOTHING Co

OPEN 7 DAYS A WEEK • NORTHBROOK COURT • CALL (800)527-5200 FOR A FREE CATALOGUE & INFORMATION

5. The Sermon

When asked how he wrote his well-regarded sermons, the preacher replied,

"First I tell 'em what I'm going to tell 'em.
Then I tell 'em.
Then I tell 'em what I told 'em."

That's pretty good advice for a copywriter.

In the Sermon, the writer acts as an authority, not merely informing, but instructing.

Many ads, articles, and essays are Sermons.

Sermons are often written in the "Corporate We." It personifies the corporation and builds a "one to one" dialogue with the reader.

Many successful advertising themes use this same "We" device. (We believe, we care, etc.)

You don't have to preach to write a good Sermon. Sometimes, you're just a good friend.

To write a good Sermon, you must feel that you have something worth saying.

And tell your story with conviction. Amen.

Here are some excellent examples:

Service Sermons.

When you're in the business of delivering service, sometimes it makes sense to deliver a Sermon.

- *Reliability*
- *Caring about customers.*
- *Commitment to doing a good job.*
- *Whatever makes you special.*

All of these are appropriate subjects for a Sermon.

Avis tried it.

Corporate Philosophy.

This ad combines facts and feelings to capture the spirit of the car, and the company that makes it.

As soon as we win, we change the rules.

On the wall near head-designer Tony Lapine's drafting table hangs his favorite design trophy.

The broken stem of a champagne glass mounted in lucite.

The same glass that Professor Porsche threw against the wheel of the 928 to celebrate the final approval of its design.

The broken champagne glass, after all, captures the true spirit of the accomplishment.

Calculated irreverence.

Like all Porsches, the 928 began as a challenge: to build a car that would satisfy Professor Porsche's obsession with technological leadership. And keep R & D entertained at the same time.

Having already built the 911, neither task would be easy.

But endless arguments later, the 928 team arrived at precisely what Professor Porsche had expected.

The unexpected.

The first front-engine, liquid-cooled V-8, transaxle, grand-touring luxury coupe ever to share his name.

A car with a top speed of 144 mph.

And an air conditioned glove box.

Of course, no sooner had the paint dried on the first production 928 in Zuffenhausen, when engineers were back to arguing over bottles of DinkelAcker at the R & D canteen in Weissach.

Someone in Engine Development with a particular fondness for working late proposed that a 4-valve design could do for the 928 V-8 what it does for the TAG F-1 engine and the 956.

Eighteen months later the first 928 4-valve turned a test lap.

Top speed: 155 mph.

The 4-valve technology had not only added 54 horsepower, it had improved everything from the torque curve at low rpm's to fuel economy.

Meanwhile, Tony Lapine sits in his swivel chair eyeing a schematic of the 928, and wonders.

What would happen, if?

928S 8-cylinder, 90 degree V, four overhead camshafts, four valves per cylinder, liquid-cooled front engine, 4957 cc's, 288 hp., transaxle. Weight: 3385 lbs. Top speed: 155 mph.

Till death us do part.

It may be beautiful to die for love in a poem.

But it's ugly and stupid to die for love in a car.

Yet how many times have you seen (or been) a couple more interested in passion than in passing? Too involved with living to worry about dying?

As a nation, we are allowing our young to be buried in tons of steel. And not only the reckless lovers—the just plain nice kids as well.

Everyone is alarmed about it. No one really knows what to do. And automobile accidents, believe it or not, continue to be the leading cause of death among young people between 15 and 24 years of age.

Parents are alarmed and hand over the keys to the car anyway.

Insurance companies are alarmed and charge enormous rates which deter no one.

Even statisticians (who don't alarm easily) are alarmed enough to tell us that by 1970, 14,450 young adults wil' die in cars each year.

(Just to put those 14,450 young lives in perspective, that is about 4 times the number of young lives we have lost so far in Viet Nam.)

Is it for this that we spent our dimes and dollars to all but wipe out polio? Is it for this that medical science conquered diphtheria and smallpox?

What kind of society is it that keeps its youngsters alive only long enough to sacrifice them on the highway?

Yet that is exactly what's happening. And it's incredible.

Young people should be the best drivers, not the worst.

They have the sharper eyes, the steadier nerves, the quicker reflexes. They probably even have the better understanding of how a car works.

So why?

Are they too dense to learn? Too smart to obey the obvious rules? Too sure of themselves? Too *un*-sure? Or simply too young and immature?

How can we get them to be old enough to be wise enough before it's too late?

One way is by insisting on better driver training programs in school. Or *after* school. Or after work. Or during summers.

By having stricter licensing requirements. By rewarding the good drivers instead of merely punishing the bad ones. By having uniform national driving laws (which don't exist today). By having radio and TV and the press deal more with the problem. By getting *you* to be less complacent.

Above all, by setting a decent example ourselves.

Nobody can stop young people from driving. And nobody should. Quite the contrary. The more exposed they become to sound driving techniques, the better they're going to be. (Doctors and lawyers "practice;" why not drivers?)

We at Mobil are not preachers or teachers. We sell gasoline and oil for a living and we want everyone to be a potential customer.

If not today, tomorrow. And we want everyone, young and old, to have his fair share of tomorrows. **Mobil.**

We want you to live.

UNFARE.

Well, it's official.
40¢ to ride the CTA.

And hard as we try to explain or apologize, a lot of people won't listen.

To some it will be one more indication that "The System" is out to get the little man.

To some it will be the last straw. They'll stop riding.

And to some it will be one more strain on an already over-stretched budget. Well, we don't like it any better than you do.

But if we don't like it and you don't like it, why raise the fares? A good question.

In the first place, the CTA is required to meet expenses from income. We're not supposed to make a profit, but we're not supposed to lose money either.

Second, expenses are up. A new wage agreement with our drivers is the largest part of generally increased operating costs.

Third, ridership has declined. If use of CTA facilities had increased proportionately to our expenses, we wouldn't be operating at a deficit. But it didn't and we are.

In a nutshell, that's why the fare is 40¢. Well, at least transfers are still a nickel.

What can you do about the fare increase? Several things:

1) Grit your teeth and put up with it. Just like you put up with the increased cost of everything else these days (car insurance, parking rates, cab fares, and new car prices for example).

2) Ride the CTA as often as possible. In the long run, the more you use it, the less it will cost.

3) Here's the hard part. The CTA operates under the limitations of existing statutes. We must find other sources of income, such as subsidies. We will propose a program, but we will need your support. Frankly, we can't do it without you.

Certainly there should be better ways for a public service to increase income than by fare increases that put the heaviest burden on those least able to pay.

Once more, we're sorry. Please remember this as the new fares go into effect at 4 a.m. this Thursday.

And remember, we're in business to serve you.

We have to be. It's a cinch we're not in it for the money.

CHICAGO TRANSIT AUTHORITY

BUNK!

That's our answer to people who say that the American Worker isn't as good as he used to be.

He's good enough to work at Zenith.

And Zenith is good enough to be picked—for six consecutive years—as the color TV having the highest quality and needing the fewest repairs.

And that's not us talking. That's the opinion of independent TV service technicians across the country. They're the ones who singled out Zenith more than any other brand.

The American Worker? He's as good as they come.

For more information about the service technicians' opinions mentioned above, write to Vice President, Consumer Affairs, Zenith Radio Corporation, 1900 N. Austin Ave., Chicago, Ill. 60639.

Zenith

The quality goes in before the name goes on.®

A NEW WAY OF THINKING
about The Same Old Thing.

Many products have to keep an idea fresh. For years.

A good reason for a Sermon.

For example, Volvo must constantly develop new ways of saying **"Volvos Are Safer"** to keep reader interest.

Before that, they said **"Volvos Last Longer."** For years.

Product Fact and **Philosophy** work together, to give the Selling Idea new dimension.

SOME SERMONS.
Usually, a philosophical point is made with a **Symbolic Visual**.

The reader is usually asked to think about something he or she may not have thought of – such as an aspect of **Product Quality**.

Often, hard facts are used as Support for an abstract concept – tangibles as Support for intangibles.

Here, similar visuals make very different points.

Ear Today.
Simple symbols
communicate.

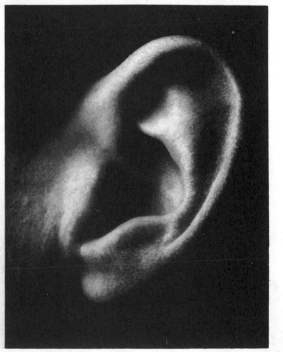

Assignment #15.

1. WRITE A SERMON FOR EACH PRODUCT.

   A. At least one should feature a **Symbolic Visual.**

   B. At least one should be a **Poster.**

   C. At least one should feature a **New Way of Thinking** about the product.

2. WORK FOR A WORTHY CAUSE.

   Pick something you care about.

   Write an ad about it.

   Think about Promotions & Publicity, too.

   How else would you try to build public support and funding?

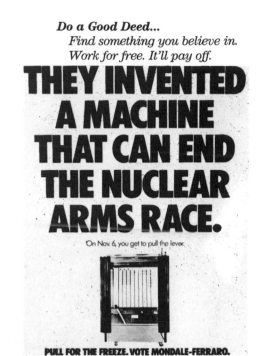

Do a Good Deed...
Find something you believe in.
Work for free. It'll pay off.

THEY INVENTED A MACHINE THAT CAN END THE NUCLEAR ARMS RACE.

'On Nov. 6, you get to pull the lever.

PULL FOR THE FREEZE. VOTE MONDALE-FERRARO.

Same Sermon.
Each of these ads won a major award. One in the U.S. And one in Canada.

FIRST, HE KILLED THE BOTTLE...

IF YOU DRINK, DON'T DRIVE.

R. Roy McMurtry
Attorney General

FIRST HE KILLED THE BOTTLE.

As part of our Healthy Virginian Program, we're out to help prevent the over 250 alcohol-related deaths that occur each year on Virginia's highways. So if you drink, don't drive. And we'll all have one more thing to celebrate this holiday season.

Blue Cross.
Blue Shield.
of Virginia

This program is jointly sponsored with the Gilmore Broadcasting Group.

SUPPORT DRUNK DRIVING AWARENESS WEEK. DECEMBER 22–JANUARY 2.

6. The Outline.

Long copy ads with large amounts of information are often Outlines.

So are short ads that list key facts. Brochures and catalogs are usually developed from Outlines, as well.

SUBHEADS TELL THE STORY.

A quick reading of subheads provides information to casual readers.

A variety of type "color," **boldface,** *italics,* and •bullets can create additional interest. (Though not all in the same sentence, please.)

Small illustrations and captions add appropriate visual information.

By the way, more people will read the caption than the body copy.

THE OPENING SECTION

This part lays out your story, with emphasis on *why it's in the reader's interest* to read the whole thing.

It's often handled with **A Boldface Subhead** that summarizes the whole ad.

THE CLOSING SECTION –
AN INVITATION TO ACTION.

Once a reader has invested effort to read your ad, he should be rewarded for his efforts.

He or she should be offered an opportunity to do something. Such as:

• Writing for a brochure or sales call.
• Receiving a free gift or sample.
• Or just coming in for a visit.

He or she should be encouraged to **Act Now!**

Research indicates that an effective encouragement to action can have a dramatic effect on the results of this sort of ad.

Here's a good way to start an ad like this…

make an Outline!

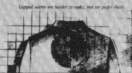

3 KINDS OF OUTLINES.

Each of these ads does a good job in the Outline format.

The "How To" Ad.

This is a great all-purpose opening that "tells 'em what you're going to tell 'em," and draws in the reader who wants to know more.

Here, each section is reinforced with a small visual.

The Visual Outline.

The ad for Midori Melon Liqueur uses large pictures and captions.

Rational / Long Copy.

The suit ad appeals to a certain kind of customer.

Copy points are made about fabrics and workmanship and the store's high level of service.

While fashionable, the ad seeks to sell fashion rationally.

For a certain kind of customer, it probably succeeds.

Act Now! Turn the Page...

Read an outstanding example from International Paper & Ogilvy.

How to write clearly

By Edward T. Thompson

Editor-in-Chief, Reader's Digest

International Paper asked Edward T. Thompson to share some of what he has learned in nineteen years with Reader's Digest, a magazine famous for making complicated subjects understandable to millions of readers.

If you are afraid to write, don't be.

If you think you've got to string together big fancy words and high-flying phrases, forget it.

To write well, unless you aspire to be a professional poet or novelist, you only need to get your ideas across simply and clearly.

It's not easy. But it *is* easier than you might imagine.

There are only three basic requirements:

First, you must *want* to write clearly. And I believe you really do, if you've stayed this far with me.

Second, you must be willing to *work hard*. Thinking means work—and that's what it takes to do anything well.

Third, you must know and follow some *basic guidelines*.

If, while you're writing for clarity, some lovely, dramatic or inspired phrases or sentences come to you, fine. Put them in.

But then with cold, objective eyes and mind ask yourself: "Do they detract from clarity?" If they do, grit your teeth and cut the frills.

Follow some basic guidelines

I can't give you a complete list of "dos and don'ts" for every writing problem you'll ever face.

But I can give you some fundamental guidelines that cover the most common problems.

1. Outline what you want to say.

I know that sounds grade-schoolish. But you can't write clearly until, *before you start*, you know where you will stop.

Ironically, that's even a problem in writing an outline (i.e., knowing the ending before you begin).

So try this method:

• On 3″x 5″ cards, write—one point to a card—all the points you need to make.

• Divide the cards into piles—one pile for each group of points *closely related* to each other. (If you were describing an automobile, you'd put all the points about mileage in one pile, all the points about safety in another, and so on.)

• Arrange your piles of points in a sequence. Which are most important and should be given first or saved for last? Which must you present before others in order to make the others understandable?

• Now, *within* each pile, do the same thing—arrange the *points* in logical, understandable order.

There you have your outline, needing only an introduction and conclusion.

This is a practical way to outline. It's also flexible. You can add, delete or change the location of points easily.

2. Start where your readers are.

How much do they know about the subject? Don't write to a level higher than your readers' knowledge of it.

CAUTION: Forget that old—and wrong—advice about writing to a 12-year-old mentality. That's insulting. But do remember that your prime purpose is to *explain* something, not prove that you're smarter than your readers.

3. Avoid jargon.

Don't use words, expressions, phrases known only to people with specific knowledge or interests.

Example: A scientist, using scientific jargon, wrote, "The biota exhibited a one hundred percent mortality response." He could have written: "All the fish died."

4. Use familiar combinations of words.

A speech writer for President Franklin D. Roosevelt wrote, "We are endeavoring to construct a more inclusive society." F.D.R. changed it to, "We're going to make a country in which no one is left out."

CAUTION: By familiar combinations of words, I do *not* mean incorrect grammar. *That* can be *un*clear. Example: John's father says he can't go out Friday. (Who can't go out? John or his father?)

5. Use "first-degree" words.

These words immediately bring an image to your mind. Other words must be "translated" through the first-degree word before you see

"Outline for clarity. Write your points on 3″x 5″ cards—one point to a card. Then you can easily add to, or change the order of points—even delete some."

An excellent example

240

"Grit your teeth and cut the frills. That's one of the suggestions I offer here to help you write clearly. They cover the most common problems. And they're all easy to follow."

the image. Those are second/third-degree words.

First-degree words	Second/third-degree words
face ————————	visage, countenance
stay —————————	abide, remain, reside
book —————————	volume, tome, publication

First-degree words are usually the most precise words, too.

6. Stick to the point.

Your outline— which was more work in the beginning—now saves you work. Because now you can ask about any sentence you write: "Does it relate to a point in the outline? If it doesn't, should I add it to the outline? If not, I'm getting off the track." Then, full steam ahead–on the main line.

7. Be as brief as possible.

Whatever you write, shortening–*condensing*–almost always makes it tighter, straighter, easier to read and understand.

Condensing, as *Reader's Digest* does it, is in large part artistry. But it involves techniques that anyone can learn and use.

• *Present your points in logical ABC order:* Here again, your outline should save you work because, if you did it right, your points already stand in logical ABC order–A makes B understandable, B makes C understandable and so on. To write in a straight line is to say something clearly in the fewest possible words.

• *Don't waste words telling people what they already know:* Notice how we edited this: "Have you ever

of the Outline format.

wondered how banks rate you as a credit risk? ~~You know, of course, that it's some combination of facts about your income, your job, and so on. But actually,~~ Many banks have a scoring system…."

• *Cut out excess evidence and unnecessary anecdotes:* Usually, one fact or example (at most, two) will support a point. More just belabor it. And while writing about some-

Writing clearly means avoiding jargon. Why didn't he just say: "All the fish died!"

thing may remind you of a good story, ask yourself: "Does it *really help* to tell the story, or does it slow me down?"

(Many people think *Reader's Digest* articles are filled with anecdotes. Actually, we use them sparingly and usually for one of two reasons: either the subject is so dry it needs some "humanity" to give it life; or the subject is so hard to grasp, it needs anecdotes to help readers understand. If the subject is both lively and easy to grasp, we move right along.)

• *Look for the most common word wasters:* windy phrases.

Windy phrases ——————	Cut to…
at the present time ———————	now
in the event of —————————	if
in the majority of instances ————	usually

• *Look for passive verbs you can make active:* Invariably, this produces a shorter sentence. "The cherry tree *was* chopped down by George Washington." (Passive verb and nine words.) "George Washington *chopped* down the cherry tree." (Active verb and seven words.)

• *Look for positive/negative sections from which you can cut the negative:* See how we did it here: "The answer ~~does not rest with carelessness or incompetence. It lies largely in~~ having enough people to do the job."

• Finally, to write more clearly by saying it in fewer words: when you've finished, stop.

Edward T. Thompson

241

Assignment #16.

1. PREPARE OUTLINES FOR EACH PRODUCT.

Each Outline should include:

    A. Headline.

    B. Subheads.

    C. Description of Visual.

       Captions if appropriate.

    D. Introductory and **Closing** copy.

    E. Do a **Rough Layout** of each ad.

A FREE OFFER.

Some of the nicest Outline ads ever done are in this series for International Paper.

You can get copies of the whole set by writing: **International Paper Co., College Survival Kit, Dept. FSE P.O. Box 954 Madison Square Station, New York, NY 10010.**

Call outs. *Another good way to make a* ***Visual Outline.***

242

And, of course, many ads are COMBINATIONS.

The one on the left has claimed more victims.

A nice, comfy floral-patterned armchair? What possible harm could that do to anybody?

According to the latest medical opinion, the answer is plenty.

The people at risk, we're told, are the retired (and nowadays that can mean mere youngsters of 55 or so).

They've worked hard all their lives. Now they feel they deserve to take things a bit easy.

Quite right, too.

The trouble begins when 'taking things easy' turns into lazing in an armchair all day.

Too many naps, too many snoozes, and the body can suddenly decide it's simply not worth waking up again.

The message from the doctors is loud and clear. Don't just sit there. Do something.

Opt for an active retirement, in other words.

You're always daydreaming about the things you wish you'd done with your life.

This will be your chance to do them.

Go ahead, build your ocean-going catamaran. Start up your vegetarian restaurant on Skye. Open that donkey sanctuary in Wales.

There'll be nothing to stop you.

Except money, of course.

And that is why you should be talking to Albany Life.

Not later on in your career. But right now, in your thirties or forties.

Start putting a regular sum into one of our high-growth savings plans and you can build yourself a very nice wodge of capital indeed.

We'll collect every penny of tax relief due to you. We'll then lump the two sums together and invest them on your behalf.

And our investment advice is arguably the best there is.

We retain the services of none other than Warburg Investment Management, a subsidiary of the merchant bank S. G. Warburg & Co. Ltd.

If you'd like to hear more about our retirement savings plans, post off the coupon.

We'd hate to see you sitting in a chair just because you couldn't afford to do anything else.

To learn more about our plans, send this coupon to Peter Kelly, Albany Life Assurance, FREEPOST, Potters Bar EN6 1BR.

Name

Address

Tel:

Name of your Life Assurance Broker, if any:

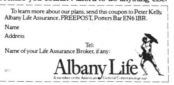

Albany Life

A member of the American General Corporation group

Here's a GOOD DEED DEMO and a SERMON.

GET A LONG LITTLE DOGGIE.

Simco's

WORLD'S LARGEST HOT DOGS.

1509 BLUE HILL AVENUE
OPEN 9:00 AM to 1:30 AM, MON. THRU SAT.
CALL 617-298-9513

Assignment #17.

1. FIND EXAMPLES OF:
  A. **One-Liner.**
  B. **News.**
  C. **Spiral.**
  D. **Story.**
  E. **Sermon.**
  F. **Outline.**

2. FIND THREE EXAMPLES THAT DON'T FIT.
What **Combinations** of formats were used?

3. PREPARE A PRESENTATION.
  Select and organize the work you've done for each of your four products – plus any others.
  Which ads worked best?
  Which types of ad formats were you best at?
  Which areas need work?

In Alaska, It's Considered A Precious Metal.

The Pixee Spoon with copper insert.

BLUE FOX

Don't hang out at the gym.

We have a wide selection of sports bras and body suits.
So you can stay in shape while you're getting in shape.

Body Language
In Calhoun Square

Introduce your husband to a younger woman.

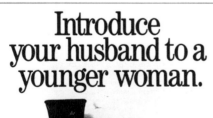

It's a scientific fact that poor moisture retention makes skin look dry, lined, and aged.
That's why many dermatologists recommend Formula 405® deep-action moisturizers, from Doak Pharmacal. The exclusive, European ingredient in Formula 405® increases moisture retention and minimizes fine lines for healthier, younger-looking skin.

Scientifically Formulated
formula 405

RESTITUTION PLANNED BY CALISTOGA MINERAL WATER CO. OF CALIFORNIA

LOST WATER RETURNS TO DENVER AFTER 50,000 YEARS.

Thousands of years ago, a sizable amount of water vanished off the face of the Rocky Mountains. It was not until this century that geologists were able to trace where it went, how it changed along the way, and in whose hands it eventually ended up.

Around 48,000 B.C., as early Asians contemplated chasing some caribou across the Bering Sea land bridge, it was springtime in the Rockies.

Much of that year's snowmelt ran into rivers and streams. Yet, a portion of this pure water disappeared into the earth, never to be seen again.

– – PATH OF UNDERGROUND RIVER TO CALISTOGA
— ROUTE OF CALISTOGA DELIVERY TRUCKS BACK TO DENVER

WHAT HAPPENED TO THIS MOUNTAIN WATER?

It trickled through purifying layers of sand and stone into an underground river slowly headed for the Pacific Ocean.

Along the way, it picked up some extremely beneficial minerals which would one day replace the ones men and women lost jumping around in health clubs or mowing the lawn. Along the way, mountain water

became mineral water. It was one of those magical transformations that only Nature can create and Man cannot clone.

"THAR SHE BLOWS!"

In 1924, this water, still underground, suddenly came upon a geothermal region beneath the town of Calistoga, in California's famed Napa Valley.

In a twinkling it popped up as a geyser, knocking a man named Guiseppe Musante off his feet and into unconsciousness. When he awoke, he capped the geyser and bottled his discovery as Calistoga Sparkling Mineral Water.

Today, it's available in bottles not only as a straight mineral water, but also with a twist of lemon or lime, or mixed with fruit juice as Calistoga and Juice.

Regardless of how you prefer it, be wary of manmade imitators. There is only one Calistoga, the original Napa Valley mineral water.

THE RESTITUTION PART.

While Calistoga has received medals and acclaim for its refreshing mineral water, Colorado, perhaps its true source, has received none.

So, in the spirit of friendship, we'd like to offer Denver residents this money-saving coupon, as our way of saying thanks.

After 50,000 years, we hope it's not too little, too late.

CALISTOGA. THE ORIGINAL NAPA VALLEY MINERAL WATER.

Finally...

*"There's no rule that there are
'Six types of print ads."*

It's been a way to teach you the *structure* of print ads and help you develop some range.

We hope the lessons covered in this section will help you become a better copywriter.

But nobody can do it for you.

That's up to you.

In addition, today's copywriter has to be aware of the increasing importance of visual communication and the entire range of media forms.

That's where it's headed.

Logos, posters, comic books, and the like may be the print of the future.

And we know that when you go to your mailbox, there will be something in it that somebody wrote.

'Til we know for sure, be sure to check whether you're saying what they should be *seeing*.

And now, we're going to shift gears a bit.

We're going to talk about *writing* what people will be *hearing*.

RADIO...

WHAT ABOUT HEADLINES?

As advertised, we did not spend much time on *"How to Write a Headline."*

I believe the major obstacles are before the headline – Objective & Strategy, and after the headline – Structure.

A good copywriter should be able to write a good headline.

What's a good headline?

A good headline is:

Dramatic.

Involving.

Interesting.

Informative.

It should be at least one of these.

With luck, it will be all of them.

Many prefer The Benefit to be in the headline.

That's hard to argue.

Some say the headline should *"relate to the reader."*

Nothing wrong with that, either.

Whatever. Just so it works.

It can be a question, a statement, an announcement, a quote, a title, or just the name of the product.

How do you write a headline?

Easy. Write a lot of them.

Then, pick the one you like best.

Sometimes it's short and sweet.

Sometimes it isn't.

Sometimes unselected headlines make good subheads or body copy.

Sometimes they become the headlines for other ads in the campaign.

And sometimes you save 'em for later, because you never know...

Generally, a good headline should give a sense of what the ad is all about.

And, usually, other people say... *"Hey, that's a good headline!"*

That's how you know.

The Pitch

The Situation

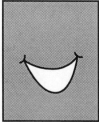

Sound Advice for Radio.

Radio is the **Theater of the Mind**.

It doesn't play on a piece of paper.

Radio is an inside game.

It plays between the ears.

While print relates to the *reader*, radio relates to the *listener*.

This relationship usually lasts 60 seconds.

TIGHTER TARGET AUDIENCES.

A radio station's **Target Audience** tends to be more well-defined: Age, sex, and music preference are examples.

Radio offers other distinct timing and geographical advantages. Like time of day.

And, other types of targeting, such as ethnic group, are more easily accomplished on radio.

You can use this information to make your person-to-person communication more personal.

THREE KINDS OF RADIO COMMERCIALS.

There are three kinds of radio commercials – The Pitch. The Situation. And The Song.

Combinations create variations.

1. THE PITCH.

It's simply an Announcer talking to you.

Your two basic tools are: the announcer's voice and your words.

Add anything else you want.

For example, **Sound Effects.**

2.THE SITUATION.

You create *an event*, a small drama that places your product in a situation of your own creation.

It's often comedic, and limited only by your imagination.

3. THE SONG.

Radio was made for music.

Music can give your words new dimension.

One of the most satisfying experiences you may have as a copywriter is to help create a memorable piece of advertising music.

The Song

> "*M*usic and rhythm find their way into the secret places of the soul."
>
> **Plato**

> "*P*eople don't hum the announcer."
>
> **Steve Karmen**
> **Jingle Writer**

COMBINATIONS.

The three types of radio commercials can be combined for good effect.

The major type of combinations are: Beds, Donuts, Tags, and Vignettes.

The Bed.

A Pitch with a Song in the background.

The Song might move to the foreground – usually to sing the Theme.

The Announcer talks, the music creates a mood and sometimes reinforces copy points.

The Bed

The Donut.

A Song with a hole in it – the Donut puts a Pitch in the middle of a Song.

It begins with a Song, then the Announcer pitches the product, which makes everyone feel like singing… so they do.

The Donut

The Tag.

The Tag puts the Pitch at the end of a Song.

Usually the announcer (often the local announcer) tells you where to get the product or provides other information – such as a special promotion.

The Tag

The Vignette.

The Vignette is a flexible format that uses *all three* types of commercials – in any sequence.

It uses short Situations, and pieces of the Pitch often held together in a Song.

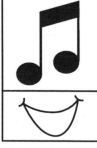

The Vignette

247

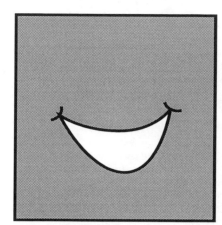

THE PITCH

Myer-EMCO: "Hear Here"
60" Radio

This Pitch utilizes a device often used by Ken Nordine, a well-known voice stylist.

A second, softer announcer track, usually with more echo, provides an answer to the main announcer voice.

In this case, the phrase *"Hear Here,"* helps keep the radio spot focused.

These days, 60 seconds is a long time. You want to stay focused on *One Idea.* In this case, "Hear Here."

This was part of a very successful local retail campaign which helped move Myer-EMCO to #1 in the market.

ANNCR: Myer-EMCO thinks you could use a new set of speakers.
(ANNCR) (Hear Here)
ANNCR: Perhaps something small like the Yamaha mini-speakers.
(ANNCR) (Hear Here)
ANNCR: or... something a bit larger. Now there's Boston Acoustics for less than $150... that might fit quite nicely.
(ANNCR) (Hear Here)
ANNCR: Extra extension speakers for the bedroom. Or a brand new pair for the living room stereo. The new JBL speakers or the Acoustat Three.
(ANNCR) (Hear Here)
ANNCR: Select your next speaker in the home-like comfort of Myer-EMCO's listening rooms.
And when you speak to Myer-EMCO's stereo experts... they listen.
(ANNCR) (Hear Here)
ANNCR: Find the speakers that will be pleasing to your eye... and *music* to your ears at Myer-EMCO, Washington's Leading Stereo Store.

Radio Structure:
Context, Content & Conclusion.

It's simple.

Beginning. Middle. End.

Context, Content and Conclusion.

Let's see how they work with the three types of radio commercials:

THE PITCH.

In the Pitch, you establish **Context** at the **Beginning.**

You may work to establish the Theme of the commercial or the Selling Idea.

Or you may work to establish a relationship with the listener. Or both.

The Middle moves to **Content**: Information, Reasons for buying. And so on.

The End is the **Conclusion**:

Stating the Theme.

Wrapping up the Sale.

Providing purchase information.

Encouraging the listener to *act.*

The Pitch on the left utilizes a device often used by **Ken Nordine**, a popular voice stylist known for "word jazz."

A second, softer announcer track (usually with more echo) provides an answer to the main announcer.

In this case, the phrase "Hear Here" (or is it "Here Here"?) is the device.

This was part of a very successful local retail campaign which helped move Myer-EMCO to #1 in the marketplace.

THE SITUATION.

The Situation is much the same.

The **Context** at the Beginning of a Situation is *Place* and *Personality.*

Where are you?

Who is speaking?

The **Content** in the Middle of a Situation is *dramatic interaction* which weaves in The Product Message.

The **Conclusion** is often some sort of *payoff* for the Situation… a punch line, a problem solved – or, of course, the Theme.

It's simple.

Beginning.

Middle.

End.

Context.

Content.

Conclusion.

SITUATION COMEDY TEAMS.

Often, you'll find the same two characters in new situations.

Often, the commercials were written by the performers. Some famous radio comedy teams:

Bob & Ray, Stiller & Meara, and **Dick & Bert**.

Dick Orkin and Bert Burdis, both creative radio superstars, now work separately.

Orkin's "Radio Ranch and Home for Wayward Cowboys" demo tape should be heard by every writer.

Collaboration can be a good way to write Situation radio.

If you're working on a radio project and find another writer who has a sense of humor you appreciate, you might want to give it a try.

Who knows? You might be the next great Situation Comedy Team.

THE SITUATION

Molson Golden
"Fridge" 60" Radio

For Molson Golden, the same two characters find themselves in new situations, usually involving his obsession with Molson Golden. She reacts.

The rapport between the two actors, plus the excellent production and performance, make each situation come alive.

SFX: Doorbell
HER: Hang on.
HIM: Hello?
HER: Hello.
HIM: Hi, I'm your neighbor, next door neighbor.
HER: Yeah.
HIM: I missed you when you moved in, I guess.
HER: Really?
HIM: I wanted to explain about that shelf in your refrigerator.
HER: The shelf? Oh, you mean the bottom shelf. The one with the whole case of Molson Golden. Boy, what a great surprise that was moving in.
HIM: It was my Molson Golden, my Molson Golden.
HER: Your Molson Golden.
HIM: Yeah, I had an arrangement with the person who lived here before you.
HER: Oh yeah?
HIM: I sort of rented one shelf in her 'fridge.
HER: You don't have a refrigerator?
HIM: Yeah, I'm a photographer. Mine's full of film and I needed someplace to keep my Molson Golden.
HER: Oh yeah, I see.
HIM: Cool, clear, smooth. I'm sure you understand.
HER: Yeah, I love it. It was terrific.
HIM: It was terrific.
HER: Uh-huh.
HIM: What do you mean *was?*
VO: Molson Golden, from North America's oldest brewer of beer and ale. The #1 import from Canada. Molson makes it golden.
HER: It really was a shame you missed the party.
HIM: I feel like I was there in spirit.
VO: Martlet Importing Co., New York.

THE SONG

Popeyes: "Dr. John"
60" Radio

This Song was written with New Orleans rock star Dr. John.

It captures the spicy personality of Popeyes – a spicy Cajun-style Fried Chicken.

There is an Intro, an Introductory Verse, a Chorus, a second Verse that develops the spicy position (usually this is "dipped" and an announcer presents a promotional offer), another Chorus, and a special ending, which in musical terms is sometimes called a Coda.

A shorter version of the same song is used for TV – so the two media reinforce each other.

MUSIC INTRO (PIANO LICK)
Girls: Dr. John for Popeyes!
VERSE 1.
Dr. John: I was raised on Cajun Cookin', that New Orleans cuisine.
Girls: Oo.
Dr. John: And the folks at Popeyes Chicken… well they know just what I mean. Help me Girls!
CHORUS:
ALL: Love that Chicken from Popeyes.
Dr. John: You'll dig the way it's fried.
ALL: Love that Chicken from Popeyes.
Dr. John: Feels so good inside
VERSE 2.
Dr. John: That New Orleans spice is *Oh so nice*, a scandalicious taste bud sin. So crunchy and spicy and juicy my Lucy, grab a piece and bite right in. Hey!
CHORUS:
ALL: Love that Chicken from Popeyes.
Dr. John: The best you ever tried
CHORUS: Love that Chicken from Popeyes.
Dr. John: Your taste buds will be tantalized.
(CODA)
Dr. John: And once you savor that eye-poppin' flavor, you'll say, this is some *serious* chicken!

THE SONG.

The Beginning of the Song is called **The Introduction** or Intro.

In this section you establish Context. This means establishing tempo and musical attitude as well as introductory lyrics.

The Middle is **The Verse** – In this section, you develop what you started. *Content*.

There may be more than one Verse.

The End is **The Chorus,** which usually features your Theme as the "Hook" in your Song.

Only. . .

Music is very flexible. For example, you may start with a Chorus, establishing your Theme at the Beginning, or you might just repeat the Theme (or Hook) throughout.

So your Conclusion could also be your Context and Content. Confusing?

Not if it sounds right.

Some musical forms, such as the Blues, can be thought of as Verse and Chorus combined.

There's a musical device to end a song called a **Coda.** And the list goes on.

Whatever you do, it should have **Structure.** Here's an example – a Song written with New Orleans' rock star Dr. John to capture the spicy personality of Popeyes Fried Chicken.

THE HOOK.

As famous jingle person Steve Karmen said, *"People don't hum the announcer."*

"The Hook" is the part of the Song that sticks in your mind (it "hooks" your memory).

For Dr. John, it was *"Love that Chicken from Popeyes."*

Sometimes it's first, sometimes it's last – it's always the part you remember.

STRUCTURE:
BEDS, DONUTS & TAGS.

The most common type of radio commercial is a **Combination** of the three basic types of radio commercials. Each has Structure.

In the **Bed,** a Song is the background for a Pitch. A major concern is matching the Structure of the Song with that of the Pitch.

For example, the words and the mood of the music should match. The Tempo and Attitude should match.

Or. . . another technique is to start with Announcer only and then bring in the music as you introduce the product.

In the **Donut,** the structure of the Song is usually already written for you. The usual concern is making your Pitch match the size of the "Donut hole" and the attitude of the Song.

You may also want to write your Pitch copy to refer to the lead in lyrics. For example. . .

Dr. John (SINGS):

'Cause Popeyes does it right.

LOCAL ANNCR:

That's right. Spiced right and priced right.

There are many Donut Varieties.

There's the **Double Donut**, with two holes, the **Donut + Tag,** with an additional Tag section. (The example at the right has a double donut and a tag.)

There's something I like to use which involves **Alternating** copy and singing...

ANNCR: Archway Cookies are made with good food.

SINGERS: Archway Cookies. . .

ANNCR: Like oatmeal, apples, dates. . .

SINGERS: The Good Food Cookie.

Finally, there's **The Tag** – the open place at the end of many radio commercials.

It's a smart way for retailers to use radio.

TWO DONUTS + TAG

Here's a commercial designed for local restaurants.

It takes the "Against" position – positioning the local restaurant against national fast food chains.

There are two donuts and a tag.

Take a Break From the Chains
60" Radio

MUSIC INTRO (One bar)
VOCAL:
Take a Break From the Chains! (Take a break) Those uniform uniforms, it's all the same.

Those clever commercials and advertising claims. (Come On) Take a Break From the Chains (Take a Break From the Chains).

ANNCR [DONUT ONE]:
At Jim & Johnny's in Oak Park, you get good food made in a real kitchen, instead of some assembly line.

Hey, a lot of places may cook up more food, but nobody cooks up better.

Real folks, real food, and real good.

Special dishes like Johnny's famous barbecued back ribs – best in town. Take a break from the chains at Jim & Johnny's, on Lake Street, in the heart of Oak Park.

VOCAL:
Take a Break From the Chains (Take a Break) Those uniform uniforms, it's all the same...

ANNCR [DONUT 2]: This week, try Jim & Johnny's barbecue Special.

VOCAL: Come on (Come On) Take a Break From the Chains!

ANNCR. TAG: At Jim & Johnny's on Lake Street, in Oak Park.

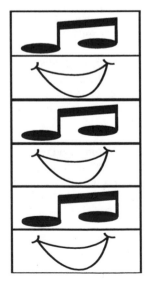

251

HOW TO PLAY TAG

Some things you can do with tags:

• **Special Promotions** – you can change them quickly and add extra energy to your image.

• **Local address information.**

• **Local phone numbers.**

• **Announcements** – Happy Birth-

day to employees and customers, or anything that adds the personal touch.

• **Community Involvement** – use your local tag to increase local involvement.

VIGNETTE:

Golden Bear – "Where."

Here's a nice little example of the vignette structure – a short song, the musical question "where?" punctuated by little situations.

SONG: Where . . .

GUY: Where can I find really good tasting food... I mean all across the menu?

SONG: Where...

GAL: Where can I get anything from a light salad to a great steak on my lunch hour... and still have time left for a little shopping?

SONG: Where...

GUY #2: Where can I get great breakfasts, you know really fantastic pancakes, perfect eggs and an endless cup of coffee or tea anytime of the day or night?

SONG: Where...

GUY #3: Where can I get a Senior Citizen's Discount on any regular menu item, from a sandwich to a meal?

SONG: Where...

GAL #2: Where can I afford to take the entire family and satisfy everyone's appetite?

SONG: Where... at Golden Bear.

ANNCR: At Golden Bear Family Restaurants you can choose what you like and be confident you'll like what you choose.

Because we take extra care to bring you delicious wholesome food every day.

Whether it's breakfast, a sandwich, a whole meal, or one of our exciting specials, and you know why? Because what's really special at Golden Bear is *you.*

SONG: You can choose what you like; you'll like what you choose.

Where... at Golden Bear!

Address and offer information helps your spot work harder in the retail environment of radio.

So give those Tags a little extra effort.

LOCAL ANNCR:

I'll repeat that. Give those Tags extra effort... starting *today!*

THE VIGNETTE.

In the **Vignette,** you can interweave all the different elements of radio.

For example . . . a **Vignette 60"**

Song Intro
Announcer Intro
Situation I

Musical Theme
Situation II
Announcer
Musical Theme

Situation III
Musical Theme
Announcer Tag

Notice.
A Beginning,
a Middle,
an End.
Structure.

STRUCTURE.

A sense of structure will improve your radio copywriting – Context, Content and Conclusion.

Before we start writing radio, let's examine two more structural ways of thinking about radio:

The *horizontal* dimension – **Time & Tempo.**

The *vertical* dimension – **Sound.**

Time & Tempo.

Think of radio as a *horizontal time line* sixty seconds in length. That's **Time.**

Now think of the pace at which you move along that line. That's **Tempo.**

TIME & TEMPO – THE PITCH.

For example, the Pitch.

The tempo of your announcer's delivery can be a distinctive part of your commercial.

Readin', Writin', and *Rhythm.* Remember?

Pay attention to how extra emphasis can be used for effect.

Use *pauses*. . . to add. . .**importance**. . .to key concepts.

Use *repetition* of certain words or phrases to tie your script together. Because *repetition* works to build both rhythm and emphasis.

The parallel construction inherent in *repetition* can help you build a solid rhythmic script.

Repetition can help people keep track of what you're saying. Need we say it again?

How many words? That's up to you.

Depending on the tempo of the announcer, you can have almost as many words as you wish.

The real question is – what's the right rhythm to deliver your message to the listener?

Mood and attitude also affect Tempo.

You can be tough and competitive. . . or. . . relaxed and friendly.

You may wish to build excitement by pushing the tempo. Or, you can add importance by moving more slowly.

Tempo is one of the major ways you can make your Pitch distinctive. And memorable.

TIME & TEMPO – THE SITUATION.

The Situation also has Tempo.

The entire sixty seconds should have form.

"I believe that the best commercials nearly always make people feel that the advertiser is talking directly to them."

Tony Schwartz

PERFECT PITCH.

Here's a pitch Tony Schwartz designed to recruit new sales people for Bamberger's department stores.

Before writing the commercial, some of Bamberger's best employees were interviewed. They were asked why they chose Bamberger's and what they liked about their job.

Also, they were asked what radio station they listened to.

Here's part of the spot.

ANNCR: Well, what are you doing with yourself now that the kids are all grown up and gone?

Wouldn't it be fun to go out and meet new people, maybe even start working again? You've got a lot to contribute. And an extra paycheck could go a long way.

You know, there's a new department store opening in September at the Lehigh Valley Mall. Bamberger's.

And they really do need people like you. People who like to shop and who like to help other people shop.

And Bamberger's will have so many different work schedules – mornings, afternoons, evenings, full time, part time, week-days, Saturdays – and they'll have employee discounts and nice benefits, too.

You know, Bamberger's really appreciates people like you, people who care and try.

So you probably won't stay at your starting salary very long...

Guess what? *Exactly the right kind of people showed up at Bamberger's looking for jobs!*

McDonald's "Chateau LeFoof."

SFX: Bell

Waiter: Good morning, Mr. and Mrs. Whifflebottom.

Whifflebottoms: Good morning.

Waiter: Enjoying your stay at Chateau Le Foof?

Whifflebottoms: Quite.

Waiter: I assume you'll be joining us for breakfast.

Whifflebottoms: Breakfast?

Waiter: Yes, one boiled egg covered with poached salmon bits and set on a slice of dry toast all for the very reasonable price of seventeen dollars and forty nine cents.

Mrs. Whifflebottom: No, no, we'll be going to McDonald's.

Waiter: McDonald's?

Mrs. Whifflebottom: They have a breakfast special for ninety nine cents.

Waiter: Ninety nine cents?

Mrs. Whifflebottom: Two farm fresh eggs scrambled in creamery butter, a toasted English Muffin, and crispy crunchy hash brown potatoes...

SFX: Feet exit

Waiter: I see, well have a good day then... Ah! Mr. HodNoggin!

HodNoggin: Morning.

Waiter: You'll be enjoying our delicious breakfast special?

HodNoggin: Breakfast special?

Waiter: Yes, an enormous boiled egg, smothered in a sea of poached salmon bits and set on a massive slice of dry toast all for only twelve dollars and forty nine cents.

HodNoggin: No!

Waiter: Nine dollars and seventeen...

HodNoggin: No!

Waiter: Four dollars...

HodNoggin: No! I'll be having scrambled eggs, an English Muffin and hash browns at McDonald's.

Waiter: Ah! Very good! (softly) You supercilious twit.

Mrs. McFarfel: Good Morning!

Waiter: Ah! Mrs. McFarfel, you'll be having breakfast here? **Mrs. McFarfel:** No, I... But I...

Waiter: I've locked all the doors... You won't be going to McDonald's! **Mrs. McFarfel:** Help! Help! **SFX:** Clatter, yelling & commotion (continues underneath). **ANNCR:** The incredible ninety nine cent Breakfast Special – at participating McDonald's.

A Beginning, Middle, and End.

In the Beginning, you must establish the Situation and introduce your Characters.

You may also wish to introduce the product. Context.

Then, you move into the Middle where the product is made an important part of the drama. Content.

And the End, with the product as hero. Conclusion.

The Tempo of the action will also affect the mood and attitude.

Dramatic structure and comedic timing are key considerations.

A fast-moving situation with people stepping on each other's lines.

Or. . . perhaps a bit more laid back. . . warm and intimate conversation with background music reinforcing the mood.

Proper Tempo will help give your situation a sense of itself.

TIME & TEMPO – THE SONG.

For the Song, Tempo is critical.

An average pop song lasts about three minutes.

Naturally, you can't stuff a whole song's worth of words and music into sixty seconds. Don't try.

Don't overwrite.

Don't rush the tempo of your commercial.

Don't try to squeeze in a few extra lyrics or a little more copy.

Find the tempo that's right for the mood and attitude you wish to convey. And stick to it.

Make your copy fit the tempo.

And to help you do a better job, let's talk about **Natural Rhythm.**

Natural Rhythm.

One of the basic principles of writing good advertising music *and* good radio is... **Natural Rhythm.**

What is it?

First, it's self-explanatory.

It means your writing and phrasing is built with the natural rhythm of the words you use.

Let's start by examining the natural rhythmic patterns of words and phrases.

For example, the word **emphasis.**

Think of three notes in an even tempo.

Now, say the word "emphasis." The first note, the first syllable has extra *em*phasis.

Three notes with an accent on *one.*

The word "emphasis" is a waltz.

Em-pha-sis. *One* - two - three.

Naturally, this varies with each word or combination of words.

Consider **serendipity** and **different.**

Seren*dip*ity – two even notes, then three faster ones, with the "dip" accented.*

One-two-*three* and four. Ser-en-*dip*-i-ty.

For the word "Different" you have a choice of two different "natural rhythms."

*Diff*er*ent* – two fast notes and a slower note. *One* and *two. Diff*-er-*ent.*

Or... two notes with the accent on the first.

Diff-rent. *One*, two.

There's more than one natural rhythm.

Phrases have rhythm, too.

For example, **"one of the best."** This useful phrase has numerous natural rhythms.

You can emphasize *"one"* to create the phrase *"One* of the best..." *One*, two and three.

Or, you can emphasize *"best"* to create the phrase "One of the *best*..." One, two and *three*.

*"If we use normal punctuation marks in written copy, it will be very difficult for someone to **sound** the words.*

Commas, semi-colons, etc., are designed for the written word...

There is a clear need for a system of oral punctuation marks that will indicate what people do when they speak...

Spoken words that make complete sense when heard, are incongruous when transcribed with written punctuation marks."

Tony Schwartz

FIND YOUR RHYTHM...
The Motel 6 Campaign
Once upon a time, a copywriter, David Fowler, enjoyed listening to radio personality Tom Bodett on National Public Radio.

Then he was assigned a radio project for Motel 6. It was the perfect match – a folksy, no-frills radio personality that was a perfect fit for the no-frills product – Motel 6.

He wrote copy that fit Bodett's rhythm – from the opening, *"Hi, Tom Bodett here for Motel 6,"* to the final *"We'll leave the light on for you."*

It could happen to you.

Keep listening.

UP BEATS & DOWN BEATS.
When counting musical beats, the **down beat** is the number of the beat (one - two, etc.).

The **up beat**, the in-between beat, is indicated as "<u>and</u>."

Thus, "One - two - three - four" indicates four down beats.

"One <u>and</u> two <u>and</u> three <u>and</u> four <u>and</u>..." indicates up beats as well.

You will find copy works well when some of your emphasis words hit on down beats.

And you will find that if you think of your copy rhythmically and match it to the music, it will fit more naturally.

Sound.

The "Vertical" Dimension.

Radio is an acoustic environment. You don't see it. You hear it.

You don't just write it, you shape it.

For example, the use of echo and sound effects can create different sized space.

The tone of your announcer, the vocal characteristics of actors, and music... they all play a part in shaping the *vertical dimension* of sound.

Sound – The Pitch.

Even a single voice in the Pitch has vertical range.

Each of the components of voice recording – presence, echo, equalization, and the voice tone itself – can help you build distinctiveness with a single voice.

Inflections and intensity add additional dimension.

Your announcer should do more than just read your words – he should "Sound" them.

Sound – The Situation.

In the Situation, the vertical component of sound can be quite important.

For example, voices in a Situation should have *tonal contrast*.

Unique voices will help establish your characters quickly and clearly.

Background noise and sound effects can also help you "set the stage" and shape your acoustic environment.

Sound – The Song.

In the Song, your sound is as wide as the sound of music.

Consider how various elements fill that vertical range:

The Low End, bass drum and bass guitar, reinforce the basic tempo, rhythmic pattern and the "root" of the chord progression.

The Middle Range is the center of your sound – melody and harmony.

This is the area where clutter can occur. Try to maintain acoustic "space" in the overall sound for your message.

Helpful Hints:

• Try to see that audio elements in the same range "take turns" (this is a standard arranging approach).

(cont.)

Or, you can string the words together into a four syllable adjective. "Oneofthebest."

(In musical terms, "Oneofthe" becomes a *triplet*. Three beats in one.)

Naturally, the words that come before and after also affect the rhythm of your writing.

And. . . you may wish to alter that rhythm to create added emphasis.

When writing for music, you will discover even more rhythmic potential, because the additional dimension that music brings offers even more rhythmic options.

It will all feel quite natural.

As you become more aware of the natural rhythm of words, you will find your radio writing improving naturally.

This natural rhythmic emphasis will merge into your message, and give your writing additional strength. Naturally.

The *horizontal dimension* of **Time & Tempo** should be an important part of the way you shape your message as you write for Radio.

And **Natural Rhythm** will strengthen your writing even further rhythmic structure.

AN EXAMPLE FOR YOU.

Look at the natural rhythm of this Steve Karmen-written song for Budweiser:

This Bud's for you!
For working hard all day
just like you always do.
So here's to you!
You know it isn't only what you say,
it's what you do.
This Bud's for you!
For all you do, the King of Beers
is comin' through.
This Bud's for you!
You know there's no one else
that does it quite the way you do.
For all you do – This Bud's for you!

SOUND CONCLUSIONS.
And that's what radio is all about:
Pitches, Situations, Songs
and **Combinations.**
Time and Tempo...
Natural Rhythm...
Sound.
And, of course, **Structure.**
Context, Content, and **Conclusion.**
Sound advice for radio.

Assignment #18.

For your Radio Assignment, you have your choice of four Products:

1. A FRUIT OR VEGETABLE.

You can use the same one you used in your Print Assignment.

2. A NEW PRODUCT.

Invent a new product, one that *solves a problem.* Describe the product and name it.

3. A BEVERAGE.

You may pick a popular beverage – a beer or soft drink, or a less popular one. No hard liquor.

4. A RESTAURANT.

Pick one of your favorite local restaurants. Pick up a menu.

5. WRITE A STRATEGY AND A THEME.

One for each product.

6. THE PITCH.

A. Write a "Hot" Script.

Announcer and SFX (Sound Effects) only.
Thirty seconds. Lots of words. Good rhythm.
How many words?

B. Write a "Cool" Script.

Announcer and SFX only. 60".
Lots of pauses... and deliberate drama.
How many words?

(Sound cont.)
•When writing announcer copy to existing music, try to find a natural sound and tempo for the announcer, that "fits" into the music.
On **The High End** of your music track, you may have additional opportunities:
•Extra percussion for a distinctive rhythm.
•Extra sound effects for extra effect.
•Soft, whispery female voice overdubs to sweeten your theme.
•Symphonic strings to give the track more size and an expensive sound.

Remember... **the voice that carries your message, whether singer or announcer, should have its own space; the music should surround and reinforce... not interfere.**

And that's sound advice for the **vertical dimension** of radio.

Here's a little more...

"Sounding."

"When you're working on the ear, you're working on sound.

And once sound penetrates the ear, then you're working on the emotions of people.

*Now, do I have to say something to stir the emotions – or shall I **sound** something to stir the emotions?*

*Certain words require to be **sounded**, not said. "What's new... whatsnew?"*

The second "Whatsnew" is slurred, but it is acceptable to you because it sounds right.

*Therefore, in commercial copy, there are certain words, certain phrases, that are not to be said, they are to be **sounded**."*

Bob Marcato, Announcer

Exercises:

Here are a few habits that can help you develop your radio writing skills:

1. Read your scripts aloud. Leave room for pauses and SFX.

2. Underline words you wish emphasized and indicate pauses… in your written script.

   This can help your talent better understand how to read your scripts.

3. Familiarize yourself with local studios. What equipment do they have available? Do they have sound effects and a music library?

4. Listen to the tapes of voice talent. Local and national.

5. Learn to announce. Don't be shy, you can do it.

6. Listen to jingle house sample reels.

7. Familiarize yourself with local musical talent.

8. Who does the jingles you like best? Track down their sample reels.

9. Listen to the demo tapes of radio specialists: Chuck Blore, Ken Nordine, Dick Orkin.

10. Listen to some old Stan Freburg recordings.

11. Finally, start producing some of your scripts in Demo form.

   Use friends at work as actors.

   This can help you develop your production skills as well as writing skills.

7. THE SITUATION.

   A. Indicate three or four situations based on your **New Product.**

   What are the Situations?

   What characters might be involved?

   Pick the characters you wish to use.

   B. Write Two Situations.

   Use the same characters in both Situations.

   Use the same "on strategy" copy as you talk about the product and the same Theme.

   C. If you want to make your commercial "funnier," read the next chapter. *Quick!*

8. THE SONG.

   Take your **Beverage.**

   A. Write three possible "Hooks."

   B. Indicate alternate rhythmic treatments of each with **underlines.**

   C. Write a Song using an Introductory Verse, a Chorus, a Second Verse, and a Closing Chorus.

   D. Write a Song with an alternate Structure.

9. WRITE A LOCALIZED COMMERCIAL FOR YOUR RESTAURANT.

   A. What ways can you localize your spot?

   B. What times or special occasions can you use?

   C. Write two localized commercials.

HA!

A Quick Course in Comedy.

What's funny?

I'm not sure either.

But even comedy has a structural basis.

You can *build* comedy into your copy.

A mathematician who analyzed jokes called it "The Disaster Effect."

If it were true, it would be a disaster.

But it ain't. So you laugh.

If it really did rain cats and dogs.

If you really had a banana in your ear. (What's that? I can't hear you.)

The quick gasp. The slight pause between the punch line and the laugh.

These are all reactions to "The Disaster."

It isn't true, but it *is* funny.

Sometimes.

Sometimes the truth is funny, too.

This is humor based on *humanity*.

The conditions we've all experienced:

Growing up.

The first date.

School, friends, work.

The characters we all know:

The Braggart.

The Cheapskate.

The Good Ol' Boy.

The Jewish Mother (or Italian, or Irish, or whatever.)

And combinations of the above.

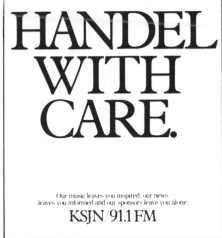

A Double Meaning Demo.
condenses consumer benefit and product performance into one strong message.

Fun with Puns.
These small space ads communicate a bright, friendly personality. In AM and FM.

These are devices generally used to create humor:

1. THE DOUBLE MEANING
2. EXAGGERATION
3. INCONGRUITY
4. HUMANITY

Let's take them one at a time.

Double Meaning.
Say one thing but mean another.

Dramatize Humorously
with Exaggeration.

**Double Meaning &
a Double-Truck Spread**
*makes this a powerful ad
for an insecticide.*

THE DOUBLE MEANING.

It is, but it isn't.

The pun, the humorous paraphrase.

A verbal misunderstanding that sets up a humorous situation.

All of these can create humor.

On the double.

260

A Double Meaning gives this single-minded ad for a bartender extra appeal.

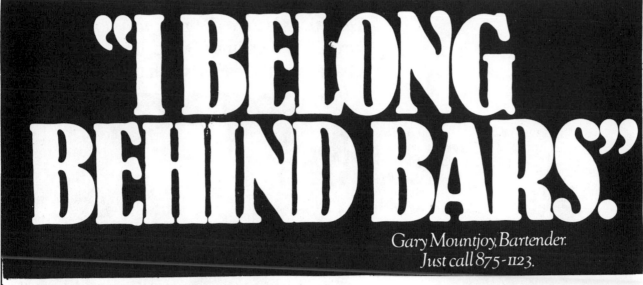

"I BELONG BEHIND BARS."

Gary Mountjoy, Bartender.
Just call 875-1123.

EXAGGERATION.

Jimmy Durante was born with it.

"If you're gonna have a nose, have a nose!"

We create it.

Exaggerated characters and situations can create comedy.

Overstatement is another humorous use of exaggeration.

So is understatement.

It's a question of degree.

Totally.

If you have a big, big craving for chocolate...

try something little.

Sure, Hershey's Kisses look little. But that's on the outside. Once you start to savor all that rich, creamy, delicious Hershey's Milk Chocolate on the inside, your taste buds will have another opinion on dimension.

———— HERSHEY'S KISSES ————

Contrast *creates* **Exaggeration.**

Exaggeration *can be powerful* **Persuasion.**
Here, a funny visual forces you to think about potatoes in a new way.

Fun with Fashion.
Terrific ad.
Very appropriate for the product.
Why be serious about polka dots?

261

"You'd have a headache, too, if someone folded your forehead."

...because relieving a headache should be as easy as getting one.

Incongruity can get attention. Here, a newspaper ad uses the fold in the middle of the paper to make you look at this experimental headache remedy ad.

Juxtaposition of major and trivial facts is a type of Incongruity that gives this humorous headline impact and drama.

This instrument simplified romance, inspired pranksters and reduced insanity among farm wives.

A twirl of the handle got you Central, the "hello girl," and suddenly, with the world at the end of a wire, even the farm was no longer isolated. You can see this early telephone and a million other fascinating indications of a changing America at Henry Ford Museum and Greenfield Village in Dearborn, Michigan.

For information, give us a call. Then pay us a visit and see how a nation grew up at the great American museum that's also great fun.

Henry Ford Museum & Greenfield Village.

INCONGRUITY.

One of my favorite commercials begins, *"Honey, let's take the penguin for a walk."* Surprise and whimsy. Surrealism. A banana in the ear is worth two in the bush.

Historical Figures who represent certain values are Exaggerations that can communicate quickly.

Guess what candy bar he would eat if he were around today.

Rich, delicious Skor. Truly a total indulgence.

HUMANITY.

The first three are *external* devices. Humanity is *internal.*

Often, the reaction is not a big laugh, but a small smile and the warm feeling of recognition.

The more you like people, the better you will be able to create this type of humor.

The easy way to use humor is to make fun *of* people. (Be careful that you don't find yourself making fun of the same people you're asking to buy the product.)

Try to have fun *with* people.

Let them be in on the joke. Get it?

Well, that's how to be funny. I think.

When developing humor for advertising, try to let it emerge from the product or the product use situation.

In much the same way that Leo Burnett sought the *"Inherent Drama"* of a product, you should seek the "inherent humor."

FOR EXAMPLE. . .

For example, let's say you're working on a lemon scented cleaning product.

Here's what you could do:

1. You could work **double meanings** off the lemon characteristic.

Like "It's a lemon." or "Lemon-aid."

2. You could create an **exaggerated** cleaning situation or an exaggerated "clean freak" type of character.

Personality & Humanity can bring extra dimension to a simple message.

Frank Perdue adds value to his product and to his advertising.

A Humorous Tone of Voice can help give your story extra persuasion – like this Perdue chicken "Reason Why" Product Story.

Exaggeration in the Visual helps to dramatize your message.

"Touching that truthful chord is at the root of all great humor."

Sharon Kirk

3. You could create a **human and humorous** situation where cleaning is important. Like Mom coming to visit a newlywed's apartment.

4. As a last resort, you could wash a gorilla. Or a banana.

As a final note, here's something to think about, though I don't know what it means...

Irony. A form of Incongruity. A serious point is made using humor as a device.

AH = ART

AHA = IDEA

HAHA = HUMOR

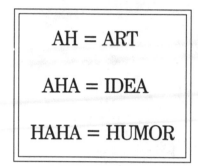

Keep it Clean. Risqué is OK.

"Mikey." This famous commercial for Life cereal has lasted for years. Why?
First, the instant recognizability of the situation with characters we all know, gets our attention.
Second, the warmth and likeability of the characters gives it staying power.

Assignment #19.

Pick a product. Any product. Have fun.

1. CREATING HUMOROUS DEVICES.
Jot down humorous ideas based on:
A. The Product.
B. Product features.
C. Product-Use or Problem / Solution.
D. A "Straw Man."

2. WORD PLAY.
Write a silly limerick or "Burma Shave-style" poem for your product.

3. INCONGRUITY.
A. Pick a ridiculous situation for your product and write a straight 30" commercial.
B. Do an ad with a gorilla in it. Or a banana.

4. CHARACTER STUDY.
A. Develop a comedic character related to some aspect of the product or usage.
B. Develop a character based on "The Problem."

5. WRITE A HEADLINE FOR THIS VISUAL.

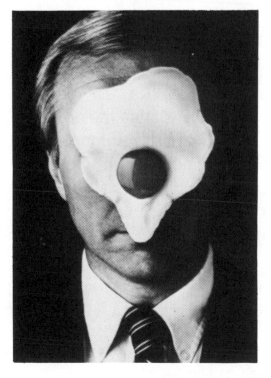

Ha. Ha. Ha. Ha.
Look at the humorous devices in this one commercial:
*1. **Juxtaposition** (Rabbit/Chicken),*
*2. **Exaggeration** (Big Chicken/ Chicken Hat) in the visual,*
*3. **Humanity** in the character, with*
*4. **A Double** in the punch line.*

VOLKSWAGEN "CHICKEN"
ANNCR: Hey, that chicken is a Rabbit.
MAN: Wrong. This chicken is a Rabbit diesel.
ANNCR: Ah, a Volkswagen Rabbit diesel. The best mileage car in America.
MAN: Yup. We get about 600 buckets to the gallon with the Rabbit. It's saving us a fortune.
ANNCR: Gee, that means you can pass the savings along to your customers.
MAN: No it doesn't.

Despite the fact you've watched television all your life, creating television is a lot different than watching it.

The task of creating television commercials is made even more complicated by the hype, glamour and pressure often associated with this important advertising medium.

And... the not insignificant fact that successful television commercials and successful careers often seem to go together.

Heavy business.

Well... take a deep breath.

Relax.

It's simpler than you think.

THE POWER OF ONE IDEA.

Maalox take the generic problem of an upset stomach and generates ownership with a single, memorable idea, "The Maalox Moment."

The problem is dramatized and then paid-off with the simple but memorable slogan.

One goal is to break through into the consumer vocabulary with a catch-phrase that dramatizes the need for the brand, as Excedrin did earlier with "The Excedrin Headache."

The advertising stays focused on this one simple, powerful idea.

It's even integrated into a consumer response program.

If you have a Maalox moment, write: Maalox Moments. P.O. Box 8388 Philadelphia, PA 19101.

Television.

To begin… start at the finish.

That's right, start at the finish.

First, concentrate on *the final impression* of your commercial.

Imagine the destination.

Many writers spend too much time thinking about the beginning of a commercial.

They worry about gags, situations, openings, attention-getting devices and the like.

Start at the finish.

You should first concentrate on the final impression of your commercial.

Try to have this clearly in mind before you start to write your commercial.

What do you want people to *see?*

What do you want them to *feel?*

What do you want them to *think?*

What do you want them to *learn?*

What do you want them to *do?*

To create the path…

first imagine the destination.

Next… a few more things to remember.

TV IS VISUAL.

This may seem like stating the obvious, but as a writer, you must learn to communicate with pictures. Words are not enough.

A good television commercial should communicate *with the sound turned off!*

What will we *see?*

TV MOVES.

Next, remember that television *moves.*

What *movement* will occur as you move from Beginning to Middle to End?

What will we see as we move along that visual path – that final moment?

Finally, remember **people aren't paying much attention.** You are. They aren't.

You must be perfectly clear.

Good television is strong and simple.

Think of the *end* of the commercial *first.*

Think *visually.*

Think of how your commercial *moves.*

Think of a strong simple *selling idea.*

And remember… your audience isn't paying attention.

These are the things you should have in mind as you write for television.

Now, let's talk about, STRUCTURE.

"Great copy and great ideas are deceptively simple."

Leo Burnett

Beginning, Middle, End.
Remember "The Problem the Advertising Must Solve" for Band-Aids? Here's the commercial Y&R developed.
The Beginning. *A child delivers the Proposition. It's pretty straightforward, but mothers (the Target) will probably pay attention.*
The Middle *delivers Support with a simple Visual Demo.*
The End *reprises the Benefit with the child stating it in a charming fashion and then the Announcer restating it in a more straightforward fashion with a product shot and a SUPER:*
"Heal up to twice as fast."

TITLE: "Boy/J&J"
LENGTH: 30 "

BOY: Wanna see the cut under my BAND-AID bandage?

Mommy said keep it covered and it'll be all better faster. Wanna see it?

Hey,

where'd

my cut go?

ANNCR V/O: Only Johnson & Johnson has proven

that BAND-AID Brand heals cuts faster.

Up to twice as fast as uncovered cuts.

BOY: It was here. Honest, I mean it.

ANNCR V/O: Cuts covered with BAND-AID Brand

are proven to heal up to twice as fast.

Only from Johnson & Johnson.

Non-Linear Logic.

Clear doesn't have to be dull.

And straightforward doesn't mean "stoopid."

Nike establishes rapport with its hip, visually sophisticated young audience with a quick-cut parody that taps into cultural forces (Mr. Roger's neighborhood and a Saturday Night Live send-up). Hip, but easy to understand.

They reinforce this attitude with a cutting style that combines formats of children's television and MTV. Plus some de-constructed type graphics.

Non-linear. But clear.

The End is the establishment of a connection – NIKE understands you.

It also marks the establishment of David Robinson as a powerful selling personality for NIKE.

TV Structure.

First, begin at the finish.

What is it exactly you wish to accomplish?

What is the final thought you wish the viewer to remember?

Well, it's a pretty good guess that one of those things is *your client's name.*

Another good guess is your *Selling Idea.*

You may have another job or two to do, too.

With your final impression in mind, you're ready to begin at the beginning.

#1. THE BEGINNING.

For openers, your television commercial must have an *Opening Section.*

It should **"open the window."**

It should provide the viewer with information about what's going on. Context.

Whether by establishing the scene or the musical "hook," introducing the characters, or dramatizing the problem, you must begin your commercial so it's easy for people to understand.

Remember, you want to be interesting, but not confusing.

That's what you *should* do.

Now, let's talk about what you *shouldn't* do.

Here are three common Opening Section problems:

1. Over-writing.

Many commercials are *over-written* in the Opening Section.

This creates time problems that last throughout the commercial.

Too much time – or too many words – in the Opening Section creates a burden that will make the remainder of your commercial less effective.

Tell 'em what you're going to tell 'em.
Quickly.

2. Lack of Clarity.

Many commercials are unclear at the beginning. While there is continuing pressure to be clever and original, an idea that took a long time to think up may take a long time for the viewer to understand.

Tricky visual or verbal footwork may be interesting – or it may be merely confusing.

Tell 'em what you're going to tell 'em.
Clearly.

3. Lack of Interest.

Many commercials are *uninteresting*.

It's not a function of dull words and graphics – or of *exciting* words and graphics.

It's a function of your message not being relevant or meaningful to the viewer.

Consumers don't care how many meetings and re-writes it took you to sell the spot.

They're considering whether to change the channel, get a beer, or go to the bathroom.

You must *deserve* their attention – and they've seen a few commercials. So it should be what's interesting to *them* – not to you.

Tell 'em something that interests *them*.

So...

You must be clear.
Quickly.
With *interest*.

THE PLAIN, SHORT STORY OF GOOD ADVERTISING.

Advertising is the business, or the art, if you please, of telling someone something that should be important to him. It is a substitute for talking to someone.

It is the primary requirement of advertising to be clear – clear as to exactly what the proposition is.

If it isn't clear – and clear at a glance or a whisper – few people will take the time or the effort to try to figure it out.

The second essential of advertising is that what must be clear must also be important. The proposition must have value.

Third, the proposition (the promise) that is both clear and important must also have a personal appeal.

It should be beamed at its logical prospects; no one else matters.

Fourth, the distinction in good advertising expresses the personality of the advertisers; for a promise is only as good as its maker.

Finally, a good advertisement demands action. It asks for an order. It exacts a mental pledge.

All together these things define a desirable advertisement as one that will command attention but never be offensive. Remember –

Reasonable, but never dull.
Original, but never self-conscious.
Imaginative, but never misleading.

And, because of what it is and what it is not, a properly prepared advertisement will always be convincing and it will make people act.

This, incidentally, is all that I know about advertising.

Fairfax Cone
Foote Cone & Belding

CHEER TODAY.

Here's a dramatic little demo that shows Cheer cleaning in cold water. No words, but a bit of opera to add drama and distinctiveness. Additional versions add different musical styles, props and outfits for our silent spokesman (who also happens to be the voice of the Pillsbury Doughboy).

Featured Personality. *The GE Dishwasher speaks for itself... dramatizing how "smart" it is in a clever spot with no spoken copy! Computer sounds and sub-titles do the job. As feature after feature is clearly and interestingly demonstrated, GE really does "Bring Good Things to Life." Including their products.*

#2. THE MIDDLE.

The Middle Section is what your commercial is all about– it's where you provide Support – the reasons, rational or emotional, for buying the product.

The basic question you must answer is **"What sort of Support?"**

You have to do more than entertain.

You have to provide something that will help motivate the consumer to pick your product in preference to the competition.

As our fun-loving friend, Claude Hopkins, warned – Sometimes it's easy:

Convincing Reason Why Copy.

A Dramatic Demo.

Strong Visuals.

Great Music.

And sometimes it's tough.

No dramatic Difference.

A difficult Strategy.

A hard-to-visualize Benefit.

A low-interest Product Category.

But whether it's easy or tough, it should relate to your Strategy.

Whether it's something in your Support Section, something important to your Target Customer, or something that's just plain memorable, it should help you get where you're going.

Strategies are synergistic – so are good TV commercials. How you do it is up to you.

Singing the jingle.

Building awareness.

Solving the Problem.

Telling us How or Why.

Delivering the Strategy.

Selling.

Telling 'em.

Remember, *you must be clear.* And, you must deliver your message *visually* and *verbally.*

Certainly, you can be cute, clever, funny, funky, hip, informative, sophisticated, or silly.

But... *you must be clear.*

Are we clear about this?

The viewer will not give your commercial the same attention that you, your boss, the account executive, or the client gave it.

BEWARE. This lack of clarity may not be clear to you, your boss or the people you work with. (After all, they have the same high interest level that you do.)

Another problem is that things that are important to people who make commercials are often not meaningful to people who watch them.

This is often not clear when you're in the third meeting and the seventeenth re-write.

That's why the most common Middle Section problem is, in a sense, "inadequate Support."

Put simply, the commercial does not *persuade.*

This basic problem is given many names: "dullness," no "Big Idea," and that old favorite, "Off-Strategy."

But what it boils down to is what is shown isn't important enough to persuade the people watching.

That's why the Middle Section of your commercial should give people some sort of reason (rational or emotional) to buy the product.

It might be non-verbal and non-rational, but it must still be *motivating.* It should make people want the product for some reason.

Humorous Overstatement Can Make for Strong Support.
Lee Jeans have invested in their position "The brand that fits."
While good-fitting jeans are the benefit, they developed powerful entertaining TV based on what happens when jeans don't fit.
Here, a popping button causes amazing havoc.
Is that a reason to buy the product? Yes.
Next time you struggle into too-tight jeans,
you just might remember Lee.

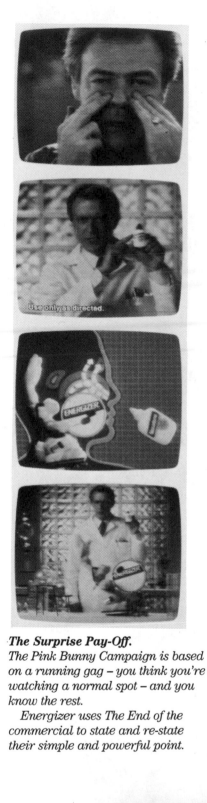

The Surprise Pay-Off.
The Pink Bunny Campaign is based on a running gag – you think you're watching a normal spot – and you know the rest.

Energizer uses The End of the commercial to state and re-state their simple and powerful point.

The Middle of your commercial should be meaningful. You should say it...

Memorably.

Rhythmically.

And *Clearly.*

And don't be afraid to say it again.

That's right, don't be afraid to say it again.

#3. THE END.

Now we finish where we began.

At The End.

The destination you first imagined.

In addition to providing the necessary information, The End of your commercial should reward the viewer.

Whether it's: a well-turned phrase, a memorable musical theme, a warm, friendly feeling, or a boffo punch line… you must tie the ribbon on the package.

Visually and verbally.

You must say it *and* show it.

Clearly, meaningfully, and *memorably.*

So your message stays with the viewer after the commercial has faded to black.

Remember, the objective of your commercial is to get people to prefer your product to the *competition* – that's the mission your commercial must accomplish.

And that's The End, my friend.

With all this in mind, let's talk about various types of television commercials.

Focus – Front to Back.
Here, Chiat/Day (the same agency that does Energizer) stays focused on a single proposition – that's restated in the final frame. "We treat you like a person. Not a prescription."

272

Types of TV Commercials:

One problem for the beginning television copywriter (and some experienced ones) is a narrow repertoire, a lack of familiarity with the range of executional solutions available.

The objective of the next section is to acquaint you with the range of executions available to you.

As far as this book is concerned, these are the major types of television commercials:

> SLICE
>
> THE TALKING PERSON
>
> THE DEMO
>
> THE VISUAL
>
> GRAPHIC COLLAGE

And of course. . .
> COMBINATIONS.

Let's take a look...

What Type of TV is this?
It's a Graphic Collage – a new TV commercial format easily understandable to today's TV generation. It uses strong music tracks and the latest video-graphic technology. By the way, the spot isn't for Bubble-Yum.

Six Types of TV Commercials?
Naturally, creating categories creates room for debate.

Yet, we think you will find these broad categories pretty well cover the range of options available in a most useful and memorable way.

Seven Types of TV Commercials?
Here's another listing of "Creative Solution Families" we ran into.
1. Product Presentation
2. Demonstration
3. Show the Need/Problem
4. Benefit in a Study
5. Tell It
6. Symbol/Analogy/Association
7. Borrowed Format/Parody
When you're done with this section, you might want to write your own list.

THE OPENING SCENE
(We see that it's a funeral.)

Male voice over: *I, Maxwell E. Snavely, being of sound mind and body, do bequeath the following:*

THE MIDDLE SECTION
(We see a sequence of spendthrifts get their just reward.)

"To my wife Rose, who spent money like there was no tomorrow, I leave $100 and a calendar.

To my sons Rodney and Victor who spent every dime I ever gave them on fancy cars and fast women, I leave $50 in dimes."

"To my business partner, Jules, whose motto was 'spend spend spend' I leave nothing, nothing, nothing. And to my other friends and relatives who also never learned the value of a dollar... I leave... a dollar."

#1 Slice.

Remember, some of the best commercials, as well as some of the worst, are "Slice of Life."

Comedy commercials, such as those for Alka Seltzer and Volkswagen are "Slice."

One of Volkswagen's best "Slice of Life" commercials was at a funeral.

The touching dramas of Hallmark, and Federal Express's surreal dramatizations are also "Slice."

So are many "McDonald's Moments."

Short pieces of Slice strung together, usually with music, create THE VIGNETTE.

The first Vignette commercial was probably Dick Greene's "Tummies!" for Alka-Seltzer, with great music and a great Theme – "No matter what shape your stomach's in."

How do you start slicing?

Imagine a situation where the product plays an integral and important part.

Then write it down.

That part's easy.

The hard part is making it special.

Situations, characterizations, and dialogue.

Any way you slice it, you have to make Slice come alive to make it "Slice of Life."

THE CLOSING SEQUENCE.
(We see the virtue of owning a VW)

"Finally, to my nephew, Harold, who oft time said:

'A penny saved is a penny earned.'

And who also oft' times said: 'Gee, Uncle Max, it sure pays to own a Volkswagen...'"

How to Slice.

Imagine a situation where your product plays an important part.

The Opening Section should establish your situation. Scene and characters.

The Middle Section builds your Sale.

It may be Problem/Solution, it may be a sequence of happy vignettes... whatever.

The key is that it's easy and interesting for the viewer to understand and that it works toward selling the product, whether it's facts or feelings.

The Closing Section is the payoff.

We know why we should buy.

We can relate to the product in our life.

The Taster's Choice Couple. *This series of "Slice" commercials was originally done in England. The sophisticated couple and dialogue serve to upgrade the image of Taster's Choice Instant Coffee. Just as in a TV series, viewers can get involved with the people in your commercial.*

"I leave my entire fortune of one hundred billion dollars." (Now <u>that's</u> a pay-off.)

E. F. HUTTON "ALPHABET"

The writer of this classic E. F. Hutton commercial found a charming way to present their name awareness mnemonic, **"When E.F. Hutton talks... people listen."**

Perhaps it was inspired by his (or her) kids. Or, noting that the first two letters of the client's name were alphabetical neighbors, the writer just created a situation where the line could be delivered memorably.

Either way, it works.

TEACHER: *Alright, children, who's going to begin to recite the alphabet? How 'bout you, Ann?*

ANN: *A... b.... c... d ... E... F. Hutton.*

ANNCR (VO): *When E. F. Hutton talks... people listen.*

1. MOM: Okay now, Harold, when you go away to college you'll have to wash all your crazy clothes.

2. HAROLD: I thought you just put them in the machine and... MOM: There's more to laundry than that.

3. Today's clothes have changed. Look at these things. New fabrics, new colors, you've got to use the right temperatures.

4. HAROLD: Sure, ma... MOM: You see this tag? HAROLD: Sure, you've sewed them on all my clothes.

5. MOM: No, this one. Permanent press, wash it in warm water.

6. This crazy thing is a bright color, and I don't want to see it all faded. Use cold water.

7. HAROLD: When do I use hot water? MOM: With these, Harold, white things.

8. HAROLD: I need three detergents?

9. MOM: No, Harold, three temperatures, one detergent... All-Temperature Cheer.

10. It's specially made to really clean in all those temperatures.

11. Hot, warm or cold.

12. Use All-Temperature Cheer. Fill it evenly, don't stuff.

13. HAROLD: Hey, mom, it did work in all temperatures. This shirt looks groovy. MOM: You're a good son, Harold.

14. (Anncr VO) All-Temperature Cheer. For the way you wash now.

15. MOM: All-Temp-a-Cheer, Harold.

276

SLICE (CONTINUED)

KODAK.

Kodak's warm, human vignettes slice life into images that Visualize the Benefit. Pictures to remember.

All-Temperature Cheer.
This was my first "Slice" commercial. Notice how it establishes the Situation, develops drama around the product, and pays it off. When they saw this commercial, the target (wives and mothers) often realized that they would have similar experiences with their children. They internalized the message.
Commercials like this helped move Cheer from #5 to #2. And it was probably the first time anybody used "groovy" in a P&G commercial.

"An advertiser's research should deeply explore the actual experiences people have with products in real-life situations, and structure stimuli in the commercials in such a way that the real-life experience will be evoked by the product when the consumer encounters it in a store.

Tony Schwartz

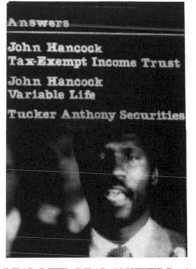

REAL LIFE. REAL ANSWERS. *An effective use of Slice dealing with turning points in people's lives. From John Hancock.*

SURREAL LIFE – *Many of Pepsi's commercials are done in the "Slice" format. The Shady Acres Retirement Home perks up when Pepsi arrives instead of Coke.*

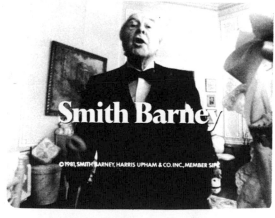

"NURSERY" 30" TV
ANNCR: *John Houseman for the investment firm of Smith Barney.*
JOHN HOUSEMAN: *Being born with a silver spoon in one's mouth is not enough.*
   How quickly it can tarnish in today's Topsy-Turvy economy.
   When it comes to growth and the preservation of capital, many prudent investors look to Smith Barney.
(SFX: BABY)
   They make money the old fashioned way, they earn it.

278

#2 The Talking Person.

The Talking Person is the *personification* of your message.
   Your commercial is the selling message.
   In person.
   Ask yourself. Who is this person?
   A celebrity?
   A distinctive character?
   An enthusiastic consumer?
   Maybe even the client himself...
   Like Lee Iaccoca or Frank Perdue.
   And how do you add dramatic dimension?
   The right visual environment.
   The right props.
   The right words.
   It's very important to add *Visual* Information to the *Verbal* Information provided by your Talking Person. It can be as simple as a nursery.
   You don't have to be limited to only one person, either. On-camera or off-camera dialogue can add additional dramatic interest.
   The Talking Person can be part of a Slice commercial, such as the continuing character dramas of P&G, General Foods and Colgate.
   How do you get started? Easy.
   First, lay out the Structure of your Sale. Beginning. Middle. End.
   Then, think of the perfect person to say it. Perhaps it's some*one* or some*thing* that represents the **"inherent drama"** of the product; like Leo Burnett's "critters."
   Finally, add appropriate Visuals.
   It walks. It talks.
   It's advertising with *personality!*

Remember, the Talking Person doesn't have to be a real person.

Charlie the Tuna, Morris the Cat, and Tony the Tiger are all excellent Talking "Persons."

A Talking Beaver for chain saws! Terrific!

Your Talking Person can even be part of a Slice commercial.

Your commercial is the selling message. In person.

The Lonely Maytag Repairman. This durable character dramatizes the durability of Maytag washers.

McCULLOCH
10" TV
BARNEY: *You've got power.*
Sharp teeth.
Even a chain brake.
Next to a guy like me,
you've got everything.
ANNCR: *See the feature-loaded McCulloch 310 at your McCulloch dealer.*

Boy Oh Boy Oh Boy! *The Pillsbury Doughboy personifies the product, represents the "inherent drama" (the product pops out of the container) and unifies a varied product line.*

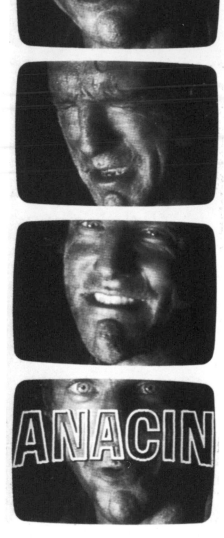

ANACIN "COAL MINER"
(A tough, good-looking actor who acts like a tough, hard-working coal miner gives Anacin's story extra impact.)
MINER: *Tell ya what, you go down a half-mile shaft… It's dark… Damp… 'bout 12 million ton o' rock on top ya. An' ya getcha a headache. Wheeh! Buddy, ya better have ya some Anacin. Yessir!*
ANNCR: *Anacin. More medicine than any regular strength pain reliever.*
MINER: *More medicine, 'at's good. But what's better is not havin' no more headache down in the hole.*

Product Presenter.
*For years, **Josie the Plumber** sold Comet in a Slice/Demo. What a combination!*

The Talking Problem.
Ikea Furniture dramatizes the benefit of not having salesmen by having them do the "the un-selling."
Title Cards (WHY IKEA DOESN'T HAVE SALESMEN) are intercut with The Problem personified.

TWO TALKING PERSONS ADD DRAMA.
   Two Talking Persons add dialogue.
   They talk to the customer and each other.
   Here's a 10" commercial that makes the
point for Polaroid. Short and sweet.
   And. . . some Lite comedy from Miller.

Mr. Butkus & Mr. Smith
Famous Lite Beer Drinkers

Lite
Everything you always wanted
in a beer. And less.
1983 Miller Brewing Co., Milwaukee, WI

POLAROID "NO REASON" 10"
*JIM: You don't need a reason to have enough
Polaroid Time-Zero Supercolor film.*
MARI: Why not wait for a reason?
JIM: Then you won't have the film.

SFX: (Bar Sounds)
*BUTKUS: I tell ya, trying to get cultured isn't
easy. We just went to the opera, and we didn't
understand a word.*
*SMITH: Yeah. That big guy in those tights sure
could sing.*
*BUTKUS: Well, at least we still drink a very
civilized beer. Lite Beer from Miller.
Lite tastes great.*
*SMITH: But us impresarios drink it because it's
less filling.*
*BUTKUS: We can't afford to get filled up.
Tomorrow night we're going to the ballet.*
SMITH: Yeah, I sure hope they do it in English.
SFX: (Crowd Laughs)
*ANNCR (VO): Lite Beer from Miller.
Everything you always wanted in a beer.
And less.*

281

*The Maysle Brothers have been
experts at this type of commercial.
Here are some of their thoughts:*

Number one in a series: How to produce commercials that are credible and creative—some thoughts from the Maysles.

Reprinted from **BACK STAGE**

On The Art Of Real People Commercials
Seven Easy Rules

Real people commercials? No scripts and no actors? But how can you be sure it will work? How do you handle the freedom? In our business, the same questions come up again and again. How do we avoid those boring old testimonials? Is there a method to our magic? We think so. After sixteen successful years of real people experience, these seven rules seem to sum it all up:

1 Know your strategy.
Remember—no client's strategy exists without extensive research. Keep the key points in mind and you'll know when to guide and—better yet—when to follow.

2 It's all in the casting.
When selecting real people, choose subjects who express themselves openly—and make sure they're people you like. Without the right people, your commercial is dead.

3 Produce small.
Put your subjects at ease by keeping their environment familiar; artificial settings, large crowds and huge amounts of equipment can intimidate anyone.

4 Guide, never push.
Treat your subjects like friends, and they'll return the favor: they'll come through with more substance and style than any script ever promised.

5 Stay spontaneous.
Every situation has more than one response—so give your subjects the freedom to come up with their own. Spontaneity equals believability.

6 Be patient.
Patience inspires confidence—and a confident subject is sure to give you the good stuff. Use time as your ally.

7 Keep it real.
Don't edit the life out of your spot once it's shot—leave room for the humor, the little comments and gestures that keep the <u>real</u> in a real people commercial.

Once you follow these rules, producing a real people commercial is easy. Easier still is to produce it with us. For us, you see, these rules aren't really rules. They're a natural expression of our work—and <u>that's</u> the art of real people commercials.

**THE MASTERS OF
REAL PEOPLE COMMERCIALS**

1. (Anncr VO) Folks are talking about Colonel Sanders...

2. ...New Improved Country Style Ribs.

3. 1ST MAN: Fantastic!

4. 2ND WM: Terrific!

5. 2ND MAN: Delicious...ha ha hee ha ha.

6. 3RD MAN: Super!

7. COUNTER GIRL: The Colonel's new cut gives you more meat for less money, don't you see?

8. 2ND MAN: Bigger.

9. 3RD MAN: Ummmmm, meaty.

10. 3RD WM: Finger lickin' good.

11. 1ST MAN: Lots bigger.

12. 1ST WM: Now that's a value

13. (Anncr VO) Try Colonel Sanders New Improved Country Style Ribs.

14. You'll say:...

15. 2ND MAN: Ha ha he he he (Etc., laugh)

An "Almost Testimonial" using actors with a Demo.

#3 The Demo.

Television is uniquely suited for *visual demonstration.* Consider.

How can your product be *demonstrated visually?* Demonstrate. Dramatically.

There are many types of Demo:

SIDE-BY-SIDE.

The traditional Side-by-Side, compares your product with another.

BEFORE/AFTER.

The Before/After dramatizes both The Problem and The Benefit.

PRODUCT PERFORMANCE.

The Performance Demo is another related type of Demo. It dramatizes how well your product works.

For example, Timex Torture Tests.

IN-USE & NEW-USE.

The In-Use Demo shows how the product is used. And how the product works.

The New-Use Demo shows people new ways to use the product.

Like a recipe or serving idea.

Demos can be real or symbolic.

For example, a graphic representation of a new product technology or a humorous over-statement.

Demos can be based on:
Test Results,
Sales Figures,
Popularity,
Uniqueness… whatever.

***Visual Demonstration* is the key.**

Don't just say it.
Show it.
Demonstrate.
Dramatically.

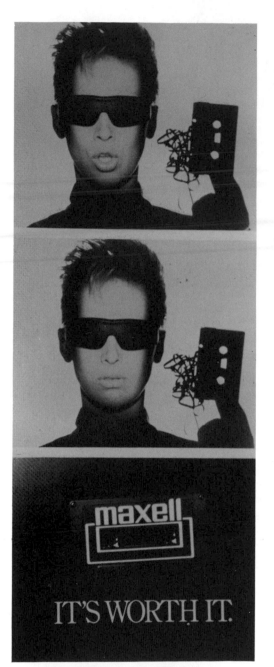

MAXELL: "PUNK TAPE" 10" TV
NEW WAVE WOMAN:
New Wave shouldn't be recorded
on punk tape.
ANNCR: Maxell, it's worth it.

284

DRAMATIZE
THE DIFFERENCE.

Mr. COFFEE "PATENT" 30" TV
(NATURAL SFX THROUGHOUT)
ANNCR (VO): *1951. Lorenzo Leeni tried to convince the U.S. Patent Office he had a way to make better coffee. He failed.*

1963. The Yunt Brothers tried to convince the Patent Office they had a better way to make better coffee. They failed.

1972. Vincent Marotta tried to convince the Patent Office he could make coffee perfectly by controlling brewing time and temperature. He succeeded.
Mr. Coffee. America's perfect coffee maker.
With a patent to prove it.

AAMCO "BREAKDOWN" 20" TV
ANNCR (VO): *Ever notice how things break down after the warranty expires?*
But if your transmission ever breaks down, you can get a warranty that lasts as long as you own your car.

AAMCO's car-ownership warranty – that provides free annual checkups.

Wouldn't it be nice if every warranty was this way?
AAMCO: (BEEP BEEP)
Why go anywhere else?

Timex Today.
The commercial on the left really breaks you up!

In fact, it breaks everything up, using broad comedy – **a face that breaks mirrors** – to freshen the "takes a licking" story.

It builds on Timex heritage – even using audio of the original announcer.

"Torture Tests."

You can dramatize product performance by dramatizing the Problem – or you can dramatize the Product Use Situation.

Above, a humorous "Torture Test" for Mr. Big Paper Towels.

And below . . .

TIMEX TORTURE TESTS.

For years, Timex had demonstrated the durability of their inexpensive watches by having them undergo some dramatic events.

Demos like this established the durability and quality of Timex watches.

"Takes a licking and keeps on ticking."

DEMONSTRATE. *DRAMATICALLY!* More Demos.

Some Products Demand Demonstration.

Glue is one of those products that does something that you can see. See?

"Fresh Mex."
The Commercial Becomes the Demo.

A symbolic Demo from a very tired creative team at Goodby Berlin & Silverstein.

To dramatize that the Mexican food at Chevy's is fresh, they get up early, shoot, and edit a commercial that runs *that day!*

Fresh copy and a spontaneous attitude reinforces the claim at the same time it communicates the casual fun of Mexican food. Fresh.

This Demo Isn't There.

We begin with a Chicago snowstorm.

Then we see the cars of Chicago Bulls buried under snow.

Then we pan to an empty space – Michael Jordan's Chevy Blazer.

Better Get It Right the First Time.

Want to demonstrate safety features?

It's easy – crash a car.

This Volvo commercial makes the point on Volvo's safety features.

Another commercial – which sought to re-create an event where a Volvo survived being crushed by a Monster Truck – caused the agency to crash and burn.

The Volvo used in the commercial was reinforced. This fact was brought to everyone's attention and the fall-out included the client driving out the door.

Before you demonstrate something, check with the Legal Department – or they'll be checking on you afterwards.

#4 The Visual.

Television is a visual medium.

Imagination begins with images.

How can you create interesting imagery for your product?

How can you *visualize* the benefit?

Or the problem?

How can you show what you say?

Remember, your audience can move, too.

You can fly them through space, so they see the Big Picture.

You can shrink them.

So small things seem larger.

Just imagine. See?

STATE FARM.

An egg on wheels is put together again by State Farm Insurance.

Here's Keith Reinhard's story on how he came up with this classic commercial.

"State Farm complained, 'You can't see insurance, so the logo is critical. But it's not big enough and it doesn't stay on the screen long enough.'

My solution?

Sixty solid seconds of logo!

I used the familiar State Farm bumper sticker to create a simple visual metaphor for the auto accident, then the full restoration of the logo to represent the car's like-new condition.

Simple? You bet.

But that simple spot won me my first Clio for State Farm.

Simplicity is the essence of unforgettable advertising."

Keith Reinhard

IBM

"Charlie" **visualized** *the average person's attitude toward a computer and was a key component of a very successful product launch.*

Visual Gags.

Traditionally, the Yellow Pages has inspired great visualizations and great advertising.

After all, it's the book that has everything in it.

This recent award-winning campaign presents visual puns. In the one above, a squad of Marines performs various dances – Rock Drills.

The theme line – "If it's out there, it's in here."

Scrubbing Bubbles.

A distinctive visual that represents a unique Product Feature.

These cute little critters don't say much, but they sure have fun doing a job that people don't enjoy much at all.

In a tough product category, they've helped Dow Bathroom Cleaner clean up.

The product itself can be visualized very dramatically. Logos and other product graphics can reinforce your selling message.

Many brands use visual **"mnemonics"*** to make themselves memorable.

Many image campaigns rely on visual impact and unique, memorable imagery.

Consider…

What is your product's visual "world?"

Study the images associated with your product.

Try to create new combinations – new relationships – that's where you may discover The Visual.

Visuals are an International language. Beauty. Smiles. Art. Fashion. Children.

Remember, the world *is* shrinking.

The visual speaks to everyone.

Show what you say.

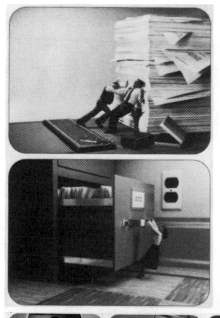

Visualize the Problem.
Making it seem bigger makes the Product seem bigger.

Visualize the Product.
Create a visual world where the product looks great.

Visualize the Emotion.

How do you feel when you hit a tennis ball?

Reebok taps into the feelings a weekend tennis player has knocking the heck out of the ball.

A unique Visual – Tennis ball faces represent all the people who bothered you the week before – a bullying boss… rude sales people… and so on.

Each shoots towards us, and we get to give 'em a whack.

This creative visualization leads to the perfect shoes for helping you get rid of all that stress.

*

Mnemonic– (ne *măn* ik) Short for "mnemonic device." A visual memory device. A common advertising technique for low-interest products.

"I NEVER MET A METAPHOR
I DIDN'T LIKE."

Look at these examples:

Babies and tires symbolizing the importance of safety – and good tires.

Rabbits symbolizing a growing business (and a large range of trucks to help).

"Bob's World" uses personalized traffic signs to symbolize a car made just for you.

A tragic toast visualizes an important message.

The new Sentra SE-R

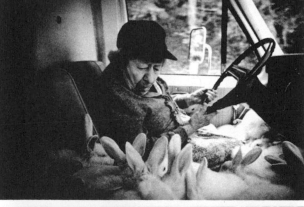

**DRINKING AND DRIVING
CAN KILL A FRIENDSHIP**

290

The Eye of The Artist.

Visual imagination can bring new dimension to your story. When the artist's eye looks at ordinary objects, they are no longer ordinary.

Here surrealistic art, a famous artist, a typographer, and a food photographer each bring their own unique contribution.

Just as Renaissance merchants commissioned portraits, modern corporations can be patrons of the arts in their advertising.

Remember, the quality of the art itself can communicate much about the quality of the advertiser.

DUE TO THE NATURE OF THIS BURGER KING COMMERCIAL, VIEWERS ARE ADVISED TO WATCH AT THEIR OWN RISK.

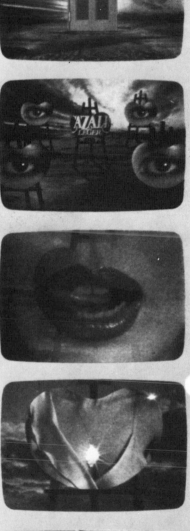

Assignment #20.

Pick three products. They may be products from previous exercises or new ones.

You may already have a Strategy and Theme from previous exercises.

The Objective of this Assignment is to help you develop range and flexibility.

Naturally, your ideas will not be of equal quality, since some TV approaches will "fit" better with some products.

Don't worry – just try to do the full range of approaches.

1. PRODUCT #1_____.

   A. Write a Strategy and Theme.

   B. Develop a **Visual.**
      Write a 10" TV spot.

   C. Develop three **Talking Person** ideas.
      Write a 30" spot using the best idea.

   D. Write a **Slice** 30".
      Single situation or Vignette.

   E. Do a **Demo** 15".
      What kind is it?

2. PRODUCT #2_____.
Same as above.

3. PRODUCT #3_____.
Same as above.

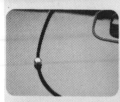

Keep it Strong and Simple.
Even an expensive and complicated product like Lexus (made by Toyota) can be dramatized with a simple Demo.

Here, a rolling steel ball dramatizes their engineering and workmanship.

And in the 90's, where advertising creates its own context, Nissan (advertised by Chiat/Day) quickly recreated the Lexus Demo using one of Nissan's less expensive models.

From steel ball to hard ball.

TV SCRIPT FORMAT

PRODUCT NAME:
"TITLE":
LENGTH:

VIDEO INSTRUCTIONS IN ALL CAPITAL LETTERS, SINGLE SPACED.	<u>AUDIO:</u> Copy indicated in upper and lower case. Double spaced.
SUPER: THEME.	<u>ANNCR (VO):</u> Theme.

292

#5 Graphic Collage.

There's another type of commercial out there, which is called **Graphic Collage**. There are **two key differences** to this type of commercial.

1. "TRACK-DRIVEN" VIDEO.

This type of commercial tends to be "track-driven." The Audio portion (copy and music) is often done first – the video develops from that.

Many MTV music videos are done this way and it has influenced the way commercials are now done. Today's audience is able to process video information at a much faster rate.

2. EXISTING VIDEO IMAGERY.

Instead of creating a commercial from scratch, the production process often involves using a number of existing images.

Footage is often re-used.

In many cases, such as local auto dealer spots, pre-produced material is provided.

Some elements you may have to work with:

> Logos and graphics.
> Existing footage.
> Previous commercials.
> Existing music.
> And other miscellaneous materials. . .

such as slides, photos, ads, and whatever else is lying around and happens to be paid for.

Many local commercials are put together this way. And a surprising number of national ones.

Video technology can re-process old images and make them look new again.

The re-editing of other people's footage with new audio tracks is also used in presentations and pitches – in what is known as the *"Steal-O-Matic."*

*Hot Doggin' at **AM/PM**. Funky animation makes this simple message fun.*

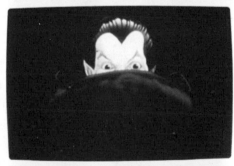

Do you feel vibration?

Start?

Rather walk?

Simple or Complex.

A Graphic Collage can be as simple as inter-cutting between film and titles – like the Goodyear commercial on the left.

The titles add an intellectual counterpoint to the message and give the message new meaning.

Or a Graphic Collage can be as rich and complex as the advertising developed by Wieden & Kennedy for Black Star Beer.

Instant nostalgia! The Wieden & Kennedy agency developed a complete history for this brand new beer with a delightful send-up of corny old advertising cliches – pictured here.

294

Many major advertisers have large libraries of produced footage which are cut into new commercials or used to produce additional spots.

Video editing techniques can also be used to make existing footage look "new."

There's another reason you may have to produce a commercial like this – *money*.

MONEY.

Often, particularly at the start of your career, your projects will have the smallest budgets.

The Look of Fashion. *Avon Calling with a variety of images for its wide variety of products. Beautiful images cut to beautiful music. Simple.*

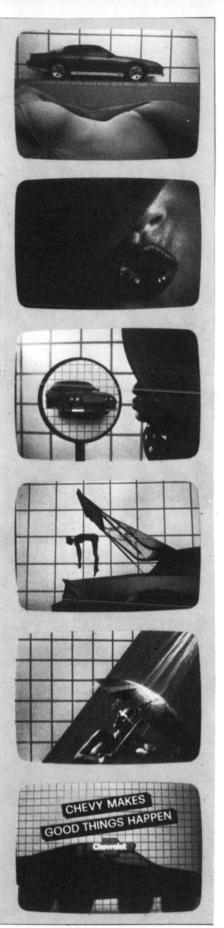

Grids, Graphics and Hot Music *made good things happen in this early Chevrolet example of the Graphic Collage approach.*

295

It's also not uncommon to be asked to solve difficult problems after the previous group has blown the production budget.

This leaves you with the task of picking up the pieces. . . which is sometimes what creating this kind of commercial is all about.

Strong editing, a good music track, graphics and your own imagination can create a rich tapestry of video communication that does a good job for your client.

The World of Chanel.

Perhaps the finest examples of this type of advertising come from Chanel.

This surrealistic effort combines multiple fantasy visions tied together through the use of color and perspective lines.

What do these images have in common?

Only the music and the vision of Chanel. Share the fantasy.

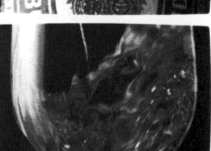

PRODUCT AS VISUAL.

A single-minded collage.

All product. Various visions.

Each shot maximizes the graphic possibilities.

Copy is classy and reassuring.

ANNCR (VO):

You could choose Heineken solely because it's far and away Europe's favorite and Europeans know their beer.

Or... you could choose Heineken because it's far and away America's number one imported beer... Americans know their beer, too.

Or... you could open it and pour it... and choose it for the best of all possible reasons.

Heineken's the best beer in the world.

Come to think of it, I'll have a Heineken.

#6. Combinations (& Variations.)

Many television commercials are Combinations and Variations of these types of commercials. Here are some examples:

SLICE / DEMO / DONUTS.

It's common to use **SLICE** to establish the Problem your Product solves.

Then, you stick a **DEMO** in the Middle.

Finally, a little **SLICE** of happy ending.

Many package goods commercials use this format. The Band-Aid™ commercial at the beginning of this chapter combined a Talking Person and a Demo.

TESTIMONIALS & DEMOS.

These two formats are also often combined.

*"It **does** taste like butter!"*

And so on.

ETCETERA.

VISUAL ideas, such as **mnemonics**, are often integrated into **SLICE** commercials.

Like the one where the crown appears when you eat the margarine… remember?

Or Parkay Margarine's *audio* mnemonic.

TALKING PERSONS emerge in **SLICE** commercials.

The list goes on…

Singing waitresses, for example, are **TALKING PERSONS**. So are singing hamburgers.

Or is that a **VISUAL?**

Whatever works.

Combinations & Counterpoint.
This beer commercial is similar to the one on the opposite page. Only, it's different. The addition of satiric supers creates a unique combination and makes a unique statement for Tuborg.

297

How cheap can you produce a TV commercial?

A Minneapolis agency used the TV studio color bars for a local supermarket – red for apples and tomatoes, yellow for corn and bananas, etc.

And the commercial above just used some titles, some intelligence and a sense of humor.

Small budget commercials can have big impact – and they'll know it's because of you, not the budget.

Remember, **you're the added value.**

These formats are not designed to limit your imagination. Hey, your job is tough enough.

They're here to give your imagination some reference points.

It's hard enough to write a good television commercial without feeling like you've got to invent the wheel. Stay calm.

The difference between a car salesman selling an old Oldsmobile in your home town and the latest whiz-bang 4-wheel drive commercial from the slopes of Mt. Kilimanjaro is one of degree.

In the beginning, your assignments may not be very exotic.

You'll be asked to sell condominiums with slides from the brochure before you'll be asked to sell Caribbean vacations on location. Your budgets will vary accordingly.

Yet, your problem is also your opportunity.

The writer on the big national car account is *expected* to do terrific work. Or it's over.

On the other hand, think how amazed they'll be at the excellence of *your* commercial.

Think about what a great job you'll do *despite* the obvious limitations. You can do it.

And it's only the beginning.

Take 'em on a trip… just imagine.

Assignment #21.

Let's try some **Combinations**.
You may use ideas from previous exercises.
Or new ones.

1. TAKE ANY TWO IDEAS FROM
ASSIGNMENT #20.
Combine them into a TV spot.
What kind is it?

2. DEVELOP A "**MNEMONIC.**"
Write a 30" **Slice** commercial using it.

3. COMBINE A **TESTIMONIAL** WITH A
DEMO.
How would you produce it?

4. DESCRIBE A **COMBINATION** WE
HAVEN'T DISCUSSED.

5. REAL WORLD EXERCISE.
Write the *cheapest* commercial you can
think of.
Any product.

6. REAL WORLD EXERCISE #2.
Write the *second cheapest* commercial you
can think of.
Same product.

7. FANTASY EXERCISE.
How would you turn this outdoor board
into a TV commercial?

TV Production.

Copywriting is a craft.

So is producing television.

Like so many things in our business, it's something you learn by doing.

It's not easy.

Producing television can be expensive and complicated, and experience is hard to come by.

Your best initial resource is people who've done it already: producers, directors, editors, and experienced writers and AD's.

Another good resource is sample reels – from commercial production houses and advertising award shows.

Study them. Be a student.

How were the commercials you liked constructed? What worked? What didn't?

Hang out. Watch. Learn.

Finally, **do animatics.**

Animatics are rough versions of commercials, usually the storyboard shot on videotape with a sound track.

Producing animatics for research or presentation can teach you many important principles of producing and editing TV commercials. It's particularly good training for producing soundtracks.

It *is* easier said than done.

But the only way to learn is to do it.

WHAT A FILM EDITOR DOES AFTER A COMMERCIAL IS SHOT TO THE TIME IT'S SHOT DOWN.

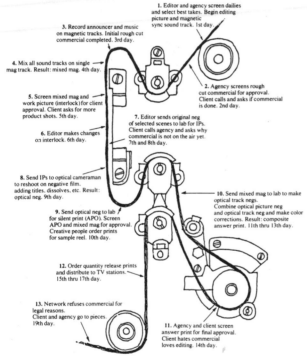

1. Editor and agency screen dailies and select best takes. Begin editing picture and magnetic sync sound track. 1st day.

3. Record announcer and music on magnetic tracks. Initial rough cut commercial completed. 3rd day.

4. Mix all sound tracks on single mag track. Result: mixed mag. 4th day.

2. Agency screens rough cut commercial for approval. Client calls and asks if commercial is done. 2nd day.

5. Screen mixed mag and work picture (interlock) for client approval. Client asks for more product shots. 5th day.

7. Editor sends original neg of selected scenes to lab for IPs. Client calls agency and asks why commercial is not on the air yet. 7th and 8th day.

6. Editor makes changes on interlock. 6th day.

8. Send IPs to optical cameraman to reshoot on negative film. adding titles, dissolves, etc. Result: optical neg. 9th day.

10. Send mixed mag to lab to make optical track negs. Combine optical picture neg and optical track neg and make color corrections. Result: composite answer print. 11th thru 13th day.

9. Send optical neg to lab for silent print (APO). Screen APO and mixed mag for approval. Creative people order prints for sample reel. 10th day.

12. Order quantity release prints and distribute to TV stations. 15th thru 17th day.

13. Network refuses commercial for legal reasons. Client and agency go to pieces. 19th day.

11. Agency and client screen answer print for final approval. Client hates commercial. loves editing. 14th day.

The more we understand each other, the more fun it is to work together.

161 E. Grand Ave., Chicago, IL 60611 (312) 321-0880

300

"The Winking Dog Syndrome"

Let me tell you a story.

When I first started out, I paid attention to everything that went into production.

And I paid attention to what came back.

I noticed that the dog food commercials were usually a bit of a disappointment.

They weren't as good as the storyboards.

Then I looked at the storyboards again.

There the dogs were smiling in anticipation, laughing. . . *winking!*

In the finished spots, the dogs were. . . dogs. The Winking Dog Syndrome is still with us.

Perhaps it's not as obvious as winking dogs, but that merely makes it harder to catch.

Consider. . . Will everything in the frame show up in the shot? It's easy to show the product a little bigger and brighter than it really is.

Will the camera lens show things in the same proportion? Or, does your board have a slight case of *"rubber pencil?"*

Does the storyboard show the time it takes to get from one frame to another? Or, is there a lot of copy with not much happening?

Will real actors smile as broadly as storyboard cartoons? Get the idea?

They say every dog has his day.

That's okay, just so it isn't your commercial.

Watch out for Winking Dogs.

Their bite is worse than their bark.

READING LIST:

How to Produce an Effective TV Commercial
Hooper White/NTC Books

How to Create Effective TV Commercials
Huntley Baldwin/NTC Books

Excellent books.
Highly recommended.

OTHER PRODUCTION PROBLEMS:

Too Many Words.
The ever-popular 33-second script. Twenty pounds in a ten pound bag. Blah blah blah.

Making Fun of the Customer.
Gee, everyone laughed at the meeting and the casting session.

"Let's Do It Both Ways."
Major sympton of the dreaded "Ad-Man's Disease."

"The Spinach in the Trombone."
Creative last-minute ideas that look strange or stupid after the film is shot.

TV Terminology:

ANNCR: Abbreviation for Announcer.

ANNCR (VO): Announcer, Voice Over

A-ROLL: The first roll of a multi-element edit or mix. Video or Audio.

ASSEMBLY (VIDEO ASSEMBLY): Combining elements and adding effects.

BG: Abbreviation for Background, as in **(MUSIC BG)**

B-ROLL: The second roll of a multi-element edit or mix.

CU: Abbreviation for Close Up.

DAILIES: The film from the day's shoot.

DISS, DS, or **DISSOLVE:** Fade from one scene to another.

ECU: Extreme Close Up.

FADE: In Audio, to reduce volume. In Video, it usually means

FADE TO BLACK which is usually the end of your commercial.

FX: Abbreviation for Effects – Sound Effects / Special Effects / Video Effects.

INTERLOCK: The edited film and sound track "locked together" on an editing machine. There may be more than one roll of each.

MATTE: Originally a film process which combined filmed images by cutting mattes to match the shape. Today it can be done electronically.

MCU: Medium Close Up.

MIX: The combining of audio elements in a soundtrack.

MORTISE: An area, usually geometric, containing a second image.
Both "Matte" and "Mortise" are often used as verbs.

MOS: Film shot without sound.

NEGATIVE: The original film stock is usually negative.

NEGATIVE TRANSFER: The process of transferring the negative film into a positive image on videotape.

OFF-LINE: Inexpensive editing – "rough cuts only," editing to prepare the edit.

ON-LINE: Expensive editing – final assembly and optical effects.

ROUGH CUT: Usually an early cut or the Editor's first cut.

SFX: Sound Effects.

SUPER: To superimpose. As in "Super the Title on the end shot."

SYNCH: To synchronize audio and video.

TWO-SHOT: A shot with both characters in it.

WIDE SHOT: (or Long Shot) a scene shot from a distance.

WIPE: An optical effect that gets you from one image to another. There are many types of wipes: clock wipe, flip wipe, iris, mosaic, page wipe, etc.

NOTE: More advertising terminology listed in the final section – "WORDS."

Onwards...

As originally planned, this book was supposed to be over by now.

But it kept on growing...

Why did this happen?

Why can't a book about writing ads stay simple?

Objective, Strategy, Tactics.

Strategy, Structure and Style.

Readin', Writin', Rhythm, and Re-Writin'.

Beginning, Middle, End.

Well... the answer is simple.

Once begun, the practice of your craft becomes a journey... not a destination.

And here's some extra baggage this book picked up while it was first written... and re-written... and...

Anyway.

We hope some of this comes in handy along the way.

*"A billion dollar hammer
pounding a ten-cent
thumb tack..."*

Here are some thoughts on our business from **Howard Luck Gossage**, a brilliant practitioner and relentless critic of advertising.

"Since ours is a competitive business in an open economic system, our services and facilities are for sale to the highest bidder; and the highest bidders are just those who have the highest profit margins – usually because they have little intrinsic worth – most of their value is contributed by the advertising they buy so freely."

"Advertising is not a right, it's a privilege. Our first responsibility is not to the product but to the public."

*"... **is advertising worth saving?** Yes, if we can learn to look at advertising not as a means for filling so much space and time but as a technique for solving problems. And this will not be possible until we destroy the commission system and start predicating our work on what is to be **earned** rather than what is to be **spent**."*

Tell the Truth.

This is a chapter my friends told me to write.

As they read early drafts of this book, each said it in their own way. . .

"Talk about telling the truth."

"Be sure to mention the need for honesty."

"You've got to put in a chapter about telling the truth."

Why is this?

Why should a writing text talk about something we all learned a long time ago?

Because all too often in our business, the truth will be unclear.

Is the product *really* better?

Is the price *really* lower?

The people who tell you are honest men.

They believe they're telling you the truth.

Yet, they may not know – for they were told by someone else. And who is to argue?

The search for advantage in business can encourage misrepresentation, overt and subtle.

And your writing is at the cutting edge.

The pressures to tell people what they want to hear are equally strong.

"The client says," says the Account Exec.

"My boss says," says the Client.

"Research says… Legal says… My wife says…"

"Will this ad work?" they ask.

"Yes, of course." you say.

As you silently pray.

This is a business shot through with fear and anxiety. The unknown is always with us.

You deal with sales projections made by optimists and budgets approved by pessimists.

Your copy is examined by lawyers who don't want any trouble, and often offered for approval to client bureaucracies who won't make a decision that isn't backed by a stack of research and legal precedents. Their guiding thoughts are,

"Don't get any on ya."

Meanwhile, consumers believe as they please, and really aren't paying attention.

Because frankly, it isn't all that important.

Is this truth? No. Merely reality.

So, what can you do?

First, be honest.

> If you think it's true, say so.
> If you think it's wrong, say so.
> If *you* were wrong, admit it.
> And learn from your mistakes.

Second, search for the truth.

> Dig for the facts of the matter.
> This business thrives on hearsay.
> You're not obliged to believe everything you hear. If it sounds too good to be true, it probably is.

Finally, don't be afraid.

It won't change a thing.

"The very bulk of advertising is its own worst enemy because somewhere along the line our immunity starts building up against imitation...

Thus we see that as the immunity builds up it costs more and more to advertise every year."

Howard Gossage

Marketing Immunity
George Lazarus/Dow-Jones Irwin

You might want to read this interesting book by the Chicago Tribune's marketing and advertising columnist.

IMMUNITY & BELIEVABILITY.

In a recent survey, advertising ranked behind toxic waste and political corruption on a list of "least liked" things.

So much for the good news.

Often, one of your biggest challenges will be to get people to believe what you have to say.

After all, consumers have heard it all before and they've been burned before, by skilled salesman, promoting dubious bargains with great skill and enthusiasm.

Overall, people are stimulated to buy more than they could afford, *if* they responded to every ad.

So we all learn early in life to resist as a matter of economic survival.

Howard Gossage had the right idea.
"People read what interests them. Sometimes it's an ad."

So did Julian Koenig...
"Tell the truth.
Make it interesting."

305

Leadership in Integrated
Marketing Communications.
Traditionally, cigarette marketers
have been innovators in advertising
and marketing techniques.

Banned from some advertising
media – such as television, they have
led the way in such areas as event
marketing and direct marketing.

This continuity-building promotion
from Virginia Slims offers fashion items
– like this leather jacket – with proofs of
purchase.

Tobacco has been part of the American economy since Colonial days.

Cigarette advertising budgets have always paid for some of the best talent and the best work in our industry.

Today we know more about the the health problems caused and aggravated by the use of cigarettes.

"Light my Lucky"
These artful ads project both youth and a defiant (perhaps death-defying) attitude. How do you feel about that?

Reinforcing the Relationship.
A continuity program from Marlboro Country.

A Word from our Sponsor.
This well-written campaign
has been the subject of controversy
from its inception.
What's your opinion?
If you were assigned this as a
project, what would you do?

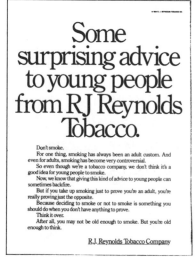

Early Appeals. "Blow some my way."
This was an innovative and effective campaign from the early days of advertising that encouraged women to smoke.

The Smooth One comes under fire.

No Ordinary Joe.
This memorable campaign uses engaging art of the Camel character.

While cigarette advertising is only supposed to target adults, some have claimed this image appeals to children. What do you think?

The Joke's on Who?
Here's a bright, funny ad from England that makes fun of cigarette advertising restrictions.

Ethical Exercise.

You're a Creative Director at an agency.

They're good people. They try to do good work. You like it there and you're doing well.

They have some cigarette business.

Suddenly, a Group Creative Director leaves and they ask you to take over the group – it's a big promotion.

You don't work on cigarettes, but guess what, one of the accounts in this group is a cigarette – which is very important to the agency.

The parent company also has other brands, some of which are also with the agency.

There are International relationships as well. What do you do?

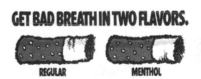

Anti-Smoking Advertising.
What is the role of advertising in either starting or stopping?

Clearly, you can write powerful anti-smoking advertising using negative appeals ranging from death to bad breath.

Which is the most effective for a younger audience?

What Strategy would you recommend?

"Our corporate goal is to do good work. We don't have enormous ambition.

It's a lousy business if you can't do good work."

Jay Chiat

Problems.

Here are my three favorite problems:

"Running Laps,"
"Moving the Problem," and...
"The Tar Baby."
There's also one very good question...
"What Business are You in?"

Running Laps...

When you're "Running Laps," you're working hard, but not really going anywhere.

Do you get the feeling that the problem was identified a while ago? It was.

Only no one will recognize it.

Meanwhile, you keep on moving on with no real idea of where you're going.

Many reasons and motives create this advertising version of the Gerbil Exercise Wheel.

Sometimes, it's as simple as bad judgement and bad decisions by the people in charge.

Sometimes, it's people who find it hard to acknowledge obvious answers.

And sometimes, people aren't as interested in solving the problem as you might think.

It gives them something to do.

It reinforces their importance as decision makers for one more pay period.

Another nasty example – clients who've become disenchanted with their agency and are getting ready to move the business.

Meanwhile, you work away. Running laps.

How do you know when it's "Laps" and when it's just a tough problem and you just have to keep on working at it?

You don't. That's one of the problems.

But. . . if you get the nagging feeling that you're going over the same ground and you keep passing the solution to the problem, you may be "Running Laps."

Meanwhile, be hopeful. Sometimes people get tired enough to acknowledge the obvious.

Try to be one of the last ones standing.

Many copywriting careers have been built on endurance and enthusiasm.

Sometimes, someone else not burdened with the clogged-up process can get it solved quickly and simply.

Don't be envious – try to become wiser.

And sometimes… you just have to tell yourself you're getting good exercise.

Running laps.

Moving the Problem.

Then there's "Moving The Problem."

In advertising, we're constantly asked to "solve problems." Usually the answer to the problem is, you guessed it, an ad.

So we write a great ad.

And we solve the problem.

Or do we? All too often, events reveal that we really haven't solved the problem at all.

We have merely *moved* it into another area where the problem sits unsolved.

"It's an operations problem."
"It's a distribution problem."
"It's a pricing problem."
"It's a product problem."
"We don't know what the problem is."

Before you run the ads and spend all that money, take a look around.

Did you solve the problem?

Or did you just move it?

The Tar Baby.

It's organizational Fly Paper – with all the entrapping potential of that cute little fellow Ol' B'rer Rabbit punched in the nose.

You never know when you'll meet one. But unlike B'rer Rabbit, you'll usually have plenty of company.

See, with the Tar Baby, everybody gets stuck.

Account Executives – probably a couple, just to add to the confusion.

Definitely more than one level of client decision-making, to complicate matters further.

And research. Lots of it… badly used. Of course.

Enough numbers and memos so everyone can collect a stack and think they're helping.

Add uncertainty, complexity, and season well with underlying panic.

It's a mess and you're stuck in it.

If you're not *in* a Tar Baby, sometimes it's fun to see one grow down the hall.

The layouts fill wastebaskets.

Storyboards by the pound.

While meetings abound.

And, as meetings get longer, people get dumber.

Send out for more research – and maybe some pizzas – 'cause we'll be working through the weekend. Again.

Suddenly there are too many people, lots of opinions, no real answers, and a problem that might not be solvable after all.

That Briar Patch starts to look pretty good.

An outdated or overpriced product is a prime candidate.

There are others.

If you think you see a Tar Baby sitting in the path… ***watch out!***

He's gonna getcha.

THAT'S NOT ALL FOLKS!
These are just some of the common problems in the advertising business.

There are more.

They're common as fleas – and they will always be with you, no matter what collar you wear.

Some you will solve.

And some you won't.

Just remember, if the problems were easy, they wouldn't need you.

The Career-Building Business.

Ads can be an opportunity to win awards and professional recognition.

Often, small advertisers and pro bono accounts offer big opportunities.

Here is an award-winning ad for Elmer's Minnows – an account that hooked 15 awards in two years.

Your Competition Can Help Define Your Business.

Don't take too narrow a view of who you're competing with.

These music teachers understand what business they're in.

New Business is Where You Find It.

Here, 3M, a company in the business of innovation, tells the story of the accidental discovery of Scotchgard™. Their record of innovation is no accident.

"What Business Are You In?"

It's one of the classic questions of marketing.

As the business school parable goes, the railroads were once all powerful in America – but they didn't realize what business they were in.

They weren't in the railroad business, they were in the *transportation* business.

By not realizing this, they became an outdated industry. So it goes.

Ask yourself the same question, *"What business are you in?"*

The advertising business?

Marketing? Communications? Promotions? Customer Relations?

You're in all of those businesses, but the real bottom line is . . .

YOU'RE IN THE BUSINESS OF BUILDING BUSINESSES.

You're in the business of helping companies talk to customers.

You're helping merchants and manufacturers, and all the people who work there.

And... you're helping the people you talk to.

You're in the business of helping people find products and services of genuine benefit.

All in all, it's a job worth doing.

Common Cents.

Here we'll deal briefly with one very important aspect of your job. MONEY.

In general, the purpose of your job is to sell goods or services.

The amount of money spent selling is an investment by your client.

He's entitled to expect results from that investment. And he's entitled to expect that you will treat every one of his dollars as though it were your own.

Your job is to help people make money.

Not only is this ethically correct, you will reap an additional benefit if you do it well.

The trust and friendship of the people you work with.

Everybody loves a profit center.

PRICE CAN BE NICE.

One of the things you will be called upon to advertise is price.

Here are some excellent examples of price emphasis advertising.

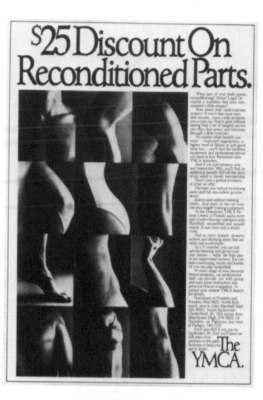

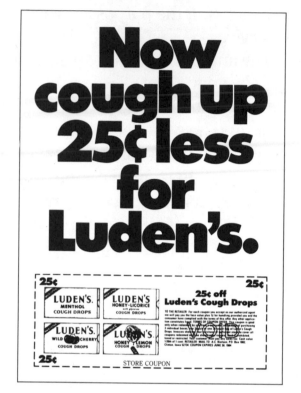

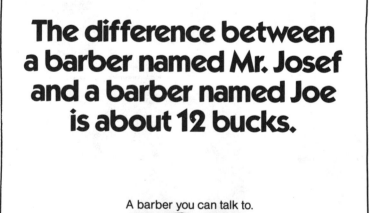

A barber you can talk to.

824 Massachusetts Ave.,   Cambridge, Massachusetts.

Add Value as You Trim the Price.

Here, Bertolli Olive Oil combines Consumer Benefits ("Eat Well" and "Live Long") with a Free Offer and a Coupon.

The result, greater value for the product at the same time that added values (a recipe booklet and a coupon)are offered to the consumer.

Maybe you really can have it both ways.

Quality Communication Keeps You from Looking Cheap.

Here, El Al uses great art direction and bright writing to avoid seeming like a "bargain basement" operation.

The clever but simple visual surprises you – you're pleasantly surprised instead of mildly suspicious.

So the price seems credible.

Be a Good Business Partner.

American Express also works to build good relationships with its "other" customers – the establishments that accept the American Express card.

One of American Express's disadvantages with this group is the fact that they charge a higher fee.

Here they work to deliver extra value to those customers by offering free advertising.

The Same Old Sale Shouldn't Be the Same Old Thing.

Pier 1 has done a great job promoting their inexpensive merchandise.

Smart writing that appeals to smart shoppers.

Here's a lesson I learned long ago.
It still works.

FCB
CHICAGO
MEMORANDUM

TO _____ FLOOR _____

FROM <u>Bruce Bendinger</u>　　EXT <u>1840</u>　DATE <u>9/29/80</u>

SUBJECT <u>WHAT I LEARNED FROM AN ACCOUNT EXECUTIVE</u>

A number of years ago, a good friend and business partner taught me a lesson.

"Principles," he said.　Repeatedly.

"Decisions have to be made from principles."

We have to make a lot of decisions in this business.

And there are always a lot of factors complicating those decisions.

How do we decide?

How do we choose between conflicting demands?

How do we build a point of view from an abundance of opinion?

Then, how do we sell it?

Principles.

Opinions vary.　Principles remain constant.

During the time we worked together, our work and our decisions were shaped by one basic principle.

<u>The agency must work in the best interests of the client's business.</u>

That is the principle on which decisions must be based.

Not short term gain.　Or "points."

Not profit or "profitability."

Not expedient personal politics based on client opinion or bias.

314

MEMO
9/29/80
PAGE 2

Not more comfortable or less controversial relationships.

Not easier meetings.

Not "safer" work.

This principle will unify a creative group. Enabling a variety of skills, view points, and personalities to focus on a common objective.

It fosters improved team work and more productive discussions between account and creative groups.

It ultimately generates the respect and trust of every client worth having.

Finally, it allows you to be utterly fearless.

When you know in your gut why you're doing what you're doing, your arguments will be strong, your logic will be tight, and your presentation will have the presence that only comes with conviction.

Naturally, you will never win every battle, or sell every recommendation the first time.

But as time goes by, the client's business will move forward.

Because every one will be united by a shared belief and a common goal.

Because the lessons you learn as you try to achieve that goal will make you wiser and more capable.

Because the feelings of mutual respect and partnership will grow, even though meetings may feature intense disagreement and controversy.

That is the lesson I learned, and it has served me well.

It is yours if you wish it.

BB/5C/929

P.S. The Account Executive was Bob Barocci, who became President of Leo Burnett International and then went on to head his own agency. Thanks, Bob.

MAKIN' BOOK.
by Rhonda Huie (*former Associate Recruitment Manager Leo Burnett; now at Ross Roy.*)

What do I look for in a beginner's portfolio? Ads, of course.

I don't look for the short story you got an "A" on, or your GPA, or what fraternity you were in.

I don't look for cute pictures of you and your dog.

I don't even look for articles from the school newspaper that demonstrate your ability to produce work under a deadline.

I look for ads. Smart ads. Interesting ads. Ads that make me want to go out and try the product.

Ads that make me happy, or mad, or misty. In other words, ads that are better than most of the produced work you'll find out there on any given day.

I don't care if you have a degree in advertising.

Or if you have any degree at all.

All I care about is if you understand what is interesting about a product, and if you can translate that into something that will make a consumer stop and think, *"Gee, that looks like something I really ought to check out."*

Good advertising doesn't have to be cute or clever. In fact, I have a rubber stamp in my office that reads, *Use a pun, go to jail.*

I don't want to see how many cliches you can come up with that relate to your product.

I want to see that you're smart – that you've considered all the possible ways to relate your message, and that you've had the sense to pick the most innovative, intelligent, interesting one.

With all the soap-box stuff over with, I'll get down to brass tacks.

Your Portfolio.

Your portfolio should consist of four or five campaigns of three or four ads each. Throw in a few one-shots if you'd like.

Make sure that you choose a wide variety of goods – everything from a big ticket item to something like toothpaste.

Pick things you know about – go to your medicine cabinet or under the sink, and look at what you buy.

Then, try to use the reasons you buy those things in your advertising.

If you want to be a copywriter, words are all-important.

Talk to your customers as if you know them.

How would you try to convince your best friend to try your brand of shampoo? How would you describe your bank to a person new to town?

How would you persuade your

cont'd

Building Your Book.

During your first years in the business, you must do your job *and* build your book.

Sometimes these aren't the same thing.

In that case, you will reap the additional benefit of building your capacity for overwork.

Your book represents your ability. It's worth all the time and effort you can spare.

A GOOD BOOK LOOKS GOOD.

Neatness and organization count.

Remember, you do meetings.

Presenting your book is a meeting.

KEEP EVERYTHING AND FILE IT.

You should have comps or stats of your best unproduced work, as well as proofs or stats of *all* your produced work.

Some of these may be large – invest in some inexpensive storage from an art supply store.

Develop a filing system for old ad ideas that never went anywhere (you never know).

MAKE SLIDES OF YOUR BEST PRINT.

As years go by, samples age. Slides will hold up better, and they can be made quickly into customized presentations.

CHOOSE YOUR CHOICEST COPY.

If it isn't produced, make sure you have a clean, crisp print-out.

Need a piece of choice copy?

Write about something you love.

There should be a fairly long piece of copy that shows you're a *great* writer.

INVENT PROJECTS.

A good idea will usually make a good ad.
Do it.

DEVELOP A "SCRAP FILE."

This is not cheating! Studying and saving other good work will help you learn to make yours better. Finally...

FREE LANCE.

Some call it "Moonlighting,"some call it "Free-lance." Some of this work is, literally, free.

Neither resent this fact nor despair. You are performing a useful economic service – revitalizing the economy, helping provide jobs and sales for new, struggling enterprises and helping ambitious politicians build careers so they can hire expensive consultants to tell them what to do.

Most important, you will be developing your skills, making new contacts, and, of course. . . *building your book.*

David Ogilvy agrees, *"If you need more income than your agency is willing to pay you, make up the difference by moonlighting... I have been moonlighting for 30 years."*

Nonetheless, discretion is advised.

Book-Building Exercises:

1. Review and UpdateYour Book.

(If you don't have a book yet, an outline for your first Sample Book is on the following page.)

2. Have Your Book Evaluated.

This is a good way of meeting people.

3. Write Additional Samples.

Write ads designed to build your book.

4. Freelance.

New businesses, relatives, worthy charities,etc. Start to build a clientele.

boyfriend or girlfriend that spending $1000 for a new stereo makes more sense than a trip for two to Aspen?

I'll bet you wouldn't say things like "phenococabromolide" or "known for many good reasons."

And, while you may not be able to draw a straight line, you should have some kind of layout.

The best ads are the ones where the copy and the art direction augment each other for an even stronger message.

Advice for Art Directors.

If art direction is your goal, you'll want to show you have interesting new ideas on how to present products.

What really counts here are the ideas, so don't spend all your time on beautifully finished illustrations, mounting and framing.

Type is important, but needn't be set. Hand renderings that are neat and handsome are impressive.

And don't think you can get away with bad headlines just because you're into art. The best young art directors – the ones that get hired – write great headlines.

I don't think you can have a great visual idea without first knowing what you want to say. So say it.

Keep Improving Your Book.

Once you have a book together, get opinions, professional opinions.

Don't ask your mother if she likes it – unless she just happens to be a Creative Director.

What's important is what people in the industry think.

Listen to them. Take their advice. Change things. Keep at it.

It may take a while for things to click, but when they do, you'll wonder why it seemed so hard back in the beginning.

Your book is what has to sell you, not the other way around. It's the only gauge we have of your talent.

It's the only thing that will get you a job in a creative department.

If you have a great portfolio, it won't matter where you went to school or who you know.

If your book is awful, it won't matter where you went to school or who you know.

The hardest thing in the world for me is to tell someone they're just not good.

When you walk through my door, I want you to have the right kind of book.

I want you to have smart, gutsy, innovative work.

I want you to be great.

That's what I look for in a great portfolio.

Sample Sample Book.

In most cases, your sample book will be the most important factor in your getting a job.

It's worth all the effort you can put into it.

The following is an outline of what a good sample book might contain.

1. An Ad for Yourself.

It can be a letter, a resume, or something more unusual. Make it bright and brief.

2. Two Parity Products.

Take 2 existing products with little or no competitive difference. (Like a beer or a bank.)

Each product should have: A short Strategy and a three-ad campaign.

3. Two "Unique" Products.

Pick affordable consumer items that you think are really special.

Write a strategy and 3 ad campaigns for each.

4. Do a Long-Copy Ad.

Show people you can write.

5. Some "One-Shots."

A few individual ads that are really terrific. Make them great.

6. Something That's "More than Advertising" – A Button, T-Shirt, P. O. P., etc. Show some "IMC" ideas that reinforce yours.

Say why you like them.

Do the next ad in the campaign.

7. New Products.

No science-fiction. It should be possible with today's technology and appeal to today's market.

Your New Product should have: a Name, a Strategy and a 3-ad campaign (2 in one medium, 1 in another, i.e., 2 print, 1 TV.)

NOTE: If you've had anything published or produced, like something in the college paper, or a brochure for your uncle's business, put it in the *back* of the book. It won't hurt. But probably won't help, either.

WRITE IF YOU WANT WORK.

1 You are the songwriter for hitmaker Poppy Putrid. She's just had three recent No. 1 hits. All love songs. For her next hit, Poppy wants a song about moldy pizza, rancid butter, and flat beer. Her agent is convinced it should be another love song. Make it both. (Don't worry about the music, or adapt a tune you know.)

2 Write a "Dialogue in a Dark Alley." (Not more than 200 words.)

3 You've just learned that the IRS is planning to lower the percentage ratio of income to medical expenses, thus lowering the tax deductions for dental, psychiatric, and medical expenses. You are the star reporter for the daily newspaper, The National Sensational. The editor wants to make this the banner story. Write your head and a two-column story.

4 A delegation of Martians has just landed in Central Park. They do not understand any Earth languages—only very basic symbols. Prepare a short speech (comprised of pictures and symbols) to welcome them and to tell them just what kind of place Central Park is. (Please enclose a plain language version of the speech in an envelope, in case we are confused!)

5 Describe, in not more than 100 words, the plot of the last episode of "Dynasty."

6 You've heard the story about the man who made a fortune selling refrigerators to Eskimos. In not more than 100 words, how would you sell a telephone to a Trappist monk, who is observing the strict Rule of Silence? (But he can nod acceptance at the end.)

7 Design/draw two posters. One is for legislating strict gun-control laws. The other is in support of the NRA.

8 The ingredients listed on the tin of baked beans reads: "Beans, Water, Tomatoes, Sugar, Salt, Modified Starch, Vinegar, Spices." Make it sound mouthwatering.

J. WALTER NEW YORK

Here's a copy assignment for beginning writers from J. Walter Thompson.

It's pretty interesting.

You might want to try it.

On the right, are some excellent examples of **Self-Promotion Ads.**

A whole campaign, in fact.

Not only did the writer win an award, he got a job. That's effective advertising.

"POST-GRAD" WORK?

If you need to work on your book before you can get work, these are some places that can help:

The Portfolio Center, in Atlanta; **The School of Visual Arts,** in New York; **Ad-Ed,** in Chicago; and **The Advertising Arts College** in San Diego are four of the better known programs.

There are also excellent advertising programs at art schools, such as **Parsons** and **The Art Center School of Design.**

Local ad clubs in many cities offer courses for beginners.

Finally, look for a *Mentor.* You can often find someone in the business to "coach" you as you work on your book.

COMPENSATION INTEGRATION?

Another problem when selecting marketing programs – some are more profitable for the agency.

Advertising has a built-in commission –many other forms of marketing communication do not.

That's why some services are performed by agencies; some are handled by the marketer; some are provided by specialized companies like PR firms or Sales Promotion agencies; and some are included as "added value" by the media itself.

The wide disparity in compensation complicates this complicated process further.

How to Think "Integrated."

You already know how.

When you got dressed this morning, you managed a complex decision-making process that coordinated a wide variety of tactics.

At the same time, you considered your target audience and your available resources.

When you went shopping, you filled your cart with a reasonable assortment – matching needs and resources to the best of your ability. Few of you filled your shopping cart with only bean sprouts or Twinkies.™

But what if you had separate divisions in charge of each item of clothing?

With a dotted line relationship between the Department of Shirts and the Tie Division (and the people in Socks always complaining about being the last to be consulted). You'd probably still be standing in front of the closet trying to get dressed.

And while a shopping cart full of bean sprouts or Twinkies may seem bizarre, many marketing budgets are dominated by a few items.

So… *you* know how to think integrated – it's the marketers and advertising agencies that have trouble.

Because organization and resource allocation make *acting* integrated a lot tougher than *thinking* integrated.

Well, here's some simple advice for complicated times.

KEEP THE CUSTOMER IN MIND.

The core of "Integrated Marketing Communi-cation" (IMC) planning is the customer.

Whether it's your current customer, or some-one you want to "recruit," the more you know about that person, the better.

So, one of the first things you might want to do is try to know your customer better.

Do some one-on-one interviews and find out what your business is *really* all about in the mind and in the lives of your customers.

Want to read a book? Check out *"Maxi Mar-keting"* by Rapp & Collins (there's also an audio tape for your car).

Want to hire someone? If you're a marketer, put someone in charge of knowing your customer – add a "Consumer advocate."

If you're an agency, try **Account Planning.** (Want to read another book? Check out *"Hitting the Sweet Spot"* by Lisa Fortini-Campbell.)

Review all your marketing programs with your customers in mind – not the division heads.

And make sure you're saying the same thing to your customers. For example, many marketers say one thing to the customer in their ads and something entirely different with their pricing.

LOOK FOR EXTRA "CONTACT POINTS."

The new IMC word is "Contact Points." This includes package copy, P.O.P., your name in the newspaper, "word of mouth" and advertising.

Mary Wells, one of the most successful adver-tising executives in history, always looked for ways to build a campaign in more than one media. She also appreciated the value of PR and brand-building promotions.

As a practical matter, try to generate extra "contact points" by taking something that works in one channel and pushing it into other commu-nication channels.

MaxiMarketing

Stan Rapp & Tom Collins, of the Rapp & Collins agency, have devel-oped an integrated approach they call "MaxiMarketing."

It moves past "Action," or "Making the Sale," to "Developing the Relation-ship." They address a world in which keeping the customers you have is as at least as important as getting new ones. Perhaps more important.

The three stages are:
• **Reaching the Prospect**
• **Making the Sale**
• **Developing the Relationship**

Rapp and Collins have a direct response/direct marketing back-ground. It's interesting to see how they apply their background to the entire marketing process.

Here's The MaxiMarketing Model:

Maximized Distribution
Adding new channels.

Maximized Sales
Through share of mind and cus-tomer database.

Maximized Linkage
Encouraging interested prospects.

Maximized Synergy
Double-duty advertising.

Maximized Activation
Inquiries and sales promotion.

Maximized Awareness
Appealing to the whole brain.

Maximized Accountability
Proving that it works.

Maximized Media
New ways to reach the consumer

Maximized Targetting
Prospecting for your most desireable customers.

MaxiMarketing
Rapp & Collins/McGraw-Hill

ARCHWAY COOKIES–
GETTING THEIR 5¢ WORTH.

Archway Cookies wants to increase off-shelf display. The grocery trade is the original target.

Now, watch what happens.

Archway develops a program called "Cookies for Kids." For every package sold, Archway donates the 5¢ a package advertising allowance to the local children's hospital.

Plus, Archway will support this program with additional advertising that publicizes the local grocery chain's support of the program.

Initial Tactics

It starts with one hospital in one market – a few public-spirited chains are "early adopters."

And Archway does some advertising.

They add a sub-theme, "Be a Good Cookie," and a jingle with music bed for customized local radio commercials.

Promotional materials are produced: In-store P.O.P. with the "Cookies for Kids" theme, and "Be a Good Cookie" balloons, buttons and T-shirts.

The Program Grows

Archway sales and PR people start to get involved with the local hospitals.

And then, because caring about sick kids is something you get caught up with, more Archway bakeries get involved in more markets. A PR professional is hired to help coordinate the growing program.

Mentions of these events pop up on local TV stations, since there are public service aspects to the program.

Archway learns more about getting extra mentions from the local media.

cont'd.

What "IMC" means to many is, *"Are there other ways to get more bang for my buck, besides advertising?"*

The answer? Envelope please… *sometimes.*

Most of the time, it makes sense to look for ways to help the "Selling Idea" in your advertising grow in a natural (and integrated) fashion into other marketing communication channels.

IMC can be complicated or simple.

The simple way is to grow successful programs and marketing ideas into new media channels.

ROLAIDS turned their ad slogan into a PR program – an award for the best "relief" pitcher.

NIKE sends clips of its commercials to sports reporters. More and more advertisers are treating the "premiere" of their advertising as a newsworthy event – with surprising results.

Need new channels to explore? Sampling and customer loyalty programs are two alternatives.

What – no elegant chart? No "White Paper?" Don't worry. Like NIKE says, "Just do it."

Start with a good idea, and then turn it into an integrated program.

PLANS VS. ACTIONS.

The Archway example (sidebar) shows how these things work in the real world.

If we'd tried to sell it, initially, as a total integrated marketing program – no way!

It's expensive, it crosses organizational lines, there's no infrastructure to handle it, and you really don't know if it might work.

Acting integrated can be complicated and expensive. From a cost/benefit standpoint, you're all-too-often "trying to catch mice with a cheese truck."

In the real world, you take a tactic and build on it however you can. Your fine mind, already integrated, keeps finding IMC opportunities.

You can do it while you're getting dressed in the morning – preparing for a new business day.

And you can do it while you're shopping – watching the marketplace at work.

Be practical. Be tactical.

And, keep the customer in mind.

That's how to think integrated.

A National Program

Then, Archway runs into a national *"Cause Marketing"* program – the Children's Miracle Network (CMN).

In some local markets, Archway becomes a CMN sponsor – and when the Telethon rolls around, local Archway bakers present checks.

This leads Archway to become a national sponsor – with more advertising, sales promotion and PR based around the Cookies for Kids theme.

The program evolves into an annual event featuring: advertising, promotion, public relations, event marketing and trade marketing.

Coordinators are assigned at each bakery. Workshops help teach sales personnel how to implement on the local level.

And, since cookies respond well to off-shelf display - sales go up.

From Tactics to Integration

In retrospect, it's smooth, superbly integrated, and very successful.

It's a program that addressed all of Archway's important "audiences:" customers, the trade, and Archway's own sales personnel.

It's also a program that does more good in the community than most.

You could probably write a "Case Histories" that makes it look integrated from the beginning.

But the initial planning and implementation wasn't "Integrated" in the classic sense - it was done in tactical bits and pieces, with people learning as they went along.

While it ended up as a national consumer promotion integrated top - to-bottom - it began with a few folks trying to figure out something new to do with a nickel on a local level.

Integrated Electronic Support.
TV uses National CMN spokesperson Merlin Olsen with localized tags.
Radio allows for easy customization in local markets.

Archway Cookies For Kids
60" Radio: "The Thank You Song"

VOCAL: Archway says…
    Thanks to you Good Cookies…

ANNCR: Thanks for supporting Archway Cookies for Kids

VOCAL:
'Cause each time you buy those Archway Cookies - You give a little help to a kid.

LOCALIZED ANNCR: (12")
    Each specially marked package of Archway Cookies results in a donation to (Local Childrens Hospital)
    It's a great way to help the people who help the kids of (Local Market).

VOCAL:
So when you get those Good Food Cookies You're gonna be a Good Cookie, too.
    From one Good Cookie to another
    A Great Big Thanks to You.

LOCALIZED ANNCR: (10")
Look for special Archway Cookies For Kids displays at (Local Store Listing) And thanks for helping (Local Childrens Hospital).

VOCAL:
'Cause each time you buy those Archway Cookies, you give a little help to a kid.

ANNCR: Archway Cookies For Kids!

A TRUE STORY.

I learned this lesson during the Pizza Hut shoot out. We competed with six other top agencies. And won.

After the big presentation, an Account Executive turned to me and said, "You know when you had 'em?"

I waited for some nifty compliment on one of my clever stories or perceptive strategic observations.

"It was the buttons," he said.

"You were talking and they were looking at those little buttons going 'Ohhh and Ahhh and Mmmm."

We won the business and I learned another important lesson.

There's more to advertising than advertising.

Even the Pink Bunny Does it!
Advertising that keeps going into Sales Promotion (like these "Self-Liquidators") that build Brand Identity.

Beyond Advertising.

Here are some of the other things you should be able to write besides ads:

**Brochures
Bumper
Stickers
& Buttons
Catalogs
Direct Mail
"P.I." Advertising
P.O.P., Merchandising & Sales Promotion
Publicity & Public Relations**

Publicity Vehicle.
The Oscar Mayer "Weinermobile" helps drive Brand Awareness.

Let's take them one at a time...

BROCHURES.

This is an important way for you to tell the whole story. And sometime during your career as a copywriter, you'll write a brochure or two.

In many ways, a brochure is an Outline ad that folds up – your headline's the cover and your copy is organized on the succeeding pages.

Brochures can be an effective way to give your sale more depth and give interested consumers additional information.

If you want to know more, **Jane Maas** has written an excellent book called *"How to Write More Effective Brochures and Sales Pieces."*

BUMPER STICKERS & BUTTONS.

They do more than motivate customers.

Another job is *motivating your own people.*

Avis did this.

Part of the effectiveness of the Avis "We Try Harder" campaign was the new enthusiasm it brought to Avis employees.

"Our only standard is excellence. In everything we do. And every time we do it.

A matchbook cover deserves as much effort, as much work, as a 30-second network television commercial."

Ed McCabe

Another important lesson, which politicians have known for years, is that one of your best media buys is a person who wears your button or drives around with your bumper sticker.

If your campaign can inspire this extra dimension of enthusiasm and commitment, it will work more effectively.

And it can make your presentation to the client a heck of a lot more effective.

Oh, and don't forget T-Shirts.

CATALOGS.

The craft of copywriting began in the world of catalogs. They're back.

Direct sales has been a real growth area during the last decade. Americans want more choices while they have less time to shop.

Even though some traditional catalogs, such as Sears, have closed their covers – this is a rich source of innovative marketing and wonderful copywriting.

The J. Peterman Company catalog is a wonderful example. Get a copy. Call 1-800-231-7341.

Catalog copywriting must replace seeing and touching the product.

See how catalogs, such as "The Sharper Image" romance their products.

There is a growing need for good catalog copywriters.

The Counterfeit Mailbag.

The secret thoughts of an entire country were carried in leather bags exactly like this one. Except this one, a copy, isn't under lock and key in a museum. It's for sale.

I borrowed an original from a friend, a retired mailman who, like thousands before him, was kind enough to test it out, for years, on the tree-lined streets of small towns everywhere. Before you were born.

The test was successful: even though discontinued, it can't be improved upon. It's simply perfect as a device for carrying important ideas and feelings back and forth. And the same as with those old and scarce and beautiful mailbags, people will look forward to seeing what you've got inside.

The Counterfeit Mailbag. Containing one vast unzippered pocket, and another zippered. Shoulder strap and handle. Size: 15" long x 7" wide x 12-1/2" tall. Strong, soft leather that will only get better. A beauty.

Price: $275.

How to take care of the Mailbag.

The first scratch will kill you, but in fact, it's the first step in the right direction: patina.

So the sooner it gets scratched, nicked, bumped, dug, hit, squeezed, dropped, bent, folded and rained on, the better. Really.

When you receive your mailbag, it's so fiercely new looking I'm almost ashamed of it. But there's no choice. It would cost too much to pre-age each mailbag before sending it out to a customer. (Antiques cost more than new, for a reason.)

Here's my recipe for "accelerating" the aging process. First, spend one day (the day you get it) the way it is. Brand new. Then, the next day, scratch it all over with your fingernails. Lightly. This will horrify you, at first. Then, spray-mist it with plain water, lightly. Let it dry. The scratches will lose their rawness. They will look old. Repeat this treatment as often as you can stand to; once a week for 5 weeks. Then once a year. (Clean mailbag with plain water only. Not petrochemicals, not oils, not detergents, not mystery solvents, not leather "cremes." It will do just fine with plain water and will outlast both of us.)

From the J. Peterman Company "Owner's Manual" No. 23.

325

The Right Message to the Right Target can Change the World.

In 1939, Albert Einstein wrote a letter to President Roosevelt – the result was the Manhattan Project (in Chicago) and the Atomic Bomb.

That's Direct Mail in action.

Person-to-person communication that hits the right target with the right message.

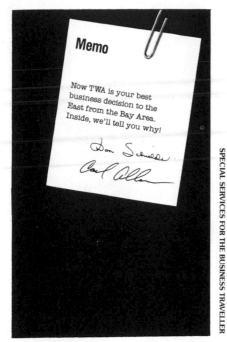

SPECIAL SERVICES FOR THE BUSINESS TRAVELLER

Good Customers Are Usually Your Best Target.

Here, TWA specifically targets West Coast business travelers.

Read All About It.

It seems like almost everyone in Direct Mail has written a book about it – which you can get by mail. Naturally.

DIRECT MAIL.

Another important way to reach your customers is Direct Mail or Direct Response.

You know what it is – you've been receiving it for years.

It invites you to get credit cards, support worthy causes and all manner of unique purchase opportunities. Catalogs, letters, sweepstakes, and so on populate the world of Direct Mail.

One of the reasons for its pervasiveness is that *it works!* The right message to the right target can change the world.

Many successful businesses have been built with Direct Mail and Direct Response Advertising.

A major advantage of this type of communication is *Targeting.* By narrowing in on qualified consumers, your audience has a higher percentage of potential customers.

And this leads to one of the few rules I know for sure in the world of Direct Mail...

"You're As Good As Your List."

There are many other "rules" and there are a lot of books available on the subject (John Caples, mentioned earlier, has been very successful in this area). If you target well and have a good list, you have a reasonable chance of success.

The second rule I know is...

"You Learn from Experience."

You count your responses, and in that way, measure your effectiveness. You don't measure CPM (Cost Per Thousand), you measure CPR (Cost Per Response).

Since each learning experience costs you money, new companies tend to "die like flies."

Still, given the right product and the right prospect list, Direct Mail may be a great way to sell your Product.

P.S. Always use a "P.S." in Direct Mail.

"P.I." ADVERTISING.

"P.I." means "Per Inquiry."

This is the stuff you see on late-night TV or on cable advertising – "Greatest Hits" albums, kitchen gadgets, or the like. They're sometimes called *"Infomercials."*

Basically, it's direct mail on TV.

Sometimes, the TV station or cable channel takes the commercial for free, and is paid "Per Inquiry."

The Newest kind of "30."
The thirty-minute "Infomercial.

Or, they take a small amount of money.

Obviously, a station would rather have cash, so P.I. Advertisers make do with marginal time and marginal channels. Unsold time is their hunting ground. And, with all the new cable channels – hunting is good.

One of Wieden & Kennedy's very first jobs was a thirty minute infomercial for SoloFlex.

A. Eicoff, a division of Ogilvy & Mather, is a major force in this type of advertising. Read *"Eicoff on Broadcast Direct Marketing."*

To find out more about this fast-growing field, I'm sure there's an 800-number you can call.

P.O.P. & MERCHANDISING*

"P.O.P." means Point Of Purchase.

It's also called "Point of Sale." Usually, it's display materials used wherever your product is sold.

It reinforces your message at the critical time when the purchase decision is being made by the customer. Some of the types of P.O.P. pieces are:

Banners, Displays and **"Shelf Talkers"**
Counter Cards, Mobiles and **"Danglers"**
Hang Tags and **Secondary Stickers.**
On-Packs and **Near Packs**
Table Tents (in Bars and Restaurants)
and, of course, **Packaging*.**

The Direct Approach.

James Webb Young, the JWT copy chief who wrote "A Technique for Producing Ideas," started his own mail-order business – *Webb Young, Trader. Santa Fe, New Mexico.*

This one ad sold 26,000 ties.

Kool-Aid™
Wacky Warehouse.

Here's P.O.P. promoting a sales promotion program designed to build frequency with Target Customers - kids who drink Kool-Aid.

It's a whole collection of neat stuff you can get by saving "Kool-Aid Points."

This is a "Continuity Program." It's designed to generate increased repeat purchase and usage.

*Package or product-based communication and display is also referred to as "Merchandising."

AEROSPACE JORDAN PR PLAN.

Here's the NIKE PR program for the Premiere of their new Michael Jordan/Bugs Bunny spot on the Super Bowl:

1/7 Mailing of Letter and Stills confirming that Michael is back with Bugs and that his opponents are Marvin the Martian and K-9. Special targetting of major marketing writers, USA Today and Ad Age.

1/8 Telephone Interviews w. Scott Bedbury, NIKE Director of Advertising.

1/13 PR Newswire Release to sportswriters that adds new element - Marvin and K-9 are coaches for the Scream Team. Art is included. Entertainment writers are also targetted.

1/18 FedEx Video News Release with selected scenes (the commercial isn't finished yet!). Plus the first Hare Jordan commercial. Plus comments from Charles Barkely, Quincy Watts and Sergey Bubka.

1/27 Satellite release of second Video News Release which includes completed commercial. To "scoop" the Super Bowl, it is possible that TV sports and entertainment media will play the commercial twice before the Super Bowl. For free!

1/31 Super Bowl Sunday! As you can see, NIKE kicked-off their campaign long before the kick-off!

In-Store PR.
Here, McDonald's addresses a critical issue with consumers.

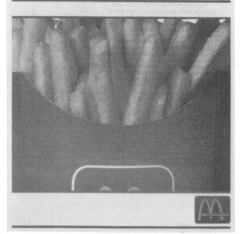

Many companies specialize in P.O.P. and many clients have departments that work in this area.

Whether you work in this area or not, try to make sure your advertising carries over into P.O.P.

PUBLICITY & PUBLIC RELATIONS

In advertising, we're so used to paying for our exposure to the public, we sometimes forget that there are other ways to build awareness.

As you develop your advertising campaign, it often makes sense to look for opportunities to get exposure in the press.

Talk show appearances, press releases, press conferences, publicity stunts and other non-advertising activities can help build public awareness and "word of mouth" for your brand.

These activities are usually supervised and coordinated by Public Relations professionals, who specialize in this area.

They have their own method of "strategic planning." In PR terms, a "target" is an "audience."

Public Relations is also very important in such areas as politics and "Issues Management."

When you create advertising that is worthy of note, it's worth working for a little publicity.

You should be able to write a Press Release and know how to put together a Press Kit.

Whatever you work on, look for opportunities to add impact to your advertising and the overall awareness of your brand with "PR"

SALES PROMOTION & "FSI'S."

Over the last ten years, promotional activities have been growing much faster than advertising.

Sales Promotion is big business.

It's common for many brands to have an Advertising Budget *and* a *Promotional* Budget.

In fact, expenditures have shifted from $2 in advertising for every $1 in promotion – to $2 (or more) in promotion for every $1 in advertising!

That's quite a shift.

A Promotion Budget pays for things like:
Coupon redemptions (Often more than the cost of the coupon ad), **P.O.P.** and other promotional material, **Trade discounts** (a big item), **Premiums** (many are "self-liquidators"), **Contests** (for consumers, the sales force and the trade) and more.

Promotions are often advertised.

Your newspaper often has 4-color sections filled with nothing but coupon ads. These are called **Free Standing Inserts** or "FSI's."

They're promotions.

If you like to have ideas that involve contests, special sales themes, premiums and so on, look into the world of Sales Promotion.

Advertising is More Than Advertising.

The total job of marketing involves using many of these important allied techniques.

Often, they can be more effective than the advertising itself.

The more you know about them, and the better you can use them, the more tools you'll have to do your job.

I didn't really learn this lesson 'til I'd been in advertising for many years.

You've got a head start on me.

A Good FSI Should be a Good Ad.
In addition to delivering the coupon offer, your FSI's message should try to add value to the brand and the promotion.
Here are some FSI's in action:
Free Product Offer *(Buy Two Spices, Get One Pepper Free).*
Discount + Brand Sell *(Coupon Offer tied into advertising theme).*
A Continuity Device *(Send in Proof[s] of Purchase, get your photo on a Wheaties Box).*
A Tie-In Offer *(Coupon Savings plus Refund).*

Assignment #22B

My Mom's Mandel Bread.

Background: Your client, Mark Cossoff, wants to market his mother's Mandel Bread – it's a traditional Jewish baked item similar to Italian Biscotti. "Mahndel" is German for almond.

Mark thinks his Mom bakes a great Mandel Bread.

He's made some money in real estate, and he'll invest $250,000 establishing this business in your market.

He's decided to make the product in three flavors: Cinnamon Nut, Chocolate Chip and Peanut Butter.

Local bakeries can produce the product for him, and he's hired you to give him good advice.

There are numerous options:

You can sell it as a traditional Jewish Deli Item (or as Italian Biscotti, Stella D'oro makes a similar product).

You can give it a new name (Snack bread?) and sell it in convenience stores.

You can sell it 6-12 on a tray or in a box, or 2-4 in a cellophane pack you can slip into your pocket or purse.

Or something else.

Your Assignment.

Mark needs your advice.

You have to decide on:

A Name. Should Mark keep this name or do you have a better one to suggest.

Your name should help establish the product position.

A Target. Should we have a narrow ethnic target or a broader target? Who would eat this product? When?

A Strategy and Selling Idea. How should we advertise Mark's product?

A Coupon Ad. Naturally, we want to encourage people to try this product.

Let's do a 4-color coupon ad that would appear as an FSI in the Sunday newspaper. Assume the FSI would use up about half your budget (production, media space, coupon redemptions).

You may have a better idea of what to do with the money.

Something Else. What can you do "Beyond Advertising" to make people aware of your product?

For example, how can you help Mark get the product into grocery stores? (Find out about "slotting allowances.")

How else can we tell the world about Mark's Mothers Mandel Bread?

P.S. Mandel Bread is nice with coffee.

Mandel Bread sort of looks like this...

Assignment #22A

Here are some ways to start thinking about the other things "Beyond Advertising."

1. BROCHURES.

Outline a brochure for one of your products. How would you distribute it?

2. BUTTONS & BUMPER STICKERS.

Design two buttons and two bumper stickers for one of your favorite campaigns.

Find a supplier in your market who makes buttons and bumper stickers.

3. DIRECT MAIL & DIRECT RESPONSE.

Pick a product. List characteristics of your *Best Prospects* for a Direct Mail campaign.

4. "P.I." ADVERTISING.

Invent a product that might be effectively marketed with "P.I." advertising. Write a 60".

5. P.O.P.

Walk through a supermarket.

List 20 pieces of P.O.P. material

Go to a franchise restaurant.

List the P.O.P. displayed.

6. PUBLICITY & PUBLIC RELATIONS.

Find two newspaper articles or items that may have been the result of a press release. (HINT: If you're having trouble, turn to the Business Section.)

7. SALES PROMOTION.

Go through your Sunday paper. Examine the "FSI"s and choose ads that catch your attention.

What other kinds of offers and contests are there besides price-off coupons?

Think up some Sales Promotion ideas for one of your products.

Beyond Copywriting.

Today, there are more opportunities than ever for copywriting skills.

They're just not all in agencies.

The traditional advertising market, while large, is not growing as it has in the past.

However, there is often growth in small and mid-size markets (where some of the most exciting work is being done) and there is a growing need *inside* companies for people who can write.

Here are some of the opportunities you might look into – in addition to advertising.

CORPORATE COMMUNICATIONS.

This can be a great place to start.

Leo Burnett was editor of the Cadillac "house organ," and moved up to Ad Manager.

David Ogilvy wrote *"The Theory and Practice of Selling the Aga Cooker,"* at age 24. It was called "...the best sales manual ever written."

Bill Bernbach worked as a writer for the head of the 1939 World's Fair.

Most companies have a wide range of communication needs: newsletters, brochures, annual reports, sales presentations... even advertising.

An "in-house" staff often handles these projects. Many companies also use "freelance" writers on a project or hourly basis.

Though "freelance" implies erratic employment, many companies employ copywriters on a "freelance" basis for years.

Just about any company with a lot of people has corporate communications needs and many have Corporate Communications departments.

"Every copywriter has a screenplay in their desk drawer."

Helayne Spivak

"Yes, I used to work at Leo Burnett."

John Hughes
Screenwriter
Producer
Director

LEARN TO DO NEWSLETTERS.

They're a great way of reinforcing relationships with your employees and your best customers.

Here's an excellent book on newsletter design by David Doty of PageWorks.

It's called **"Basics of Designing and Producing Newsletters with PageMaker."** They also publish a newsletter on newsletters, "The Page."

PageWorks • P.O. Box 14493 • Chicago, IL 60614 • 312-348-1200

*In-House Creative Departments
are now in fashion.*

> *"For me, copywriting was the
> key to building an $80 million
> a year business.*
>
> *Look around, many successful direct mail companies
> were founded by copywriters.*
>
> *I've found that if you have
> something to say, and can say
> it well, a lot of people will
> send you money."*

**Jeff Salzman, Co-founder
CareerTrack Seminars and Tapes**

> *"Too many able, creative
> people have turned their time
> and talent to selling.*
>
> *Too few are doing the work
> on which all sales should be
> based: manufacture.*
>
> *It is not false flattery when I
> say to people in advertising
> that there are more interesting,
> able and creative people in
> your business than any other
> business in America.*
>
> *I urge some of you to get out of
> the business of selling and into
> the business of producing...*
>
> *For God's sake, go <u>make</u>
> something."*

Andy Rooney, CBS

"IN-HOUSE" CREATIVE DEPARTMENTS.

Other large advertisers, such as department stores, and direct marketers like catalogue houses (Land's End, Sharper Image, L. L. Bean, etc.), also have complete in-house ad departments. Large marketers from Apple Computer to Xerox also have in-house departments.

The excellent advertising for The Gap, Calvin Klein and Esprit is done *"in-house."*

TRAINING AND DEVELOPMENT.

It's called "T & D." Many organizations need training videos, brochures, A/V presentations, and related communications tools in the growing business of helping people learn.

The whole field of education offers additional opportunities. You can make a good living and a real difference helping people learn.

SALES PROMOTION.

As we've mentioned, advertising is just one of the ways writing and strategic and tactical thinking can help sell.

Sales promotion offers many opportunities.

Promotions, sales meetings, presentations, and events from store openings to fund-raising usually need some sort of copywriting help.

OTHER FIELDS.

Copywriting is a brash young entry in the larger field of journalism and literature.

Your copywriting job might just be a step on the way to other writing.

While I was at Leo Burnett, I knew two copywriters who went on to success in other fields.

The writer/director John Hughes made his living as a copywriter while he worked on the scripts that got him to Hollywood. Some, like *"Trains, Boats and Planes"* and *"Mr. Mom"* were based partly on his agency experiences.

And Don Novello, whom you may know as

Father Guido Sarducci, was also a copywriter.

In Detroit, novelist Elmore Leonard and screenwriter/director **Lawrence Kasden**, *("The Big Chill," "Indiana Jones and the Temple of Doom," "Grand Canyon.")* began as copywriters. So did **Cathy Guisewaite**, who writes and draws the comic strip "Cathy."

SOME GOOD ADVICE.

In general, when you're writing what someone else wants written, you get paid.

But you can write for yourself, too.

Even if it doesn't pay as well.

So if you truly enjoy writing, why not write a bit on the side? It offers satisfactions you might not get from that ball-bearing brochure.

And don't forget the lost art of letter writing – you'll improve your skills and brighten the lives of the people you care for. It's nice to get mail.

In general, I offer this advice. Try to find the right "fit" with your skills and interests. Then...

- Find the best job you can.
- Do the best job you can.
- Work hard.
- Work to expand your range.
- Work to improve your abilities.

You may find a job that has everything you're looking for – or you may write hardware catalogs by day and science-fiction novels by night.

Hopefully, you'll enjoy both.

Whatever writing you do, many of the principles of copywriting can help you do it better.

And one more thing.

Whatever you do, try to have fun.

Father Guido Sarducci:

How would you like to sit around all day long, drinking espresso with friends and talking about stuff you know absolutely nothing about?

If the answer is yes, you'd like to do that, perhaps you should become an artist.

You get to wear old clothes all the time and if you don't want to talk to somebody, you say to him, "Hey, I don't feel like talking to you now, I'm an artist."

You see, that's what artist means.

You could do whatever you want to.

Right here I have a chart – this is the rising times of various occupations.

Doctor, 6:30 in the morning you got to get up. How about that?

Lawyer gets to sleep 15 minutes more; a quarter to seven.

Engineers, 7:30. Big deal.

But artists, on the average, don't get up until a quarter to noon, even better than priests, 10:30, 11:00.

Looks like I missed the boat there, but you don't have to.

You could become an artist.

Write to San Francisco Artist Institute and ask for a folder and maybe they'll send it to you.

Who knows?

Supervision.

Advertising is a team sport.

Sometimes you play. Sometimes you coach.

As a supervisor, part of your job is to help grow other people's good ideas.

Many talented creative people never make this important step. They are too preoccupied with their own ideas.

It's understandable, since it's your job to have ideas, but to do your job as a supervisor...

LEARN TO BE #2 ON A GOOD IDEA.

This means you must learn to recognize good ideas that come from other people as well as your own good ideas.

Identifying good ideas and making them better. . . this is the art of creative supervision. It was one of Bill Bernbach's strengths.

Jim Riswold at Weiden & Kennedy heard one of his people connect Bo Jackson and Bo Diddley.

You should too.

Good supervision principles are much like good coaching principles:

EMPHASIZE THE POSITIVE.

People naturally respond to the chance to win. A winning attitude builds winning teams.

Emphasize ideas worth keeping.

Minimize time spent criticizing.

When you do criticize, try to do it well.

Is there nothing there? Look again.

For a start, there is effort.

That's a start in the right direction.

Emphasize the *positive*.

DEVELOP SHARED OBJECTIVES.

People enjoy winning together.

Focus on goals – make them *shared* goals.

334

We are social animals. The interaction of people working toward a common goal can be one of the most joyous experiences in business.

Again, it's a team sport.

Try to answer important questions together.

WHAT'S *OUR* OBJECTIVE?

WHAT'S *OUR* PROBLEM?

Work to develop a shared vision.

A key to establishing this common goal is to involve people in the strategic process as much as possible. Let them feel a part of it.

This need not be a "group grope," or yet another committee (just what we need).

Sometimes a quick, concise update can be enough to let people feel they are being included.

Focus efforts on goals, then focus attention on the fun of getting there. Together.

SET ACHIEVABLE GOALS.

Idealistic but unachievable standards are usually demoralizing, not inspirational.

Tom Peters in his *"Excellence"* books talks about looking for "easy wins."

Keep raising the standard higher, but don't start too high. Once you've got a win under your belt, the next one is a whole lot easier.

Don't put people in situations where they will probably fail – unless you want to get rid of them.

Putting people in over their heads, or in erratic work situations, merely reveals talented individuals who would have succeeded anyway.

If you want to *grow* people, gauge their abilities and design their workload accordingly.

Some may disagree with this "coddling," but I believe that you "grow" creative groups.

The desire to improve is natural. (After all, that's why you're reading this book.)

Good people engaged in productive activity will improve naturally.

"Except for the fact that the work should be fresh and on the button, to the point, do the work, the selling job, I definitely didn't look for a Doyle Dane Bernbach style.

The thing I prided myself on in those years was bringing out the best in other people.

We didn't want to make little carbon copies of me.

To say don't do it like this, do it like me, I think is deadly.

But to say to someone, I don't think this is right because of such and such and to turn it back and say look back inside yourself and find the answer – that helps a person grow and gets a better job right away.

To have them search for themselves for the answer, that's the way you get people to develop their own schtick, their own style.

A garden needs more than one kind of flower."

Phyllis Robinson,
Hall of Fame copywriter
Doyle Dane Bernbach

> *"You don't do it with memos and rules; you do it by example.*
>
> *If the people who run the agency work hard, enjoy the business and are optimistic; then the rest of the people will work hard, enjoy their work and they'll share the optimism.*
>
> *I try to manage by example."*
>
> **Jerry Della Femina**

READING LIST:

You might add a few Management books to your reading list.

Some current recommendations – which I'm sure are already out of date.

A Passion for Excellence
Thomas Peters.
A terrific book, full of stories about how companies and their people really made a difference.

Corporate Cultures
Deal and Kennedy
Interesting insights into the dynamics of companies. Did you know marketing is a "Macho Culture?"

The Art of Japanese Management
Athos & Pascale.
How do the Japanese do it?
This book will tell you.

Good Work
E. F. Schumacher
A personal favorite.
Schumacher also wrote "Small is Beautiful. Economics as if People Mattered." Thought provoking.

The key is to structure their activity so that they're steadily busy doing useful work. This fosters good work habits and continually improving skills.

THE "ENOUGH ROPE" THEORY WORKS.

Good people will work to their own high standards. Given the opportunity, *bad* people will also work to *their* standards.

Give them the opportunity, too. You will help a few "turn it around" and the others will have had a fair shot. When you have to let them go, it will be a lot easier on both of you.

BE AS HONEST AS POSSIBLE.

No one likes rejection, yet a certain part of your job requires it.

Hey, you can't like everything.

Here's a thought: Focus on the *work*, not the person. It's easier and more effective to talk honestly and objectively about the work itself.

Criticize *structurally* . . .

"Here's why the Beginning was confusing."

"The Support doesn't tie to the Benefit."

"The End doesn't really meet the Objective we agreed upon."

Help people get perspective on their work. And along the way, let them know you care about *their* success.

You have a responsibility for the success of the people who work for you.

Show it. Honestly.

Demonstrate your honest concern for their success and your reward will be loyal and honest effort from the people you work with.

Remember, successful people have successful people working for them.

Don't try to make them junior versions of you.

Every supervisor has a personal style that has brought them success. So it's natural to encourage people along a path that's worked for you.

336

Furthermore, your influence in their lives is large. Be careful. Don't be too quick to say, "Do it my way."

BE CONSISTENT.

Don't tell different stories to different people. Keep it straight. Be clear and consistent as to what you think represents good work.

Put examples up on the wall. Give the best work extra praise to reinforce the values you seek.

The Trouble With Surrounding Yourself With Yes-Men Is That The Results Are Usually Negative.

Creative people can create what "the boss" thinks is good work if they get consistent signals.

If you are moody, change your mind without telling people *why,* or seem to like alternate approaches on alternate Tuesdays, you'll create a confused creative group. *This is dangerous!*

It wastes time and energy. It encourages office politics – since there's no consistent standard, people look for other ways to "win."

It defeats the winning team feelings you're trying to create. It demoralizes people who need to be up for a tough job every day.

Finally, it destroys your credibility.

If your judgements are viewed as fickle, you'll never develop the enthusiastic cooperation that builds winning teams. In this business, you've got to stay steady. People need to count on you.

SET AN EXAMPLE.

Set an Example. Work hard.

Show enthusiasm for the good work of others.

Take criticism and helpful "suggestions" gracefully and with appreciation.

Yours is a tough job, but don't take your frustrations out on the people who work for you.

Be the kind of person people want to work for. And they will.

"Young creative people start out hungry.

They're off the street; they know how people think.

And their work is great.

Then they get successful.

They start to make more and more money, spend their time in restaurants they never dreamed of, and fly back and forth between New York and Los Angeles.

Pretty soon, the real world isn't people – it's just a bunch of lights off the right side of the plane.

You have to stay in touch if you're going to write advertising that works.

Ride a subway.

Stand up on a bus.

Buy a hot dog on the corner.

Stay in touch."

Jerry Della Femina

Team Work.

Advertising is a team sport.

Most successful advertising has been created by more than one person – it's the product of many talents working together.

Not just copywriters and art directors, but creative directors, account executives, research assistants, consumers… and even clients.

The better you integrate the thinking of the people you work with into *your* thinking, the better your chances of success.

It's simple. Others have good ideas, too.

And the more ideas you have to work with, the better your chances of having the best idea.

You'll be taking advantage of maximum Input at the Preparation stage.

And whether or not the final work includes others' contributions (it probably will), acknowledging and respecting their point of view will increase the chance they acknowledge and respect yours. Cynical, but true.

Finally, the better you learn to work with others, the better you'll do in a people-oriented business like advertising.

We've already discussed working with Art Directors.

Now let's talk about working with your other business partners: Account Executives, Clients, Research, Media, and your fellow Creatives.

Here's the ad that announced the team of Fallon McElligott Rice.

338

How to Work with Account Executives.

First, remember, they're a little nervous.

Their job, to some extent, depends on working with *you*. No wonder they're nervous.

You must work to understand everything they know about your client's business.

Listen. Pick their brains.

And through your efforts, you must work to earn the AE's confidence and trust.

How do you do this?

Develop these four habits:

1. UNDERSTAND THEIR POINT OF VIEW.

Whether you agree or not, they must know that you acknowledge their concerns.

You'll find it difficult to get anyone to understand *your* point of view until they feel you understand theirs.

2. TIE YOUR WORK TO OBJECTIVE AND STRATEGY.

Account Executives tend to operate in the left brain (rational), as do most clients.

Give them left brain reasons.

The more emotional (right brain) the work, the more you have to emphasize the rational (left brain) reasons for this approach.

3. GIVE A *REASON* FOR EVERYTHING YOU DO.

Even if no one asks, give a reason.

"Here's why we picked the type face, here's why we should use a photo (or an illustration), here's how we relate to our "Target Audience."

Even though no one has asked the question, the client might.

"We look for account people who understand advertising. It's amazing how few do. All account people are interviewed by creative people.

It's tougher hiring account people than creative people."

Jay Chiat

The traditional semi-hostile attitude that "Creatives" have toward "Suits" is indicated in this recruitment ad by "hot" creative shop Chiat-Day.

4. REHEARSE THE PRESENTATION.

Before the ad is presented to the client, everyone should be rehearsed and ready.

And, if the AE's going to the client without you, make an extra effort to help see to it that he's going to come back with a sale.

If you do all this, an account executive will be your friend for life... or the next meeting.

Whichever comes first.

How to Work with a Client.

The client may or may not be your friend. Particularly at first.

If he's been a client for a while, he's heard many agency promises.

And he's been burned more than once.

However, *you are the client's friend.*

You are a business partner dedicated to making him money. Show it.

Show it by knowing his business and *caring* about it. That'll show, too.

Show it by being gracious when you don't get everything the way you want it.

When you disagree, show it by defending your work in terms of what it can do for *his* business.

Honest emotion, when shown while caring for the client's business, is permitted.

Temper tantrums are not.

David Ogilvy advises,

"Do not grudge your client the right to contribute ideas and criticism. It is his product, his money and his responsibility."

And Bill Bernbach used to go to client meetings with a piece of paper in his pocket.

It said, *"Maybe he's right."*

In the course of your career, you may find that some of your best friends and biggest fans are people who started out as clients.

A smart business person appreciates someone who helps his business make money.

And someone who appreciates you makes a pretty good friend.

If you show you're dedicated to making your client money, you will find you will work with clients very well.

Think small.

Our little car isn't so much of a novelty any more.

A couple of dozen college kids don't try to squeeze inside it.

The guy at the gas station doesn't ask where the gas goes.

Nobody even stares at our shape.

In fact, some people who drive our little flivver don't even think 32 miles to the gallon is going any great guns.

Or using five pints of oil instead of five quarts.

Or never needing anti-freeze.

Or racking up 40,000 miles on a set of tires.

That's because once you get used to some of our economies, you don't even think about them any more.

Except when you squeeze into a small parking spot. Or renew your small insurance. Or pay a small repair bill. Or trade in your old VW fo. a new one.

Think it over.

"Some ad agency people think clients are dumb because they may not know about type, art, media, the rest of it.

Look, how dumb can some guy be when he's managed to build a business that's worth millions?

You know, agencies aren't big businesses. So they ought to have a lot of respect for people who are smart enough to build big businesses.

Remember, success for an agency is a sale in someone's conference room... clients have to succeed in the open marketplace.

That takes someone who's very very smart – and if agency people don't understand that – they're dumb."

Jerry Della Femina

THE "THINK SMALL" STORY.
Once upon a time, Julian Koenig was working on an ad for Volkswagen.

He was thinking about what to write when he read a speech by his client, the VW ad director, Helmut Schmitz.

Mr. Schmitz said that Volkswagen needed to remain small in spirit, to think small, in order to deal with all the important details involved in building and marketing cars.

And **"Think Small"** was born.
The client helped write it.
How about that?

How to Work with Research.

No other agency function has affected the job of the Creative Department as much as research.

John B. Watson, one of the founders of Experimental Psychology and Behaviorism, left the academic world in the 20's to join Stanley Resor at J. Walter Thompson.

Advertising has always had a close relationship with the information research provides.

While research has been a part of advertising since the days of Hopkins, Caples and Rubicam, it was first used as a *measurement* function.

Research *measured* coupon responses.

Research *measured* sales results.

Research *measured* readership with services such as Starch.

But as making advertising decisions became the function of bureaucracies instead of entrepreneurs, research was asked to do more than *measure*. Research was asked to *predict*.

Research was no longer measurement after the fact, as in the early days, when people made ads, ran them, and learned from the experience.

Those days are over, at least in the big agencies, though they are still alive and well in the fields of direct mail and response.

Today's advertisers and advertising agencies want to know how well an ad will work *before* they run it.

Research now occurs *before the fact*. In this environment, one does ads for research, and, if the research scores are good enough, the ads run.

There is a lot wrong with this system, but we will not be able to change it.

The good news is there is a lot we can learn from research to make our work better.

Here are my guidelines for working successfully with research:

1. EARLIER IS BETTER.

Since research's involvement is inevitable, the sooner you use it to gather Input, the better your chances of doing work that "works."

Often, the right kind of research can help you know your target customer better.

For example, experiences like **Focus Groups** can give you a deeper understanding of your customer.

Previous research can be enlightening, too.

Occasionally, research will even give you a few "trial runs" at the concept stage.

In short, research can help make you smarter. The sooner the better.

2. BE A FRIEND.

Often, some of the most interesting people you will meet in this business are the people in Research.

They have active and inquiring minds.

They're not nervous about losing the account (that's the Account Executive's job).

And they're genuinely interested in helping you find the right answer.

Even while they try to remain objective (that's their job), I've found many research people to be genuinely enthusiastic about good work.

And the best news yet, they're usually positive and helpful with their insights and contributions.

People like that make good friends.

Don't blame research itself for every bad research score.

Sometimes the idea isn't right, or isn't done well enough. Sometimes the product really isn't that interesting to consumers.

And, of course, sometimes the research really didn't measure the advertising's potential.

MALE (VO): C'mon old Trademark, time for your walk. Where will you take me? Sure wish you could talk.

I know what you'd tell me. How your family began with

Your family's future — sure looks like it should.

the same Levi's blue jeans worn by this man.

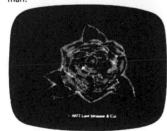

Levi's don't have to be blue — just have to be good!

3. SHOW WHAT YOU SAY.

Audio-Visual Integration means that the words (the audio) must relate clearly and dramatically to the picture (the visual).

The words and the pictures work together.

Sounds simple. Looks simple.

But this can be more difficult than it seems.

First, creative minds tend to be attracted to subtler metaphor and visualization.

Second, the obvious visualization can be unexciting and uninteresting.

For example, talking about the product for 30 seconds while you show the product for 30 seconds is integrated but may not be interesting.

And, as Julian Koenig said, our job is to, *"Make it Interesting."*

4. MAKE IT BETTER.

One of research's real values is as a "Feedback" mechanism – it can give you information to make your work better.

Research can give you a second chance.

Find out what people really remember from your ad. It might not be that clever turn of phrase or subtle visual.

Research can help put the real world into focus for you – take advantage of it.

Give yourself a second chance.

5. DO IT AGAIN!

Every new insight, every new piece of "feedback," is a chance to do more advertising.

It may be better, it may not.

Don't worry, just do.

Train yourself to go quickly and effortlessly into the "do" mode.*

Just do it.

Do it in the now.

And do it again.

*

Become as the Zen swordsman, Musashi. "Aturo" means to strike without thinking of doing it.

6. LEARN.

A major purpose of research is to learn... to become smarter.

You should take advantage of every learning opportunity.

When you have a chance to hear a research "overview," like Yankelovich... go.

Have a cup of coffee with the Research Director on your account.

You might learn something.

Become familiar with Case Histories in the category and research on old commercials.

What worked?

What didn't? Why?

More Input = Better Ideas.

Experience brings wisdom.

What's Wrong with Research?

Researchers tend to be bright, honest, helpful, well-intentioned people.

So, what's wrong?

First, research doesn't do what people want it to do.

Research does not predict the future.

It cannot, with accuracy, predict the success of an advertising campaign in the marketplace.

It cannot even guarantee the selection of the best ad among many in a testing situation.

For example, most research measures a single exposure while most good TV commercials work with repeated exposure.

Furthermore, a "correlation" is not a guarantee.

At best, you've hedged your bets and added a "disaster check."

7 THINGS THAT HELP ADVERTISING "RESEARCH" WELL.

More lists. More "rules."
Who knows, they may help.

1. An Easy to Remember Plot.

It doesn't have to be a "Slice" commercial, but it should have solid Structure.

Generally, the plot structure should revolve around the product.

2. A Clear, Dramatic, and Easy to Remember Benefit.

It should be easy for the consumer to answer the question "What's in it for me?"

The answer to this question should be an important part of your commercial.

3. A Good Animatic Presentation.

Many commercials are damaged in research by sloppy presentation in **animatic** form.

For example, the situation might not be clearly established.

Or a storyboard frame doesn't make it clear who is talking to whom.

A confusing editing rhythm can throw the viewer off the track.

You should be able to understand the commercial with the sound off!

4. Clear, Attractive Visualization.

If you're advertising food and you want appetite appeal, don't expect a drawing to do it for you.

Appetizing film or photography is necessary to communicate appetite appeal.

Likewise, dull ordinary storyboard frames will not help your commercial.

Looking at your commercial should make you want the product.

5. A Good Audio Track.

One of the best things about TV research is that it gives you an opportunity to develop your audio production skills. Go for it!

Get good voices with good readings of your script... nice music... great sound effects.

Your sound track should work as a radio commercial.

6. "Spirit!"

The process of research can take a lot of the fun out of this business.

Don't let it.

Keep your energy level high – even when it's only a test.

Let it show in your work. *cont'd*

At worst, you've missed opportunities research can't measure.

For, as McLuhan said,

"Research is a rear view mirror."

While there is merit in knowing what has gone before, it can be paralyzing when it comes to considering a truly new idea.

We cannot measure the future with research. We cannot see six months into the marketplace.

Yet research is used to make decisions by people who hope that they can see the future in a rear view mirror.

Second, all too often...

Research Replaces Judgement!

"Paralysis by analysis" is a common bureaucratic disease.

Sad to say, over-reliance on research is one of the symptoms.

One substitutes a decision, "Let's do something," with a non-decision, "Let's do some research to find out what we ought to do."

On the face of it, this is a rational, responsible act.

But it also gets the bureaucrat off the hook.

As David Ogilvy said,

"Some people use research like a drunk uses a lamp post. For support instead of illumination."

Cumulatively, however, something insidious happens...

Research Slows The Pace of Decision-Making.

The rhythm of the business becomes the rhythm of research, with long lead times provided for research and short bursts of time provided for getting work done.

You're "putting it into research" or "waiting for it to come out of research."

And sometimes you get to do some work.

But there's an even bigger problem...

People No Longer Make Decisions.

The saddest result is the gradual emasculation of agency and brand management.

Research implicitly makes decisions or "recommendations." A "good score" means "yes," a "bad score" means "no."

This is the essence of non-decision.

The decision itself is abandoned to a process that decides for us.

Now, on a case by case basis, this may be a rational and responsible act. After all, millions of dollars may be riding on these decisons.

And the decisions themselves may be no worse than the ones people would make.

But the people become worse – untouched by vision or courage, uncertain, passive, protected. They are made neither stronger nor wiser by the school of experience.

These points are well-acknowledged by many thoughtful research professionals.

They are equally concerned about the mis-use of research for decision-making.

Yet, they're also trapped in a process created by bureaucracies doing business in tough times.

You may be trapped in it, too. Participating in that modern advertising ritual known as *Feeding the Research God.*

"More ads," says the Research Machine.

"More scores," say the clients.

And so it goes.

Yet, in your journey, you may find that some of your most valued business partners, and maybe a few friends, work in the Research Department.

Look at some animatics.

You can tell who had fun doing them and who didn't.

Remember, the final commercial decision is affected not by which is the best commercial, but by which is the best animatic.

Finally, you should hope for…

7. Bad Competition.

In research, your advertising is generally compared to other advertising.

If you're competing with talented people who have been working hard, you just might lose even though your work is quite good.

"TWO BOXES."

You might also lose if the competition happens to include what I call a "Two Boxes" commercial.

In a "Two Boxes" commercial, a flat-footed comparison is made between Product A and Product B.

With mind-numbing clarity, the point is made that one box is better than the other box.

This point is made as often and as obviously as time allows.

In many "forced viewing" situations, this sort of commercial has been known to do rather well.

There is, in my experience, little you can do about it.

You might try mentioning that this type of commercial often scores low in "On-Air" testing, and that people don't pay much attention to things that aren't very interesting.

But don't hold your breath.

The good news is that, chances are, you'll get another shot at the problem when "Two Boxes" is a dud in the marketplace.

How to Work with Media.

The people you see least often are the people who work to see to it that your ads are seen most often – the Media Department.

From a *quantitative* standpoint, their business is pretty well worked out to the decimal point – Cost per thousand (CPM). Gross Rating Points (GRP). Target Rating Points. Reach. Frequency.

From a *quantitative* standpoint, there's not a lot to discuss. And, since Media people seldom lack for people to take them to lunch, you might not see them much.

However, from a *qualitative* standpoint, you might have some fun talking.

Because Media people are smart – but bored.

Everyone has pretty much the same computer programs with the same information. Good Media people are looking for a *qualitative* edge – maybe as much as you are.

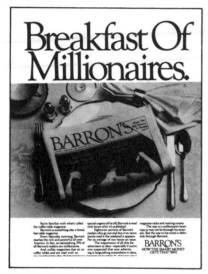

Media Accounts.

They can often be an opportunity to do great advertising – your Target is a sophisticated marketing audience.

Media Audiences.

This is often the "product" Media Vehicles sell to advertisers – they're not just selling the magazine – they're selling the people who read the magazine – the audience.

MEDIA TERMS.

Some of the most common media terms and what they mean:

CPM. *Cost Per Thousand.*

The cost of reaching 1,000 of anything – Men, Women, Households, etc.

REACH. Unduplicated audience, expressed as a percent.

FREQUENCY. Number of times your message is heard – usually expressed as an average.

GRP. *Gross Rating Point.*

A rating point is a percent of homes tuned in to a program.

GRP is the sum of rating points purchased.

TRP. *Target Rating Point.*

Rating points delivered against the target, as opposed to the entire audience.

MATCH THE MEDIA WITH THE MESSAGE.

Certain campaigns may execute with greater strength in different media.

For example, a campaign with a great piece of music might lend itself to radio, as well as TV.

A strong theme line might put you in outdoor.

A narrow target audience might put you into direct mail as well as specialized magazines.

A sudden piece of product news might have you both racing to produce an exciting, "newsy" TV spot or newspaper ad in just a few days.

And "New Media" opportunities are happening all the time – like "Place-based Media," such as advertising in the store or at the stadium.

Advertising as Context.

Here, the media buy itself – small space – is used creatively to support the quality claim.

The Smaller The Ad, The Better The Restaurant.

This thought is brought to you by the elegant Georgian Room at the Four Seasons Olympic Hotel. Call 621-1700 for reservations.

INTEGRATING MEDIA.

Here are some thoughts from Media Guru, Ron Katz, about "Integrated Media Planning"– noting some of the strengths of various media forms, and how they might work together.

Network TV – Delivering a strong brand identity.

Direct Response TV – Offering more information.

Brochures – Providing this information.

Radio – Reminding consumers to act.

Store Displays – Stimulating action at the Point of Sale.

The Package – Reinforcing with consumers the wisdom of their decision and reasons to repeat the action.

Media Vehicle as Context.

Here the media vehicle itself is used as context to get your Attention.

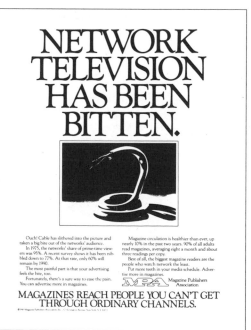

It's a Jungle Out There.

Media vehicles battle each other for a relatively fixed amount of money. One wins. Another loses.

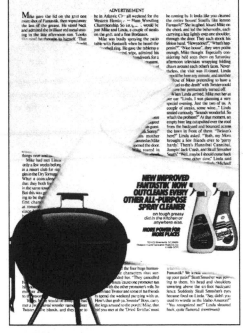

A MEDIA OPPORTUNITY CAN BE A CREATIVE OPPORTUNITY.

Keith Reinhard of DDB/Needham calls media *"The New Creative Frontier."*

This covers both media selection and the creative use of that media.

DDB/Needham integrates Media Selection into their "R.O.I." System.

Here are some examples of the creative use of media in print.

And there are many others – in print and in the other media vehicles.

Each media buy is an opportunity – make the most of it!

Media Vehicle as Context II.

Again, the media itself is used to get your Attention and then make a point.

This time, it also helps to demonstrate a Product Benefit.

Creative Media Space.

Some media vehicles provide unique and interesting space units – and sometimes you have to make your own.

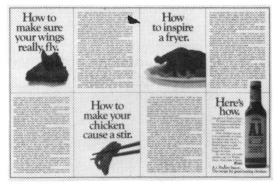

Virtual Reality.

Don't forget sampling – the Product as Media Vehicle.

MEET YOUR MEDIA PEOPLE.

Get to know media people at your agency. Develop an understanding of what they're trying to accomplish.

And help them understand what *you're* trying to accomplish.

Don't dispute the *quantitative* – they'll drown you in data and they're trained to defend media budgets and recommendations tenaciously.

But together, you can contribute to enriching the *qualitative* dimension of your media program, and do a better job of matching the media to the message.

Good Agencies. Good Media People.

Some of the most creative agencies also do some of the most creative media planning and buying.

Even Chiat/Day's Help Wanted advertising is first-rate.

A TRUE MEDIA STORY.

Many years ago, I was assigned some radio commercials for The Chicago Transit Authority.

I looked at the media list. *"Why are we using these stations?"* I asked.

"Well," said the Media guy, *"we're advertising to suburban commuters during drive time."*

"Oh." I thought about it for a while. Next day, I walked into his office with a cup of coffee.

"Hey," I said. *"I been thinkin'."* (I had.) *"We've been saying the same thing to this same bunch for a while now, and I'd like to talk about our Target Audience."*

"What do you mean?" asked the Media guy.

"Well, a lot of people riding mass transit are younger and less well-to-do. Some might be listening to different stations than the ones on this list."

The Media guy looked thoughtful. Media people *like* new ideas. They get to hear them so seldom.

"Hmmm," he said, *"I'll get back to you."* He did.

And that's how the Chicago Transit Authority got into rock 'n roll radio back in '68.

People loved the spots.

So what's the message?

Massage the Media.

You might rub 'em the right way.

Consumer Advertising.

Media vehicles advertise for readers, viewers and listeners.

Here, The New York Post addresses an Image Problem.

TAKE A BUS TO LUNCH THIS WEEK

Whether it's downtown or Old Town, east or west, we'll be happy to accommodate you.

Just sit back and pat your hair into place one more time. Or powder your nose.

And then when you get to where you're going, you'll be even happier you took the bus.

You won't have to park it. Or give it a tip.

With all the money you'll save, maybe you can order the squab. Instead of the tuna fish salad.

A message from Chicago's largest restaurant delivery service.

The Chicago Transit Authority

Alex Osborn.
Founder of BBD&O.
Inventor of "BrainStorming."

**GUIDELINES FOR
BRAINSTORMING:**

1. Suspend Judgement. No
negative comments. No critics.
   Evaluation and criticism is
postponed during the session.

2. "Free Wheel."
The participants have to let go of
traditional inhibitions. Wild ideas are
encouraged. It's easier to tone down
an idea than think one up.

3. Quantity not Quality. The
objective is to generate the most
ideas you can think of.

4. Cross-Fertilize.
Participants are permitted and
encouraged to work off of other
people's ideas.
   Authorship is not a concern.
   Ideas are tossed around in the
group and new versions are
developed.

*Notify participants of the meeting and
topic in advance – it enables them to
start thinking about the topic.*

> **TO:**
>   **YOU ARE INVITED TO ATTEND
> A BRAINSTORM MEETING ON
> (DATE) AT (PLACE) AT (TIME).
> THE PROBLEM/TOPIC IS**
> _____
> Looking forward to seeing you.
> JOHN DOE (Phone #)

Team Creativity.

BrainStorming & "The Brain Wall."

This section is about having ideas with other
creative people.

   "BrainStorming" is a technique that was
invented in the 1930's by Alex Osborn of Batten,
Barton, Durstine & Osborne.

   Basically, it's a method of unlocking creativity
in people in such a way as to generate a lot of
ideas in a short amount of time.

   "The Brain Wall" is a variation I use (as do
many others – under a variety of names) and it's
covered in the upcoming sidebar.

   For a session, you need a group, a Leader, large
sheets of paper, and a room with lots of space. Let
people know the topic ahead of time – to prepare.

   Here's how BrainStorming works:

   THE SIX STAGES OF BRAINSTORMING.

1. The Problem

   The Leader states the problem.

   For example, "Today, we're going to *talk* about
new ways to sell hamburgers."

   We discuss the problem to be addressed.

   Questions are answered, and the problem is
discussed in more detail.

   *"The hamburger business is suffering from no
news and increasing concerns about eating red
meat. Plus, there are too many burger places."*

2. "How To..."

Now, we step away from the problem and restate it in a "How to" format.

The problem is *"How to end the Ho-Hum Hamburger."*

The problem is *"How to establish the Tradition of the Hamburger."*

The problem is *"How to put more fun on a bun."* And so on.

They are written on large sheets of paper, in large letters, and displayed around the room.

This stimulates more thoughts.

This opens participants' minds to the possibilities, and is usually upbeat and stimulating.

All statements from this point on are written down and displayed prominently.

3. "How Many Ways..."

The group selects the first statement to be "BrainStormed."

The selected statement is written down in a "How many ways..." format.

"How Many Ways Can We End the Ho-Hum Hamburger?" Etc.

Solutions are called out and written down.

As ideas dry up on the first restatement, you may move to another.

The ideas are numbered and reinforced and "built on" as you move into the session.

Now, take a step back. Pause and leave the Basic Restatement up on the wall.

It's time to get the group ready to "storm."

4. The Warmup – "Other Uses For..."

There should now be a short session to "step away from the problem." About five minutes.

Participants throw out ideas like *"Other Uses For..."* a paper clip, an ash tray, whatever.

The idea's to get the mental muscles warmed up and create a positive, free-wheeling atmosphere.

For naturally "creative" people, this stage can

"The Brain Wall."

For major advertising projects, here's a good technique called **"The Brain Wall."**

It's not a formal technique, like Brain Storming or Synectics, just a general approach to creative problem-solving within an agency Creative Group.

(If you're in a Student Agency or Campaigns Contest, your Team will be the "Creative Group.")

Others use this technique – under many different names.

Here's all you need:

1. People.

Art, Copy, even Account Executives and people from the Research Department.

2. Flexible Leadership.

Don't force your will on the group. "Go with the flow," as you look for the strongest lines of development.

3. Paper (not too big) and Markers (lots).

Get everything possible on paper. And get as many possible pieces of paper on the wall.

4. A Room with a Cork Wall.

It could be your office, or a conference room. You should be able to leave the stuff up on the wall.

5. Lots of pins and thumbtacks (tape, too.)

6. Multiple meetings.

Here's how the process works...

MEETING #1.

The assignment is presented.

"Just got the account... we need a new campaign."

"We need to show the client some new product ideas."

"If we don't come up with something new, we're going to lose the account!"

Note the use of the word "we."

This begins to build a group approach to the problem.

The problem is discussed. Perhaps the AE or Research person gives some background.

Relevant material is shown or handed out. A business summary can also be helpful.

A good set of handouts for the first meeting gives it substance – but... not just piles of data.

If the time is right, you might kick it around in a pleasant, casual and optimistic way. Set the tone.

And set a time for the next meeting.

cont'd

353

MEETING #2.

Everybody gets together and you go around the room.

Thoughts and impressions are stated, shared, and put up on the wall as Headline Ideas.

Some may be rough layouts or key frames. Or scrap. Or samples.

Put 'em up.

At first, they will be placed randomly on the wall.

As the meeting develops, ideas and approaches will begin to "cluster."

Move them around and begin to organize them: Benefit Ideas. Target Consumer Ideas. Graphic Ideas. Theme Ideas. And so on.

Add some "Title" heads for each cluster.

You will see the thinking begin to pattern. Strengths and "lines of development" will emerge.

Often, certain people will show up with a similar approach – they may actually have the same idea.

Terrific. This helps defuse the Authorship issue, and you can begin to form creative teams.

After all the ideas are up, ask for new thoughts or variations.

People should "work off" of each other to stimulate new lines of thinking. Put 'em up.

Now, take a deep breath and head into the second part of the meeting (a short break here is fine).

In this part of the meeting, ask for reaction to others' ideas.

At first, compliments only.

Strengths are reinforced.

Initially, people are asked to refrain from "selling" their ideas. (That's for the next meeting.)

For now, they can only be positive about *someone else's* idea.

Leadership at this point can be tricky, particularly if the group has never worked this way before.

There can be initial discomfort.

But if you promote a positive attitude toward everyone's contribution, you can solve the problem *and* strengthen your group.

Don't expect the problem to be solved at this meeting – but the beginnings of an answer may appear.

You're accelerating the ideation process – creating an "Input Soup."

Keep an upbeat attitude.

It's the beginning of the journey–

cont'd

sometimes be eliminated, as they'll be "chomping at the bit."

But even with people eager to begin, an additional shift in perspective can be helpful.

Then, the Leader turns to the basic restatement and the "BrainStorm" begins.

5. "BrainStorm!"

The Leader reads the restatement and calls for ideas. Write them down as quickly as possible and put them up on the wall.

Displaying ideas stimulates additional ideas.

Laughter and noise should be part of it as ideas are continually written down.

As it slows, take a short time out – a silent minute. Stretch. Let people look at the ideas that are displayed around the room.

The flow of ideas should start up again.

Then, select another restatement.

And do it again.

Ideas are continually generated, written down and "built on."

The Leader is also allowed to contribute ideas as well (but don't get in the way of other participants). The idea is to keep the storm going.

In a good session, one feels like one is riding a surging mental wave.

Traditionally, the leader then ends the session with a technique called "The Wildest Idea."

6. The Wildest Idea.

The group takes the "wildest" idea and tries to turn it into something useful.

This tends to brighten up the session again, and a few more ideas are usually generated.

It will become obvious when the session has run its course.

Ninety minutes to two hours is good for a first session – a morning or afternoon is usually plenty.

Don't make them marathons!

Everyone is thanked and given positive feedback. Now it's time for the next step – Evaluation.

"AFTER THE BRAINSTORM."

Evaluation is a critical, logical left-brain process. The search is for *quality* in the *quantity*.

And naturally, the next steps are up to you.

The BrainStorming technique has been quite helpful over the years in generating fresh, new perspectives and new ideas. It has also generated new variations on the technique.

SYNECTICS™ & "STORYBOARDING."

Synectics is a copyrighted technique developed by W. J. J. Gordon and George Prince.

It's a more focused version of BrainStorming, concerned with practical problem solving.

Specific exercises, such as analogy metaphor and discontinuous stories are used to stimulate fresh, rich beginning connections.

It is practiced by Synectics, Inc., and licensed users around the world – casual, non-licensed versions of Synectics' technique are commonly used in "Idea Sessions," or "BrainStorms."

A related technique is **"StoryBoarding,"** which relies on visual display.

It's not like a TV storyboard – it's more of a visual outline. It looks like this...

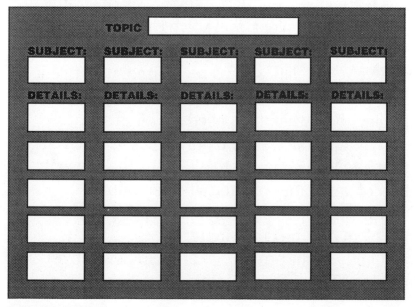

don't expect the problem to be solved right away.

Next Steps.

Compliment the Group. "A lot of good ideas here." Etc. Indicate ideas you think are particularly interesting.

Give out some assignments ("pull this together... expand that idea," etc.), but keep it flexible.

If possible, leave the ideas up on the wall. Save them for the next meeting.

MEETING #3

This is the water-shed meeting. Unless the problem is complex, or wide-ranging, it's the meeting where you "pull it together."

Generally, you'll begin to see developed approaches, theme lines, a few new ideas, and some ad roughs.

Major lines of thinking will start to become clear.

Here's how to handle it. Take down the old cards and put them in a pile(s).

Let people present.

First, the new work is put up on the wall. Then the best of the old – with your comments.

Now, people can sell their ideas and promote their point of view.

Enthusiasm is encouraged.

When everything has been presented, take a deep breath – say "Wow," (or words to that effect).

Look around at all the good work. Talk about what you like, and why.

Gently ignore ideas that, in your judgement, aren't working.

Give people permission to work on those ideas further, if convictions are deeply held – but it's time to start thinning the garden.

Focus on the strongest approaches. Hopefully, it will become obvious.

Now, start to organize it into a Presentation. (If you want help on that, look back at "Selling Ideas.")

You can kick it around in a pleasant, casual, and optimistic way, or turn it into a real "Let's Win One for the Gipper" type of team effort.

Make an outline of the order of presentation for your next "work session" with Account Executives or Clients (or both), and proceed to develop a final presentation in whatever way is typical for your agency or group.

The "Brain Wall" can be a fun way to build a strong campaign –

And a better, stronger group.

There are other business uses for these techniques; as part of annual marketing meetings, or to help people in structured jobs stretch their mental muscles.

Companies are finding it's very productive for groups of people to be creative and have good ideas.

Under proper circumstances, it can be an effective way of dealing with business problems.

If you're interested in learning more, there are books with techniques and guidelines as well as training programs available. (See Reading List.)

A TRUE STORY.

One day, I ran into someone who'd been involved in the successful **"Weekends are Made for Michelob"** campaign. I asked him about it.

"Well," he said, *"We had a lot of things up on the wall… one said 'Weekends are Special' and another said 'Michelob is Special.' So we put them together."*

And that's where that campaign came from.

Do these techniques work?

Certainly they don't work every time, and they probably don't work for everybody.

But they've worked for me.

In a wide variety of circumstances, I've seen this technique identify the key issues of a difficult advertising problem, and solve that problem with a variety of approaches.

I've seen relationships revitalized, new talent identified, and sad to say, those in the group not pulling their weight exposed for all to see.

This approach should only be used when the problem is big enough to allow for the presentation of a number of alternative solutions.

Inviting too many people to work on a small problem can be demeaning.

On the right project, it can help develop an upbeat **"Team Spirit"** within a creative group.

A HELPFUL THOUGHT.

Remember, there will be only one winning idea.

Here's a positive way of discussing a negative subject.

Share your disappointment ahead of time that there's going to be a lot of good work and probably more than one good answer – but only one "winner."

Many contributions will not be "bad" ideas, just good ideas that didn't make it.

Happens all the time.

Try to make everyone feel better about the inevitable, and positive about their contributions.

Not only will people enjoy working together more – they'll get better with each new problem.

And in this business, the more problems you solve, the better you get.

Learn to solve problems – they keep us all in the business.

I remember my freshman year at JWT.

Sears had just assigned us a new battery.

"I was thinking," said Tom Hall, "a battery doesn't wear out… it *dies.*"

Marion Dawson looked up from strumming his baritone ukelele.

"Let's call it **The DieHard.**"

And they did.*

Advertising *is* a team sport.

The better we learn to work together, the better we'll do. Together.

Assignment #23.

Organize a BrainStorming session.
- Pick an assignment – New Product, Fund-Raising Project, Original Party, etc.
- Get everyone together in a room with all the tools you need.
- Follow the steps and **BrainStorm!**
- Implement the best idea, if practical.

Reading List:

Some books about BrainStorming and Group Creativity.

Applied Information
Alex F. Osborn
Charles Scribner & Sons, 1957

Your Creative Powers
Alex F. Osborn
Charles Scribner & Sons, 1948

Synectics
J. J. Gordon Williams
Harper & Rowe, 1961

*Creative Thinking
and Brainstorming*
S. Geoffrey Rawlinson
Halsted Press
John Wiley & Sons, 1981

*

Years later, I found out that Marion had been kicking ideas around a bit earlier with his baritone uke and Howard Rieger, the talented art director who developed the original DieHard graphics. Howard says he said it first – and the uke's not talkin'!

IF THIS IS WHAT YOU THINK ABOUT VOLVOS, YOU'VE GOT ANOTHER THINK COMING.

THE NEW VOLVO 850 GLT

Coming October 24

Slow and Steady Wins the Race.
Over time, **Brand Equity** *slowly*
builds in the mind of the consumer.
It takes a while, but you get there.
Ultimately, this allows you to do
advertising that builds upon itself –
resonating *with the consumer's*
existing feelings and attitudes
toward your Brand.

The Campaign.

This is about making it all work together.

That's what an advertising campaign is all about.

Advertising rewards those who do it right over the long haul – the effect of your advertising becomes cumulative. Each ad builds.

Which leads us to repeat our final truth –

"You're not in the business of making advertising, you're in the business of building businesses."

That means building brands and building ***"brand equity."***

And that means a lot more than just the next ad or the next meeting.

It's "The Campaign."

It's the whole thing.

It means maintaining a strong, consistent **Selling Idea,** and building each ad around that idea, making your message cumulatively stronger with each additional ad.

It means establishing a **graphic rhythm** that builds recognition and awareness - even when the ad isn't read!

It means developing a **brand personality** that people come to regard as a friend.

Together, they build **brand equity** – the result of all the things people know and feel about your brand from initial Attention to final Action.

None of this is done overnight.

Not even at Federal Express.

It's *"Keeping Everlastingly At It,"* as N. W. Ayer has done since 1869.

Here are a few examples of successful long-term advertising campaigns and one new one:

VOLVO

Durability was the initial Selling Idea of a campaign that worked hard and endured.

Along the way, it helped build Volvo into one of the major auto imports.

Support for their message was product-based – beginning with the Durability of Volvos and then moving to newer technology.

Their Durability message evolved, to one of Safety. It was an evolution, since durability of construction contributes to this additional Benefit.

As they became a manufacturer with more cars and more features, they broadened their approach.

But they maintained their Brand Character, a solid stance in the marketplace.

Volvos held up.

So do their ads.

A NICHE CAN BUILD A BIG BUSINESS.

If you can find the right niche in the marketplace and your competition lets you keep it, you can build a dominant brand.

But remember, the niche has to translate into a genuine consumer benefit, and the product must deliver.

In the case of Volvo, a longer-lasting (and safer) car was the benefit.

Below, one of Ed McCabe's early ads on the "Durability" strategy. A variation on "Fat cars die young."

A gripping crash scene in a Volvo spot underscores the make's construction.

THE VOLVO TURBO
AS MOST COMMONLY
VIEWED FROM A
BMW 318i.

THE TURBO+
By Volvo

How often do you buy a new car?
That's too often.

Buy a Volvo, keep it a long time and get out from under car payments for a change.

How long can you expect a Volvo to last? We're not sure yet how long a Volvo will hold up here in the States. In Sweden, Volvos are driven an average of eleven years. When you consider that there are no speed limits on the Swedish highways, there are over 70,000 miles of unpaved roads, and that driving is almost the national pastime in Sweden, you can understand why we have to bite our tongues to keep from making some rash promises.

One more thing. You won't *mind* keeping your Volvo a long time. Its body style doesn't change every year. It's uncomplicated and requires very little maintenance. It runs away from other popular-priced compacts in every speed range, yet gets over 25 miles to the gallon like the little economy cars (even with automatic transmission).

And your Volvo will look good standing next to your swimming pool. The one you build with the money that used to go for car payments.

See the Yellow Pages for the dealer nearest you.

Mr. Spleen: Okay, Eunice, travel plans. Ineedto be inNewYork Monday, LAon ThursdayandNewYorkonFridayGotit? Soyouwanttoworkhere?Well, whatmakes youthinkyoudeserveajobhere?
Guy: WellsirIthinkonmyfeet. I'mgoodwith figuresandIhaveasharpmind.
Spleen: CongratulationsWelcomaboard. **(SFX)** Wonderfulwonderfulwonderful. AndinconclusionJimBillBob PaulDonFrankandTed, businessisbusiness andweallknowinordertogetsomethingyou've gottodosomethingyou'vegottogettowork solet'sgettowork. Thankyoufortakingthis meeting. **(SFX)** Peteryoudidabangupjob. I'mputtingyouinchargeofPittsburgh.
Peter: Pittsburgh'sperfect.
Spleen: Iknowitsperfect, Peter, thatswhy IpickedPittsburgh. Pittsburg'sperfectPeter . MayIcallyouPete?
Peter: CallmePete
Spleen: Pete.
Secretary(OC): There'saMr. Snitlerhere toseeyou.
Spleen: Tellhimtowait15seconds.
Secretary: Canyouwait15seconds?
Man: I'llwait15seconds.
Spleen: Congratulationsonyourdealin DenverDave. I'mputtingyoutodoadealin Dallas. Donisitadeal?Dowe?It'sadeal Ihaveacallcomingin.
ANNCR: In this fast moving high pressure get-it-yesterday world, aren't you glad there's one company that can keep up with it all?
Spleen: Dickwhat'sthedealwiththedeal. Arewedealing?We'redealing. Dave it's adealwithDonDorkandDick. Dorkit'sadealwithDonDaveand Dick. Dickit'saDorkwithDonDealandDave. Davegottago, disconnect Dorkgottago, disconnecting Dickgottago, disconnecting.
ANNCR: Federal Express. **(SFX)** When it absolutely positively has to be there overnight.

Federal Express

Here's an example of how fast you can build Brand Equity if you do it right.

By establishing themselves with *"When It Absolutely Positively Has to Be There Overnight,"* they've changed the way America does business.

It was a Big Idea – a nationwide airline designed for freight – originally submitted as a graduate school term paper by Fred Smith, the man who founded the company.

He got a "C."

In the real world, he made the grade.

He identified a genuine need in the marketplace and met it.

He founded a company on a simple well-executed benefit and delivered. Almost overnight.

The Federal Express Vision. Every person in the target group has some need related to making a deadline. Here, a businessman's A/V presentation doesn't make it, and he has to fake it. Funny, but terrifying. It could be you.

UNDERSTANDING THE TARGET.

"Absolutely positively" was the fourth ad campaign for Federal Express, but it's the one that connected.

People loved the commercials because they could see themselves.

They could identify with the anxiety whether they were a clerk or a CEO.

THE FUTURE OF FEDERAL EXPRESS.

It is a fast-paced, fast-changing world.

Watch Federal Express to see how a #1 player responds to competition.

UPS, a strong #2 player, is establishing itself with good service and a position based on its well-deserved reputation for efficiency and its leadership in the large business of shipping.

Their line – *"We run the tightest ship in the shipping business."*

Meanwhile, new technology, the FAX, changed the way America does business again. Overnight.

SFX: *CAR FLAT*
ANNCR: *You can't count on anything these days...*
MAN: *Did you type the letter I told you to type.*
SECRETARY : *No.*
ANNCR: *With possibly one exception: Federal Express. When it absolutely positively has to be there overnight.*

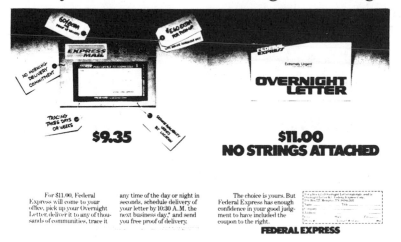

Hard Ball. *Federal Express went after its competition – even though some of its competition was the Federal Government. Here, they compare their overnight letter with Express Mail.*

Soft Ball. *A pleasant, humorous ad announcing a new service. More relaxed, since the service is for things that don't "absolutely positively have to be there."*

Apple Macintosh™

ANNCR: *This is a highly sophisticated business computer. And to use it, all you have to do is learn this...*
(STACK OF MANUALS DROPS INTO FRAME.)
ANNCR: *This is a Macintosh from Apple. Also a highly sophisticated business computer. And to use it, all you have to do is learn this...*
(SINGLE MANUAL DROPS INTO FRAME.)
ANNCR: *Now, you decide which one's sophisticated.* **Macintosh.**
The computer for the rest of us.

Apple Computer, has established itself as a dominant force in the computer industry with their unique Macintosh.

One reason is that Apple's top people are all deeply involved in the advertising program.

As a result, their advertising is an accurate reflection of the company's beliefs.

It's designed to speak to their target – which includes me and you, as well as a lot of people who aren't like us at all.

A UNIQUE TONE OF VOICE.

Look at the graphic rhythm, a friendly serif type face that is contemporary, yet comfortable, and a personal tone of voice that speaks to the individuals who make the purchase decision.

We've added a piece by Chris Wall, of BBDO/L. A., that describes the Apple Tone of Voice.

It works for a wide range of material: television, print, brochures, direct mail... all done with a consistent point of view and all consistently tasteful.

SOME EXAMPLES.

Everybody remembers **"1984,"** the introductory commercial for the Macintosh.

It only ran once (during the Super Bowl), but it set the stage for the product introduction in a dramatic and memorable way.

The follow-up TV and the print was very product-oriented, like the spot on the left.

The piece that sold me was an **8-page insert.**

I needed an easy to use word processing with graphic capabilities. By the fifth page, I was sold.

Their introductory promotional program was also a breakthrough.

Take Macintosh out for a test drive.

Promotional Events. *Macintosh tries to make their marketing activities events. In this early promotion, people were invited to sample the product by taking it home for a* ***"Test Drive."***

IT'LL TAKE US AT LEAST SIX PAGES TO EXPLAIN DESKTOP PUBLISHING.

"DeskTop Publishing."
This important "niche" market helped Apple establish the Macintosh inside companies that had already bought other computers!

& More...

The Macintosh family keeps growing, with new machines and capabilities.

As computers become appliances, Apple works to defend their unique product and position and hit more and more "niches."

New Products.

Look to see how Apple matches specific products against specific areas of the marketplace - from mass retailers to universities.

New Competition.

Though they sell hardware, their position is based on software – the *Macintosh Graphic User Interface.*

Watch as the competitive framework shifts from IBM vs. Apple to a battle with Microsoft's MS/DOS-based "Windows."

New Formats.

CD's will become a more common playback format for computers as well as other forms of home entertainment and information.

For example, now your snapshots can come back on CD and your daily newspaper can come in over the phone line on a "modem."

Whatever happens, it sure isn't "1984" any more.

This piece was originally written to help new writers on Apple get up to speed.

It provides an excellent view of what it takes to develop a long-term stance and tone of voice for a brand.

As Chris says, "It's wonderful to win an award for an ad. It's far better to win two awards: one for the great individual ad, and one for the great campaign."

It's reprinted with apologies to Chris and to you - we really had to cut it down.

But, as Chris says, "write copy to fit the layout."

There were also some very funny illustrations and captions that we had to cut.

Trust us, they were very funny.

But most important, there are a lot of smart insights in here.

It's a great framework for helping you "Find a voice" for your brand.

This article was set in "Apple Garamond," which is Garamond condensed 80%.

The Communicator's Guide to Success and Survival.

by Chris Wall, BBDO/LA

Preface.

It's the best of times.

It's the worst of times. It's Apple.

Seldom will you have the opportunity to work with products that are so good and so clearly different in vision from their competitors.

Never again will you have the chance to work so many hours on so many tasks that are so vaguely defined, that can change at the drop of an offhand remark by an industry pundit; where your clients applaud your great work on Monday and tell you on Tuesday that you were totally off the mark.

Working on Apple is like trying to nail Jell-O to a bulletin board – like driving on a freeway where the posted maximum is 75 and the posted minimum is 85.

1 Apple year = 5 human years = 35 dog years.

Working on Apple, you will have the chance to make your career, win major awards and make a real contribution to the success of a *Fortune 100* company. You will also have the opportunity to destroy your personal relationships, raise your blood pressure and take advantage of those psychology benefits in the health insurance.

The good news is, Apple will do incredibly exciting advertising, take calculated risks and give you the chance to do the unexpected.

The bad news is, they will change the assignment on you, they will change the assignment on you again and quickly dismiss great advertising if it doesn't say exactly what they believe it should say in exactly the way they think it should be said.

Apple exists in an industry where monumental change takes place overnight.

Where the life of even a successful product can be less than a year.

Don't expect a lot of time to develop your ideas. (They develop entire products in a matter of months, so it's not unreasonable for them to expect you to do an ad in a week or two.) The faster you can develop your communications, the quicker you can adapt to change, the greater success you will enjoy.

The purpose of this guide is to give you a little perspective on Apple communications and help you understand the basic ingredients that go into any successful Apple ad.

I. The Apple Voice.

The very best Apple communications have one of the most distinctive voices in all of business communications.

It sounds a whole lot like Steve Hayden in a good mood.*

It isn't easy to pick up the Apple Voice.

The Apple Voice has three basically different moods that you need to understand. All three can be found occasionally in a single piece.

1. The Hopeful, Optimistic Apple.

This voice is serious, intelligent and human. It has the quality Steve calls *ponderosity.* It has a profound quality and relates the way Apple builds products to the ambitions and aspirations of our readers and viewers.

It espouses that one person with the right tools and a great idea can accomplish anything, and that people working together with the right tools can change the world and make dreams come true.

This is not b---s---. The people at Apple believe this. The people who have written really great Apple communications believe it.

If you have a point you want to make and you can make it with this voice, it is almost impossible to go wrong. It makes people feel good about Apple. It gets test scores that are off the charts.

Best of all, it truly reflects the spirit of Apple people and the products they make.

This voice belongs to Apple and you are its custodian. This is the voice you will use if you're working on an education ad. For an example of this voice, see *Industrial Revelation, MacWorld, I'm Different* and most education print ads.

2. The Practical Apple.

This voice wants you to know why the particularly bright engineers at Apple build computers the way they do. How those computers work. And why the way they work is better than the way other computers work.

This is the voice that easily relates complex technology to real-world benefits.

It works very well in business ads, new product ads, and in product television spots.

Examples of the Practical Apple can be found in *Manuals,* most of the product TV spots), *Testing 1-2-3, Testing 4-5-6,* and the original Macintosh introduction insert.

---

* *Steve is head of BBDO/LA and a long-time Apple creative force, beginning at Chiat/Day, Apple's first agency.*

3. The Radical Apple.

This is the nitroglycerin of Apple communications.

Funny, flip, roguishly smart and confident that we have a better way of working. The best thing about this voice is that it attracts lots of attention. It is fun to read and watch. And it has a certain charm in a world of bland, predictable corporate communications.

The worst thing about it is that it is taken as arrogant and condescending.

Without this voice, Apple would never have created perhaps the single most successful ad of the last decade – *1984*. Don't be afraid to use this voice.

Just use it with care.

Examples where it has worked well include the print ads *Just what the world needs...* and *Welcome IBM. Seriously.* And the TV spots *Testing 1-2-3, Testing 4-5-6* and *1984*. Where it backfired was *Lemmings* and *The Berlin Wall* ad.

II. The Apple Advantage Points. The Evidence for Any Argument.

In 1989, a lot of people spent a lot of time defining the Apple Advantage Points (also known as the "points of light"). These points serve as the outline for the body copy of any Apple ad thusly:

1. Powerful technology that is easy to use.

Although this point wasn't discovered until 1989, it's really the basic idea behind Apple since the days in the garage.

Macintosh – with its simple, graphic interface – made the personal computer useful to millions of people who couldn't or wouldn't invest the time to learn the peculiar syntax personal computers had borrowed from their mainframe cousins.

Everything about Macintosh was designed around a real-world metaphor – the desktop. Instead of you having to adapt to the way the computer works, the people who designed Macintosh adapted it to the way that you work.

This was a revolutionary concept.

Ultimately, it is this philosophy that continues to distinguish Macintosh from other computers and Apple from other computer companies.

Each subsequent version of Macintosh has increased the power and sophistication of its technology enormously with only a small increase in complexity to the user.

2. Thousands of programs that work together.

Prior to the arrival of Macintosh, every computer program worked differently, according to the whims of its author.

The command to save a document in one program could be the command to erase a document in another – even though you were using the same machine.

On a Macintosh, programs are consistent and they work together. Although there are thousands of Macintosh programs there is only one way to print, open, save or close a document. You can copy information from one program and paste it into almost any other program, so you never have to do the same work twice.

3. Built-in networking.

At its most basic level, Apple makes it easy to connect a Macintosh to other computers so you can share information, send electronic mail etc.

You can use a very sophisticated, complex network without a lot of training.

This gets back to Apple Advantage #2; networking software works exactly like all other Macintosh software.

4. Growth without disruption.

In the DOS world, each subsequent iteration of the operating system has required users to get new versions of their applications. Or, a new version of a program would be incompatible with previous versions and would have entirely new commands. This is disruption.

In the Macintosh world, it's much simpler. The Mac interface is basically the same today as it was in 1984. New features have been added, improvements have been made, but the basic way of working is still the same.

The basic benefit of this is that you can add new features and capabilities as Apple improves the system software – quickly, easily, inexpensively, without enormous interruptions in your business.

III. The Basic Reader Perspectives.

Every Apple ad is written to one of two perspectives.

1. The User Perspective.

People who use computers want to know what's in a Macintosh computer for them. You can talk to them with any Apple Voice that is appropriate.

They care about the emotional appeal of Apple as well as the practical. The User Perspective is in the Chiat/Day spot *Basketball* and more practically focused spots like *Macintosh Office* and *Manuals*.

2. The Management Perspective.

These guys don't care about the hopeful, optimistic Apple. Spare them anything remotely philosophical unless, of course, you relate it to a practical benefit. The benefit to them is that people use Apple computers more and get more done with them with less training. *Testing 1-2-3* is a particularly successful example of this perspective.

IV. Three Ways to Explain the Advantages of a Macintosh.

When it's all said and done, you've got three choices:

1. Product.

Explain how a Macintosh works. Demonstrate point by point why it does what it does and how that differs from other computers. Show it. Explain it. Demonstrate it. This is your basic new product ad.

2. Task.

Explain why a Macintosh is a better way to accomplish any particular task. For example, Macintosh is a better way to work with numbers not only because it has great spreadsheet programs (any computer has them) but because it's easy to learn and set up (so you spend more time working and less time learning); because all the programs work together; because it makes it easy to work with other people. And so on.

3. People.

Explain innovative ways real people are actually using Macintosh.

V. The Basic Arguments Against Macintosh. (Circa 1991)

(NOTE: This is a discussion of the counter-arguments to the following four "Arguments Against Macintosh:" 1. It's not affordable. 2. It's not compatible. 3. It doesn't connect. 4. No applications.

VI. Art Directors Who Write, Writers Who Art Direct.

You are inheriting a unique tradition of advertising.

Apple ads are frequently better written and more interesting than the articles in the magazine in which they appear.

It is your responsibility to maintain that tradition.

Any copywriter good enough to get a job working on Apple knows the basic cliches of copywriting. Lots of fragments for emphasis. Clever word plays and jokes. Quite simply, the use of phrases like "quite simply."

Use them to help make your points. But don't kid yourself into thinking these little devices are a substitute for hard facts, insightful analysis and passionate reasoning.

Detail is everything. Apple ads have achieved no small measure of notoriety among copywriters for the bright, amusing quips in the legal copy. At first blush, they seem to just be one of the more charming manifestations of the Radical Apple Voice. But they tell the reader something very important: that everything in an Apple ad is written to be read and enjoyed, that Apple, as a corporation, pays attention to the smallest detail.

I'm a copywriter, so this has mostly focused on writing.

Art directors are also responsible for good writing. They should read the copy and, if it isn't as good as they think it can be, they should say so.

Much of the print work of the late 1980s was influenced by the clean, dramatic Apple look. As an art director on Apple, you are following in the steps of the best: Lee Clow, Yvonne Smith, Houman Pirdavari and Brent Thomas, to name a few.

It never hurts to study their work and measure yours against it.

Don't fall into the trap of changing the Apple look just for the sake of change.

Every time someone played around with the "Apple look" to "make it better" we have come away with something far less satisfying than we had before. I know, because I've fallen into this trap.

Apple ads should be beautiful and consistent. The best Apple ads of 1983 bear a striking resemblance to the best of 1986, which look a lot like the best of 1989.

It's wonderful to win an award for an ad. It's far better to win two awards: one for the great individual ad, and one for the great campaign.

The beauty of Apple ads isn't just "an art problem." Copywriters are responsible, too. That means you should do things like write copy to fit the layout.

Don't present a layout with half as much room as you need and wind up with an ugly ad filled with eensie-weensie type.

This sound obvious. But it's amazing how often a really good concept winds up weak and unsatisfying because the members of the team don't work together.

VII. Apple. Where the Future is Tomorrow, Every Day.

The next decade is going to be at least as exciting as the last – technologies are going to come together very quickly – computer, telephone, television, fiber optics, cellular, photocopy, laser printing, maybe more.

Imagine a Macintosh with a television, cellular telephone and VCR built into it, small enough to fit on your desk. Or in your briefcase.

I'm not letting you in on anything confidential, you can see most of the pieces today at any MacWorld Exposition. It's just a matter of time – and not much, at that – before someone will pull it all together for you, eventually at a reasonable price.

In the next few years, it's important that we help Apple win not just market share, but mind share. We must expand and redefine what " " stands for that is consistent with our "computers for people" heritage.

We must protect those values and attitudes and we must find new ways to express them as others clamor to jump on our bandwagon.

If we do, if we continue to make Apple communications relevant, dynamic and innovative, we will help Apple become one of the first great global brands of the 21st Century.

Chris Wall/BBD /January 1991

We haven't talked much about retail in this book, yet it's one of the most exciting and demanding areas of advertising.

So, we'll use this Case History to spend a bit more time talking about the strategy and implementation of this local retail campaign.

The Insider's Guide to:
STEREO
COMPONENT BUYING
by Edward Myer

1st Edition

This is an inside view of the world of quality stereo and video components. It tells you what's good and what's bad about the manufacturers and the stores. It gives you the solid insider's information you need to get your money's worth. It tells you what to look for and more particularly what to look out for. Here are the plain unvarnished facts about quality component buying—warts and all.

The Client Wrote This.
It criticized inflated "list" prices and some other common practices in the stereo business.

It helped establish credibility for Myer-Emco's "expertise."

Myer-EMCO

This is a small chain of stereo (now audio-video) stores in Washington, DC. I helped move them from #3 to #1 back in the 70's.

The campaign was originally based on the strong central idea that Myer-Emco provided the highest quality equipment supported by the best stereo service department in town.

They even tested the equipment before you took it home!

This unique combination of quality and service, and their well-earned local reputation, led to a simple straightforward Selling Idea that was the basis for all their advertising.

"Washington's Leading Stereo Store."

At the time, they were #3 in the market and the stereo business was exploding with mass merchandisers and heavy discounting.

They grew with a small but consistent ad campaign and *one sale a year.* (No kidding.)

Here's how they did it.

STAGE ONE.

It started small and simple. But classy.

• **Read All About It.** Ed Myer, the head of Myer-EMCO, wrote a little booklet –
"The Insider's Guide to Stereo and High Fi."
We promoted the book.

• **Small Space Print**, with nifty headlines based on unique selling points from the booklet ran in the upscale city magazine.

• **Radio Commercials**, often funded by co-op money, used each individual brand to feed to Myer-Emco's quality position.

• **Promotions.** A Free Turntable Clinic, which let people get their turntables checked, was a consistent traffic builder.

We stuck with this program for almost two years, adding a few radio stations and gradually increasing the frequency of our print.

Business increased slowly but steadily while the competition outspent us with advertising that featured screaming discounts.

The contrast between the quiet and steady expertise of Myer-EMCO and the "Everything Must Go" attitude of the competition served to further reinforce Myer-EMCO's position – so when they did run a sale, it blew the doors off.

During that time, one of the major competitors went out of business and Myer-EMCO made their move.

STAGE TWO.

We maintained the focus of the campaign, but added *impact* as our budget grew.

• **Print Advertising.** Myer-EMCO began running full pages that continued to reinforce their expertise. Some examples. . .

• **Tape Talk.** Myer-EMCO responded to the move to audio cassette players with this informative and helpful long copy print ad.

It also promoted a new event that was added to the Turntable Clinic – a Free Tape Deck Check.

• **Hear Here/Print.** We dramatized our audio selection *visually* by featuring a variety of the speakers offered and positioning Myer-EMCO as the source for every speaker need.

• **Radio Ads.** We kept the distinctive sound of our spots,

MYER-EMCO
"PRE-CHRISTMAS RADIO."
ANNCR: [Christmas Music Under]

'Twas the sale before Christmas
and all through the store.
The samples were moving
from off of the floor.
Components were nestled
all snug in their shelves.
While shoppers went shopping...
just for themselves.
Ma in her Gucci
was looking quite nifty.
Look, Pa, she said,
"We can save 10 to 50."
So visit our stores,
if it's bargains you seek.
But hurry, my friends.
It's only this week.
Myer-EMCO'S Pre-Christmas
Clearance Sale. At Myer-EMCO.
Washington's Leading Stereo Store.

continuing to add stations (reach) and increase *frequency*.

Various components were advertised in the Myer-EMCO style using co-op ad dollars.

• **Hear Here/Radio**. This commercial, which was featured in the Radio section, was a complement to the print advertising with the same headline and turned this effort into a mini-campaign.

• **Promotions.** In addition to continuing the Turntable Clinic, and adding the **Tape Deck Check**, we developed a *Seasonal Promotion*, "**Have a Myer-EMCO Christmas**," supported with print, radio and direct mail.

• **Mailer.** An engaging mailer, sent to Myer-EMCO customers, featured a wide variety of items, many selected for appropriateness as gifts.

It made an already strong selling season even stronger.

• **Myer-EMCO Pre-Christmas Radio**.

Even though we tried to keep it to one sale a year, every once in a while there was a chance to grab an extra selling event.

Here, we turned a small demo clearance into a major event which also stimulated Christmas shopping traffic.

During this period, Myer-EMCO moved into the #1 position in the marketplace.

WHY IT WORKED.

Here are the reasons I believe this campaign succeeded in the marketplace:

Start with a quality product.

Myer-EMCO's quality point of difference was the basis for our message.

It's hard to do great advertising if you don't have a great product.

And most brands and businesses build with *repeat* customers.

If Myer-EMCO hadn't been keeping customers, the campaign wouldn't have worked.

Establish leadership as quickly as possible.

Even though we weren't the #1 store by volume, we were, by our definition, the *leading* store according to quality. (Myer-EMCO had, in fact, a national reputation.)

We weren't shy about exploiting and pre-empting our position, turning a *niche* into a "#1" position.

Differentiate dramatically.

We used both creative and media differentiation to good effect. If we'd played the competitors' game, we probably would have been buried.

Our low, slow radio commercials were much different than any competitors' advertising effort.

Our unique print ads competed with large amounts of screaming newspaper.

Consumers noticed we were different.

Stick with it.

The first year, it was hard to know whether the advertising was really working or not.

Business was good, but not great.

It would have been easy for a client who was greedy or nervous to change.

We kept it up and were able to tap into the *cumulative* power of a good campaign.

Be lucky.

For the first three years, nobody else in the market went after our position.

Two big competitors punched each other out, discounting themselves out of business, while degrading their image with their own money.

This served to further reinforce Myer-EMCO's high-end image and position.

Finally, Washington, DC, is somewhat insulated from the economic realities that affect the rest of America and Myer-EMCO was well-positioned for this affluent market.

THE NATION'S NEWSPAPER

USA TODAY

Breaking the sound barrier at home

By Anita Manning USA TODAY

There is nothing quite so vulnerable as a non-technie in a hi-fi store.

■ Rack systems—stereo components made by a single manufacturer that fit together on a rack or stand—are easy to buy. But at $500 to more than $1,000, they aren't cheap—and audio experts warn that, in most cases, they're no bargain. Behind knobs, meters and lights are what one engineer labels "a consumer trick—the trick is to produce a lot of wattage at the expense of everything else."

Manufacturer's of rack systems cut corners by producing cheap speakers, and speakers "are probably the component that will make the largest single difference" in your audio system, says Edward Myer, president of Myer-Emco, a Washington, D.C.-based chain of audio specialty stores.

Go for components, experts advise.

■ Speakers. Buy this component first. "Speakers vary a great deal in the quality of sound," Myer says. "The average person is an excellent judge of the accuracy of a speaker. All you have to do is listen, but you have to listen under good circumstances."

Not all speakers are made to be accurate. Some are designed to appeal to people who want "a boomy bass and overemphasized high," a sound Myer calls "showroom brilliance." It might dazzle the listener initially but "will get on your nerves after a while."

■ Receivers. "A receiver is a very complex product, probably as complex as buying a computer," Myer says. Unless you can decipher manufacturers' specification sheets, it's one area where you might have to rely on an honest salesman. Expect to spend $275-$400.

The power output of a receiver's amplifier is expressed in watts but, Myer warns, "the average store does a con job—they say the 30-watt is better than the 25. That's sheer engineering nonsense."

■ Tape deck. Experts recommend a unit that appears wellbuilt. Don't be dazzled by lots of dials and buttons. Sound quality varies, so be sure to listen to decks from two to three companies. Expect to spend $300-$400 for a good one since recording quality is reflected in cost differences. "Don't just listen to a recorded tape," Myer advises. "Make a recording and listen, then you'll hear the difference."

■ CD Players. "Even the worst CD is better than the average phonograph record," says Myer. "There are important differences among CD players."

It wasn't only advertising.
Publicity like this and Direct Mail to customers worked to reinforce the Myer-EMCO position.

More about calcium and McDonald's good food.

New McLean Deluxe. Hold the fat.

McDonald's.

Through the years, their consistent, high-quality **brand personality** has been matched by consistent, high-quality service in their stores.

McDonald's pays attention to **QSC&V: Quality, Service, Cleanliness** and **Value.**

They also pay a lot of attention to their advertising, combining the best of big national agency marketing with the kind of local market attention you only get from a local agency.

The result is a wide range of work on a wide range of products and promotions that manages to be both consistent and effective.

The warm glow of the Golden Arches sheds its light on everything from their terrific French Fries to Cheeseburgers, and big Big Mac's to a McDonald's Breakfast.

And the people in their commercials enjoy the McDonald's experience in a way that entertains at the same time it sells.

Everybody works hard to keep it fresh – from the folks at Leo Burnett to all their local and regional agencies.

And it all works. Together.

EARLY ADVERTISING.

Yesterday's advertising is part of today's brand image. Two of McDonald's classic early campaigns were **"You Deserve a Break Today"** and **"We Do It All For You."**

Each additional campaign builds Brand Equity.

NATIONAL AND LOCAL ADVERTISING.

McDonald's largest agency, Leo Burnett, has to produce, literally, hundreds of commercials.

But that's just the beginning.

CHILDREN'S ADVERTISING.

In addition to the part they play in the national advertising, this important group has its own campaign, with Ronald McDonald.

And it pays off in the store. A child wants to go to McDonald's and get a "Happy Meal" with a toy or game-oriented packaging.

McDonald's also has two other young targets – Teens and "Tweens."

Each has their own ad program.

OTHER MEDIA.

It's not just TV.

From outdoor boards to the sign behind the cash register, McDonald's communication efforts give attention to every dimension of the McDonald's experience.

Family Values.
McDonald's communicates its role as a place where families and friends get together – it's not just food, it's the whole "McDonald's Experience."

Here are some frames from the classic "Little Sister" by Jack Smith at Leo Burnett.

SOCIAL RESPONSIBILITY.

In many areas, McDonald's has responded positively to the pressures facing today's marketers – large and small.

It hasn't been easy. Moving from styrofoam to recycled and recyclable packaging involved a massive logistical effort.

PROMOTIONS.

Logistics of another sort occur in all the markets where McDonald's does business.

Many commercials you see are product promotions. There's probably one going on right now.

"Big Mac Attack" focused on Bic Mac sales. **"Mac Tonight"** focused on dinner.

"McBreakfast at McDonald's" opened up a whole new meal opportunity.

Games like **"Monopoly"** help bring customers in more often.

Local Promotions.
McDonald's Field Marketing Staff, local Franchisee Co-ops and Regional advertising agencies maintain a full calendar of events that maximize local opportunities. Here, a national promotion gets extra impact by tying-in with a local radio station.

Building Brand Equity.
Another example of the strength of McDonald's Brand Equity – the McKid's clothing venture.

Creative License.
With some projects, there's always a new opportunity on the menu.

376

Starbucks

Even in flat or declining markets, there can be great opportunities for growth.

All it takes is the right idea done right.

For example, while coffee is not a growing category, Starbucks is a fast-growing business.

It all started when a young man from Seattle had an idea while on a visit to Europe – he noticed the popularity of corner Espresso bars.

Returning to Seattle, **Howard Schultz** asked the small coffee roasting company he worked for if they'd be interested in expanding into retail locations. They declined, but indicated that he could proceed if he wanted to. He did.

A sound concept and excellent execution resulted in Starbucks Coffee.

Consistent graphics and smart merchandising are just the beginning.

Starbucks markets intelligently to all its targets, from their employees to their customers to the investment community.

It's also a pretty nice cup of coffee.

Well-Located. Well-Coordinated.
The green logo is integrated into the store decor for Retail Graphics that work to create a pleasant environment for coffee-drinking.

Good margins serve to make good locations affordable.

Well-Marketed.
Handsome advertising reinforces product quality.

Individual ads usually feature a Product Story.

Well-Sampled.
"Star Bucks" are handed out regularly to stimulate customer traffic.

Well-Invested.
The investment community is also a target market – providing Starbucks with capital for aggressive expansion.

STARBUCKS COFFEE
OVERVIEW

Starbucks Coffee Company is a Seattle-based privately owned and operated chain of over 100 retail outlets, merchandised around two concepts: espresso bars, and stores offering whole bean coffees and brewing accessories. Starbucks is committed to dominating the specialty coffee market in each city where they establish operations. Quality, service, speed, and cleanliness are the vehicles of Starbucks' success in implementing this strategy.

Starbucks is the largest company-owned specialty coffee roaster/retailer in North America. This powerful position is supported by a vertical corporate structure combining all elements of bean buying, roasting and retailing. At the core of this structure is Starbucks' new state-of-the-art roasting plant. The facility, located in Seattle, Washington, has 68,000 square feet, designed and built to meet the special needs of Starbucks Coffee. The new plant can roast and process up to 11 million pounds of coffee each year, to meet the demands of more than 300,000 customers who visit Starbucks' stores each week.

Familiarity breeds contentment.

Cappuccino   Espresso Con Panna   Caffè Latte   Caffè Americano   Caffè Mocha   Espresso Macchiato   Espresso   Latte Macchiato

Well-Merchandised.

Here's an inside spread from an in-store brochure. It's also an in-store poster. This Product Story encourages the customer to become more of an expert on the product. This doesn't just make the sale, it builds the relationship.

Well-Served.

A key dimension to Starbucks product is the people who serve it.

Internal communications and training are critical.

Because a commitment to quality demands a commitment to people and a company culture that is rich with shared values and team spirit.

This in-house company magazine has a modern upbeat feel that demonstrates that commitment and salutes the people of Starbucks.

Well-Packaged.

Starbucks doesn't miss an opportunity. Shopping bags, coffee cups, grinders, packaging, even little extras like candy and granola. Each one is an opportunity to make the point that Starbucks is a special place – and each one is an opportunity to build the sale.

Well-Informed.

These informational brochures are available for anyone who wants one.

Topics range from how to make Espresso to product information to consumer concerns like caffeine.

Next Steps:

The essence of the journey is progress...
Next Steps...

Yet, in our business, we often seem plagued with slow, clumsy decisions multiplied by last minute deadlines.

Too often, we deal with institutional inertia interspersed with intense periods of panic and uncertainty. Reactions instead of actions.

Does this sound familiar? Are you reacting instead of acting? Try this...

While you cannot control previous events, you can get in touch with current events.

Think about things as they are...

Now, think about possible future events and actions you could take which *might* make things better... take a deep breath.

As Louis Pasteur said,

"Fortune favors the prepared mind."

Vaccinate yourself against the future.

Where do you want to go?

What are *your* Next Steps?

For example...

Before you write an ad, you should have a sense of what you want the ad to do.

In every meeting, look for the new things that need doing. Seek the chance to do them.

Do not expect too much. Find the small steps that will help put things on track.

And do not be too big to take small steps:

Improve the copy. One more time.

Find a way to do more. Show how that big idea works as a small piece of P.O.P.

Do another ad.

Do another campaign.

Do it again. And again.

By focusing on Next Steps, you will begin to manage change – whether what you have to change is someone else's mind or your own habits.

There is change with every next step.

Do not avoid tough problems and tough accounts.* Look for them.

Solve a few, and it can make your career.

People may even begin to seek you out to help them with their problems.

Naturally, they will be people with problems, generally a pre-occupied sort, but **if people didn't have problems, they wouldn't need you.**

I still remember the new business campaign a young writer had written for his former agency.

The theme... *"We're Looking for Trouble."*

It was targeted at clients with problems – just the type searching for a new agency. Smart.

Sadly, his agency decided to play it safe.

Happily, he quickly got a new job with that campaign as the centerpiece of his book.

I bet he's doing quite well.

He understands the business.

Savor each challenge and do not despair that you cannot solve every one – it's a tough business.

Many impossible problems, particularly in tough times, are just that... impossible.

And many smart, talented, imaginative people have found satisfaction somewhere other than the advertising business.

Remember, you're being paid cash money to give it your best shot. Give it gladly.

You'll do a better job.

And you'll feel better doing it.

Develop a healthy appetite for tough problems and your reward will be more of them.

*

*These can often be confused with **impossible** problems and accounts, which should be avoided.*

Experience alone will help you tell the difference between the tough and the impossible.

Unfortunately, this new wisdom is often acquired after the fact.

As your journey progresses, so will your career. Hopefully.

It can be a good living *if* you can develop an appetite for hard work and constant frustration.

This will be punctuated by the brief satisfaction of a job well done and the lasting satisfactions that come with helping to make a business grow.

Your reward will be a growing wealth of knowledge and experience, a job that may pay fairly well, and friendships that often last longer than the jobs and the agencies.

Now this book is over.

The Next Steps are yours . . .

What is your Objective?

What is your Strategy?

What is your Style?

What Tactics will you use to help your client's business? Think about it.

Think about how you can help your friends and business partners.

Help them and you will help yourself.

It's a team sport.

Give your gift.

Good luck.

Bruce Bendinger

Words

Advertising and marketing has its own vocabulary – here are some common words and acronyms, and their generally accepted meanings.

A

AAAA: The "4 A's." American Association of Advertising Agencies.

AAF: American Advertising Federation

"A" Counties: Larger urban counties.

A & B Roll: The use of two rolls of film or videotape to achieve some sort of "wipe" or "dissolve" between the two.

Account Executive: The person who is in charge of running a piece of business (the account) at an advertising agency.

ADDY: Advertising award given by local ad clubs / regional advertising groups through the American Advertising Federation.

ADI: Area of Dominant Influence. Geographic definition of markets based on TV viewing.

AFTRA: American Federation of Theater and Radio Artists. The performance union for talent appearing on audio or videotape.

AFM: American Federation of Musicians. The musician's union.

Animatic: A rough commercial, usually a storyboard laid off onto video tape and the frames matched to a rough soundtrack.

An animatic which uses photos is also called a **"photomatic"**– An animatic which uses pieces of other commercials is called a **"steal-o-matic."**

Attention: An initial objective of an advertisement.

Attitude: The feelings people have towards a product or service.

Audio Mix: Combining or "mixing" of audio elements to produce final soundtrack.

Auto Assembly: A type of videotape assembly that is automated by use of "time-code" numbers on the videotape.

A/V: Audio Visual Presentation. Once exclusively slides with an audio track, this now refers to a number of formats.

B

"B" Counties: Smaller urban and suburban counties.

Back Light: Dramatic lighting technique in which much of the light comes from behind the object.

Bait and Switch: Illegal practice of baiting customers with low priced goods which they are then unable to buy or discouraged from buying.

Bells and Whistles: Usually referring to special electronic effects used in video editing. Or extras in general.

Benefit: In advertising, this is usually short for "Consumer Benefit," the benefit the consumer receives from the Product.

Bite: A short segment of sound track.

Bleed: When the "live" area of an ad, such as the photograph "bleeds" off the page, this is a bleed ad. A non-bleed ad has a white border around it.

"Blooper Soap": Description of overdone reading of copy. It refers to an old comedy tape in which the announcer ends up shouting every single word of the phrase "Blooper Soap is Real Good!"

Boilerplate: Standard legal copy, often used on coupons.

Bold Face: Type style that is darker than the regular "reader" face to give the copy emphasis.

Broadside: One page promotional flyer, folded for mailing.

"Buckeye": Uncomplimentary description of crude, obvious graphic treatments (except in Ohio).

• **Bullet Points:** Way of listing multiple points in presentations or print ads.

Burke: A type of "day after recall" research practiced by Burke Research in Cincinnati and used by P&G and other package goods marketers.

Often used as a verb. To "Burke" something. Or "it won't Burke."

Business to Business: Advertising of products and services from one business to another (as opposed to Consumer Advertising). "B to B."

C

Call-Outs: Small captions next to items or features in an ad.

"C & D" Counties: Predominantly small town and rural counties.

ChromaKey: Way of "Matting in" backgrounds by shooting against a Chromakey blue. This is commonly used on TV news shows. On film, the technique used is **"UltiMatte."**

Clearance: or "Network Clearance" procedure of submitting scripts or storyboards to television networks for approval before they are shot. A wise step if there are legal questions about the commercial.

CLIOS: Another advertising industry award. There are many.

Color correction: Technical process of altering color values of film or videotape.

Comp: A "tight" or comprehensive layout, including type.

Contingency: Part of production budget (often 10%) set aside for unknowns.

Copy: The words in an ad.

Copy/Contact: A copywriter who works directly with the client instead of through an account executive.

© **Copyright:** The exclusive right to a publication, literary, dramatic, musical or artistic work. The copyright to an ad is generally owned by an advertiser and a copyright symbol plus the year of publication must appear on the ad.

Cut: Going from one scene to another with no intervening effects. Also used as a verb, i.e., "It doesn't cut."

D

Dailies: The film that was shot that day. One usually views dailies the day after they were shot. Also used to refer to all the film from the shoot.

Demo: 1. A demonstration in a TV commercial. 2. A rough version of a jingle submitted by a music house. 3. A sample tape submitted by a film house. 4. Short for *demographic profile*.

Demo Rates: Lower rates which apply to the production of Demos.

Demographics: The statistical data about Target Consumers, i.e., Age, Income, Family size. Usually *quantitative*.

Dissolve: Fading from one scene to another.

Dog & Pony Show: A big presentation for a client or prospective client.

Dominance: Often an objective in many areas of advertising. In media – dominant space. In business – dominant share.

Donut: A form of TV or radio commercial in which a "hole" is left in the middle for special local or promotional use.

DTP: Desktop publishing.

Dub: 1. A copy of an audio or video tape. 2. To substitute a new voice track.

Dummy: Mock-up or layout of brochure or other multi-page piece, such as an Annual Report.

Dupes: Tape copies. Same as Dubs.

E

Echo: An audio effect in which echo is added to give the voice and acoustic space more size.

Effects: A common advertising phrase used to describe a wide range of audio and visual (optical) effects.

Empty Suit: A person who adds little.

Emulsion: The part of the film that holds the image.

EQ: Sound equalization or re-adjustment.

Eye Brow: A small pre-head at the top of a print ad.

Eye Camera: Research device used many years ago, which measured the dilation of the pupil when a person looked at an ad.

F

FCC: Federal Communications Commission.

FDA: Food and Drug Administration.

Fill: Lighting used to fill in dark areas.

Flip Wipe: Optical effect where one scene flips to another.

Focus Group: A research technique where 10 –12 consumers are invited in for a discussion which focuses on issues related to the product and its advertising. Usually observed from behind a one-way mirror.

Four Color: Full color printing derived from 4 separate plates – Black, Yellow, Red and Blue.

Frame Count: A numerical record of the number of frames in a commercial or a part of a commercial. Often used for animation or music scoring.

Frequency: Media statistic measuring the number of times various percentages of an audience see a commercial.

FSI: Free Standing Insert. Common media vehicle for delivering coupons. They often appear in Sunday newspapers.

FX: Common abbreviation for "effects" in scripts.

G

Generation: A measure of how far removed a dub is from the master. The master tape is first generation. The dub is second generation. A dub of that dub is third generation. And so on. There is a gradual diminution of quality which varies depending on type of tape, tape speed, and equipment quality.

GRP: Gross Rating Points. A way of buying and measuring media. The cumulative number of ratings points (usually Neilsen) are the criteria.

H

Half-Track: A two track tape recording.

Headline: The "Titling" words in an advertisement.

Hook: The part of a song (or jingle) that "hooks" your memory.

Hype: Generally negative statement describing empty claims and enthusiastic selling with no substance. Sometimes used as a verb meaning add excitement or energy, i.e., "hype-up the product shot."

I

ID: A short commercial message. Usually 10 seconds. . . or less.

Image: A combination of factors that add up to the way people think and feel about a product. Also used as an adjective to describe advertising that is more attitudinal than factual.

Impact: Initial attention-getting. Often a result of powerful visual imagery or graphic treatment.

Inherent Drama: Advertising philosophy of Leo Burnett. He believed it could be found in every product or service.

ips: Inches per second. Audio tape speed.

J

Jive: Slang for phony, empty, trying to be hip but not.

Jump Cut: Type of edit where continuity is sacrificed for effect.

K

Kem: Common film editing machine. The editing table or the "table."

Keyline: Final assembly of type and art for printed piece. (Stats of art and photography are often pasted in place "For Position Only.")

L

Layout: Graphic representation of an ad. Can be rough or tight.

Lead Time: Amount of time needed to complete a job.

Leading: The amount of space between lines of copy. Pronounced "ledding." (Typesetters used to put bits of lead between lines of type.)

Leakage: In recording, occurs when material recorded on one microphone leaks over to another microphone.

Left Hand Side: Scene and action description in a TV script.

Library Music: Pre-recorded music classified by tempo and mood, formerly available on records, now usually on CD.

Local Tag: A part of the commercial with no announcer to allow local station announcers to read appropriate local copy.

Locator Copy: Address information in a tag.

Logo: Short for logotype. The identifying graphic treatment or graphic device for a product or service.

M

"Marionette Effect": Bad copy does this. It turns actors into phony people saying words they would never say.

Master: The original, usually referring to first generation film print, video assembly or audio mix.

Matte: A film effect where one image is overlaid onto another. A "matte" is used to block out the underlying film image.

Maven: Noun. Yiddish word for "expert."

Mechanical: Type and artwork pasted on a board for reproduction by printer.

Mnemonic: Memory device usually used to register product name or benefit.

Mortise: In film, similar to a matte. Usually a hole in which a product or scene appears. As a verb – "Mortise in a product shot."

Multing: Repeating vocal or instrumental parts on additionl tracks to create the illusion of a larger group.

N

NAB: Newspaper Advertising Bureau.

NAD: National Advertising Division of the National Advertising Review Council, a self-regulatory body which reviews advertising.

NARB: National Advertising Review Board. Reviews decisions of NAD.

Needle Drop: Use of library music in a commercial – originally you paid each time you dropped the needle on the record.

Neilsen: Refers to data from A. C. Neilsen Company. May refer to data which measures TV viewership or retail sales (the prime source of brand share information in retail sales.) Neilsen does both types of research.

Negative: The film in the camera is negative film. Also, photostat that has been reversed (i.e., white on black).

Negative Transfer: The process of transferring film negative to a positive videotape image.

Nine Wheel Logic: Type of Support which seems to prove a point, even though it doesn't. "Daddy, why does the locomotive go so fast?" "Because it has all those wheels." For example, new colors are sometimes added to a product to symbolize a new ingredient which may be colorless and may be technically difficult or uninteresting to explain.

O

Objective: The mission or goal of an advertising or marketing program.

Off-Line: A type of tape editing that is free-standing.

On-Line: Tape editing where all elements and effects can be used.

Opticals: Various visual effects (dissolves, supers, etc.) performed during the final part of the post-production process.

Outdoor: Advertising which appears outside. Also out-of-home.

P

Paste Up: Same as keyline.

Penetration: As in market penetration or media penetration.
The depth or degree to which you have made your presence felt, if referring to distribution, expressed as a percentage.

PDQ: Pretty darn quick. A rush job.

"Permission to Believe": Concept credited to Leo Burnett.
The reason the audience allows itself to believe your commercial, or believe your product is superior. It may be real, though minor, i.e., peas picked in the moonlight. May be tonal and totally executional, i.e., Keebler Cookies "made by elves."

P.I.: Per Inquiry. Type of advertising, usually television, in which the media is paid for the number of orders or inquiries.

P.O.P.: Point-of-Purchase. Also called "P.O.S.," Point-of-Sale.

Portfolio: Folder containing samples of writer's, artist's, photographer's, or model's work. Also known as the "book."

Post-Production: Activities which occur after production, i.e., Editing, Mixing, Optical work and final Assembly. Also called "Post-pro."

Post-Scoring: Writing the music **after** the film is edited to match or reinforce visual timings and cues in the edit.

Pre-Production: Activities necessary to get ready for production. "Pre-pro."

Production: The actual filming or recording of a commercial.

Psychographics: Psychological description of Target Consumer, i.e., Nurturing Mother, Adventurous, Sensate, etc.

Q

Qualitative: The non-numerical aspects of a situation, i.e., attitudes, "image," and types of research which give a "feel" but are not statistically accurate, such as Focus Groups.

Quantitative: Numerical data. Market share, customer demographics, "hard" research numbers from large sample research.

R

® : Registration Mark indicating name or logo is legally registered and owned.

Reach: The percentage of an audience reached by a media buy.

Reason Why: Facts which provide support for consumer benefit or product performance.

Right Hand Side: Voice script broken out for reading.

Rim Light: Lighting technique in which the edges are highlighted.

Rough: Anything in rough form: layout, mix, edit, etc.

Rough Cut: The initial edit of a film or tape without optical effects. Often, splices and other marks of assembly are visible.

Rough Mix: Early mix of audio elements.

S

SAG: Screen Actor's Guild. Performers' union for actors in filmed commercials.

"schtick": Yiddish vaudeville term for a piece of "business." Groucho Marx's cigar and eyebrows were his "schtick."

Scratch Track: A rough representation of a jingle soundtrack submitted by a music production house.

SFX: Abbreviation for Sound Effects. Sometimes used as an abbreviation for Special Effects.

Share: Percentage of market held by a brand.

Share of Voice: Percent of ad weight held by brand in product category.

Side Light: Lighting that comes predominantly from the side.

Side by Side: Type of comparison commercial or Demo.

Slogan: Phrase used to advertise a product. Usually it's the theme of an advertising campaign, though many products have numerous slogans, some quite old.

Slogo: Slang. A combination of slogan and logo.

Small Space: Print advertising utilizing small-sized media spaces.

SMPTE: A standard electronic time code used in video editing. SMPTE stands for Society of Motion Picture and Television Engineers, the professional group which established the code. Also known as "Time Code."

Spec: Two meanings. 1. Short for "Specifications." 2. Short for "Speculative" work done to get new business, generally, with no payment from the prospect.

Spread: An ad covering two pages. A full page spread uses up two full pages. A horizontal spread uses two horizontal half pages.

SRDS: Standard Rate and Data Service.

StockMusic: Pre-recorded music which can be used for sound tracks or commercials for a small fee. Also called "Needle Drop."

Stop Motion: Animation created by images or objects moved and filmed frame by frame. A form of stop motion using clay is called "Clay-Mation."

SubMaster: Master missing certain elements, usually supers (video submaster) or announcer (audio submaster) which will be used in the final version or versions.

Super: Words "super-imposed" over the picture. Also used as verb, to super-impose words over the picture.

T

Table Tent: *Point-of-sale* signage intended to sit on a restaurant table or bar-top.

Tag: Copy, often localized, used at the end of the commercial. Usually used to supply purchasing information.

Target Audience: The audience to whom you are aiming your media message.

Target Market: The group of people in the marketplace who are the best prospects for your product.

TBD: To Be Determined.

Telemarketing: Selling, soliciting or researching via phone. Can be *inbound* or *outbound*.

Temp track: A rough track used temporarily in an edit.

Time-Code: Numerical code used to indicate a frame of videotape. There are many types of time code, such as SMPTE, not all compatible.

™Trademark: Symbol used to distinguish a product, usually protected by law and indicated by a ™symbol. Any word, symbol name or device used to identify goods and distinguish them from those sold by others.

Transit: Advertising associated with mass transit. Usually, bus cards inside busses, the outsides of busses and at bus stops.

Turnaround (Time): Time necessary to implement revisions. Usually integrated into a production or approval schedule.

Turn-key: An event that includes all materials required so that the program is easy to implement, i.e., you just "turn the key."

TV Safe: Area of TV screen for clear title read.

Typo: Typographical error.

U

UltiMatte: Film technique, similar to ChromaKey, where a Matte of the film image is generated along with the negative.

UltiMatte Blue: The background color on which UltiMatte is shot.

UPC: Universal Product Code. Those bar stripes on packaging.

USP: Unique Selling Proposition.

V

VALS: Research which emphasizes Values and LifeStyles.

VCR: Any video recorder.

VHS: Popular 1/2" video format.

VFX: Abbreviation for Video Effects.

Video Assist: Video Hook-up on a film camera that shows what's filmed.

Videotape: Tape used to record video. Used in many formats. Common professional formats are 1", 3/4" and 1/2" (BetaCam). Current common home use formats are Beta and VHS. Both 1/2".

VO: Abbreviation for Voice Over.

W

Wipe: A video effect which provides a transition from one scene to another, sometimes indicating passage of time. Some examples are: Clock Wipe, Flip Wipe and Page Wipe.

Work for Hire: Unless otherwise specified, creative work that is paid for is the property of the person or company that pays for it, not the creator. The work is regarded as "work for hire."

Work Print: Film used in editing. Usually a "one-light" copy of the dailies, with no color correction or special printing. This is usually the same film viewed as "dailies."

"Wrist-Radio": Slang for obvious advertising device, referring to Dick Tracy cartoons where the wrist-radio was indicated with both an arrow and caption.

X-Y-Z

X-Acto™: Type of razor-blade knife used in mount rooms.

YUPPY: Name for Young Upscale Professional. Also YUPPIE. This sort of naming of target markets and consumers is fairly common.

Zap: Change channels.

Zoom: Film or tape production term, to "zoom in" on subject - usually with a "Zoom" lens. Used as noun or verb.

Some Numbers . . .

Audio Tape Speed is measured in inches per second – *"ips."*

30 ips is used for highest quality audio mastering.

15 ips is used in most professional audio studios.

7.5 ips is used on broadcast tape recordings.

3 3/4 ips is used to record things such as Talking Books.

1 7/8 ips is the usual speed of audio cassettes.

Film Speed: Film plays at **24 frames per second.**

Tape Speed: Videotape plays at **30 frames per second.**

30" TV Commercial: On tape, about 29", with fade up and fade to black. Allow for about .5" on either end of the spot. (i.e., a 10" is 9". Get it?)

30" TV Commercial: On film, about 28.5", with fade up and fade to black.

30" Radio Commercial: 30" in length.

60" Radio Commercial: One full minute.

10" ID: About 9" – if you push it, 9.5"

Billboard: 6-8" Audio. Usually used with a still.

Agate Line: Unit of print space – 1 column inch wide by 1/14". There are 14 lines to 1 inch.

Point: Type size – There are 72 points to 1 inch.

Additional Definitions:

You may run into some additional terms and phrases that you want to remember. Write them here.

Books & Articles:

Here's a handy place to write down the names of other books to read or magazines to subscribe to.

It's also a handy place to put interesting articles or add examples until you file them (you do have a Scrap File, don't you?)

Names & Addresses:

Forgot your address book?
Clip in the business card or jot down the information.
There's an old saying, "You're as good as your Rolodex".

Acknowledgments

This book is the result of many lessons learned from agency professionals and clients over the last twenty years.

I'm grateful to all of you for your help and experience. (You know who you are.)

A few people are entitled to specific thanks:

H. J. and **Babette K. Bendinger** who taught me that life is a team sport.

Dave Berger and **Norm Brown** of FCB for help on early versions and **The FCB Library** for valuable assistance. **The Leo Burnett Company** for a great 4 year education.

Howard Cutler and the "Adopt a School" program, **Jim Gilmore** and **Kensinger Jones** of MSU, the late **Prof. Larry Baricevic** of St. Louis U., and other dedicated educators.

Cynthia Burns formerly of Kellogg School of Management, Northwestern and **Paul Geisler** of Kimberly-Clark, for help and assistance in the Strategy section.

Apple Computer, (Rich Binell and Mike Markman, particularly) for their support of a Strategy Seminar that resulted in improving this edition greatly and **Chris Wall** of BBDO/LA.

The Portfolio Center, for hosting a week to class-test some of the New Edition.

Dave Glick & Linda Kirsch for their help, talent, and friendship.

Roy Sandstrom & Keith Longino for type and cover design.

Harant Soghigian, an agency professional dedicated to quality. Thanks for use of 8 Quince Street on Nantucket, where the initial version of this book was written...

The Copy Workshop Crew, for going above and beyond every day.

And most of all... **Lorelei.**

For More Information:
If you'd like to know more about The Copy Workshop, write:
The Copy Workshop
2144 N. Hudson
Chicago, IL 60614
We'd love to hear from you.

P.S.

We'd like to know how you liked the book.

So, send us a note.

Tell us what you've learned. Tell us what you'd like to know more about.

Who knows, you might inspire us to publish another book or two.

Free Newsletter.

Every once in awhile, we send out a newsletter – full of news you can use if you write or teach advertising – plus other interesting items from "The Biz."

We'll be glad to send you a free copy.

More Books!

Did you know that we also publish a few other books on advertising and marketing?

True. Good ones, too.

If the fine folks at your bookstore don't have them in stock, or you need information, fill out one of our cards and send it to us.

Or, call us anytime at

The Copy Workshop

2144 N. Hudson, Chicago, IL. 60614
312-871-1179 FAX 312-281-4643